MAMBO KINGDOM
LATIN MUSIC IN NEW YORK

Max Salazar

SCHIRMER
TRADE
BOOKS

New York London Paris Sydney Copenhagen Madrid Tokyo Berlin

To my wife, Gerri, who, along with the *son montuno*, enriched my life.

Copyright © 2002 by Max Salazar

This edition published 2002 by Schirmer Trade Books,
an imprint of the Music Sales Publishing Group.

All rights reserved. No part of this book may be
reproduced in any form or by any electronic or mechanical means,
including information storage and retrieval systems,
without permission in writing from the publisher.

Order No. SCH 10115
International Standard Book Number: 0.8256.7277.5

Exclusive Distributors:
Music Sales Corporation
257 Park Avenue South, New York, NY 10010 USA
Music Sales Limited
8/9 Frith Street, London W1D 3JB England
Music Sales Pty. Limited
120 Rothschild Street, Rosebery, Sydney, NSW 2018, Australia

Printed in the United States of America by
Phoenix Color Corporation

Contents

FOREWORD V
PREFACE IX
THE DEVELOPMENT OF LATIN MUSIC IN NEW YORK CITY 1
RAFAEL HERNÁNDEZ 13
GABRIEL OLLER 19
CONJUNTO CANEY 27
ALBERTO IZNAGA 31
MIGUELITO VALDÉS 37
ALBERTO SOCARRÁS 51
ANSELMO SACASAS 59
MARCELINO "RAPINDEY" GUERRA 63
NORO MORALES 69
JOE LOCO 75
FEDERICO PAGANI 81
THE PALLADIUM 87
JOSÉ CURBELO 95
MONCHITO MUÑOZ 101
JOHN "BIG DADDY" RODRÍGUEZ 105
TITO RODRÍGUEZ 111
TITO PUENTE 125
JIMMY FRISAURA 133
FRANKIE COLÓN 139
VICENTICO VALDÉS 143

Vitín Aviles	147
Gilberto Monroig	151
Santitos Colón	155
Tony Molina	159
Orlando Marín	163
La Lupe	169
Two Centuries of Charanga	175
José Fajardo	187
Charlie Palmieri	193
Joe Quijano	205
Eddy Zervigón	209
Hector Rivera	219
Tony Pabón	223
Joe Cuba	227
Willie Torres	239
Cheo Feliciano	243
Joe Bataan	249
Salsa Origins	255
Jerry Masucci	261
The Corso	265
Willie Rosario	269
Hector Lavoe	273
Willie Rodríguez	279
Index	283

Foreword

Once Afro-Cuban music evolved into the early stages of its current form in the late 1920s, it quickly became a popular item on the world stage, and it continues to have a unique and profound effect on the world of music and dance. Thanks to phonograph records, dancing to Cuban music became wildly popular wherever the music was heard, causing local "Latin" bands to spring up everywhere. Now you can find talented and original Cuban-style bands practically anywhere on this planet: Finland's Salsamania, Sweden's Hot Salsa, Amsterdam's Paradis, Scotland's Salsa Celtica, England's King Salsa, Haiti's Haitiando, and Italy's Battisticoco, just to name a few. And of course there is Mother Africa, where the familiar-sounding returning rhythms gave rise to a thriving African Afro-Cuban music scene, with its own golden era from the 1950s through the 1970s. In Congo in the late 1950s, Le Grand Kalle's African Jazz, a Congolese rumba band modeled on Cuba's La Sonora Matancera, set the tone for the entire continent. Today, bands and bandleaders such as Congo's African Fiesta, Senegal's Orchestre Baobab, and Benin's Gnonnas Pedro are finally being discovered on this side of the world. The guitar-driven soukous of Congo, Africa's most enduring and influential dance music, has its roots in Cuban *son* and rumba, having taken shape as guitarists like Dr. Nico, Papa Noel, and Franco improvised, added local rhythms, and pushed the sound further.

Of all the fertile soils that Cuban musical seed landed on, none has had the importance of New York City. In fact, until Cuba established its own recording industry, it was here that many of the seminal Cuban recordings were made. As early as the 1920s, RCA and Columbia were recording *son* groups like Sexteto Habanero and Septeto Nacional in New York. As one of the world's major cultural crossroads, New York was the place where things that couldn't happen anywhere else came together. It was in New York, many miles north of Havana, that Afro-Cuban musicians met musicians from Puerto Rico and Central and South America, along with other multiethnic artists doing creative work in this city.

New York's Latin music, like Cuba's, has gone through distinct eras, sending original recordings and styles all over the world. The clave thrives here, and many of the most influential artists lived and worked here, among them Machito and Mario Bauzá, Orquesta Broadway, Charlie Palmieri, Tito Puente, Tito Rodríguez, Lou Pérez, Pete Terrace, Ricardo Ray, Henry Fiol, Joe Cuba, Johnny Pacheco, Mauricio Smith, and Monguito "El Unico." Their innovations are the direct result of the brilliant musicians from Cuba who settled here and simply played their music. That's all they really had to do; the rest followed naturally, in ways peculiar to New York.

Max Salazar was born in 1932 in Spanish Harlem, an immigrant neighborhood alive with the syncopations of Cuba and Puerto Rico. He was nine years old when he heard "Anna Boroco Tinde" by Miguelito Valdés with the Xavier Cugat orchestra, "Sopa de Pichon" by Machito and his Afro Cubans, and "Serenata Rítmica" by Noro Morales. Thus began a lifelong fascination with the musicians and with all the facets, fusions, and possibilities of Afro-Cuban music. It wasn't until the 1960s, while taking an English literature course at the City University of New York, that he started writing about the music.

Max was sort of a salsa fly on the wall. He was the only New York writer who tried to fill in the gaps by asking the men and women who were there at the beginning (and already getting on in years)—musicians like Machito, Mario Bauzá, Alberto Socarrás, Chico O'Farrill, Federico Pagani, Victoria Hernández, (sister of Rafael Hernández), Gilberto Calderón, and Alberto Iznaga—about New York's Afro-Cuban experience, as well as their musical lives in Cuba and Puerto Rico. It is because of Max that we have so much of the anecdotal and oral history that documents the distinct and original eras that make up the New York experience.

Of equal importance, Max began a parallel radio career as the host of *The Latin Musicians Show*, giving voice to those often-unsung heroes of Afro-Cuban music, the arrangers and sidemen. As was too often the case, albums would be released with no identification of the personnel. Max would not write about or give airplay to these records until he could credit the sidemen by name.

When these two media approaches come together in a truly independent person without any kind of hidden agenda or any feeling of servitude to the few who really control what you hear, the insights, breadth, and scope can be amazing. It is this freedom and honesty that over the years has made Max stand out as one of the best in a field that is often dishonest and laden

foreword

with ulterior motives. Countless talented artists from New York, the United States, and the rest of the world who did not stand a chance of recognition or airplay in the small monopoly that is the New York Latin-music world got them from Max.

Max grew up in an era where Spanish-language radio was sporadic, playing mostly boleros and *rancheras*, and ignoring the Afro-Cuban sounds so deeply imbedded in this city. Here, dancers partied in apartments and basements with Victrolas and 78-rpm records. There was a blaring jukebox at the Weekend Bar on 108th street and Madison Avenue, where the kids gathered out front to listen and dance to the hits of the day. Then there were the local record stores, with their own small labels, where they played the discs before you paid. Two stores that live in New York City Afro-Cuban legend are Almacenes Hernández, established by Rafael and Victoria Hernández, and Tatay's Spanish Music Center (SMC), run by Gabriel Oller. It was Oller, years later, who let Max rummage in the chaotic backroom, where he found a copy of Arsenio Rodríguez's classic "Tumba Palo Cucuye," perhaps his most African recording. It was through Max's research that I learned why Arsenio's music was so different from other Cuban musicians', and why some of his compositions, such as "Bruca Manigua," have African words. Arsenio's grandfather was born in Congo and taken to Cuba as a slave, where he lived until the age of 103. Thanks to Max, we know the story behind Arsenio's beautiful lament "La Vida Es Un Sueño" (Life Is But a Dream). While staying with friends in the Bronx, the blind musician was told by his ophthalmologist, Dr. Ramón Castroviejo, that there was no hope of ever regaining his sight. He took a nap, and when he awoke he wrote the haunting lyrics and melody.

Max has always maintained contact and friendship with his colleagues around the United States and the world, particularly in Cuba. During the cold war, an era of an almost complete blackout of music from where it all began, Max corresponded with and printed the articles and observations of Cuban writers such as Leonardo Acosta, Cristóbal Díaz Ayala, and Radames Giro. Important contemporary Cuban innovations, new artists, and trends were made known to American aficionados.

Max has lived through and chronicled most of the eras that make up the New York Afro-Cuban experience. He was the first to note the fascinating fusion of African-American West Harlem with Caribbean East Harlem, in which soul and R&B melded with *guajira* and *son* to produce the popular hybrid called the boogaloo. The many awards and honors he has received include recognition from European and Caribbean governments, the cities of Los Angeles and Denver, and the Smithsonian Institution in Washington, D.C., where he is a featured lecturer. Only New York hasn't been heard from, and perhaps this book will help bring about official recognition for a true living catalog and font of this city's remarkable part in one of the world's most popular and beloved musics.

Al Angeloro
New York, June 2002

Preface

El Barrio, the Spanish phrase for "the neighborhood," is a term immediately recognized by Hispanics who have lived in New York City's East Harlem—the section of Manhattan's Upper East Side that runs northward from Ninety-sixth to 125th Streets and eastward from Fifth Avenue to the East River Drive. For writers like Piri Thomas, El Barrio is a haven, a place where Puerto Ricans feel emotionally secure, wanted, and as though they belong. There are locales inside and outside the city where living conditions are better, but in their hearts, first-generation Puerto Ricans know where their roots are. In his autobiographical book *Down These Mean Streets*, Thomas recalls the day he left Harlem to live in Long Island.

"As we got our belongings ready for the moving van, I stood by watching all the hustling with a mean feeling…my face tried hard not to show resentment at Pappa's decision to leave my mean streets forever.…I felt I belonged in Harlem, it was my kind of kick.…I didn't want to move out to Long Island.…'Moms why do we gotta move outta Harlem?'…we don't know any other place better'n this."

Thomas and family escaped from the mean streets of El Barrio to their own home in Babylon, Long Island. But he soon learned that the better life they sought—with green trees and grass, open spaces, and cleaner air—was not enough to fulfill him. For Thomas, these abstract luxuries could not replace El Barrio's "faded, multi-colored building façades along Madison, Park and Lexington Avenues…the unique spicy *sofrito* aromas of street vendors' *pastellios* and *alcapurrias*…the friendly greetings: 'Buenos días,' 'Cómo andas?'…or the music emanating out of juke boxes from the restaurants, bars and cafes on the avenues." Wrote Thomas: "This Long Island was foreign country. It spoke a language you couldn't dig…you always felt on the rim of belonging.…I came back to New York…the first place I went was to El Barrio…I heard all the noises I'd missed for so long."

Since the early 1920s, El Barrio's inhabitants have been surrounded by sounds that could be heard nowhere else but in *los barrios Latinos* of New York: utterances from Cheo, Tito, Belén, *mavi*, *piraguas*, the words of a Pentecostal preacher forewarning a small crowd about God's day of retribution, the *jíbaro* music of Ramito, the mellifluous harmonizing of Ismael Rivera and Rolando Laserie inducing fantasies of *Borinquen* via Rafael Cortijo's recording of "Los Carreteros," the arousing sounds of Noro Morales performing "Serenata Rítmica," the Machito orchestra's exciting Afro-Cuban jazz sounds in "Tanga," the mambos of Tito Puente, Tito Rodriquez, and Joe Loco, the Latin-soul sounds of Johnny Colón's "Boogaloo Blues," Joe Cuba's "Bang Bang," Joe Bataan's "Gypsy Woman," and Landy Nova's "There's No One to Blame," the blind Arsenio Rodríguez's lyrics for "Fuego en el 23," "Come Se Goce en el Barrio," "La Gente del Bronx," and "La Vida Es Un Sueño," Ray Barretto's erotic "Cocinando," the pride instilled by Ismael Quintana and Eddie Palmieri's recordings about Puerto Rico.

These are just a few of the many sounds heard in El Barrio since the 1920s. They are the background to daily life in East Harlem—of street chatter and other rhythms that went unnoticed until they were no longer audible. Spanish Harlem means many things, most of them unpleasant to people who believe what they read in the daily papers. But for Latinos, Spanish Harlem was a casbah, a refuge beyond the ghettos of the Lower East Side, Washington Heights, Brooklyn, and the South Bronx, where Puerto Ricans and Cubans squeezed together to feel at ease. This book is about the musical sounds of El Barrio and the people who made those sounds, beginning in the 1920s.

Max Salazar

ONE

THE DEVELOPMENT OF LATIN MUSIC IN NEW YORK CITY

In 1919, two years after Puerto Ricans were granted U.S. citizenship, a small number migrated to the United States. They left the island to escape its deadly tropical diseases and to improve their standard of living. Afro-Cubans, meanwhile, were leaving their country for the United States to escape racial discrimination. As U.S. corporate interests grew in Cuba, wealthy Americans were buying businesses and tourist resorts that hired Americans only. The Cuban legislature proposed a law requiring that for every non-Cuban working in Cuba, two Cubans must be employed. But black Cubans did not have to worry about whether or not these laws passed, since they were not wanted anyway—by Americans or white Cubans. Hotel and resort owners employed only mulattos who could pass for white.

So Afro-Cubans worked mostly in menial jobs, but even those qualified as musicians lost out because of their brown or black skin. In the early twentieth century, silent movie theaters throughout the island provided employment for Afro-Cubans trained in classical music. But when the first talking movie, *The Jazz Singer*, arrived in Cuba in 1928, black musicians sensed that their employment was coming to an end. Artists such as Vicente Sigler, Nilo Menéndez, Alberto Iznaga, Alberto Socarrás, and René Edreira were among the Cubans to leave their homeland and live among the African-American community in New York City's West Harlem neighborhood.

Among the first wave of Puerto Ricans to live in the United States was the island's most famous composer, Rafael Hernández. He and his sister Victoria were pioneers in East Harlem when it was a still a predominantly Jewish neighborhood. According to Victoria, Puerto Ricans were hired as building superintendents there, and as rooms became available, the superintendents rented them to fellow Puerto Ricans. The earliest newcomers rented rooms on Ninety-ninth Street and Second Avenue.

Months later, a bodega opened; it became the social center where news of the island was exchanged. Victoria maintained that her brother was the first Latino to sound a Latin musical note in New York—in 1919, when his trio performed at a house party. Hernández did not perform at dance halls; he and two guitarists played a few house parties. Later he left New York for Cuba, then Mexico, where he was inspired to compose his famous songs.

Arsenio Pagani, who would become famous two decades later as a dance promoter under the name Federico Pagani, left Puerto Rico for New York in 1925. He has said that the Vicente Sigler orchestra was the first to perform Latin music there, in 1926. Sigler, a six-foot-tall, light-skinned Cuban mulatto, attracted Latinos to his monthly dances at the Astor, Governor Clinton, Waldorf-Astoria, and McAlpin hotels in midtown Manhattan. Each verbal announcement or written ad was accompanied by the words "*gallegos* only"—meaning that only people supposedly of white Spanish extraction were allowed to attend. Sigler's orchestra played stock (store-bought) arrangements such as "Amapola." The trumpeter-bandleader was popular because he was the only Spanish-speaking musician at the time whose band played Latin music. Sigler's band marked the beginning of burgeoning careers for Puerto Ricans Augusto Coen and Alberto Calderón, and for Cubans Alberto Socarrás, Nilo Menéndez, René Edreira, Alberto Iznaga, and Mario Bauzá. The Vincent López orchestra had also been performing in New York City since 1922, but during its thirty-year span, it recorded only five Latin tunes, all of them with the Hispanic elements watered down.

Cuban bandleader Don Azpiazu and his vocalist Antonio Machín made history on the afternoon of April 26, 1930, at the RKO Theater at Broadway and Forty-sixth Street, with their version of Moisés Simón's composition "The Peanut Vendor." After a few introductory bars, Machín appeared from behind a curtain and proceeded to the blinding spotlights while melodiously singing *"manís"*—peanuts—while throwing nuts to the audience. On May 13, 1930, RCA Victor recorded Azpiazu's version of the song. The record was released seven months later, and with it, popular Latin dance music was born in New York. In 1931, Warner Brothers filmed Mexican actress Lupe Vélez, American opera star Lawrence Tibbett, and entertainer Jimmy Durante for the movie *Cuban Love Song*. The background music throughout the film was "The Peanut Vendor."

Alberto Iznaga, an Afro-Cuban musician, recalled that "for most musicians during the early 1930s, music was a means of supplementing their primary income. After finishing work in a factory, as a house painter, a porter, a dishwasher, musicians hurried to El Billar de los Músicos [a billiard parlor] at 113th Street and Madison Avenue, which served as an employment agency and hangout for El Barrio's musicians." Inside the premises was a five-by-five-foot blackboard that listed musicians' names and instruments in chalk. Space was provided for remarks like "engaged." If the space was blank, the musician was available. Next to the blackboard was a large bulletin board covered with three-by-five index cards, listing jobs for a trio, quartet, a vocalist, or a musician who played a specific instrument, and the name of the person to contact for the job.

Rafael Díaz, a barrio resident said: "It was July 1932. Cuba's Kid Chocolate was the world's featherweight [boxing] champ. I was among a crowd outside Simon Jou's restaurant near the corner of 115th Street and Fifth Avenue. Two guitarists, a maraca player, and a muted trumpeter attracted a crowd. A car rolled to a stop. The door was opened by an Afro-Cuban chauffeur named Brinca, and out onto the pavement stepped Kid Chocolate. The Kid always visited Jou's place for black coffee and Cuban pastries. The musicians stopped traffic with a performance of 'Son de la Loma.'…Miguel Matamoros, one of the guitarists, was embracing Chocolate.

"For reasons unknown, musicians of the 1930s used nicknames such as Chinchita [bedbug], Conejo [rabbit], Lobo [wolf], Caballo (horse), Pajarito [little bird], Pepe El Sapo [Joey the Toad], Chino [Chinaman], Negrito [Little Blackie], and Indio [Indian]. When musicians died, some surviving colleagues learned their departed friends' true names for the first time." Díaz added that the Monge Funeral Parlor, located on Madison Avenue between 114th and 115th Streets, would claim the body at the morgue and—depending on the family's finances—deliver the cadaver to the funeral parlor or the decedent's apartment for a one-day wake. When a trumpeter named Armandito died in 1932, there was a religious ceremony before the body was placed in the hearse. Latin musicians lined up in front his apartment building to fulfill his last wish—to be buried to the accompaniment of music. They played "La Borinqueña," the Puerto Rican national anthem. The funeral procession wove through the streets of East Harlem on the way to the West Side pier from which the body was shipped to Puerto Rico for burial. Such New Orleans–style sendoffs ended during the early 1940s.

Gabriel Oller, born in Santurce, Puerto Rico, in 1903, came to New York City in 1919. He was a font of information regarding Puerto Rican life in Spanish Harlem. "In 1933, Julio Cuevas bought Casa Hernández," he said. "I opened the Spanish Music Center next to El San José Theater at 110th Street and Fifth Avenue. I sold RCA, Columbia, and Decca records, pianola rolls, and guitars. I just couldn't compete with the Hernández name, so I decided on a gimmick to attract attention. I founded the second

Puerto Rican recording company, the Dynasonic label, and I recorded in the back of my store. I recorded the music of the neighborhood trios and quartets. I paid each musician three dollars for the session. Business always picked up prior to the Christmas holidays. Puerto Ricans bought every *aguinaldo* recording."

Latin music was much more than entertainment; it was an indispensable crutch for Puerto Ricans and Cubans determined to survive in an alien environment. More importantly, the sounds of *son, danzón, bomba, danza,* and *aguinaldo* were reminders of the two islands in the Caribbean. One could always tell which Puerto Rican and Cuban families had higher incomes: one or more members were musicians. Poor families who could not afford to rent a hall for a wedding, baptism, or birthday party held the festivities in their apartments.

During the 1930s a house party in El Barrio was a ball. The apartment and hallway reeked with the aroma of garlic and oregano emanating from the fresh hams in the oven. Thin slabs of *pernil* (roast pork shoulder) accompanied plates of steaming rice and pigeon peas. The elders drank beer that flowed from a wooden keg kept in the kitchen sink on top of a twenty-five-cent block of ice. The bathtub, filled with cracked ice, cooled the several flavors of soda pop the children drank. Unemployed Cubans and Puerto Ricans raised rent and food money by holding dances in their apartments. The entrance fee was twenty-five cents. Musicians were paid with the money earned from the sale of beer, *mavi, pastelillos, alcapurrias,* and *pasteles.*

Despite the great number of proficient Latin musicians, English-language radio stations refused to air Spanish-language music; they claimed there was no market for it. In early 1934, Marcial Flores, a wealthy *boletero* (numbers runner), opened the Club Cubanacán at 114th Street and Lenox Avenue. Alberto Socarrás, Flores's friend and favorite musician, directed the house band. Months later Flores rented the closed Mount Morris Theater at 116th Street and Fifth Avenue, renamed it El Campo Amor, and had people standing in line for a chance to see the Tango King—Carlos Gardel—in person and on screen in *Cuesta Abajo,* one of the nine films Gardel made for Paramount Pictures. The crowd urged Gardel to sing, but he refused. Instead, he sat in the first box seat to the left of the stage and watched the movie for the first time. On June 24, 1935, Gardel was killed in a plane crash on his way from Medellín, Colombia, to Panama.

During the early 1930s, entertainment stars were being incubated at La Milagrosa Catholic Church, in a program called *Estrellas del Futuro* (future stars). Ernest "Tito" Puente and Olga San Juan were ten years old when they acted, danced, and sang in plays performed at the church. Meanwhile, Diosa Costello's beauty and talent were discovered on stage at Teatro San José. José Estévez (Joe Loco), Lou Pérez, Charlie Palmieri, Luis Varona, Pete Terrace, and Johnny "La Vaca" Rodríguez were dividing their time between children's games at La Casita María and music studies.

It was in the mid-1930s that competition for housing, employment, and political identity in Spanish Harlem began straining relationships between Puerto Ricans and Cubans. Puerto Ricans, who are U.S. citizens by virtue of a congressional proclamation, traveled to and from the mainland without problems. But Cuban visitors could not remain in the United States longer than twenty-nine days for fear of being arrested and deported. Relations between Puerto Ricans and Cubans seemed to improve in 1941, after word spread throughout Harlem and Brooklyn that a Cuban man and a Puerto Rican woman had wed. It was rumored that the marriage of Cuban bandleader Frank "Machito" Grillo to Hilda Torres, a Puerto Rican, contributed to the end of the hostilities.

Machito's band had Puerto Rican musicians, Noro Morales's orchestra employed Cubans, and Cuban vocalist Miguelito Valdés was singing the songs of Puerto Rican composer Pedro Flores. These were just a few of the goodwill gestures that ended the Caribbean version of the Hatfield and McCoy feud. The cease-fire resulted in intermarriages, and many families joined the caravan of vehicles on weekends from Spanish Harlem to Rockaway Beach in Long Island. But in the mid-1940s, a serious traffic accident en route to the beach ended these weekend trips and rerouted barrio natives to "Las Villas." These were New York City Latinos' version of the Jewish "borscht belt" resorts of the Catskills. Las Villas were also upstate and in the mountains. They featured large quantities of Cuban and Puerto Rican food, endless live music, and a chance for young, unmarried men and women to meet each other.

By 1937 El Barrio had ballrooms that featured the music of Alberto Socarrás, Augusto Coen, Jose Morand, Vicente Sigler, Nilo Menéndez, Juanito Sanabria, and Los Happy Boys. Tito Puente was then living on East 117th Street. When he heard Anselmo Sacasas's piano solo on Casino de la Playa's recording of "Dolor Cobarde," he decided to study the piano. That was the year the word "disc jockey" was first used, in an article about music in *Variety*. A "record hit" competition every bit as intense as a horserace developed among commercial radio stations as their "jockeys" tried to play a disc as many times as possible and thus "ride" it to success. For Puerto Ricans, it was a special treat when guitar-and-vocal groups like those of Rafael Hernández, Pedro Flores, Davilita, Johnny López, and Pedro Marcano sang "Vereda Tropical" and "Incertidumbre."

Harlem's Latinos had their music. Thick ten-inch 78-rpm records were played through a megaphone-shaped horn that extended from an RCA Victrola that had no electricity. The Victrola's spring drove the turntable. To hear a recording at its proper speed, the spring had to be wound tight; otherwise, the music would sound slow and lethargic. The turntable spring was rewound with a crank after each record was played. Phonograph needles were sold in packets of twenty-five for five cents. They had to be changed after every two plays because the needle tips quickly became blunt and dull.

In October 1937, Frank "Machito" Grillo left Havana for New York City to live with his sister Estella and her husband, Mario Bauzá. At about this time, the career of Alberto Iznaga began rising as he became Augusto Coen's music arranger. Iznaga recalled the importance of top billing: "The Hollywood and Broadway-stage-show methods of listing screen credits of names in order of their supposed importance is what urged Latin bandleaders to demand their names on the top line of marquees, posters, and announcements." Bandleaders used every possible stratagem to place their names at the very top.

In 1938, the world's fair in Flushing, Queens, attracted tourists from all over the world. Cuban singer Miguelito Valdés became Latin America's most exciting recording artist. His recording of "Babalú" was heard throughout Latin America, and he was hailed as the Latin Bing Crosby. Meanwhile, the handsome Cuban vocalist Desi Arnaz was spotted at La Conga Club, which led to a part in the Broadway revue *Too Many Girls*. Arnaz soared in popularity via his Columbia recordings and became a barrio hero. In 1940, Arsenio Rodríguez introduced the conga drum to Cuban popular dance music, and that instrument quickly became a part of Cuban trumpet *conjuntos*.

The conga rhythm, popularized by Miguelito Valdés with the Casino de la Playa, was recorded by every Latin and American pop band. According to Decca Records' 1939 *The History of La Conga*: "The conga dance is of African origin. It was introduced into Cuba by slaves....The name conga was derived from the African Congo [and] later applied to a narrow barrel-shaped Cuban drum....The rhythm's four-four time accents the fourth beat. The drum accent was created to prevent a unison movement to prevent accidents....Slaves were chained by their feet to the others in a long line and—urged by the tempo of a beating drum—had to drag that chain in an even, forward movement to prevent tripping."

The most important event in the history of Cuban popular dance music occurred in 1938. It was then that Orestes "Macho" López and his brother Israel "Cachao" López created the *danzón*-mambo while they were members of Antonio Arcaño's charanga orchestra.

The cultural influence of African-Americans on Puerto Ricans became obvious in 1939. Latinos were moved by the vocal harmonies of the Ink Spots, by Avery Parish's piano solo on Erskine Hawkins's "After Hours," and by Count Basie's "One O'Clock Jump." Thirty-five cents enabled Latinos and others to jitterbug on Sunday afternoons from 3 to 7 P.M. to the music of Chick Webb's band and other well-known jazz groups at the Savoy Ballroom. After this matinee dance, the same crowd headed to the Park Palace at 110th Street and Fifth Avenue. From 7 P.M. to 1 A.M., they danced the rumba, *rumba abierta, guaracha,* paso doble, bolero, *son,* and *danzón.* Above the middle of the dance floor, a large mirrored ball spun, reflecting colored lights throughout the fully lit ballroom. In most East Harlem dance halls, the lights were never dimmed. It was a question of morality.

After the dance, most dancers ate at one of the Cuban restaurants along Lenox Avenue. For the famous artist, there was Valentino's, an after-hours eatery at 116th Street off the corner of Fifth Avenue. Every well-known black and Hispanic artist ate there after a night's work. Valentino, a five-foot-seven-inch white Cuban of medium build, had transformed a basement apartment into a cozy cabaret and restaurant. Anyone waiting to enter was first examined through a peephole. A window near the entrance door was an altar, with glowing candles and statues of Santa Barbara and La Virgen de la Caridad del Cobre. The sanctimonious setting was designed to discourage the pious Irish policemen from closing the unlicensed restaurant. Every night one could see Desi Arnaz, Pedro Marcano, Noro Morales, Alberto Iznaga, Diosa Costello, Mario Bauzá, or Machito eating a specially prepared dish. "Cab Calloway, the Cotton Club chorus girls, and I ate here often," Alberto Socarrás, a frequent visitor, once told me.

It was during the late 1930s that three Harlem teenagers were making their mark on New York City's Latin-music scene. Sixteen-year-old Tito Puente had dropped out of high school to work as a full-time musician. José Estévez (Joe Loco) was a pianist much in demand by dance bands. Luis Varona had the same name as his Cuban-born father, a symphonic violinist. His mother was Maria Luisa LeCompte, a concert violinist of Puerto Rican descent. She taught Luis to play piano at the music school named after her at 116th Street between Park and Lexington Avenues. Varona went on to perform with the orchestras of Machito, Marcelino Guerra, Pupi Campo, and Tito Puente before settling in Miami, where he became a Latin-music idol.

When the 1940s began, Latin music was still restricted to Spanish-speaking communities. Downtown theaters, nightclubs, and ballrooms were owned by non-Hispanics. The Xavier Cugat orchestra was based at the Waldorf-Astoria Hotel, but the other bands worked the Spanish Harlem clubs—the Park Palace, El Obrero Español, the Odd Fellows Temple, Club Tampa, Borinquén Hall, Club Ponceño, Laurel Gardens, Carlton Hall, the American Legion Hall, and El Cubanacan. Outside Harlem, they also worked Hunts Point Palace in the Bronx. Popular Latin entertainment on radio was *La Hora Continental,* in which a man with a pleasant baritone voice recited love poems to the accompaniment of orchestral string music.

During the summer of 1940, the course of Latin music was altered when radio networks publicized their unhappiness with the American Society of Composers, Authors and Publishers (ASCAP) over performance rights. The broadcasters had long objected to the fees they paid annually to ASCAP, and they were threatening not to renew their contract in 1941. Without ASCAP music, there would be no *Your Hit Parade,* a program sponsored by Lucky Strike cigarettes. Yet, *Variety* magazine wrote in 1939, radio networks paid publishers only $218.50 a week to air the top ten hits. Unless a compromise was reached before January 1, 1941, ASCAP tunes would no longer be heard on radio. The networks advised bandleaders to set aside ASCAP tunes and prepare new songs for broadcast. On New Year's Day, 1941, the ban became effective. A scramble ensued for non-ASCAP music. The music of Stephen Foster became unrelenting: the networks noted that his songs, written before the Civil War, were in the public domain. After weeks of listening to "I Dream of Jeanie with the Light Brown Hair" and other moldy Foster tunes, the public was bored out of its mind. Months later an agreement was reached between ASCAP and the networks.

Realizing, however, that more confrontation was bound to erupt, broadcasters established BMI (Broadcast Music, Incorporated) in 1940 to avoid similar situations. BMI was responsible for exposing Latin music nationally. BMI contracted material from the Music Corporation of America (MCA) and aired rumbas, congas, and Xavier Cugat ballads over English-language radio stations. BMI's airing of "Bésame Mucho" in 1946 made a wealthy man of its composer, Chelo Velázquez, and a star of Mexican vocalist Andy Russell.

Latin music began making inroads into Hollywood. The 1940 movie *Down Argentine Way* marked the American debut of Brazilian vocalist Carmen Miranda, whose versions of "Mamá Yo Quiero" and "South American Way" pleased Latinos. Dick Gilbert, an English-speaking radio host who was born and raised in Arizona, began playing sambas from the movies. He also aired songs like "Tico Tico," "Amapola," "Adios," "Incertidumbre," and "Vereda Tropical," as well as Latin tunes that did not include Spanish lyrics. Gilbert is credited with popularizing the term "disc jockey."

One person who helped put Latin music into the movies was Ralph Peer, a non-Hispanic music publisher who began recording African-American "race music" in the 1920s. Peer noticed that tunes originating in Cuba, Mexico, Puerto Rico, and Brazil were copyrighted and not published in the United States. He visited the Caribbean and South America and bought the copyrights for less than a dollar. In 1940 Peer was the only American to own a voluminous catalog of Latin American songs. That year BMI acquired Peer's music catalog for use in motion pictures. A few of the songs used were "Babalú" (*Two Girls and a Sailor*, 1944), "Tico Tico," "Alma Llanera," and "Bim Bam Bum" (*Bathing Beauty*, 1944), "La Bamba" (*Fiesta*, 1947), and "Cuánto Le Gusta" (*A Date with Judy*, 1948).

In April 1940, Miguelito Valdés and pianist/arranger Anselmo Sacasas left Cuba for New York. Valdés landed a job with the Cugat orchestra. Sacasas became an immediate success with his own band. On December 3, 1940, Machito rehearsed his newly formed orchestra at the Park Palace ballroom. Mario Bauzá, its music director, introduced jazz arranger Edgar Sampson to Machito to orchestrate the Machito sound.

Thanks to James Petrillo, president of the American Federation of Musicians, music makers' livelihoods improved. In June 1942, Petrillo notified U.S. record companies that in order to insure maximum employment for the 138,000 members of his union, he would no longer allow them to make recordings that would be played again and again on jukeboxes or the radio without adequate compensation. Petrillo wanted a fee for each playing of a tune that had been made with union member participation. The federal government challenged his recording ban, but the union prevailed, and the strike, which began in October 1942, lasted fourteen months. In response, a few companies recorded artists in Mexico or Canada and released the recordings under pseudonyms. In late June 1943, Frank Sinatra recorded "You'll Never Know" and "People Will Say We're in Love" accompanied by vocal ensembles without instrumentation—and sales were minimal. On October 11, 1944, the record companies agreed to pay a royalty of five cents for each playing of a recording. As a result, the musicians' union received half a million dollars, which became a fund for unemployed musicians. In turn, these musicians performed free concerts.

In June 1942, ten days before the AFM strike started, the Machito orchestra went into a studio for a Miguelito Valdés recording session. By

July 27, it had produced two dozen 78-rpm recordings. Tito Puente's timbal is heard on the tracks "Oye Negra," "La Rumba Soy Yo," "Eco," "Nague," and "El Botellero." A few weeks later, Tito Puente and bongo player Chino Pozo left the Machito band to join Jack Cole's dance troupe in Chicago. Bauzá replaced them with Pedro "Pulidor" Allende and José Mangual. During his short stint in the Machito orchestra, Pulidor became the first North American Latin musician in an orchestra to play a conga drum. One month later, Tito Puente returned to the Machito band, where he remained until he was drafted into the U.S. Navy during World War II.

If the Spanish Harlemites of 1942 had voted for the year's favorite recording, Noro Morales's "Serenata Rítmica" would have won easily. The excitement it caused prompted Morales to make it his theme song. Wherever he appeared, he opened and closed his shows with "Serenata Rítmica." The next year, 1943, some of the top recordings were Machito's "La Paella," "Tingo Talango," and "Chacumbele" and Miguelito Valdés's "Zarabanda," "Drume Negrita," "Rica Pulpa," and "Rumba Rumbero." That was the when year Puerto Ricans were branded with the epithets "marine tiger" and "spic," and when wearing a zoot suit or pegged pants in Los Angeles was dangerous to one's health.

The year 1943 was also when Seeco Records came into being. "Sidney Siegel was the proprietor of Casa Siegel, a jewelry, furniture, and record store located at 1393 Fifth Avenue, near the corner of 115th Street," recalled Siegel's cousin Howard Roseff. "I started as a delivery man in 1941. In 1943, shellac, an ingredient necessary for the manufacture of records, was difficult to get. The little which was allowed to be bought was given to RCA, Columbia, and Decca to record American pop bands. Foreign music recordings were reduced drastically, to the point [where] Latin orchestras were let out of their contracts. The once-Jewish community of Harlem was now predominately Puerto Rican and Cuban, and [people] were desperate for Latin-music recordings. Mr. Siegel signed up Latin-music artists. The first was Pedro Marcano, then Miguel Matamoros, Johnny Rodríguez, Trio Los Panchos, Trio San Juan, and the artists abandoned by RCA, Decca, and Columbia.

"The recordings took place at the Joe Smith studios at Fifty-seventh Street. The recordings were released three weeks after…manufacture. Salesmen of jewelry and music stores came to Casa Siegel and bought the records to resell. We never paid a cent for promotion. Program directors of radio stations dropped by the store to pick up free copies of the latest releases to air on their programs. I'm talking about radio hosts such as Santiago Grevi, Rafael Díaz, and Raúl Alarcón. In the late 1940s, Art "Pancho" Raymond, Dick Sugar, and Bob Harris aired our releases. We recorded the Puerto Rican trios and the Cuban *conjuntos*. Eventually Seeco catered more to the Afro-Cuban sound, as it sold the most. We had Celso Vega, whose "La Ultima Noche Que Pasé Contigo" was a big seller. Seeco became ninety percent Cuban. Ansonia Records was the opposite; it became ninety percent Puerto Rican."

Roseff continued: "Our market was Puerto Rico, and it was buying the Cuban sides. *The Make Believe Ballroom*, a music show hosted by Martin Bloch, aired a few of our instrumentals. Petrillo's 1942 recording ban did not affect all of the recording industry, because of supply and demand. Musicians recorded after hours. Doors were locked in case a Local 802 [musicians' union] delegate came around. It was business as usual. Gabe Oller made recordings which were manufactured in Mexico and Canada. A box [of twenty-five 78s] cost $12.25, or fifty cents a record. The retail price was usually one dollar. Between 1943 and 1945 we recorded mostly Puerto Rican artists. For a record to go gold, it had to sell five thousand copies. I remember one gold recording which was recorded by Davilita. Way over five thousand were sold in Puerto Rico.

"Song titles were created on the spur of the moment. During a Noro Morales session, Mr. Siegel urged Noro to improvise on a melody which was sung by an unknown composer. Noro was incredible; he ad-libbed as he played. The composer, a Puerto Rican, proudly declared he was one of many Borinquen sons born near Stop 21. The title of Noro's recording became "Stop 21." Noro recorded for us many years, and he would never sign a contract…everything was done on a handshake. The recording scale was twenty-five dollars for a four-hour session. The Seeco label was the most popular seller of Latin recordings until the early 1950s."

Between January and April of 1943, the Machito orchestra was ravaged by the World War II draft. In January, tenor saxophonist Jose "Pin" Madera was the first to go. The following month, alto saxophonist Johnny Nieto, pianist Gilberto Ayala, and Tito Puente were called into active service. On April 23, 1943, Machito reported to Camp Upton, New Jersey, for basic training. Six weeks later, while on a weekend pass, Mario Bauzá told him he had composed "Tanga" the week before, and it was now the orchestra's opening and closing theme. Bauzá's "Tanga" kicked off the era of Afro-Cuban jazz.

The third most important event in the history of popular Latin dance music occurred on January 23, 1942, when the Dreamland Dancing Academy at Fifty-third Street and Broadway, a k a the Alma Dance Studios, became the Palladium Ballroom. It was at the Palladium that a new Cuban rhythm—the mambo—exploded. Soon it would be heard around the world. In the fifty years that followed, new musical trends would come and go, but none would outshine the mambo. Today, popular up-tempo Latin dance music is called "salsa" and is enjoyed the world over. But the sound of salsa is rooted in the Palladium Ballroom, in Cuba, and especially in New York City's Spanish Harlem.

Originally published in Latin Beat *magazine, May 1997.*

TWO

RAFAEL HERNÁNDEZ

If a vote for the most popular Puerto Rican in the music world had been held in early 1940, songwriter Rafael Hernández would have won easily. Songwriter Pedro Flores and musicians Pedro Marcano, Augusto Coen, Daniel Santos, and Noro Morales couldn't compare with him—no doubt about it.

In 1939, I was seven years old and living in Spanish Harlem. Some of the events that stuck in my mind from that year were the world's fair in Flushing, Queens; world heavyweight boxing champ Joe Louis getting up off the canvas to brutalize Tony Galento; the movie *Wizard of Oz*; and Rafael Hernández tunes like "Cachita," "Preciosa," "El Cumbanchero," and "Campanitas de Cristal." "Cachita" was heard everywhere—on the streets and at house parties, weddings, and dance halls. Xavier Cugat's up-tempo hit version, sung by Machito, was a happy tune that dancers enjoyed. Its tempo and lyrics were markedly different from the romantic and protest songs Hernández was known for.

According to his sister Victoria, Hernández's melodies and lyrics were reflections of his moods at the time he composed them. If this premise is correct, he was happy when he wrote "Cachita," "El Cumbanchero," "Ahora Seremos Felices," "Campanitas de Cristal," "Cuatro Personas," "Buchi Pluma Na' Ma'," and "Capullito de Alelí." When cupid's arrow found his heart, he may have been inspired to write "No Me Quieras Tanto," "Romance," "Lo Siento Por Tí," "Corazón No Llores," "Tú No Comprendes," "Dos Letras," "Qué Te Importa," and "Ausencia." He could not have been angry often, since he only wrote a few protest songs. Still, the emotionally stirring lyrics of "Preciosa," "Los Carreteros," and "Lamento Borincano" suggest that he was a political activist.

Of all the hundreds of tunes Hernández wrote, these three raise one's blood pressure more than any others. Their lyrics are a history of life in Puerto Rico at the turn of the century. They lament and protest colonial oppression and widespread poverty—the lack of electric lights, running water, indoor plumbing, paved roads, and modern transportation. After the sun went down in the evening, oil lamps provided light in the wooden shacks. Water was fetched from wells or brooks. Stagecoaches traveled over bumpy roads. And deadly, tropical diseases kept the average life span down to only thirty-five years. In New York City, on the other hand, many fatal bacterial diseases had been eradicated by 1916. Tap water was available, and so were electric lights and trolley cars. Nightlife was filled with entertainment, and restaurants delivered steaks minutes after customers gave the waiters their orders. Technologically, New York City was a hundred years ahead of Puerto Rico.

As a member of a U.S. Army band, Hernández served in France and Germany during World War I. After the war he returned to Puerto Rico, then left for New York and began composing songs that are now classics. In mid-1928, his sister Victoria opened the Hernández record store on Madison Avenue between 113th and 114th Streets. She sold 78-rpm records, pianola rolls, maracas, guitars, and guitar strings. A room at the back of the store housed a piano used to teach students.

One summer day in 1929, Victoria urged Rafael to leave the room so she could instruct a student. Rafael took his guitar and a tin can of black coffee out onto the sidewalk, sat near the edge of the curb with his feet in the gutter, tuned his guitar, and began to sing and write lyrics on a piece of paper. His melodic words and phrases came straight from the heart of a man who was separated from his beloved and who could assuage his loneliness and lovesickness only by holding a guitar in his left arm while searching for the notes with his right hand. The lyrics to the tune he composed that day, "Lamento Borincano," suggest that Hernández was hopelessly in love with an island in the Caribbean—with its scenery, folkways, and all the intangibles of Puerto Rico that simply could not be experienced in East Harlem. While singing and playing his guitar, Hernández seemed to mentally transport himself to his beloved Borinquen anytime he wanted to. "Lamento Borincano," would arguably become the most popular composition that Hernández ever wrote.

In 1937, while living in Mexico, he wrote "Preciosa," a song that caused controversy with its expressed resentment toward the American government. In 1947, Puerto Rico's governor, Luis Muñoz Marin, requested that Hernández change the lyric *"del tirano la negra maldad"* (the American tyrant's wickedness)—a reference to U.S. colonialism—to *"del destino la negra maldad"* (the destiny of the wickedness). The government then hailed Rafael Hernández as a Puerto Rican hero.

And there is more to this legend's life worth telling. On September 17,

1981, I interviewed Rafael's sister Victoria, who was then seventy-four years old, in her apartment on Manhattan's Upper West Side. The following is her version of the Rafael Hernández story.

"Rafael was born on October 24, 1896, in Aguadilla, Puerto Rico. I was born in the same town on March 3, 1907. Our parents, María and Gaspar, had two other children—Jesús, whom we called Pocholo, and Rosavida. The four of us were raised by my grandmother Chrisanta, whom we called Tata. Rafael began studying music with my grandmother at age ten. He reached the tenth grade, the highest grade in school. During this time period a child had to become what his parents desired, not what the child wanted to be. The popular music during this time period was the *danza*, waltzes, mazurkas and paso dobles.

"Rafael's first instrument was the cornet, then the violin, and finally the trombone for the San Juan band of Manolo Tizol. He was tutored by Professor Pepe Legreti. He enjoyed kid games like swimming. At age thirteen he wrote his first song, a waltz he titled "Virginia," a tribute to a beautiful Mexican actress. Radio did not exist at the time. The only live music we heard was by the trombonist Cocolia. Rafael's first girlfriend was Nicolosa Cruz. In 1915 he left Aguadilla to join the San Juan municipal band.

"In 1917, when World War I broke out, an American black musician was in Puerto Rico to recruit musicians for the Sixty-fifth Regiment, stationed in South Carolina. From there Rafael went to France, where he remained for close to two years before returning to South Carolina, then to Puerto Rico. He came to New York in 1918. The following year the rest of the family followed. We lived at 1735 Third Avenue....The few Puerto Rican families settled around Ninety-ninth street and Third Avenue. Shortly thereafter, more Puerto Ricans arrived and occupied apartments at Ninety-eighth Street through 103rd Street and Third Avenue.

"In 1919 all of the Puerto Ricans in the area congregated daily at a bodega on 102nd Street between Second and Third Avenues to buy groceries and to socialize. Other Puerto Ricans lived at 135th street near Broadway. The first orchestra to sound a Latin music note was my brother's, which consisted of a few musicians of the Sixty-fifth Regiment. It was a quartet then, which performed at a house party on Ninety-ninth Street. The quartet then backed Rosita Morena, a Spaniard, at El Rivoli theater. Rafael continued to work house parties with a trio or quartet or with a band in a Bronx dance hall. Rafael's last dance was in 1920, when a riot broke out between Puerto Ricans and Anglos, who resented the Latin dances at a Southern Boulevard dance hall. Many people were hospitalized. This discouraged Rafael and prompted his move to Cuba with his girlfriend Juanita.

"In Cuba, Rafael fell in love with the Cuban bolero. For the following four years he studied Cuban music and rhythms. When Rafael returned to New York in 1925, I was already married and living at 102nd Street and Second Avenue. At this time the only band playing Latin music was the big band of trumpeter Vicente Sigler, who played the downtown hotels only. He and Rafael became good friends. Rafael rented an apartment at 102nd Street and Second Avenue, where he and Juanita lived. At this time he formed El Trio Borinquen, which included a Dominican named Señor Mesa, who was first voice and claves, and a Puerto Rican from Cataño named Salvador Ithier, who was second voice and maracas. Rafael played guitar. The trio was contracted to perform in Puerto Rico, the Dominican Republic, then back to Puerto Rico to record Rafael's compositions 'Canta Pajarito,' 'Capullito de Alelí,' 'Ausencia,' and 'Tú Siempre Detrás de Mí.'

"I opened my record store on September 2, 1927, at 1635 Madison Avenue near 114th Street. Before the year ended, Mesa and Ithier left the trio to form their own groups. Rafael earned money writing arrangements of *danzas, danzónes,* and boleros for pianola rolls. I became the first to record Latin music in New York in 1927, when I founded the Disco Hispano label. Four musicians recorded the tunes 'Elena,' 'Menéalo Que Se Empelote,' 'El Reloj,' and 'Ya No Te Quiero.' Because Puerto Ricans had house parties, pianola music was important if they could not hire a live group. They held rent parties, where music was the attraction. There was a twenty-five-cent entrance fee. The *pasteles, pastelillos,* and *coquito* were extra. As the Puerto Rican population increased, musicians replaced the pianola.

"In 1928 Rafael recorded 'Capullito de Allelí' for RCA Victor. In 1929, after a trip to Puerto Rico, Rafael wrote 'Lamento Borincano,' which was inspired by the misery he saw. He also wrote 'Desvelo de Amor,' which was dedicated to me. 'Buchi Pluma Na' Ma'' was dedicated to the people of Curaçao, inspired by a Curaçao rhythm.

"In 1930 we moved to a larger store at 1724 Madison Avenue. Here I sold records, radios, and Victrolas. In the back of the store were women's hats and clothing, and a piano, which I used to teach music. During the mid-to-late 1930s, two of my students were Tito Puente and Joe Loco. Tito told me to tell his mother that he liked to play drums instead of the piano.

"In 1933 Rafael formed El Cuarteto Victoria, which I managed. It consisted of Davilita as first voice; Rafael Rodríguez, second voice; Paco López, first guitar; and Rafael, second guitar. At this time the Puerto Rican population in East Harlem outnumbered the Jewish population in this once affluent Jewish community. El Barrio came alive with Puerto Rican culture. There were many places Latinos could enjoy themselves—El Teatro San

José at 110th Street and Fifth Avenue, the Park Plaza on the same corner, El Campo Amor theater at 116th Street and Fifth Avenue, El Toreador restaurant at 110th near the Park Plaza, and Valentino's restaurant at 116th Street, which only catered to entertainers. For unexplained reasons, El Cuarteto Victoria only lasted a few months.

"There is a bit of history attached to Rafael's composition of 'Malditos Celos.' The popularity of 'Capullito de Alelí' led to an invitation to visit Mexico in 1933. Many people believed he was referring in the song to the jealousy of rival composers Pedro Flores of Puerto Rico and Mexico's beloved Augustín Lara. He wasn't. They were all the best of friends. The tune is about a woman's jealousy. Rafael lived with a Puerto Rican woman, Juanita, for fifteen years. When they moved to Mexico, Rafael fell in love with a Mexican woman, María Pérez. Juanita suspected she was losing Rafael. She became jealous, she got drunk, and she humiliated him in public. Rafael then wrote 'Malditos Celos.' He married María and had four children with her. In Mexico he studied at a conservatory and directed a big band.

"In 1939 he visited Puerto Rico, formed the second Cuarteto Victoria, and replaced Davilita with Bobby Capó. Pepito Arvelo became the first guitar. I spent Christmas with [Rafael] in Puerto Rico in 1939. Right after New Year's Day we left for Curaçao and did radio and theaters; then Barranquilla, Colombia, where vocalist Myrta Silva joined the group and became a star. In July 1940, Rafael was in New York, then Panama, then Mexico, where he divorced Juanita and married María. I moved to Mexico in late November 1940. I tried to open a business and could not: Mexican law provided that only Mexicans could own businesses in Mexico. The same people who told me I could not operate a business told me that for a fee I could have someone front the business for me. I returned to New York City in 1941 [and ran] a women's clothing store at 736 Prospect Avenue between 1942 and 1964.

"Rafael was doing fine in Mexico. He loved it there, was moved by its warmth and the affection of its people, and said it was his second home away from Puerto Rico. He wrote many more tunes in Mexico, performed in nightclubs, and acted in motion pictures. In July 1947 he returned to New York City because of problems with another jealous woman named Celia Luna. A Spanish newspaper reporter asked him if he wanted his four children to be musicians. Rafael said, 'No, because a musician's life is a lie, a bitter disappointment.'

"He lived with me at my apartment on Prospect Avenue until the end of the month, then left for Puerto Rico. Shortly thereafter, he became the music adviser for the newly formed Puerto Rican Symphonette, then later musical adviser of the government-owned radio station WIPR. He held that position until his retirement.

"In 1962, when it became known that he was diagnosed with terminal cancer, Puerto Rico's senate honored him. The senate asked the Institute of Puerto Rican Culture to record a compilation of his popular tunes. He was presented with an honorary doctorate from the Inter-American University of Puerto Rico. One evening, the entire island saw a television show that paid tribute to him. I was in Puerto Rico for five months during his hospitalization at the Veteran's Hospital in San Juan. I visited him every day. He knew he had cancer and was going to die. At times I rolled him around in his wheelchair so he could see the sunset, the moon. He recalled episodes of our childhood, the moments we shared together. Many nights I slept in a chair next to his bed. He mentioned that the only woman he truly loved was Juanita. He was a proud Puerto Rican. Borinquen was his main inspiration."

Rafael Hernández died on December 11, 1965. He was honored with a state funeral attended by thousands. Anyone wishing to understand why so many people came should listen to Ismael Rivera and Rolando Laserie's rendition of "Los Carreteros." Doing so will make apparent Hernández's deep love of Puerto Rico.

Originally published in Latin Beat *magazine, May 1997*

THREE

GABRIEL OLLER

Machito, my mentor for the subject of Latin music in the Big Apple, once advised me, "If you write about the history of New York's Latin music world, you must speak to Gabriel Oller." So on May 21, 1973, I visited the Spanish Music Center in the lobby of the Hotel Belvedere off Eighth Avenue. Oller, a short seventy-year-old, looked like a man in his early fifties. In between customers, he answered my questions in fluent Spanish and English as I took notes. Over the next seven years, I visited Oller so many times that I felt I was absorbing his experiences through osmosis. Each time we spoke, he gave me historical material, rare 78-rpm recordings, and photos, which I copied and returned. They dated from the 1920s and summed up Oller's view of New York City's Latin music world.

Eight decades after those early years, you can turn on a radio any time of day and find Latin music playing. You can dance every night of the week in several places throughout metropolitan New York. Numerous stores sell recordings of all sorts by orchestras and vocalists. There are musicals, television documentaries, concerts, and sophisticated space-age recording equipment that produces the highest possible sound quality. None of these conveniences were available sixty years ago.

Latin music has indeed progressed, and Gabriel Oller is a big contributor to the phenomenon. He is one of a few people who can truthfully claim firsthand knowledge about what was happening musically in Spanish Harlem during the 1920s and 1930s. He was the second Puerto Rican to own his own recording company, the Dynasonic label, and the second to record Puerto Rican folkloric music in New York City, which he began doing in 1934. He and a partner founded the Coda label in 1945; two years later he started the SMC (Spanish Music Company) label with Art Raymond. Oller made early, now-priceless recordings of Noro Morales, Marcelino Guerra, Alfredito Valdés, Alberto Iznaga, José Curbelo, Johnny

Seguí, Juan "El Boy" Torres, Tito Rodríguez, and the Cubans Los Jóvenes del Cayo, Cheo Belén Puig, Olga Guillot, Chano Pozo, Mongo Santamaría, Alberto Socarrás, Miguelito Valdés, and Arsenio Rodríguez. Machito's orchestra (who never wanted their name on the Coda records because of their contract with Verne Records) backed the recordings of Chano Pozo, Olga Guillot, and René Hernández.

Oller's appreciation for a variety of musical sounds began when he first heard a rooster's *kikirikí*, the Puerto Rican alarm clock that wakens the island at dawn each day. Oller was born in Santurce on October 12, 1903. His father, Gabriel Oller Sr., was a teacher who had come to Puerto Rico in 1898, after Spain and the United States agreed in Paris to end the Spanish-American War. The senior Oller arrived in Puerto Rico to teach in a correctional institute. Teachers were badly needed on the island because the Spanish government for centuries had ruled by the "Three B's"—*baile, botellas y barajas* (dancing, liquor, and card playing). With the exception of Cuba, Spain had never enhanced its colonies. As for Borinquen (the old name for Puerto Rico), its first governor, Ponce de León, was not interested in improving life there. All he wanted to do was ship the island's riches back to Spain.

The Puerto Rico of Oller's youth was rural, with streets that were still unpaved. "Half of what the people ate was grown on the land," he said. "Puerto Ricans depended on each other for survival. They raised big families so their children could work the farm and produce the essential agricultural needs. Spain exported clothes, cloth, codfish in barrels, *carne cocida* [*ropa vieja*], soap, perfumes, olive oil, *turón* candy, and guitars. Rice and beans have been our main dish since the days of Christopher Columbus. Taking rice and beans from Puerto Ricans would be the same as taking away their civil rights."

On March 17, 1917, Puerto Ricans were granted American citizenship. Immediately, Puerto Ricans began leaving the island for the United States mainland. The Oller family came to New York City later that year, shortly after World War I was declared. The city's streets were paved with cobblestones, and the clip-clop of horses pulling wagons with beer barrels could be heard for blocks. Compared to the single train track that circles the island in Puerto Rico, New York had four—the Second, Third, Sixth, and Ninth Avenue elevated trains, traversing the length of Manhattan. The ten-cent, double-tier, open-air bus ride up and down Fifth Avenue provided one of the most exciting thrills of the day.

New York City was known as the entertainment capital of the United States and the center of everything. The entertainment district was crowded between Thirty-fourth and Fiftieth Streets. Here is where the best plays were staged, the most fashionable clothes displayed, and the latest dance steps, slang, and fads introduced. It was the era of "Funny Girl" Fanny Brice, composer Irving Berlin, Broadway song-and-dance man George M. Cohan, the dance team of Vernon and Irene Castle, and the gorgeous Ziegfeld girls. It all overwhelmed young Oller.

One day, after reading an ad about opportunities in the field of electronics, he decided that he would develop a career in the entertainment industry by recording performances for posterity. For years, Oller studied electronics at night at a Brooklyn trade and technical school. During this time, the exodus from Puerto Rico began to intensify. Rather than settling in Brooklyn, where they had first gotten off the boat, *borinqueños* began moving into East Harlem, between Ninety-ninth and 116th Streets. The area west of Lexington was inhabited by Jews. To the east lived Italians.

Oller's knowledge of electronics enabled him and his brother Vicente to open the second Spanish music store in Harlem in 1934. Located at 1318 Fifth Avenue, on the corner of 110th Street, it was named Tatay's Spanish Music Center. The brothers sold 78-rpm records, pianola rolls, and guitars; they also charged for guitar lessons. The store was a few feet away from El Teatro San José and the Park Palace Caterers, where Spanish Harlemites in the late 1930s could see musicians like Noro Morales and his brothers, Fernando "Caney" Storch, Pedro Flores, Bobby Capó, El Canario, Pedro "Davilita" Ortíz, Augusto Coen, Alberto Iznaga, Polito Galíndez, Los Hermanos Marcano, Montecino, Mario Bauzá, and Machito—all standing on the corner of Fifth Avenue and 110th Street.

The crowd was there to get work. Anyone wanting to hire a group or a musician who played a specific instrument would phone Oller at his store, and he would tell the musicians standing outside. Bandleaders or star musicians would earn as much as ten dollars for a night's work. A sideman earned three dollars. Very few musicians could depend on music for their livelihood. Music was a means to supplement their income from other work.

Opened in 1927, Casa Hernández, the first Spanish music store in East Harlem, was owned by Puerto Rico's renowned songwriter Rafael Hernández and his sister Victoria. Hernández directed the most popular group in 1933, El Cuarteto Victoria, named after his sister. The store was a twenty-by-sixty-foot space on the west side of Madison Avenue facing uptown, between 113th and 114th Streets. It sold 78-rpm records as well as guitars and the popular pianola rolls. In the back of the store was a piano that Victoria used to teach aspiring musicians. One day in 1929, Hernandéz was composing a tune on the piano when a student appeared for lessons. He took his guitar and a tin can of black coffee out onto the sidewalk, sat down near the edge of the curb, and continued to compose. As a result, "Lamento Borincano," Hernández's most popular composition, was born on the sidewalk outside Casa Hernández. Oller says he was a witness.

"With a name like Rafael Hernández to compete against, I had to have a gimmick—the Dynasonic test records," Oller said. "During the 1930s, New York Puerto Ricans were different than today—they were dyed-in-the-wool Puerto Ricans. They lived by their folkways, they spoke Spanish, they ate Spanish food only. It was like one big family. Although there were some problems with other people, we became friendly neighbors with Jews, who learned to speak Spanish. The Jewish people were our only outside influence. The Puerto Ricans stuck to their own culture until the early 1940s; we became Americanized in a few aspects in order to compete in the labor market."

From 1934 to 1941, Oller sold his Dynasonic recordings of Noro Morales, Caney, and the neighborhood trios and quartets. These recordings helped popularize artists who would later begin recording for Decca. Dynasonic never pressed more than two hundred copies of any particular recording. The quality of the shellac used to make them was such that each record could survive at least fifteen good plays. But during the 1930s, radio networks saw no need to air Spanish music. They said the Hispanic population was too small to constitute a market.

In the early 1940s, violinist/bandleader Xavier Cugat got nationwide recognition with his recordings of "Ojos Verdes" (Green Eyes) and "Amapola." Cugat's music became a favorite among non-Hispanic American listeners, and Hollywood put his orchestra into motion pictures. Cuban vocalist Miguelito Valdés, Colombian baritone Carlos Ramírez, and Brazilian singer and dancer Carmen Miranda gained worldwide fame by appearing in motion pictures with Cugat. His music paved the way for Latin music and musicians.

After World War II began, record manufacturing was restricted, as shellac and wax were needed for wartime purposes. Major American record labels released Latin artists from their contracts so that popular swing bands could make records using the rationed material. As a result, Latin bands had to mail their masters to Canada and Mexico, where their records were pressed, labeled, and shipped back to the United States.

The public's thirst for Latin music was partially quenched by the weekly CBS radio show *Saludos Amigos*. During the war years, it hired the most popular orchestras in Latin music. Even the U.S. military overseas could hear the show. Then, toward the end of 1944, the United States began clearly winning the war, and restrictions on recording materials were eased.

In January, 1945, Gabe Oller founded the Coda Recording Company at a new location, 1291 Sixth Avenue, at the corner of Fifty-second Street. In 1947, Oller and WEVD radio talk-show host Art Raymond formed the Spanish Music Center recording company. Raymond became known as "Pancho" and hosted a one-hour program, *Pancho's Club Tico Tico,* on which he aired SMC and Coda label recordings exclusively.

On February 23, 1947, the orchestras of Machito and Alfredito Valdés became the first bands to kick off the Sunday rumba matinee dances at Oller and Raymond's Club Tico Tico. Beginning at 1 P.M., dancers paid a dollar and fifty cents to enjoy themselves for five hours. The Sunday-afternoon ritual became a gold mine that week, when more than five hundred dancers occupied the dance floor of the Manhattan Center, at the corner of Thirty-fourth Street and Eighth Avenue. For reasons unknown, however, Oller and Raymond's successful venture ended in 1948. Oller bought out Raymond and became sole owner of the SMC label.

The following are Oller's recollections of his experiences with some of the artists he recorded.

> Noro Morales: "On January 16, 1945, Noro was the first to record for Coda. He recorded 'Rumba Rhapsody,' 'Bangin' the Bongo,' 'Linda Mujer,' and 'Begin the Beguine.' Our friendship began in the 1930s when he hung out on the corner of 110th Street and Fifth Avenue. He was always well dressed—shoes shined, nails polished—and he reeked of expensive men's cologne. He loved women. He had to work steadily in order to pay the alimony his three wives collected. Noro always needed money. He sold me a half interest of the copyrights of two of his tunes, 'Montuno in A-Flat' and 'Bangin' the Bongos,' for a hundred and fifty dollars. He didn't like to sign contracts. He used to say 'Are you American or Puerto Rican? Don't you trust me? Come, let's go to the studio.' Noro made great recordings for me."

> Miguelito Valdés: "Miguel and I were friends since he came to the United States. He was respected by everyone in his profession. I was able to record Olga Guillot and Chano Pozo because of him. Cuban artists always asked Miguel for his advice. Valdés was one hundred percent Cuban. He thought Cuban, he bought from Cuban merchants only, and Cuban goods only. His recording 'Harlem Special,' which was first called 'Gateando,' was his biggest seller. 'Mondongo' was second.

> Alfredito Valdés (vocalist and brother of Vicentico and Marcelino): "Alfredo was one of Los Bravos de Cuba before he came to America. Alfredo, Cheo Marquetti, and Abelardo Barroso were Cuba's best *soneros*. His Coda recording

of 'Guantanamera' was a big seller. Of all my SMC recordings, Alfredo's 'Encanto Cubano' sold the most. Tito Puente arranged this tune and 'El Mambo de Broadway' for Alfredo's June 1949 recording session. Backing Alfredo was Tito Puente's orchestra, the Picadilly Boys."

Tito Rodríguez: "Tito and I became friends around 1940, when he first came from Puerto Rico. He lived at 110th Street, one block away from my store. He was sixteen or seventeen and would join the musicians every day after 2 P.M. on the corner of 110th Street. He was short, thin, and very handsome—a pretty boy. He and Miguelito Valdés attracted the women to this corner. I got him a singing job with Conjunto Caney. After Caney it was all upwards for Tito. He was so good looking he had women fighting over him at the China Doll when he sang there with Noro Morales. In June 1948, he recorded four records for me at the Beltone studios. René Hernández [Machito's pianist] was one of a few people responsible for Tito's success; he arranged music for Tito's recordings. On August 31, 1949, Tito recorded four more sides, which were arranged by Tito Puente. I paid Puente ten dollars for each arrangement. As payment for the recording session, Tito Rodríguez asked for thirty-five dollars and the four Puente arrangements. Months later Rodríguez was recording for Tico Records."

Arsenio Rodríguez: "During the late 1940s, Arsenio was tied to RCA Victor. Through a mutual friend of ours in Cuba, Arsenio sent me tapes of eight *son montunos* he recorded in 1948. He first tried to sell them to RCA, but RCA was only interested in mambos, because Pérez Prado caused quite a stir with his 'Mambo No. 5.' Arsenio sold me the recording because he needed money. This incredible man supported himself, his wife, and his two brothers. He loved his family like some people love wealth. His music, which is priceless today, was recorded for peanuts. He wasn't a good businessman. After a while, his wife began to negotiate for him to help him from being robbed.

The first of his records to be released by SMC were 'Yo No Engaño a Las Nenas' and 'Tocoloro.' Since he was under contract to RCA at the time, he urged me to list his *conjunto* as Estrellas Cubanas [Cuban Stars]. In 1950 he left Cuba and stopped off in Miami en route to New York City. He spent a few days in Miami and left. He never went back to Florida because of the way he was treated. He couldn't stay at certain hotels, he couldn't eat at certain restaurants, and he suffered all the indignities that black people have endured in a Southern state. He was always searching for a new sound and never forgot the people who were kind to him. He would always mention their names in his recordings. He immortalized Luis Cora, a Bronx barber, in a *son montuno*, because Cora always cut his hair free of charge.

I recorded Arsenio with Chano Pozo, the Machito orchestra, and Marcelino

Guerra's Conjunto Batamu. During the '60s he came to me with a tape of four tunes other record companies were not interested in. I added some of his other recordings and released *Fiesta en Harlem*, a twelve-inch SMC LP. The *pachanga* was popular at the time, so he changed the title of a fast *son montuno* he called 'Gozando en el Barrio' to 'Son Pachanga.' This tune reveals the gaiety and spirit of El Barrio, the only place he felt comfortable in. Arsenio Rodríguez is the best musician to come out of Cuba. No one will ever top the legacy he left us.

In 1988, Gabriel Oller retired and relocated to Las Vegas to live with his brother Vicente Tatay. At the time, Oller was suffering with Alzheimer's disease. In late 1988, he was struck and killed by an automobile while crossing Las Vegas's main boulevard against the traffic light. His brother's nephew, Andrew Tatay, inherited Oller's estate. Part of it was a six-story warehouse that held thousands of 78-rpm recordings—twenty-five to a box—as well as session recording contracts, which included musicians' names, dates, salaries, titles of tunes, photographs, and other historical documents. Unaware of this memorabilia's value, the nephew emptied the warehouse of the "garbage" and had it hauled off.

Originally published in Latin Beat *magazine, March 2000*

FOUR

Conjunto Caney

In 1940, a fill-in tune needed to finish a Decca recording session ended up making Conjunto Caney a star attraction. At that time, Caney, the thirty-five-year-old bandleader, resembled movie star Errol Flynn, with his handsome face, wavy black hair, and dark, impeccably trimmed mustache. His Conjunto Caney had finally become a headliner after years of struggle. The group went on to sell thousands of Decca and Columbia 78-rpm discs, featuring vocalists Machito, Panchito Riset, and Johnny López.

On June 24, 1974, I was at Gabriel Oller's Spanish Music Center in the lobby of the Hotel Belvedere, off the corner of Forty-eighth Street and Eighth Avenue. In the store sat Caney, listening to his old Coda recordings and reminiscing about his heyday. He was dressed in a gray sharkskin suit, blue sport shirt, and a yellow fisherman's cap that covered most of his cotton-white hair. The portly, white-mustachioed Caney looked like Santa Claus on a summer vacation. He was passing through New York City en route to Lake George, an upstate summer resort where he would play his last gig. He mentioned that he had reached the point where he could no longer tolerate hustling for gigs and being underpaid. He was having a hard time locating three sidemen who would accept earnings of $110 a week, with room and board, until Labor Day. His own cut would be only $150 a week.

"Why," I asked him, "will you work for these low wages, when you used to earn the same amount for a night's work during your peak years?"

"Used to," he replied in Spanish, the language he preferred to speak. "The music industry is similar to prizefighting. You are a champ for a short duration, the competition is tough, a new rhythm emerges, a new trend is started, and if a bandleader ignores it, he fades into obscurity. I know nothing else but music. Music enables me to meet my daily expenses."

Caney is one example of how a musician must live when he is compelled into semi-retirement for lack of work. He drives his blue 1965 Mercury to entertainment spots where Latin music is featured. He organizes a four- or five-piece group of local musicians. He gets paid, pays the sidemen, and hits the road again, traveling the length and width of Florida looking for more gigs.

In addition to his conga drum and *tres* guitar, Caney makes certain he has his brown briefcase. He holds on to it as tightly as if it contained a million dollars. Inside are his links to yesteryear—a variety of mementos that permit him to relive unforgettable events of the past. Feeding the nostalgia are a few yellowed photos of his many bands, faded and wrinkled Spanish and English newspaper clippings, a few old music sheets, and a ten-inch Decca LP whose yellow cover says "Caney" in bold black lettering. These memorabilia are not only a ticket to the past; they are also documentary evidence that Caney was once the musical director of a popular band.

Born Fernando Storch on May 30, 1905, Caney is a Cuban of German ancestry. In a proud voice he said, "I was raised in El Barrio Santos Suárez in Havana, Cuba." He began studying the saxophone at age sixteen, when the big band of Los Hermanos Palau influenced him with its versions of American jazz. At this time, the Sexteto Habanero were the kings of Cuban music. In 1925 Caney formed a septet, Los Krazy Kats, but disbanded the following year when one of the sidemen died.

In early 1927, Caney left Cuba without his family and settled in the Bronx. A friend of his father's taught him to play the *tres* guitar. In 1929, unable to find work, he relocated to Wilmington, Delaware, to take a factory job. Six months later he moved to Detroit, Michigan, and worked for the Ford Motor Company. In 1930 he returned to New York and rented an apartment on Lenox Avenue at 111th Street. For a ten-block stretch, only Cubans lived on Lenox. A regular dance, begun a few months earlier at the Park Palace Caterers at 110th Street and Fifth Avenue, had made it possible for many musicians to work steadily.

Caney formed El Cuarteto Borinquén and worked every weekend from ten o'clock at night until three in the morning at house parties throughout Spanish Harlem. Puerto Rican and Cuban families staged these parties to help pay the rent and buy food. "Upon entering the apartments, guests were pinned with a small strip of colored cloth, indicating they paid the twenty-five-cent entrance fee," said Caney. "We played boleros, *guarachas*, and tunes like 'Son de la Loma' in a slow swing. The two guitarists would set the tempo and sing in unison. The muted trumpet, rattling maracas, and claves rounded out the sound. We were paid with money collected from the sales of *pastelillos*, *pasteles*, beer, *coquito*, and *mavi*. On good nights we earned earned five dollars."

Before 1930 ended, Caney was directing a sextet, Los Ecos de Cuba. He kept the group intact for three years until he met a transplanted Cuban from Tampa named Elio Osácar, one of the few Cuban musicians at the time who played string bass in place of the traditional *marímbula* (an African-derived instrument similar to the kalimba, or thumb piano). Together they persuaded Mr. Roldan, the proprietor of El Toreador Restaurant at 110th Street and Fifth Avenue, to give their newly formed Fernando Storch Quartet a chance to play. Roldan did not like the name of the group and suggested it be changed to Caney as a tribute to a section of Santiago de Cuba famous for its fruit.

In 1933, El Cuarteto Caney debuted at El Toreador. In those days it was an exclusive, high-priced Spanish restaurant whose specialty was paella, a delicious rice and seafood dish. In addition to their ten-dollar salary, the quartet earned tips as they strolled from table to table playing requests.

The incident that resulted in national recognition occurred in 1939 at Chicago's Colony Club. Latin bands during this period were "relief bands," filling in while the American pop band took a twenty-minute rest. The Latin bands were responsible for reminding the featured groups that their short break was over. When the time was up, Caney's pianist, Rafael Audinot, would signal the featured band with an ad-libbed melody as the rest of Caney's group started leaving the bandstand.

One evening, after Audinot began his signal, Elio Osácar began plucking his bass, Johnny López chimed in with his maracas, and Audinot ad-libbed a lengthy piano solo. The result was later titled "Rhumba Flamenco," and in 1940 it was recorded as a fill-in tune when Caney's trumpeter's lip went numb after recording five tracks. The tune, which Audinot retitled "Rhumba Rhapsody," became a smash hit, selling thousands of copies. It became the band's theme and got them top-dollar gigs. The 1940 strike by ASCAP (the American Society of Composers, Authors and Publishers), in which the better-known Broadway and Tin Pan Alley composers refused radio stations permission to broadcast their songs, added exposure for "Rhumba Rhapsody."

A few months later, while working at the Latin Quarter in midtown Manhattan, Caney was searching for a vocalist who could play maracas and sing second voice until Manolo Suárez arrived from Cuba. Gabriel Oller suggested he utilize Pablo Rodríguez, a teenager who had sung with Placido Acevedo's Cuarteto Mayari a few months earlier in Puerto Rico. Rodríguez was given the job for two months and went on to join Xavier Cugat's orchestra after being replaced by Suárez. "If I knew then that Pablito would later becomes the famous Tito Rodríguez, I would have had him record with me as a lead singer," said Caney.

In 1943, Caney gave up a lucrative steady job at the Havana-Madrid because he could no longer tolerate the steadily increasing crime rate in his Bronx neighborhood. He moved to Florida and has lived there ever since, although he occasionally returned to New York to perform. Danton Walker, a columnist for the New York *Daily News*, honored Caney as an important bandleader. In his May 7, 1957, column, Walker wrote, "After fourteen years, Caney's back in New York City at the Chateau Madrid."

One of the saddest moments in Caney's life occurred in 1957, when his dear friend Elio Osácar died. Caney recalled the day in October 1936 when Osácar's wife gave birth to their son in an apartment at 111th Street and Lenox Avenue. "My wife and I were the first to see the baby a few minutes after he was born," Caney said. Elio Osácar Jr. grew to be six-feet-four-inches tall, a handsome and accomplished musician who played piano for José Fajardo, Willie Bobo, Rafael Cortijo, Louie Ramírez, and Típica 73. Later he was known as Sonny Bravo and played keyboards for Tito Puente's orchestra.

Caney's wife, Lydia Storch, is of Puerto Rican descent; the two were married in New York City in 1934. They have two sons—Fernando Jr., an accountant who lives in Jacksonville, Florida, and Ronnie, who lives in Miami.

"After working the last thirty years as a musician, I have little to show for it," lamented Caney. "I made over two hundred recordings for several companies, and I never received one cent in royalties. It's going to be rough for me to quit and never play again after Labor Day. I won't have any money coming in, but I just can't succeed against the odds."

Caney said this in July 1974. He is just one more example of why a musician should have another skill besides music in order to earn a livelihood in case his musical career is cut short. Hard-working musicians like Caney grow old. The efforts they put into their art should be repaid with assurances that they will still live in dignity. [Editor's note: Fernando "Caney" Storch died of a heart attack in Jacksonville, Florida, on December 24, 2001.]

Originally published in Latin Beat *magazine, August 1997*

FIVE

ALBERTO IZNAGA

On a mild day in late May 1929, a passenger ship moved slowly out the harbor in Havana, Cuba. As it headed out to sea, everything left behind began to shrink in size—the castle fortress, the tinted, two- and three-story Spanish-style houses, and the cross crowning the convent of San Francisco. On the deck, a tall, handsome young Afro-Cuban stood staring at the increasingly distant city. His gleaming, bitter eyes were the only evidence of how much he despised the country of his birth. As the Havana skyline disappeared from sight, Alberto Iznaga thought to himself, "Good-bye Cuba, I hope I never see you again." He was heading for the United States, where blacks were given a chance to work and succeed in life. He could no longer tolerate his own country's covert policy of racial discrimination.

Not all white Cubans believed in the separation of the races. Ten percent of the population of Cuba's *solares* (tenements that housed Afro-Cuban slaves) were indigent white Cubans. But since childhood, Iznaga had seen racist attitudes at work and heard the rationalizations used to deny black Cubans the inalienable rights of man. Throughout Cuba, blacks were not allowed to stay at hotels. Santa Clara's Vidal Park was segregated; only whites could walk in it. Although Afro-Cuban musicians entertained at a few clubs, they could not socialize with the patrons. During a break, a musician either stayed in the kitchen or off the premises until it was time to perform again. Afro-Cubans were denied entrance to all the prominent entertainment spots because tables were reserved for members only. To get a university scholarship or a bed in a good hospital, brown and black Cubans had to have political patronage. All this was a quiet fact of life until 1959, when Fidel Castro took control of the government and officially abolished segregation.

Nature seems to contain a mysterious force that rights wrongs. This invisible force enables a blind person to develop a keen sense of hearing, touch, and smell. It makes it possible for a person with one arm to have the strength of a person with two. This same force rewards good deeds and punishes evil ones. People whose congenital defects do not permit them to achieve fame on the athletic field often succeed as painters, sculptors, scientists, and writers.

In Iznaga's first-floor apartment, adorned with his own oil paintings, this writer saw certificates of musical achievement from Cuban conservatories, private tutors, and New York's Juilliard School. He has commendation notes for his diligence in the study of theory, sight-reading, diction, harmony, composition, and arranging. He still had the books he used to teach himself to play the clarinet and alto saxophone. Iznaga has always been driven by a will to succeed, to strive for excellence in his work. He possessed such determination even as a child.

Alberto Iznaga de Palacios was born in Havana on July 25, 1906, to Germán Iznaga and his wife, Catalina Palacios. A year and a half later, Germán died. As a child, Alberto was always in trouble, and his mother was always in school explaining why he was out fishing instead of in class. His behavior improved at age fourteen—the same period when wealthy white Americans, mostly Southerners, were buying hotels and businesses and establishing new industries in Cuba. It was at this time that Alberto began to notice the preferential treatment of whites to the detriment of blacks. After studying for two years at the San Alejandro Academy of Art and Culture, he gave up painting for music as form of expression, believing that "a proficient musician could never be denied."

He was wrong. There were many proficient Afro-Cuban musicians who never received the recognition due them. An example was that of accomplished concert violinist Estrella Socarrás, the sister of renowned musical maestro Dr. Alberto Socarrás. Estrella sat in the twentieth seat and second row of the Havana Philharmonic Orchestra until the protestations of several white- and dark-skinned orchestra members resulted in her being moved to the first chair, first row. Virgilio Diago, whose violin virtuosity was known throughout Cuba, was first chair of the Symphonic Orchestra of Havana, but he never received the recognition due him because he was black.

At the Fernando Carnicer Conservatory, Iznaga learned to play the violin under tutelage of Demetrie Vladescu, a white Romanian. Vladescu, whom Iznaga still holds in very high esteem, helped the young musician complete a four-year violin course in half that time. Vladescu was always criticized for seating Iznaga in the first chair of the academy's orchestra. Iznaga paid for his lessons from money he earned as a valet at the Hotel Almendares. He learned to speak English from the American owners of the hotel. After he finished his studies, he got a job with the Havana Philharmonic. The orchestra traveled the concert hall and theater circuit of Havana. On June 10, 1928, Iznaga played a concert at Teatro Nacional with his childhood friend, Mario Bauzá, the orchestra's bass clarinetist. Bauzá would later become famous throughout the Latin-music world as co-leader and musical director of the Machito orchestra.

While reading the Cuban newspapers over a period of several months, Iznaga noticed that blacks in the United States were winning scholarships to universities and cash prizes in concerts, and that they were allowed to compete with Caucasians and be recognized. He decided he wanted to live in the United States, even though Vladescu tried to persuade him to live in France.

His first job in the U.S. was as a clerk for a black-owned insurance company in Washington D.C. Two months later he became a violinist for an all-black jazz band that played for black audiences at the Howard Theatre. Months later, El Barrio in Manhattan came alive with music after a community dance, organized at Park Palace Caterers to raise funds for the Latino community, proved breathtakingly successful. Iznaga moved to New York and settled in an apartment in the Puerto Rican enclave at 114th Street and Madison Avenue, in front of the Almacenes Hernández record store. At that time, musicians frequented El Billar de los Músicos (the Musicians Billiard Parlor), a poolroom at 113th Street and Madison Avenue, which also served as an employment agency. Whoever wanted to hire a musician would simply fill out a three-by-five white index card and indicate the instrument needed, the salary, the hours, the place, and the person to contact. The card was tacked onto a plywood board and removed by the musician who accepted the job. This is how Iznaga got gigs with Vicente Sigler, the first Latin bandleader to direct a big band in New York City during the 1920s. "Sigler was a grand person," said Iznaga, "but we never knew what he was going to pay us."

In 1933, Iznaga taught himself to play the clarinet and alto saxophone. He played dance dates in clubs throughout the five boroughs for three years, until he joined the International Workers Order Symphony Orchestra in 1936. He started as a violinist with the I.W.O. and graduated to assistant conductor and assistant concertmaster. The orchestra played concerts in theaters and high schools and always raised money for a cause. Before the year ended, Iznaga learned the cause was a communist one, and he resigned from the organization.

Latin music during this period was evolving in Cuba, and new trends were emerging due to the innovations of the very popular Casino de la Playa orchestra. In addition to introducing the ad-libbed lyrics, charts, and riffs of vocalist Miguelito Valdés, Casino de la Playa presented the swinging, up-tempo piano of Anselmo Sacasas, whose solo on the recording "Dolor Cobarde" in 1936 was a landmark in Cuban music. Sacasas was also one of the most influential Cuban arrangers.

Iznaga learned arranging, and in early 1937 he became a sideman and arranger for trumpeter/bandleader Augusto Coen. After he got married the next year, he formed New York's first cooperative band, La Siboney, and debuted at La Toja Cabaret in Staten Island. The band's personnel consisted of Gilberto Ayala (piano), Rafael Pesante (bass), Tony Escollies (bongos and timbales), José Budet (violin, clarinet, and tenor sax), Alvaro Felix (trumpet), and Frank Grillo (the vocalist who later became famous as Machito). La Siboney established itself as a popular band immediately through musical battles against other bands, a popular gimmick during this era. Iznaga's battles with Montesino, a Cuban percussionist and leader of Los Happy Boys, are legendary. But the bands did not need gimmicks to fill dance halls. Their fiercely contested battles revealed how strongly they felt about each other. They musically knocked each other's brains out to prove which group was better and who deserved top billing on the marquees and posters.

In 1940, the Club Cuba opened in midtown Manhattan and hired Machito to lead the house band. Machito became La Siboney's leader until the club went bankrupt six months later. Iznaga then resumed the leadership of La Siboney. Later in 1940, Machito and his brother-in-law, Mario Bauzá, formed the historic orchestra Machito and his Afro-Cubans.

Also in 1940, the atrocious behavior of Adolf Hitler in Europe caused great unease in the United States. Americans tried to push such things out of their minds, but newsreels showed fearsome images of rumbling tanks, goose-stepping Nazis, exploding shells, and roaring cannons. The U.S. government took a step to protect American shores by establishing the draft, which selected men younger than age thirty-eight by lottery and inducted them into the Army.

A few months before the year ended, La Siboney began to play out-of-town engagements. Their road trips ended in early 1943, when Iznaga opted to remained in New York and enroll at the Juilliard School. "I've studied under several men in Cuba who were considered musical geniuses," he said, "but after studying at Juilliard I realized I did not know much about music....Americans take music much more seriously."

In June 1943, while Iznaga was attending a class, his wife was visited by an FBI agent named O'Connor in their plush Central Park West apartment. After a half-hour of conversation, the agent left a note instructing Iznaga to report to his draft board. At the draft board, Iznaga learned he had been on the FBI's wanted list since 1940. The bandleader was shown a draft board notice dated December 17, 1940, which read that he was number eighty-seven of the first hundred men selected in the draft lottery. The notice was mailed to "Alberto Palacios"—Palacios being his mother's maiden name. Iznaga escaped a prison term by producing letters, pay stubs, bank records, and his 1942 American citizenship papers, all of were in the name Iznaga. The board members had sent FBI agents through El Barrio for three years to seek the phantom Alberto Palacios. Now they looked at Iznaga with raised eyebrows. He was given three months to settle his affairs, then report to Fort Dix, New Jersey, on August 1. But seven days before his induction date, Iznaga celebrated his thirty-eighth birthday and thus was exempted from the draft.

That year saw a demand for Latin music arrangers. Since 1940, violinist/bandleader Xavier Cugat had been titillating this nation's non-Spanish-speaking public with his recordings and movie appearances. Requests for Latin music from pop orchestras and college and high school bands created a great deal of work for Latin music composers and arrangers. Stock arrangements—printed sheets of music—sold at music and record stores for $1.25. Iznaga arranged tunes such as "Voodoo Moon" (Enlloro), "Chupa Chupa," "Nague," "Goin' Conga," and many others for the Pan American, Antobal, Marks and Robbins music-publishing companies. Iznaga's nationwide exposure as an arranger, his danceable arrangements, and his commendable reputation earned many gigs for La Siboney. Some of the most notable were at the exclusive Monte Carlo Cabaret at Fifty-sixth Street and Madison Avenue, and at Grossinger's summer resort in the Catskills.

In 1952, while mambo was increasing in popularity, La Siboney disbanded. Iznaga became a violinist for the orchestra of flutist Gilberto Valdés at the Bronx Tropicana Club. Valdés's orchestra was the first American charanga, but it was hard to impress dancers with flute-and-string-based *danzónes*. After a year of struggling, Valdés joined the Katherine Dunham Dance Company as musical director, and left his band to Iznaga. In 1957, Iznaga relinquished the group to Arsenio Rodríguez, then picked up his tenor sax and became arranger and musical director for vocalist Carlos Pizarro.

On April 13, 1974, after playing an Easter Sunday Eve dance at the Bronx's Colgate Gardens, Iznaga closed his saxophone, clarinet, and violin cases for the last time. This marked the end of a thirty-five-year career, during which he recorded a number of hit tunes for the Decca, Coda, Standards, Davis, Columbia, Lopati, and RCA labels. He shared credits with vocalists Machito, El Boy, Dioris Valladares, José Luis Moreno, Bobby

Rivera, Macucho, Payo Flores, and Yayo el Indio. He arranged music for Augusto Coen, Rafael Hernández, Bobby Capó and Carlos Pizzaro. His tune "Goin' Conga" was recorded in 1940 by Cab Calloway and Anselmo Sacasas.

"Being a musician has been frustrating at times, but it has been good for me," he concluded. "I earned $260 a week during the 1940s, banked $10,000, always had a new car, and learned from Demetrie Vladescu that not all white people are alike. I've made many white and black friends during the course of my career....Today I am not bitter toward anyone."

By the time Alberto Iznaga reached adulthood, nature was countering the inequities wreaked against black Cubans with the beats those same blacks had been crafting for generations. Cuba's most valuable commodity is not its rum, tobacco, or sugar cane. It is the Afro-Cuban rhythms created in Cuba's black ghettos. The *danzón*, *son*, *son montuno*, afro lament, *rumba*, *guaracha*, mambo, *guaguancó* and *cha-cha-chá* have brought joy to people all over the world and are responsible for the creation of Japan's Orquesta de la Luz, Holland's Nueva Manteca, Sweden's Hot Salsa, Germany's Connection Latina, Finland's Septeto Son, and the funky salsa sounds of Al DeLory in Nashville, Tennessee.

Alberto Iznaga, heir to this rich tradition, successfully strove to be twice as good as the average musician. Dr. Iznaga died on April 16, 1995, in Bayamon, Puerto Rico, after a lengthy illness. But while he lived, he gained and nourished the universal respect that Afro-Cuban rhythms bring to every person of color from the island.

Originally published in Latin Beat *magazine, December/January 1997*

SIX

MIGUELITO VALDÉS

It was a cold, gray morning, February 11, 1976. Icy winds and snow covered the streets and discouraged the usual human activity. I was sitting near the large, Fifty-fifth Street window of *Latin New York* magazine's office, looking out from the second floor onto the street, awaiting the arrival of renowned vocalist Miguelito Valdés. At 11:05 A.M., Gary Elter, the magazine's sales manager, greeted Valdés by exclaiming "Mr. Babalú!" Valdés, attired in a black scarf and sweater, blue trousers and navy blue overcoat, removed his wide-brimmed black hat, smiled, extended his hand, and said in a heavy Spanish accent, "Hi, I'm Frank Sinatra." We all broke out in laughter. I directed him to an empty office where the interview would take place. "Miguelito," I said, "I am extremely pleased by this opportunity." He replied that "Machito and Mario [Bauzá] said you were the only one who would write it objectively" and in a way that "would not embarrass me...besides, I am reading your five-part story about rivalries...it is one hundred percent accurate....I love it."

For the next four hours, I recorded our conversation. More time was needed, and it was granted. We met on four consecutive Mondays at Victor's restaurant on Columbus Avenue. Flutist/pianist/bandleader Lou Pérez joined us twice. Despite the hours allotted this interview, it was not possible to learn everything about Mr. Babalú, whose career spanned fifty years. Still, there should be enough here about the handsome, five-foot-eleven-inch Cuban musician to leave you well satisfied.

On September 6, 1910, Miguelito was born Eugenio Zacrias Miguel Valdés in *el barrio de Belén,* Havana, Cuba. His father, Emilio Izquierdo, a white Spaniard, was a colonel in the Spanish army. His mother, América Valdés, was a beautiful Maya Indian born in Yucatan, Mexico. She reared Miguelito, five brothers and one sister in *el barrio Cayo Hueso,* a neighborhood full of splendorous Spanish architecture. The grocery and meat stores were owned and operated by *gallegos*—white Spaniards. The

37

Chinese operated the vegetable stores, while black Cubans and other indigents worked the sugar and tobacco fields. Miguelito received only six years of formal education, at Havana's Zapata Grammar School. At age eleven he was working as an automobile mechanic. "I wanted to help my mother…she and my father had separated years before. I earned two dollars a week."

In 1926, when he was sixteen years old, Valdés was inspired by the boxing feats of Cuban featherweight Kid Chocolate to try ring combat. Subsequent to winning his twenty-third bout over a promising fighter, Valdés was interviewed at the Casa del Deporte radio station. After explaining how he beat his opponent, he asked permission to sing a song. In Cuba, if one was not involved in politics or sports, one was enmeshed in music. "When I was a kid, Santería music was the most popular music in Cayo Hueso, but I listened to classical music also," Valdés recalled.

He decided to try singing after attending a performance by Mexican vocalist José Mojica. In 1927 he became the vocalist for El Sexteto Habanero Juvenil. Two years later, after he studied guitar, solfeggio, and voice with female bandleader María Teresa Vera, she made him part of her chorus, which worked dime-a-dance academies—in effect, ballrooms—such as Sport Antillana, Havana Sport, and El Rialto.

The early 1930s were rough years for Cubans. Government corruption, bribery, and the 1929 American stock market crash contributed to Cuba's high unemployment rate. The sparse work offered musicians resulted in disbandments, and those groups who managed to stay together reduced their personnel. In 1933, immediately after President Gerardo Machado was ousted from power, Valdés accepted a singing job with a Cuban band contracted to play a carnival in Panama. "I lived in Panama from the end of 1933 to the end of 1936," he said. "After the carnival was over, most of the bands returned to Cuba. I fell in love with Vera Eskilssen-Tejada, whom I married. We had a son named Juan, who I call Chengue. I washed dishes, waited tables, and sang at El Moderno Cubano restaurant. Every time I waited on a Cuban, I learned what was happening in Cuba and what it was like living in [dictator Fulgencio] Batista's regime. One night the popular Panamanian bandleader Lucho Azcárraga heard me sing at the restaurant. While I took his order for dinner, he offered me a job. I sang with his orchestra at the Union Club from 1934 to 1936."

During his two years with Azcárraga, Valdés made many friends. The Panamanian media loved him. Over the radio, in newspapers, and in magazine articles, they would report how the "handsome Miguelito Valdés" charmed an audience with his warm and pleasant sense of humor. Word of his Panamanian success filtered back to Cuba. "In September

1936, I returned to Cuba. It was the right time. I knew I had made it big. My two trunks were full of expensive clothes and shoes. I went back with presents for my family and a little money....I put on a show like I had made it big."

Shortly after his return to Cuba, alto saxophonist Manolo Castro, the bandleader of Los Hermanos Castro, engaged Valdés to sing at a private club for a ceremony honoring Alfonso Hornedo. He said he would accept only if he could select the songs. "I always dressed in a tuxedo when I presented Afro-Cuban music to society. I tried to present it in the best light."

At the Hornedo ceremony, Valdés overwhelmed the audience with a singing style never heard before. It was his innovations (he called them "routines") during a *montuno*—in which he inserted fast double-talk like *"mamacita de mi vida, puchungita de mi vida...no me llores...pree-con-con"* that drove the listeners wild. "A vocalist must know the story [in the song lyrics] first before he can improvise during the *montuno*," he said. "One of the best today is Ismael Rivera. Some of the vocalists of today just make sounds that mean nothing because they do not know the story. It takes time before a vocalist can get in our book...when I say 'our book' I mean Machito, Tito Rodríguez, and myself. We know the story about the song and we never lose the syncopation. There are many stories to sing about. The people in the many *solares* [inner-city tenements] in Cuba have one to tell. I believe in Santería. and I know what I am singing about when I open my mouth. Whoever sings about Santería or *Náñigo* should know about these religions."

After singing for about a year with Los Hermanos Castro, Valdés and six members of the band decided to leave and form a corporation. "Three of us had more contact with people. The others had other interests. What made our orchestra popular was not so much good recordings...but the friends we made off the bandstand, with good will. Musicians should always be gentlemen...be well dressed. The Castro organization was good, but it was too strict...most of us wanted something flexible, so we organized our corporation."

In June 1937, the corporation formed a twelve-piece orchestra. Its personnel were Guillermo Portella, violinist and director; Miguelito Valdés, administrator and vocalist for both up-tempo and Afro material; Anselmo Sacasas, pianist and music arranger; Walfredo de los Reyes, second trumpet and ballad vocalist; Luis Rubio, first trumpet; José Peña, bass and trombone; Liduvino Perieda, first alto sax, and Ernesto Vega, handling guitar and maracas.

"A few days after we formed our group, I visited Pepe Vásquez, one of the owners of the Summer Casino Corporation in Marinao, Havana. In his office I told him that I was part of Cuba's most progressive orchestra. He asked 'What's the name of the orchestra?' I told him we had no name yet, but if he gave us a five-year contract, we would call it the Summer Casino Orchestra. His eyes opened wide; he invited me to sit and offered me a shot of whiskey. He realized the potential value of a good orchestra publicizing his resort. He didn't like the name I suggested. He suggested Orquesta Casino de la Playa. I liked it, and we signed a five-year contract.

"The next day, I went to the office of Mr. Ramon Crusellas, the manufacturer of *el jabón Candado*—Candado soap. A security guard stopped me in front of [Crusellas's] office and asked me if I had an appointment. 'I'm Cuban,' I said. 'Do I need an appointment to see another Cuban?' So I walked by him into a big office. I said to the man sitting behind the desk, 'Mr. Crusellas, I'm Miguelito Valdés.' Crusellas, a portly six-foot-tall man with light hair and mustache, said, 'I never heard of you. Good day.' I said, 'Wait a minute...I have a proposition you may like.' When I said I was a singer, he cut me off and asked if I ever sang for the Castro Brothers. After I said yes, he asked me to sit down."

Valdés negotiated to have Casino de la Playa become part of the daily comedy hour that promoted Candado soap on radio station CMQ. The show featured the comedy routines of two white men named Garrido and Piñeiro; one of them wore blackface makeup. The band performed in between the comedians' routines. Valdés accepted ten dollars per musician, fifteen dollars for himself, and an extra five dollars for expenses. From the moment of their first performance, Casino de la Playa was a hit. There were trips through Cuba, the Dominican Republic, Puerto Rico, and various South American countries.

A few months after the band's CMQ debut, Havana's RCA Victor representative, Daniel de Folis, approached them at the radio station and signed them to a recording contract. "The recordings were made at the Montmartre nightclub," said Valdés. "The walls were soundproofed. The microphone that was suspended from the ceiling over the band recorded the instruments, and a second one recorded my voice. I sang the fast tunes and Walfredo sang the ballads. At this time we recorded four records—eight sides—which were sold as an album. We recorded others that sold as singles. For three years we recorded eight records every two weeks. We had no union...no agents to protect us. We were paid twenty dollars each and never received royalties...but the exposure it got us was priceless. Our first recordings, I believe, were 'Bruca Maniguá,' 'Fufulando,' 'Yo Te Saludo,' 'Taboga,' and 'Dolor Cobarde.' I wrote 'Dolor Cobarde,' a ballad, and gave it to Anselmo Sacasas to orchestrate. You see, when I wrote this tune, it was at a time vocalists and guitars would take turns soloing. Anselmo had another idea. He composed a *montuno* and I listened to his lyrics. I said, 'Oh my God, it is beautiful, let's do it.' Anselmo included a piano solo for himself and he told me that when he nodded his head, I was to stop singing. All of us remained quiet so the microphone hanging from the ceiling could pick up his solo."

Tito Puente, a fourteen-year-old fledgling musician at the time he first heard "Dolor Cobarde" in 1938, said, "It was the first time I had heard a piano solo.…It was a new innovation to me, and it started a new trend in Latin music; after this, arrangers included piano solos in their orchestrations."

The piano solo did not originate with Sacasas. Antonio María Romeu, a turn-of-the-century Cuban musician, is one of a few pianists in *danzón* orchestras who soloed, but the solos were not as arousing as Sacasas's. Valdés added, "Anselmo may have gotten the idea from Arsenio Rodríguez. On the day we were going to record Arsenio's "Se Va el Caramelero" [The Candymaker is Leaving], we invited him to the session. Anselmo got an idea to include Arsenio on *tres* guitar. Midway through the tune we reached a break, and Anselmo nudged Arsenio to take a *tres* solo. Immediately after the recording, all of us congratulated Arsenio and Anselmo. We realized that Arsenio's solo was a historical innovation that had taken place in front of us."

At this point in our conversation, Valdés seemed not to be directly answering questions I asked about racism in Cuba. I rephrased my questions and was able to deduce from his answers that he had really left because he could not tolerate his country's racial policies. Although he would not admit it, the facts he mentioned indicated that he had been waging a tacit war against Cuba's overt discrimination toward Afro-Cubans. Since returning from Panama, Valdés had been singing the Afro laments of Arsenio Rodríguez, Chano Pozo, and other composers whose lyrics depicted the Afro-Cuban experience. Evidence of his struggle against racism is audible in the more than one thousand recordings he made over five decades. Protest lyrics, such as *"Yo soy carabalí negro de nación, sin la libertad no puedo vivir,"* are found in the songs "Bruca Maniguá," "Tierra Va Temblar," "Tambo," "Negro," "Cabildo," "Africa Canta y Llora," and many others. The Afro-Cuban lifestyle is described in his recordings of "Angelitos Negros," "Drume Negrita," "Yo Saludo," "Enlloro," "Indio," and "Sabor y Africanerías," to name a few. In a tone that clearly showed his annoyance, he noted that Arsenio Rodríguez's *tres* and Ramon Castro's bongo playing were good enough for Casino's recordings, yet neither musician was permitted to work any gigs with the band.

The tenor of our conversation made it clear to me that Valdés was fed up with racial prejudice. He probably suffered a guilt complex whenever he thought about the money, fame, adulation, and international recognition he was enjoying because of Afro-Cuban composers' music. It must have been difficult to cope with. He waited for an opportunity to leave Cuba. It came in late 1939, a few months after his recording of Margarita Lecuona's "Babalú" was released to record stores.

New York Latinos bought every available copy. A young, handsome Cuban living in New York named Desi Arnaz capitalized on the hit recording by singing it everywhere he appeared during the following year. It helped his show-business career immensely. By early 1940, the "Babalú" mania had not subsided. Someone wrote to Valdés from New York City that Arnaz was the hottest Latin artist in the city and was headed for Hollywood because of the popular Cuban conga rhythm and the impact "Babalú" had in all Hispanic communities.

"In March 1940," said Valdés, "I decided to leave Cuba and live in the United States. I had been in love with the United States for a long time...I wanted to be a citizen. The [Casino] orchestra would meet once a week to discuss business, new business, problems, and ideas. At the end of one meeting I announced that I would be leaving the organization in thirty days to live in the United States. They didn't believe me. My expected departure was mentioned on the radio and printed in a small newspaper article. In May I left. My family and the entire orchestra came to the pier to see me off. We embraced each other...choked up...and tried to hold back the tears...but we couldn't. I took all of my belongings in a lot of luggage...I had no intention of returning. During the trip to Florida aboard the SS *Florida*, I rested in a lounge chair in front of an open bar. Men and women were sipping drinks and listening to a small group of musicians. In Miami I had to use the toilet facilities. In the restroom, some black men told me I was in the wrong place."

Days later in New York City, his three-hundred-dollar bankroll dwindling, Valdés was in the office of Angel López's Havana-Madrid at Fifty-first Street and Broadway, in the basement below the Winter Garden Theatre, trying to land a featured singer's job. López would not agree to Valdés's price. "I received offers from Nano Rodríguez and Enrique Madriguerra, which I declined," said Valdés. "I was waiting for one offer. It came during the second week. One afternoon, Xavier Cugat visited the Havana Madrid and said to Angel, 'I hear Miguelito is in town...where is he?' I was sipping a brandy when Cugat entered Angel's office. He said, 'I've been looking for you.' I said, 'And I've been waiting for you.' He said, 'You want—' and I cut him off with 'How much?' I signed a five-year contract for $150 a week."

Reminiscing in his third-floor apartment at 1750 Rosedale Avenue in the Bronx on November 14, 1978, Machito said, "I first met Miguelito when he and I were in María Teresa Vera's group. Miguelito and Anselmo Sacasas came to New York together in April 1940 with the intention of working at Ben Marden's Riviera Nightclub in Englewood Cliffs, New Jersey. Mario [Bauzá] was their English interpreter in negotiations with the William Morris Agency. The Valdés-Sacasas combination never did get a start. Miguelito was very disappointed....Sacasas was a great musician who was not only capable of writing hit tunes but arranging them also.

"It was after this that he tried to get a job with López at the Havana-Madrid. Valdés's first job in this country was with Alberto Iznaga's La Siboney at a Sunday dance at the Audubon Ballroom. I was singing with La Siboney at the time." Machito was interrupted by his wife, Hilda, who reminded him that "Miguelito just sang one song....Iznaga asked him to sing a song after he introduced him. I remember the day as if it was yesterday...this gorgeous hunk of a man, very handsome, in a black pinstripe suit with an intoxicating aroma of expensive cologne. The women were crazy...they grabbed him...would not stop screaming....They kissed him...took his handkerchief....He smiled through it all...he enjoyed it."

Machito smiled adoringly at his wife, thanked her, and continued. "Miguelito was the hottest name in Latin music at the time, because of 'Babalú.' He appeared as a special attraction with La Siboney at the Park Plaza and the Bronx's Grand Plaza. Weeks later I left La Siboney to lead my own band."

"With Cugat," said Valdés, "I performed in five shows a day at the Paramount Theatre for two weeks. I sang every night at the Waldorf-Astoria's Starlight Roof and sang on the Camel cigarette show, *Rumba Revue*. At the beginning of the second week I asked for more money and I got an extra fifty dollars." For the May 27, 1940, RCA recording session, an RCA discography shows that Valdés replaced vocalist Nico López on the recordings of "Blen Blen Blen," "Rumba Rumbero," "Macurijes," and "Nueva Conga." The Cugat orchestra worked six days a week, filled two and three engagements a day, and recorded every month. The RCA contract expired on October 10. A new contract with Columbia Records began with the October 14 recording session.

During the first six months of 1941, Miguelito Valdés became a household word in every Hispanic community that heard his voice. His rise in popularity began with the January 10 recording of "Negra Leona"; continued with the March 14 session, which included "Babalú" and "Bambarito"; and peaked after the March 28 recordings of "Yo Tá

Namorá" and "Anna Boroco Tinde," two smash hits that were constantly heard throughout Spanish Harlem. Valdés was the popular topic of the day. Hispanics of all ages spoke about him. Dick Gilbert, Latin music's first English-speaking disc jockey, would announce "Miguelito Valdés with the orchestra of Xavier Cugat." That was the first time a sideman received billing over a popular bandleader.

Later in 1941, the Cugat orchestra was contracted to appear in the movie *You Were Never Lovelier*, which would feature Fred Astaire and Rita Hayworth. In February 1942, aboard a luxurious train complete with sleeping compartments, lounge, and bar, the Cugat orchestra headed for Hollywood, stopping off at Chicago's Palmer House for a three-month engagement.

"In Hollywood," continued Valdés, "I made it my business to learn that the picture's budget allowed two thousand dollars for me. I refused the four hundred dollars a week he was paying me and settled for fifteen hundred dollars for the two weeks' work. Cugat and I did not speak to each other after this. Before we headed for the coast, it had been decided that I would sing "Bim Bam Bum" and a serenade for a love scene in which Astaire would dance while Hayworth watched from a balcony. I was cut out of the scene after it was filmed…only my voice is heard. Cugat is the king of upmanship. No one would get publicity at his expense. Our work was completed in March and we headed back to the Waldorf. When I refused to work the Paramount Theatre, the radio show, and the Waldorf without an increase, he let me out of our contract.…I owe much to Cugat. I respect him. He taught me many things about business which prepared me for future business deals."

Valdés received national attention when his photo appeared on the cover of the April 1942 *Billboard* magazine. One week after leaving Cugat, Valdés was working at La Conga club with billing over Puerto Rican vocalist Bobby Capó and the Machito orchestra. It was mid-July when James Petrillo, president of the American Federation of Musicians Local 802, called a strike against the jukebox industry. He ordered a recording ban in which musicians would not record until a five-cent royalty was paid for every recording pressed. To beat the ban deadline, Valdés, backed by the Machito orchestra, recorded twenty-four tunes, most of them already recorded with Cugat and Casino de la Playa.

For the July 20, 1942, Columbia recording session, Pablo "Tito" Rodríguez replaced Valdés in the Cugat orchestra and recorded "Bim Bam Bum." The William Morris Agency made it possible for Valdés to perform at La Martinique, Hollywood's Mocambo, La Conga (with Diosa Costello), and every other prominent supper club across the nation, at three times the amount he earned with Cugat. In order to keep earning huge salaries, publicity and media exposure was necessary. The Machito recordings were top sellers, but only in New York City. Motion pictures offered mass exposure.

"At the end of 1942," Valdés remembered, "I got permission from the U.S. government to visit Mexico. During my two years in Mexico City, I had roles in twelve motion pictures. In June 1944, I married for the second time, to a French woman named Elyane. I had met her in Los Angeles while on location for the Astaire-Hayworth movie."

In September 1944, after Valdés finished his work in the Mexican movie *Imprudencia*, the family relocated to Los Angeles. By now, exposure in the twelve motion pictures had made him the most talked about, most popular Hispanic musician in the United States. His Seeco recordings with Noro Morales's orchestra and La Sonora Matancera contributed to his popularity. South American heads of state honored him with deals and proclamations. The rerelease of old Cugat recordings prompted Valdés's threat to take Cugat to court to stop him from benefiting from their recordings together.

In a September 1945 *Daily Mirror* column, Walter Winchell wrote that "Valdés was commended for cementing goodwill ties with Cuba." A month later, Musicraft Records signed him to record twelve tunes. The recordings, the same songs he recorded with Cugat years earlier, were released during 1946.

At the end of 1945, Valdés was hailed as a hero throughout Cuba when he received a medal from President Fulgencio Batista. At this time, he promised percussionist/dancer Chano Pozo and vocalist Olga Guillot that he would help them launch their careers in the United States. "After the medal ceremony, Chano and I went to my hotel," Vadés said. "He was already a famous song composer and earning good money as a choreographer for hotel revues. But he wasn't satisfied. He had to make it big in the United States. He and Olguita had wanted to come to New York ever since they heard my recordings with Cugat."

Back in New York, Valdés recorded eight sides for Verne Records, backed by the Machito orchestra. The tunes "Cabildo" and "Tierra Va Temblar" hit big. He also recorded eight sides for Musicraft, including "Rhumba Rhapsody," which received airplay on a few American pop music stations in New York City.

The following May, Pozo, his girlfriend Cacha Martínez, and the composer and dancer Pepé Becké arrived in New York city. Valdés turned to Machito's musical director, Mario Bauzá, for help in getting Pozo employed. Bauzá, aware that Dizzy Gillespie was working on creating a sound like the Machito orchestra's, convinced the trumpeter that the Cuban percussionist was what he needed. Betty Reilly, a blonde Mexican actress who appeared to be infatuated with Valdés, had a Latin music sequence for him written into her Monogram Pictures movie *Night in the Tropics*. Valdés persuaded Reilly to film the Machito band also.

Probably the most significant turning point for the Machito orchestra occurred late in 1946, when Valdés made it possible for Machito to be interviewed and have his records aired by popular New York disk jockey Fred Robbins. "Robbins," said Valdés, "who had never heard "Tanga" before, acted crazy while the transcription recording was going out over the airwaves. 'Ooh, wow!' he said. 'I never heard this kind of jazz before.' He asked Machito, 'What do you call it?' Macho said 'Afro-Cuban jazz.' Robbins told him to keep recording it."

At year's end, Valdés, dissatisfied with Pozo's progress in the Gillespie band, tried his hand at promoting him. He lined up special appearances at Hispanic theaters and dances promoted by Federico Pagani. He approached Gabriel Oller of Coda Records for recording dates and special appearances at Oller and Art "Pancho" Raymond's Sunday dance matinee "Tico Tico" dances at the Manhattan Center. Oller agreed, provided that Valdés and the recently arrived Olga Guillot would be part of the deal and that Valdés would pay expenses. They shook hands.

On February 4, 1947, the Machito orchestra, Valdés, Chano Pozo, Arsenio Rodríguez, Tito Rodríguez, Gabriel Oller, and Olga Guillot congregated at the Nola Penthouse Studios on West Fifty-seventh Street to record. A group picture was snapped before the Guillot and the Machito orchestra began their twelve-hour recording session of ballads. It started at noon, and at 2 P.M. the "Chano Pozo y Su Ritmo de Tambores" session commenced, with Pozo, Carlos Vidal, Miguelito Valdés, and Arsenio Rodríguez on congas, and Bellingi Ayala on bongós.

On February 7 at the same studio, the Machito orchestra became "Orquesta Chano Pozo," featuring Tito Rodríguez on vocals, Arsenio Rodríguez on tres guitar, and Pozo on congas, for the Coda label recording of "Cómetelo Tú," "Pasó en Tampa," "Porque Tú Sufres," and "Rumba en Swing." The Pozo recording commitment was completed on February 10, when Pozo recorded "Serenade" with Marcelino Guerra's Conjunto Batami. All of these priceless recordings were made without the participating musicians ever getting paid. A spirit of brotherhood to "help one of our own" prevailed. Tito Rodríguez, the only non-Cuban musician, donated his services to help a friend of Miguelito Valdés. "I remember it was a cold day," said Valdés, "I bought a few bottles of whiskey to warm up. The whiskey was payment for the Machito orchestra…they donated their services to help Chano and Olguita."

Gabe Oller, whose only expenditure was the rental of the studio, became co-owner of Coda, along with his partner at the Sunday dances at Manhattan Center, Art "Pancho" Raymond, who played all the recordings every evening on his WEVD Latin Music program *Tico Tico Time*.

Hundreds of 78-rpm records were sold. Guillot's and Pozo's careers began. Raymond, dissatisfied with his share of the proceeds, dissolved the partnership of Coda Records, and the Sunday afternoon dances at Manhattan Center came to an end in late 1947. Oller then formed the SMC (Spanish Music Center) label.

In 1948, Latin music orchestras were performing in every nightclub that had a bandstand in the tri-state area, playing hot rumbas and *guarachas* that were the attractions at clubs La Conga, China Doll, Ambassador, Embassy, Gloria Palace, Roseland, Alma Dance Studios, the Plaza, Havana-Madrid, Bill Miller's Riviera in Englewood Cliffs, New Jersey, and at Broadway theaters and swank hotels and resorts. Valdés, tired of his solo act, decided to lead an orchestra. While in Los Angeles during August, he selected specific musicians for a twelve-piece orchestra that debuted at Lake Tahoe, Nevada. Two months later they were at New York City's La Martinique, Apollo, Strand, and Paramount theaters, as well as all the popular ballrooms.

At 11 P.M. on December 2, 1948, Valdés asked the desk clerk for the key to his room at the Woodrow Hotel on Sixty-first Street and Broadway and was given two telephone messages, one from Mario Bauzá and the other from Cacha, informing him that Chano Pozo had been shot dead. He drove to Chano's Harlem apartment, picked up Cacha Martínez and Pepé Becké, then headed for Bauzá's apartment. They discussed the funeral and the plan to ship the body back to Cuba. The following morning they identified Pozo's body at the morgue. Days later, Chano Pozo was buried in Cuba.

On January 18, 1949, the Valdés orchestra plus vocalist Paquito Sosa recorded six sides for Oller's SMC label between 3 and 6 P.M. at the Harry Smith Recording Studio. The tunes were "Mondongo," "Está Frizao," "Qué Me Pasa," "Cose, Cose, Cose," "Sahara," and "Chano Pozo." The Valdés orchestra became flaming hot. SMC recorded three more sessions on March 18, June 1, and June 30, 1949. Valdés was exceptionally pleased with his recording of "Gandinga." "It was a mix of riffs," he said, "that René [Hernández] and I put together at the time René lived in the west seventies. He had a piano in his living room where we worked things out. What I most remember about René was his smile…he always had a smile. "Harlem Special" was an idea of mine that René transformed into an unbelievable orchestration. Very few musicians have an imagination like René's. He is different…he had his own trademark. I would sing a phrase and his imagination would create and build it up."

In early 1950, a few of the SMC recordings were performed for film and shown in movie houses in every Hispanic community in New York, Los Angeles, and Miami. When his big band appeared at the Strand Theatre during the first week of April, the audience's reaction to his rendition of "Chang" (Tito Puente's "Picadillo") persuaded Valdés to record it, along with "Palladium Stomp," for the Monogram label. Demand for the Miguelito Valdés orchestra continued for the next four years. There were a few recording dates from time to time, but only for a soloist. One such date occurred in 1953, when Valdés fronted the René Touzet orchestra for the Tico label recording of "Te Venido a Buscar."

The fourteen-piece band's popularity subsided in 1954, when it was apparent that the nightclub and big-band business was in trouble due to the high costs of labor. An entertainment tax was added to the cost of food and drinks. Dancers and aficionados remained home and watched television. Valdés was in New York City when Chris Courtney of the William Morris Agency summoned him to his office. Courtney told him that if he wanted to continue as an orchestra leader, he would have to reduce his personnel to eight or nine men. "In a respectful tone," said Valdés, "I told him he knows administrative work and the nightclub business. I told him I know the music business and suggested he leave it to me. When he said he could no longer book my orchestra, I disbanded, because without my trumpets and saxophones I wouldn't have the sound that I wanted. I gave everyone one month's notice. I rested for one month. I needed it, since I was so damned angry at what had happened. I became sick; it was my nerves. The following month I made plans to continue as a single." With pianist Luisito Benjamín and *bongocero* Ray Romero, Valdés traveled cross-country playing engagements.

The mid-1950s saw a new era for North American music with the emergence of Elvis Presley, Fats Domino, and rock 'n' roll. The diehard Sinatra fans remained loyal. Latin music had gone through some changes. The Cuban mambo rhythm caught fire and so did the *cha-cha-chá*, enabling new young musicians to gain fame on stage.

In 1955, Miguelito Valdés was no longer the dominant Latin vocalist. Latin music had singers such as Tito Rodríguez, Vicentico Valdés, Vitín Aviles, Willie Torres, Gilberto Monroig, Santos Colón, Tony Molina, and a crop of Cubans like Beny Moré and Fernando Alvarez, whose ballads and up-tempo recordings sold well.

Then, in 1957, while in Mexico, Valdés heard the voice of Chilean singer Lucho Gatica and said to himself, "This is the new Frank Sinatra." Valdés recommended Gatica to the president of Panart Records and—without any fanfare—went into retirement in Los Angeles.

In 1963, Valdés received a phone call from Mario Bauzá in New York with an offer to record. "I told Miguelito," said Bauzá, "that I spoke to Morris Levy of Tico Records about my ideas to record an album entitled *Reunión*. I told him to select the tunes, give me the key he sings in, and send them to me so that René Hernández, Frankie Colón, and I could orchestrate them. When he arrived in New York, he asked me and Macho what had transpired in the seven years he had been away. We told him of the top billing wars that were going on (bandleaders fighting for the top line on marquees or in ads), the humiliation of promoter Federico Pagani by specific bandleaders because of money, and the bull....Someone started to get Puerto Ricans and Cubans at each other's throats." This gossip prompted Miguelito to write "Qué Pena Me Da."

The album *Reunión* received little airplay. Two tunes, "Qué Pena Me Da" and "Africanerías" aroused listeners, and word of mouth was the best publicity they received. "For "Africanerías," said Valdés, "I tried *Náñigo* and Santería together." "Qué Pena Me Da" made listeners to choke with emotion with lyrics that appealed to bandleaders Tito Puente and Tito Rodríguez to end their top-billing feud. In the tune, Valdés sings about a dream he had in which Machito, Puente, and Rodríguez meet for a reunion dinner at Machito's home. Graciela, Machito's sister, answers a knock on the door; it is Tito Rodríguez, who enters and embraces Machito and Puente like brothers. Valdés's lyrics emote: "We are all brothers...we have the same blood...overcome the retardation of jealousy and envy...use your heads before it is too late...in unity there is strength."

The *Reunión* album rekindled Valdés's career. Three years later he starred in his own weekly television show, which ran for ten years. Although Fania Records artists dominated the popular sounds of the 1970s, there were still Valdés contemporaries throughout Latin America who preferred to see and hear him sing songs evoking pleasant memories of yesteryear. When Valdés was not on the road, anyone looking for him could find him at one of two Cuban restaurants—the Asia No. 1 at Fifty-fifth Street and Eighth Avenue, or Victor's Café at Seventy-first Street and Columbus Avenue.

On May 26, 1978 (two months after suffering a mild heart attack in Mexico), Mr. Babalú was honored by New York City's Latin music industry for his forty-two years in show business. One third of the more than four thousand people who crowded the Roseland Ballroom were widely known Latin music personalities. Weeks later, Valdés was a featured act for a concert tour of Puerto Rico that included the Machito orchestra, Charlie Palmieri, Johnny Pacheco, Ray Barretto, and Lalo Rodríguez. It was disastrous and cost Valdés about five thousand dollars. Recalling the tour, Machito said, "The promoters booked us at the same time that the Puerto Rican government-financed Fiestas Patronales showcased the best bands in free concerts throughout the island. We didn't get paid…the promoter cried poverty. Miguelito never collected the six thousand dollars owed him."

At 1 A.M. on November 9, 1978, Miguelito Valdés was singing to over three hundred people in the Monserrate Room at the Hotel Tequendama in Bogotá, Colombia. He loosened his black bow tie while singing a medley of tunes he had made popular. Valdés gestured with his right hand while singing into the microphone he held with his other hand. *"Echale bruca manigua, ayé!"* were the lyrics he sang before a painful expression began spreading over his face. He stopped singing and closed his eyes briefly while his left hand pressed his chest near his heart. "Excuse me, gentlemen," he said in Spanish. Those were his last words before he collapsed at center stage. A doctor in the audience rushed to his side, removed his bow tie, and loosened his shirt. Valdés had died right there. A half-hour later at a military hospital, he was officially pronounced dead.

On November 11, the remains were flown to Los Angeles for burial. Meanwhile, in New York, many Latin-music luminaries attended a mass in midtown Manhattan, where Charlie Palmieri performed Valdés's tune "Letargo" without accompaniment. The next month, Al Santiago, the founder of Alegre Records in the 1960s, enshrined Mr. Babalú for posterity with his Guacho label recording of "Luz a Babalú." The tune featured Machito on vocals, Mario Bauzá on alto sax, Charlie Palmieri on piano, Luis "Perico" Ortiz on trumpet, José Fajardo on flute, Bobby Rodríguez (of Bobby Rodríguez y La Compañía) on clarinet, and Johnny "Dandy" Rodríguez and Tito Puente on timbales.

At the end of our taped interview of February 11, 1976, Valdés had said "People, I want you to know that I am shaking hands with Max Salazar…then I am shaking hands with you. I know that you love me, and I love you."

Originally published in Latin Beat *magazine, February, March, and April 1992*

SEVEN

ALBERTO SOCARRÁS

"If I am to be discriminated against in my own country," mused the young Afro-Cuban musician, "I would be better off in the United States, where black musicians like Duke Ellington are given a chance to earn a living." These were his thoughts when he wrote a letter to his mother from Havana. The letter ended with the line, "The next letter you get from me will come from New York."

These were the first recollections of the mild-mannered, soft-spoken Alberto Socarrás during our initial interview on January 16, 1974, at his music studio at 322 West Fifty-third Street in Manhattan, where he taught his students. Seated comfortably in a chair, he explained the reasons for his anger in 1927.

In Cuba then, a person's skin color attracted more attention than his or her intelligence, skills, or character. During this period, the island aped the Southern United States by perpetuating a double standard—one for whites and the other for its population of color. There were parks that Afro-Cubans were forbidden to walk in, water fountains they could not drink from, areas in cities they could not live in. And even though Afro-Cubans provided the music, black Cubans were not permitted in many nightclubs or ballrooms. These and many other racial injustices prompted the young Socarrás to leave the country of his birth.

On April 26, 1927, Alberto Socarrás left Havana by boat. He intentionally bypassed the racially segregated city of Miami, Florida, and proceeded to New York. Justo Baretto, a friend who earned his livelihood as a pianist, met him at the crowded pier filled with happy white and black faces. While riding the Seventh Avenue IRT subway uptown to Baretto's apartment, the multiracial faces of the other riders assured Socarrás that he had finally escaped the restrictions of discrimination. Possessed of good feelings and wonderful expectations, he got off the subway with Baretto at 125th Street and Lenox Avenue. After walking a few blocks and seeing nothing but black faces, an uneasy feeling overcame Socarrás. He stopped, laid his luggage down, and asked his friend, "Where are we?" and "Why are there only black people here?"

"Harlem," retorted Baretto. As he quickly explained the neighborhood's history of segregation, Socorrás's eyes opened wide in disbelief.

Had it been turned into a script, Socarrás's flight from Cuban discrimination to unexpected New York segregation would have given Rod Serling's TV show, *The Twilight Zone*, a high Nielsen rating. But this was no fantasy; it was stark reality. Even so, Socarras's shock at conditions in New York was ultimately a good thing for the United States, and for U.S. Latinos. After all, he ended up contributing to the evolution of popular Cuban dance music in this country. Had he not left Cuba, he would not have directed one of New York City's most popular Latin music orchestras during the mid-1930s, in which musicians like Augusto Coen, Fausto Curbelo, René Edeira, Rogelio Martínez, Noro Morales, and Pedro Ortíz-Dávila (Davilita) acquired valuable experience.

Since 1927, this Cuban classical-music flutist, alto saxophonist, and clarinetist has made too many 78-rpm recordings for him to remember. The archives of the Institute of Jazz Studies at Rutgers University in New Jersey lists "Bottomland," recorded with the Clarence Williams orchestra in late June 1927, as his first recording. Socarrás then played with Lew Leslie's Blackbirds (1928–1933, including a European tour in 1929), Eva Taylor (1928), Mary Dixon (1929), Margaret Webster (1930), Benny Carter (1933), and Sam Wooding (1935). In 1928, he became the first flutist to record a jazz solo, on Clarence Williams's QRS label recording "Have You Ever Felt That Way?" He composed more than one hundred songs, including music for stage shows and symphony orchestras. He was a studio musician for the Columbia and Decca record companies and orchestrated music for Vincent López, Cab Calloway, Enric Madriguera, Tommy Dorsey, and Miguelito Valdés.

During the 1930s and 1940s, when nonwhite bands were described as "sepia orchestras" and the labels of their recordings bore the "race music" inscription, Socarrás's Afro-Cuban rumbas tumbled the color barriers and crossed into forbidden territory. In 1939 his jazz octet worked the prestigious Glen Island Casino, where bands like those of Glenn Miller, Charlie Barnet, Benny Goodman, and Tommy Dorsey performed. After nineteen months at Glen Island, his orchestra moved on, overwhelming larger white audiences in cities in the Northeast. The Columbus, Ohio, daily newspaper *The Citizen* published a lengthy article about Socarrás, calling him a "great showman," a "musical technician," and a "showstopper." The trade magazines named him "musician of the month" on several occasions.

A 1940 Boston newspaper article, headlined "Cuban Music Thrilling," enthused: "If two weeks ago anyone had told us that staid Bostonians would go strongly for a flute player with conga and rumba rhythms, we might have been polite, but not impressed. Yet after one session at the Beachcomber with Socarrás and his magic flute, even our jaundiced expression changed to one resembling joy everlasting." The music section of the January 3, 1944, issue of *Time* magazine quoted renowned flutist Georges Barrère on the difficulties of flute playing. "Thousands play the flute," Barrère said, "but few play it well." Included among those few was Socarrás.

The Socarrás story begins on September 19, 1908, when Alberto Socarrás-Estacio was born in Manzanillo, Oriente, Cuba. In Manzanillo, the Socarrás name was synonymous with music. His mother, Dolores (known as Lolo), was his first flute teacher; she began teaching him when he was seven. Years later, at the musical conservatory of Santiago de Cuba, he mastered the instrument. Alberto, his mother, grandfather, four uncles, three cousins. and two sisters made up La Familia Socarrás Orchestra, which was hired to play all the town's social functions. Their symphonic and violin music accompanied silent films in the town's only movie house.

But by the time Alberto reached his late teens, he began to feel the sting of racism. "Prior to 1920," he said, there were provinces where "discrimination never existed." Without emotion or even a trace of rancor in his voice, he went on to explain that "whites, Afros, and Orientals lived as equals and in harmony in the same community. I guess we had a common bond—we were all poor." But that harmony ended when white Americans acquired businesses and began employing white Cubans exclusively. Formerly integrated Cuban pop and jazz orchestras, which had played the prominent Havana nightclubs and resorts during the lucrative winter tourist season, were replaced by white American bands and music. The Cuban government passed a law requiring that every American-owned business must employ two or three Cubans. In response, the integrated Cuban bands disbanded and reconstituted themselves as "white" groups by utilizing light-skinned mulattos only. As a result, brown and black Cubans were thrown out of work. When this process first started happening, Socarrás was a featured soloist in the Arquimedes Pous orchestra, which was acclaimed as one of the world's best classical orchestras. On his recommendation, his sister Juana was given a violinist's chair, and her legend as "Estrellita" (Little Star) Socarrás began.

Then Alberto and Estrellita performed with the Creole Stars, a jazz orchestra, and toured throughout Cuba. But in early 1927, after Havana's

Hotel Seville was bought by Americans, Socarrás witnessed the replacement of the Seville's integrated Cuban band. At this time he was working at the famous Montmartre nightclub, which was also American-owned. "I thought it was just a matter of time before our band would be replaced," he recalled. "So I decided at that moment to leave Cuba."

One day during his first week in New York, he was roaming the streets, searching for the famous Broadway thoroughfare in midtown Manhattan that he had heard so much about. After his tour along the bright, neon-lit streets, with their flashing signs, theaters, vaudeville houses, and cabarets, he found his way back to Harlem by following the same signs and train stops. His first job was with Cuban trumpeter-bandleader Vicente Sigler at the Hotel McAlpin in midtown Manhattan. At this dance was José LaCalle, director of the Latin-music department of Columbia Records. LaCalle, who is best remembered for his composition "Amapola," was impressed by Socarrás's proficiency on four instruments. He got Socarrás two jobs—one as a studio musician and another with Cuban pianist-bandleader Nilo Menéndez, whose house band played Cuban shows at the Harlem Opera House at 125th Street between Seventh and Eighth Avenues. Socarrás's multiple skills got him work and recording dates with the Chicago Serenaders, Carl Webster's Yale Collegians, Walter Bennett's Swamplanders, Russell Wooding's Grand Central Redcaps, and the Lazy Levee Loungers.

In late 1929, immediately after Spain's violinist-bandleader Enric Madriguera replaced LaCalle as director, Socarrás left Columbia to begin his first of four years as a featured soloist with Lew Leslie's Blackbirds, a jazz band whose *Rhapsody in Black* and *Blackbirds Revue* toured Europe on the same bills with Bill "Bojangles" Robinson, Josephine Baker, Duke Ellington, Cab Calloway, and Louis Armstrong. Socarrás's mastery of the alto sax, soprano sax, clarinet, and flute, along with his original compositions and arrangements, made him one of the most sought-after musicians of the early 1930s.

During the spring of 1934, Marcial Flores, a wealthy Puerto Rican, opened El Club Cubanacán at 114th Street and Lenox Avenue. Socarrás's newly formed rumba band, which included ex-Blackbirds trumpeter Augusto Coen, became the house band. Months later, Flores rented the empty Mount Morris Theater at 116th Street and Fifth Avenue. He reopened it as El Campo Amor Theater and gave the Cuban flutist's band a second daily job backing the stage shows. For the last half of 1934, Hispanic New Yorkers were treated to Afro-Cuban music every evening between 10 and 10:30 P.M. and from 3 to 3:30 A.M. over radio station WMCA, which broadcast live from El Cubanacán. The airwaves were filled with live renditions of rumbas, *sones*, boleros, and Afro laments with such titles as "Masabi," "Africa," "Porque Lo Dices," "Tabú," and "Pacto Con El Diablo," all recorded for Brunswick Records in 1935.

"In 1935," said Socarrás, "Noro Morales, the famous Puerto Rican pianist, left Venezuela to live in New York. I gave him a job. I was working seven days a week playing jazz and blues at the Savoy, Cotton Club, Small's Paradise and Connie's Inn. I was also playing Cuban music at El Campoamor, El Cubanacán, and Park Plaza. Noro couldn't play jazz, so he left the band."

During the same year, Dávila and Coen left the Cubanacán to form a group Coen planned to direct. Coen was a smashing success at the Golden Casino Ballroom directly underneath the Park Palace, whose entrance was near the corner of 111th Street and Fifth Avenue. Fernando Luis, El Campo Amor's talent director, was constantly talking about how he wanted to buy a new car. He convinced Socarrás and Coen that a musical battle between the two of them would pack a dance hall, and that each would get a percentage of the receipts. The battle, a war between Cuba and Puerto Rico, was promoted at El Campoamor in the spring of 1935. A movie had just ended in a theater when suddenly the audience was startled by a message on the screen: "Flash! Flash! Flash!" then "War! War! War!— between Cuba and Puerto Rico—at the Park Palace…between Alberto Socarrás of Cuba and Augusto Coen of Puerto Rico."

During the evening of their battle, Socarrás performed on one stage and Coen on another at the extreme ends of the ballroom. A third band played the Casino. The event was so successful that the fire department was summoned to the premises as the dance hall bulged from the overcrowding. Fernando Luis kept the door receipts while the proprietress, Mrs. Hersh, managed the bar. Dancers, unable to find space on the crowded floor, moved to the music wherever they stood. The magnet attracting them was the dislike the two groups had for each other. Puerto Ricans, who were American citizens under a 1919 U.S. government proclamation, could travel to and from Puerto Rico with no problem. But visiting Cubans could stay in the United States for only twenty-nine days. Meanwhile, Cubans and Puerto Ricans who were U.S. citizens constantly clashed as the two groups competed for New York City's menial jobs and housing, and for ethnic control of the area known as El Barrio.

Recalling the musical war at El Campoamor, Socarrás started grinning. "Because there were more Puerto Ricans in Harlem," he said, the organizers "were going to appease them by declaring Puerto Rico won the war…but the Cubans threatened to wreck the place…so no one won.…The ironic thing about this is [that] my band was made up mostly of Puerto Rican and Dominican musicians, and Coen's was mostly Cuban and Panamanian."

By 1 A.M., Mrs. Hersh had sold all her liquor and soft drinks. A half-hour later, Luis hurriedly walked up to both bandleaders and told them "Here, hold this!" He handed each of them $150 in a wad, then left in a rush. At 4 A.M., as the dancers were going home, Socarrás and Coen, euphoric with visions of splitting a large sum of money, were unable to find the promoter. The twenty-eight musicians who made up both bands angrily accepted eleven dollars each for a night's work—not bad, considering that the going rate at the time was two dollars. The following day, the bandleaders found Luis, who sadly told them he had lost money and that the huge turnout consisted mostly of gatecrashers who did not pay. A month later, Socarrás saw Luis park a shiny new silver Ford on 116th Street. Luis was not allowed to promote anything else again until the 1940s.

From 1935 to 1937, Socarrás gave up Latin music to play jazz with the orchestras of Sam Wooding, Benny Carter, and Erskine Hawkins before resuming his role as a bandleader in September 1938. In January of that year, Messrs. López, Ferrer, and Blanco had opened the Havana-Madrid club at Fifty-first Street and Broadway. On the bill was vocalist Alfredito Valdés, who formerly was with Ignacio Pineiro's Septeto Nacional and the all-female jazz band La Anacaona Septet of Havana. Clifford Fisher, the musical impresario who contracted for entertainment spots in Europe, believed the all-woman group would be a hit in Paris. Concepción "Cuchito" Castro, the septet's leader, knew no English, and she asked Socarrás to interpret Fisher's proposal. The impresario offered each woman eight hundred French francs (eighteen dollars U.S.) for transportation, and a villa to stay in. The union scale for New York City musicians was between two dollars and four dollars per gig, depending where one worked. Socarrás suggested thirty dollars a week for each musician, sixty dollars a week for the leader, and three hundred dollars for himself to write music, arrange, and rehearse the band.

On March 25, 1938, La Anacaona, accompanied by Alberto Socarrás, was in Havana to prepare for the European trip. In the Havana newspaper *El País*, reporter Portuondo Cala wrote: "Tomorrow, fifteen [musicians] will embark for Paris's Les Ambassadeurs club under the direction of maestro Alberto Socarrás, a Cuban saxophonist who resides in New York. The Anacaona orchestra consists of the seven Castro sisters, whose parents are Chinese and Afro-Cuban. Ana Permuy, Graciela Pérez and Hortensia Palacios will also perform at the London Casino under the competent baton of Socarrás." La Anacaona spent ten weeks in Havana rehearsing each arrangement with a twelve-piece orchestra. The group then returned to New York, boarded the SS *Île-de-France* for Le Havre, and headed for Paris. The band included the now-famous Graciela (Machito's sister), and it was a smash at Les Ambassadeurs. Anacaona alternated with Django Reinhardt's group at the Chez Florence in Montmartre. Meanwhile, Adolf Hitler's Nazi war machine was terrorizing Europe. After eight weeks, La Anacaona declined invitations to play other European countries. The group returned to Cuba, and Socarrás went to New York.

The orchestra Socarrás and His Magic Flute, which included a trumpeter named John "Dizzy" Gillespie, performed in all the prominent New York nightspots. The Socarrás name appeared in the popular daily gossip columns of Walter Winchell, Nick Kenny, and Ben Gross. Every performance, whether classical, jazz, or Latin, was written up in the newspapers and trade magazines. In 1947, RCA recorded Socarrás's "Rumba Clásica," whose melodious flute phrases were enhanced by Machito's pianist René Hernández. But by the mid-1950s, the sounds of jazz and Latin music had changed, increased taxes had closed many clubs, and rock 'n' roll dominated the American music scene. So Socarrás decided to give up the role of active bandleader. Even so, he was still in demand. The flute virtuoso soloed at Carnegie Hall symphony concerts, performing classics like "Hora Staccato," "Rhapsody in Blue," Chopin's nocturnes, and his favorite tune, "Satin Doll." There were record dates for the Spanish Music Center, for a ten-inch LP titled *El Gringo and His Brazilians*, and with pianists Marco Rizo and Eddie Bonnemere. Socarrás's flute also soared on "Call of the Jungle Birds," "Velorio," and "Jungle Holiday," all on Tito Puente's RCA LP *Tambo*, recorded in 1960. Three years later, during the charanga-*pachanga* era, Socarrás's flute inspirations appeared on all twelve tracks of Oscar Boufartique's Columbia LP.

The soft-spoken, pleasant doctor of music closed our interview with praise for the Machito orchestra and Tito Puente. He recognized Mario Bauzá for having created Afro-Cuban jazz. He noted that though he played Latin music and jazz, it never occurred to him to merge the rhythms. "The secret to being a good musician," Socarrás said, "is being able to read music and acquiring experience....Learn to read the bass and treble clef before touching the instrument."

After his semi-retirement in the mid-1950s, Dr. Socarrás taught hundred of students music and how to play the flute. In 1983 he was filmed in Central Park playing flute for Gustavo Paredes's one-hour documentary *Música*. He was already suffering from Alzheimer's disease, and the police occasionally had to bring him home when he forgot where he lived. In June 1987, he was hospitalized.

He died on August 26, 1987. Four days later his body rested at St. Peter's

Lutheran Church at Fifty-fourth Street and Lexington Avenue. The Reverend John Gensel eulogized him. Socarras's wife, Carol, and son Dwayne asked me to speak about his life. I recalled the hard times Socarrás had experienced and how he overcame them. I noted that his photo album, which was filled with letters and telegrams from W.C. Handy, Xavier Cugat, Bill "Bojangles" Robinson, Desi Arnaz, Cab Calloway, Tommy Dorsey, Miguelito Valdés, and many other famous names, showed that Socarrás was not an ordinary musician. Most of all, I recalled his kind and friendly demeanor, and the fact that although some disliked him because of the color of his skin, he never disliked anyone. Musical tributes were rendered by Marco Rizo, Eddie Bonnemere, and alto saxophonist Charlie Frazier. Bonnemere's performance of Duke Ellington's "Satin Doll" closed the service. On September 1, Socarrás was interred at Ferncliff Cemetery in Hartsdale, New York.

The civil rights movement triumphed in the 1960s, and Socarrás's life contributed to it. When his rumba, jazz, and classical sound started demolishing ethnic barriers in 1939, it was the beginning of his tacit war against racial discrimination. Judging from the huge number of repeat performances he gave before white audiences, it is safe to say he triumphed. From the first day Socarrás's mother, Lolo, taught him to play flute, he prepared himself to teach the world that the only colors music lovers need be concerned with are the shadings from a muted trumpet, the pastel pianissimo of a pianist, the dark wail of a saxophone, and the bright fluorescence of violins and flutes. If white Cubans of the 1920s had realized what colors really count in life, Socarrás would never have had to come to New York. Still, many of us are grateful that he did.

Originally published in Latin Beat *magazine, January 1993*

EIGHT

ANSELMO SACASAS

By the time the 1970s rolled around and up-tempo Latin music was experiencing a popularity surge with salsa, one of its pioneers had been forgotten by nearly everyone—but not by Dr. Ken Rosa, an accomplished pianist known in New York City as "the musicians' doctor of chiropractic medicine." Rosa had a radio program, *Latin Nostalgia*, every Saturday afternoon on WBAI. He was one of New York's most popular DJs because his format mentally transported one to yesteryear.

I did not know who Anselmo Sacasas was until Rosa reminded his listeners of the man who, during the late 1930s and early 1940s, was Latin music's most popular pianist. Rosa took a reel-to-reel tape recorder to Puerto Rico and interviewed Sacasas in the ballroom of the San Juan Hotel, then returned to New York. One summer afternoon in 1975, he thrilled Latin New York by playing the Sacasas recordings of "Mala Lengua" and "Koki Koka," which led many to the opinion that the great Puerto Rican pianist-bandleader Noro Morales was influenced by Anselmo Sacasas.

Immediately after listening to the program, I researched Sacasas. Charlie Palmieri, Tito Puente, Machito, Miguelito Valdés, Mario Bauzá, and Alberto Iznaga are just a few who placed him on their all-time-best lists. Sacasas and I corresponded, and what follows is proof that he is one of the greats of Latin music.

By mid-1937, Sacasas's reputation had begun to spread from one Cuban city to another. In 1939 he and vocalist Miguelito Valdés were responsible for the Casino de la Playa orchestra's immense popularity. Yet he had very little to show for it. As someone whose musical arrangements resulted in hit recordings that made others wealthy, he should have ended up rich. But that did not happen in Cuba. So he moved to the United States, where the life of this Cuban musician, who speaks fluent Spanish and English, changed drastically.

Born to Enrique and Rosario Perez-Sacasas on November 23, 1912, in Manzanillo, Cuba (in Oriente province), he joined a family of three brothers and two sisters. He graduated from Manzanillo's music conservatory at age sixteen, then moved to Havana, where he studied harmony and composition under the tutelage of Pedro San Juan, director of the Havana Philharmonic Orchestra. In New York in the early 1940s, his skills were honed by the great Italian musician Domenico Savino of the Robbins Music Corporation, whose job was to arrange and enhance music of the company's best composers. Sacasas showed talent for this work, and would orchestrate music for the music publishing company Peer International.

In 1929 young Sacasas was in the pit orchestra of Havana's Gloria Theater, which provided the music for silent movies. Three years later, when silent movies faded into history, Luis Carrillo, a flutist and charanga music specialist, taught him to orchestrate music. Sacasas worked with several bands when he joined the charanga of flutist Tata Pereira at the Havana Sport Academy, a dance hall on Galiano and San José Streets. In the early 1930s, Tata's charanga was what Arcaño y Sus Maravillas would be in the 1940s. The orchestra consisted of Havana's best musicians, including Pedro López (the father of Orestes López and Israel "Cachao" López) and Abelardo Valdés (composer of "Almendra") on bass, Virgilio Diago on violin, Ulpiano Díaz on timbales, Remberto Beicuz on tenor sax, and a Mr. Viera on trumpet (this last fact suggests that Orquesta Francesca de Tata Pereira may have been the first to utilize trumpet and sax in a charanga, as early as 1933). For three years, every tune Sacasas played was a *danzón*. "It was in this orchestra," he noted, "that I became an accomplished pianist....I was a *charanguero* and I am proud to say I'm still a *charanguero*."

In September 1936, after a three-year absence, vocalist Miguelito Valdés returned to Cuba from Panama. "At that time," said Valdés, "Anselmo was known throughout Cuba. What made him outstanding was the unique sound of his arrangements....I don't know what he did to a tune, but it sounded different and better. Shortly after I joined Los Hermanos Castro band, I convinced Manolo [Castro, the music director] that his brother Juanito's piano playing was weak. The brothers had an argument and Juanito left the band. I took Manolo to the Havana Sport to hear Anselmo. At first Manolo had doubts and asked, 'Can this *charanguero* arrange music for a jazz band?'" After one hour at the academy, Castro was convinced that he could. Los Hermanos Castro gave up playing American pop hits and concentrated on Cuban music.

Anselmo gained attention for the band by creating swinging

orchestrations, yet he suffered financially. "At the Havana Sport, I earned $3.75 a day," he said, "and for Sunday matinees and nights, $6.50. Castro paid me two dollars a day, and I had to pay him back for my uniform." After months of frugality, seven musicians left the Castro Brothers to form a corporation headed by Guillermo Portela, the violinist-director of the band, which subsequently became Casino de la Playa.

Between 1937 and 1940, the orchestra earned more money than any other musical group in Cuba because of its daily radio transmissions, its dance hall appearances, and the eight recordings it made every two weeks for RCA. Sacasas's arrangements and Valdés' innovative vocals were largely responsible for this monetary success. But Sacasas said that his three years with Casino were "the most miserable time of my life...linked to memories I do not want to recall...things I try to block out of my mind. All I did was work, work, work in order to meet my expenses. I got married at the time and I didn't have a honeymoon because I couldn't afford one. While other musicians slept, I was writing new arrangements. I was paid one dollar per arrangement and I had to supply the paper, which cost me twenty-five cents. This is why I never speak about Casino de la Playa...those were sad times for me." According to Miguelito Valdés, RCA sold thousands of recordings and split the proceeds between itself and Portela. The Casino corporation paid each musician ten dollars a week.

In April 1940, after the tremendous success of Casino's 1939 recording of "Babalú," Sacasas and Valdés joined Xavier Cugat's orchestra, and Sacasas formed a band that debuted at Chicago's Colony Club. He still has a photo of the group, including its drummer—a seventeen-year-old from Spanish Harlem named Ernest "Tito" Puente. In 1941 the Sacasas orchestra was selected over others (including Machito and his Afro Cubans) for the house band job at La Conga Club in midtown Manhattan. A year later Sacasas received word from Cuba that his father was ill, and was given two weeks off. Weeks before he found out about his father, Sacasas had signed a one-year contract to appear at La Martinique Club. He already had urged Jack Harris, La Conga's owner, to replace him with the Machito orchestra.

Upon his return from Cuba, his orchestra at La Martinique played shows, dinner music, and the fiery *guarachas* that today we call salsa. In 1944, RCA recorded Sacasas's "Koki Koka," which placed him among the top five Latin bandleaders. Three years later the orchestra moved to the Havana-Madrid, where his music was aired nightly over WOR radio. "During this time," recalled Sacasas, "I divided my year...four months in Miami, four months in New York City, four months at the New York mountain resorts. No matter where my orchestra appeared, WOR would broadcast my performances....I have copies of the transmissions."

From 1950 on, the pianist lived in Miami, where he became the musical director of the Fontainebleau Hotel. At El Club Ronde his orchestra accompanied Latin and non-Latin recording artists. In 1963, Sacasas moved to Puerto Rico to fill the artistic director position at the Hotel San Juan; he decided what orchestras and acts would perform there. He organized a band that appeared at the hotel and at El Tropicoro. After thirteen years in San Juan, he retired in 1976 and moved to the Kendall section of Miami, where he and his wife are enjoying life and the Havana-like atmosphere.

Originally published in Latin Beat *magazine, September 1991*

NINE

MARCELINO "RAPINDEY" GUERRA

On October 10, 1992, Cuban-music historian Cristóbal Díaz Ayala was in the town of El Campello, Alicante, Spain, to interview the legendary Marcelino Guerra. Seated across from Guerra, Díaz asked the seventy-six-year-old musician, "Which is the one song that has gotten you the most royalties?" Guerra, who had probably composed more than seventy-five tunes, replied, "About one week ago I got a royalty check for $2,347....Included in there are royalties for 'Pare Cochero,' 'A Mi Manera' [his biggest hits], and others....I never received a royalty payment like that before." Fifty-nine years had elapsed since he wrote his first tune, and his publisher, the Edward B. Marks Music Company, was paying him two and a half cents for every recording sold that contained his music.

Guerra is one of the best musicians Cuba ever exported to the United States. His orchestra was among the five most popular groups in New York City, and many aficionados believe that it was the best one during the years immediately following World War II. In 1940, Guerra's tune "Pare Cochero" was recorded by Cuarteto Caney for Decca Records, featuring Machito on vocals. It was also recorded by the orchestra of Mariano Mercerón for RCA, featuring Guerra on vocals. Since then, "Pare Cochero" has been recorded many more times and has become a standard that most Latin bands include in their repertoires. Verne Records recorded Guerra's orchestra seventy times. His melodious tenor voice is also on the recordings of Ignacio Piñeiro's Septeto Nacional, Mariano Mercerón, Chano Pozo, Machito, and the La Playa Sextet. In the mid- to late 1940s, New York's most popular orchestras were those of Machito, Noro Morales, José Curbelo, Pupi Campo, and Marcelino Guerra.

Guerra was born in Cienfuegos, Cuba, on April 26, 1914, the youngest of four brothers and four sisters. His father was a soldier and his mother a housewife. In 1921, his parents died within a few months of each other. Juana, his maternal grandmother, reared the orphaned children. At the age of eight, Guerra acquired the nickname Rapindey. "Whenever my sister's boyfriends would visit, they would get me out of the house by giving me a peseta to buy *tres de azúcar y dos de café* [three cents worth of sugar and two cents worth of coffee]," said Guerra. "I rushed to the store and returned home within minutes. One day a man who saw how fast I ran said that I was a 'Rapindey,' and the nickname stuck."

His interest in music began at age fourteen, when he attended rehearsals at a studio a few doors from where he lived. Every Friday evening, young Marcelino listened and learned the words of songs made popular by Septeto Habanero. One evening the band's lead vocalist did not appear. The musical director, a policeman who owned the studio, invited Rapindey to sing. Thus began Guerra's career as a vocalist.

In 1931, the seventeen-year-old Guerra was Septeto Cienfuegos's lead vocalist for four months at Havana's Infierno cabaret. The seven musicians rented a room in a four-story *solar* (tenement) at Amistad 17 and took turns sleeping on one of four beds while the rest slept on cots. After a year, the group returned to Cienfuegos without Guerra, who had landed a job as a tailor's delivery man, earning a dollar and twenty-five cents a day. The following year the musical director of Sexteto Cauto needed a maraca player to sing chorus. He was introduced to Rapindey, to whom he gave ten dollars to purchase an orchestra uniform consisting of a suit, shirt, tie, and shoes. On the bandstand of the Sans Souci nightclub, Rapindey met Panchito Riset, the band's vocalist, and the two established a close friendship.

Months later, in 1933, Havana's serenity was disrupted by a revolution in which Fulgencio Batista toppled the government of Gerardo Machado. Guerra was one of many unemployed *habaneros* when he was introduced to Julio Blanco, a dancer whose troupe was called Batamú. Guerra bought a guitar for three dollars at a pawnshop and learned to play it. Blanco convinced Guerra to form a partnership in which Blanco would write lyrics and Guerra would compose the music. Their first effort was "La Clave Misteriosa," which was transcribed by Oscar Boufartique. That was followed by the compositions "Batamú," "Volví a Querer," "Amor Gigante," and "Buscando la Melodía."

"There was a time," said Guerra, "when many of the tunes heard over Havana radio were Guerra-and-Blanco compositions." Their lyrics appeared on the back of fliers from merchants promoting their products or businesses. The print shops paid royalties for the lyrics, and for months the songwriters split the earnings. Then Blanco collected the weekly royalties and kept Guerra's share. Rapindey confronted Blanco and asked for his portion of the five dollars. "Well, Rapindey, I collected on the lyrics," said

Blanco. "When the printers print the music of one of your tunes, you can collect royalties." So after months of lucrative collaboration, greed parted Guerra and Blanco.

In 1933, Guerra was the second voice for Sexteto Habanero when it appeared at the Havana Sport, a popular ballroom where men danced with "hostesses" for five cents a dance. Guerra left Sexteto Habanero to join the sizzling Septeto Nacional de Ignacio Piñeiro. Guerra was earning enormous sums of money via dances and two daily radio broadcasts. In 1938, Miguel Angel Banguela, a dancer with the group Batamú, approached Guerra and gave him lyrics that he wanted music for: *"Soy un chico delicado / que nació para el amor / Este coche me ha estropeado / Pare en la esquina, señor."* Guerra wasted no time composing music for the tune he titled "Pare Cochero." Shortly thereafter, Banguela dropped out of sight and was never heard from again. A year later, the six-foot-tall vocalist left Septeto Nacional and joined Isolina Carrillo's Quinteto Siboney, which comprised Facundo Rivera on piano and the four voices of Carrillo, Guerra, Alfredo León, and Joseito Núñez.

In 1940, Rapindey sang with Conjunto Hatuey for a few months before joining Arsenio Rodríguez's newly formed *conjunto*. After four years of recording inactivity, Guerra came to New York City to record four of his songs for the Robbins Music Corporation. "Robbins sent for Marcelino," said Mario Bauzá. "At that time, Spanish-language songs like 'Adios,' 'Perfidia,' 'Frenesí,' 'Ojos Verdes,' and 'Siempre en Mi Corazón' were recorded by American pop bands with English lyrics. So I told Robbins about Marcelino, and they sent for him."

Although Guerra entered the United States with what Cubans described as a "V-29" (a twenty-nine-day tourist visa), he ignored the twenty-nine-day restriction and remained in New York. Machito and Mario Bauzá helped him find shelter and employment. An old photograph is evidence that Spanish Harlem's musicians got to know Rapindey; it was snapped in front of Marcano's photo shop at 111th Street and Fifth Avenue.

At times he sang chorus with Machito's orchestra. Machito and Bauzá organized the second version of their Afro Cubans for Guerra, who agreed to give ten percent of his salary to Bauzá, ten percent to Machito, and ten percent to pianist Luis Varona (whom Bauzá selected as Guerra's musical director). The agreement also allowed the use of Machito's music charts as well as the words "Second Afro Cubans." Of the twenty-five dollars that Rapindey was paid, Machito, Bauzá, and Varona collected two dollars and fifty cents each, which left Guerra with seventeen dollars and fifty cents. The Second Afro Cubans performed at La Conga Club on Mondays, when the Machito orchestra had a day off, and on Tuesdays, when the José

Curbelo orchestra was off. The ten-piece orchestra consisted of Guerra on vocals and maracas, Varona on piano, Rogelio Valdés on bass, Steve Berrios on drums, José "Belingi" García, Frank "Hot Lips" García, and a trumpeter and three saxophonists who were non-Hispanics. Guerra's band rehearsed at El Babalú, a restaurant owned by dance promoter Federico Pagani, and performed at the Park Palace, Golden Casino, Club Cubanacán, Odd Fellows Temple, and Audubon Ballroom, as well as in stage shows at Harlem theaters.

But before 1944 ended, the U.S. Immigration and Naturalization Service informed Guerra that he had to return to Cuba. He returned to Cuba, bought twenty original tunes, applied for legal residency in the United States, and was back in New York by the fall of 1945. Luis Varona greeted him with a proposition: Varona would direct the orchestra for fifty percent of the money earned. Guerra stunned Varona, saying, "No, I will direct my orchestra without partners." A Cuban musician, Frank Gilberto Ayala, became the pianist, arranger, and director. With twenty new charts, the twelve-piece *conjunto* made its debut at the Odd Fellows Temple on 106th Street between Park and Lexington Avenues.

In 1945, Luis Cueva founded Verne Records. The Verne discography indicates that the Guerra orchestra recorded four tunes in 1945—the boleros "Miedo de Tí" and "Impression" and the *guarachas* "Comparsa Baracón" and "Dice Mi Gallo."

Jazz trumpeter Doc Cheatham recalled, "In 1945 I met Marcelino. He signed up as one of my students. He was difficult to teach...so after months of tutoring him on trumpet, I told him to learn another instrument." Cheatham became part of Guerra's horn section, and his trumpet is heard on every one of Guerra's Verne recordings of the 1940s. Guerra signed an exclusive contract with Cueva, which meant that he could record for Verne only.

In January 1945, the newly founded Coda label recorded Noro Morales's "Rhumba Rhapsody" and "Bangin' the Bongo." The Coda recordings "Bruca Maniguá," "Tierra Va Temblá," "Sin San Sore," and "Yenye" were made by Conjunto Rapindey. Shortly thereafter, Rapindey's Sexteto Batamú recorded the tunes "Un Poquito Más," "Sin Comprender," "Tú Baila Con Ella," and "Mátala." Guerra's popularity soared. The band was working in all the top Latin clubs of Spanish Harlem and the Bronx, including the Martinique, Lincoln Square Center, and St. Nicholas Arena, plus the Sunday "Tico Tico" dances at the Manhattan Center. Federico Pagani's battles for top billing between the Machito and Guerra orchestras were sold-out performances.

After his Verne recording of "Rumba Rumbero" in 1946, Guerra was one of the most popular Latin musicians in New York. The recording was heard for many years thereafter. In 1947, Chano Pozo's *conjunto*—which included "El Mago del Tres" (Arsenio Rodríguez) and Rapindey—recorded "Serende," "Seven Seven," "Contéstame," and "Sácale Brillo al Piso."

In February 1947, Arsenio Rodríguez was in New York to record with Chano Pozo's *conjunto* (composed of members of Machito's orchestra). "Arsenio had been blind since the age of eight," said Mario Bauzá. "Miguelito [Valdés] learned about a successful operation in which Dr. Ramón Castroviejo had restored a man's eyesight. Miguel asked Macho, Federico Pagani, and me to promote an *El Rayo de Luz* (Ray of Light) dance, which would raise funds for Arsenio's eye operation. On July 12, 1947, the dance at the Hotel Diplomat featured orchestras led by Guerra and Machito, along with guest artists Miguelito Valdés, Noro Morales, Bobby Capó, Olga Guillot, Chano Pozo, Graciela, Daniel Santos, Juan "El Boy" Torres, and Xavier Cugat. Five thousand dollars were raised. Arsenio was examined and told that his eyesight would never be restored. Hours later, at an apartment in the Bronx, Arsenio composed "La Vida Es Un Sueño" (Life Is But a Dream).

In 1950, the new sound of mambo dominated the dance scene, and Guerra included mambos in his repertoire. In 1954, after years of tolerating his sidemen's problems with drugs and alcohol and the racism of some midtown club owners who thought his sidemen were "too black," Rapindey left the music scene. He turned over his orchestra to pianist Ayala, then joined the United States Merchant Marine and began traveling all over the world.

In the 1960s, Guerra started making guest appearances with Machito's orchestra during downtime between his merchant marine voyages. He was the vocalist for the tunes "Convergencia," "La Florecita," "Echa Martín," and "Busca Lo Tuyo" for La Playa Sextet's 1964 United Artists LP *Sí, Sí, La Playa*. Weeks later, he was the lead vocalist on the tunes "Yo Soy La Rumba" and "Así No Se Quiere A Nadie," and sang in the chorus on "El Guardia Con el Tolete," "Baja del Caballo," and "Entre Juanita y José" for Machito's 1965 United Artists label LP *Mucho Mucho Machito*. While docked in Madrid, Spain, he met Julia, whom he married in 1967. To spend more time with his wife, he left the merchant marine and landed a night job as a maintenance worker at Rockefeller Center. He supplemented his income with the hundred and fifty dollars he earned as a vocalist on Fridays, Saturdays, and Sundays at La Viña, a Cuban Club in Union, New Jersey.

During the summer of 1976, Mario Bauzá was directing his own orchestra. Bauzá attempted to convince Guerra to become a bandleader again. He introduced him to conga drummer Armando Sánchez, who became the first member of Guerra's Septeto Son de la Loma. The group debuted on June 15, 1976, but after a few appearances, Guerra left the band to Sánchez and moved to Spain with his wife. He died there, in the town of Alicante, on June 30, 1996. A few months later he was cremated, as he had requested. Back in New York, fourteen people, including his wife, Julia, rode a ferry to the Statue of Liberty and carried out a provision of his will by scattering his ashes at the foot of the monument. Why had he wanted them dispersed in the United States instead of Cuba? The answer lies, perhaps, in the lyrics of a song he never completed:

> *Nueva York, Nueva York*
> *Ciudad donde fuí tan feliz*
> *Nueva York, en tu suelo también sufrí*
> *Algún día he de morir*
> *Y desearía fuese en tí*
> *Adorada Nueva York.*

> New York, New York
> The city where I was so happy
> New York, the land where I suffered as well.
> One day I will die,
> And I hope it will be
> In you, my beloved New York.

Originally published in Latin Beat *magazine, April 2000*

TEN

Noro Morales

For New York Latinos during the 1940s and early 1950s, the name Noro Morales represented exciting, up-tempo dance music. Morales was a rotund man who measured five feet eight inches and weighed 280 pounds during his peak years. Noro was a Puerto Rican hero in the 1940s, partly because some of the titles of the tunes he wrote bore the names of Puerto Rican cities and also because of Rafael Hernández's lyrics, which celebrated the island's culture. For the first half of the 1940s, Morales's and Xavier Cugat's groups were the most popular bands around; after 1945, Morales's main rival as a bandleader was Machito. During this period, Noro's band was regularly paid the highest compliment an orchestra can get: wherever Morales and his group appeared, musicians from other bands would come just to watch the performance. That was what Tito Puente, Tito Rodríguez, Charlie Palmieri, Hector Rivera, Lou Pérez, Pete Terrace, Frankie Colón, and Ken Rosa did on many occasions.

Noro was died very young, in his forties. He might have lived longer had he controlled his alcoholism. It was rumored that he was consuming a bottle of rum a day. Obesity, diabetes, and alcohol abuse were the causes of his early demise.

Born on January 4, 1911, in Puerta de Tierra, Puerto Rico, Norberto Morales came from a family of musicians. His father, Luis, a violinist, and his sister Marina were his first tutors. In 1924, Luis Morales, his wife, and their nine children moved to Caracas, Venezuela, and Luis joined the official orchestra for President Juan Gómez. Months later, Luis Morales died, and Noro became musical director.

The family returned to Puerto Rico in 1930 after the orchestra disbanded. Back on the island, Noro performed as a freelance pianist for Rafael Sánchez y Su Sinfónica, the Midnight Serenaders, Carmelo Díaz, and Rafael Muñoz before relocating to New York City in 1935. His first stateside job was with the red-hot Alberto Socarrás orchestra, which performed at jazz and Latin nightclubs. Noro could not play jazz. He left Socarrás for stints with the bands of Augusto Coen, Leo Marini, and Johnny Rodríguez (Tito's brother), with whom he made his first recordings on January 2, 1936, for Columbia Records.

The Morales Brothers Puerto Rican Orchestra emerged in New York on May 19, 1938, with drummer Humberto and flutists Esy and Pepito (a k a Mandinga). The orchestra made its first six recordings for Columbia Records. Noro was then living in an apartment at 116th Street between Fifth and Lenox Avenues. On the floor above him lived Puerto Rican composer Rafael Hernández and his sister Victoria. Whenever Hernández felt an inspiration for a new tune, he would go downstairs and compose the music on Noro's piano. As a gesture of goodwill, Hernández made sure that Morales and his vocalist Davilita got the first chance to record the new tunes. The first one that they took him up on was "Ahora Sí Somos Felices," recorded for Columbia on June 15, 1938. Two months later, the band began appearing in clubs as the Noro Morales Orchestra. On September 11, 1939, Machito served as Noro's vocalist for "Con Tu Negro," a song with a conga rhythm.

By the middle of 1940, Morales was no longer recording for Columbia. He signed with Decca Records and utilized bandleader Machito's vocals for the July 29, 1941, recordings of "Como Yo No Hay Quien Baile El Muñeco," "Bim Bam Bum," and "Rueda." Then, on January 30, 1942, came that once-in-a-lifetime chance for international stardom, when Noro recorded his composition "Serenata Rítmica." The tune's melodic richness aroused the passions, and for months it was heard daily in Latin communities. But the orchestra was also suddenly getting offers from the Anglo world to play in downtown Manhattan—an area theretofore closed to Latin bands.

This writer can easily imagine the enthusiasm "Serenata Rítmica" must have provoked at a downtown club. When I was eleven years old, my family was at Spanish Harlem's Hispano Theater, on 116th Street and Fifth Avenue. A movie featuring Mexico's most popular artist, Jorge Negrete, ended, and the house lights came on. After a few seconds the piano vamp of "Serenata Rítmica" sounded and the theater became a din of noise. The stage's maroon drapes opened and revealed the Morales orchestra, with Noro playing piano, smiling and nodding to overzealous fans. The audience rose to its feet screaming, yelling, applauding, and behaving madly while Noro's fingers stroked the black and white keys, raising a fever pitch of Puerto Rican pride. Like Rafael Hernández's "Los Carreteros," "Serenata Rítmica" became a reminder of how great it felt to be Puerto Rican.

Months later, in September 1942, Morales's orchestra was contracted to play the New York *Daily News*'s Harvest Moon Ball, an annual event showcasing the city's best dancers. The orchestra also played in movie shorts such as *The Gay Ranchero* (1941), *Cuban Pete* (1942), *Ella* (1942), and *Mexican Jumping Bean* (1942), two of which featured a teenaged Tito Puente on percussion. During the same period, the Stork Club became the first downtown club to open its doors to Morales's music. At the Stork one evening, renowned *Daily Mirror* columnist Walter Winchell spoke to Noro in English. With a bewildered look, Noro replied, "Scoose me, me English is not so nice looking." Winchell roared with laughter and mentioned it in his column the following day.

Great-selling recordings and exposure in Winchell's column enabled the Morales band to appear in many prominent Broadway nightspots and to earn top dollar. But World War II was reaching its peak, and in 1943 the country experienced a vinyl shortage. Major labels concentrated on American pop bands and vocalists, and Latin recording artists (except for Xavier Cugat) had their contracts cancelled with Decca and Columbia. In response, two new labels, Seeco and Verne, started up and signed individual Latin artists as well as the top two Latin bands. Machito and his Afro Cubans signed with Verne, and Noro signed with Seeco.

In early 1945 the Noro Morales Orchestra was appearing at La Conga Club, featuring vocalists Tito Rodríguez, Juan "El Boy" Torres, and Pellín Rodríguez. Morales's Seeco 78s of "Walter Winchell Rumba," "Noro in Rumbaland," "Rumbambola," "Stop 21," and "Serenata Rítmica" placed this band in contention with Machito's for the most popular Latin music orchestra. John "Big Daddy" Rodríguez (a k a "La Vaca") said, "I was Noro's *bongocero* at the Copacabana when the band recorded for Seeco. During the mid- to late 1940s, Noro recorded using phony names. He needed the money for the alimony he was paying to ex-wives. He started to gamble....In 1952, while the orchestra appeared at Havana's Montmartre Casino, Noro exchanged ten hundred-dollar bills for ten chips. I saw him lose a hundred dollars a minute for ten minutes on roulette."

Gabriel Oller, proprietor of the Coda and SMC (Spanish Music Center) labels, recalled a business deal with the pianist-bandleader. "After a lengthy discussion on January 16, 1945, I convinced him to sign a contract to record 'Rhumba Rhapsody,' 'Begin the Beguine,' 'Montuno in A-Flat,' and 'Bangin' the Bongo.'" On February 14, 1945, Morales sold Oller a half interest in the musical copyrights of "Montuno in A-Flat" and "Bangin' the Bongo" for $150. This maneuver permitted Oller to share in the composer's royalties. "At this time," said Oller, "Noro lived at the Hotel Victoria in midtown Manhattan. He was a diabetic, he drank rum every day, was always well groomed, and spent large sums of money on expensive colognes. He was naïve when it came to women. He fell in love with every pretty face he looked at. He married three women. They divorced him and collected alimony. On a few occasions he was threatened with imprisonment for missing alimony payments. Noro did not like to sign contracts. He used to say, 'Let's go to the studio....What do we have to sign a contract for? Don't you trust a fellow Puerto Rican?'"

The Coda recordings of the instrumentals "Bangin' the Bongo," "Montuno in A-Flat," "Begin the Beguine," and "Rhumba Rhapsody" became bestsellers. They garnered huge sales because of the exposure they received on daily radio programs, especially the Arthur Godfrey show. In 1946 Morales signed a contract with Majestic Records; his recordings were released in 1947. Bestsellers were "Ten Jabón," "Jungalarero," "Montuno in G," "Temptation," "Tambó," "Escucha Mi Son," "Tea for Two," and "Opus Esy."

Noro's brother Esy Morales was born in Puerta de Tierra, Puerto Rico, in 1916. At age eight, Esy was performing on sax, clarinet, and flute. In 1930, at age twenty, he moved to New York. He would spend the next eight years on and off with Cugat and the Morales Brothers Orchestra before organizing his own band in 1947. In 1949, the Esy Morales Orchestra would have a cameo role in the motion picture *Criss Cross*, featuring Burt Lancaster. Five minutes into the movie, Yvonne De Carlo and Tony Curtis are seen dancing to "Jungle Fantasy," a fast rumba that includes the legendary Cuban pianist René Touzet. Scarcely a year later, on November 3, 1950, Esy Morales would die in New York of a heart attack. A year after that, Tito Puente's orchestra would record Puente's composition and arrangement of "Esy" for Tico Records.

In September 1946, Club London (formerly La Conga) reopened as the China Doll Restaurant at 52nd Street and Broadway. Its employees were of Asian ancestry, and the restaurant served Oriental, Cuban, Puerto Rican, and American dishes. The bands of Noro Morales and José Curbelo supplied the music for the shows and for the diners, who were Latin dance music aficionados. The China Doll capitalized on Morales's popularity. Noro's live broadcasts from the China Doll kept his fans home.

On Sunday afternoons at exactly 4 P.M., the shows always began with "Serenata Rítmica." The announcer would then say, "Live from the China Doll in midtown Manhattan, Noro Morales and his orchestra!" The orchestra would play Noro's charts for thirty minutes. Then the sound of "Serenata Rítmica" would signal that the show was ending. Noro's "Tea for Two" was the recording heard most often in 1947 and 1948. Before 1947 ended, Gabriel Oller signed Noro's quintet to record four Rafael

Hernández boleros: "Campanitas de Cristal," "Silencio," "Malditos Celos," and "Perfume de Gardenias." These Coda label gems left no doubt who Latin music's most popular orchestra was with Puerto Ricans.

In January 1949, the Machito orchestra recorded "Tanga" for Mercury Records; it was heard nationwide on jazz stations. Months later, Machito's recording of "Asia Minor" placed that tune in contention for best recording of the year. Meanwhile, Noro's orchestra was selected to play at the inauguration of the governor of Puerto Rico. An official of MGM Records who attended was bowled over by Noro's music and signed him to a contract. Noro's recordings of "Puerta de Tierra," "Chen Chen Ko," "Isla Verde," "Capullito de Alelí," "El Soplón," "The Peanut Vendor," "Ponce," and "110th Street and Fifth Avenue" made Noro into Machito's rival. "Ponce," composed by Ruben Berrios, and "110th Street and Fifth Avenue," by Morales and his lead trumpeter, Paul Lopez, received the most airplay throughout Spanish Harlem—whether via radio or simply through open windows.

"One evening," said Lopez, "the band was on stage at the China Doll. A comedian of Turkish descent named Guilli Guilli opened his show by saying, 'Guilli Guilli…tonight's the night…come to the Ali Baba.'" Noro composed music called 'Guili Guili' and recorded it for Columbia Records in 1951. Jazz trumpeter Doc Severinsen replaced Lopez on the 1952 Decca session *Mambo with Noro*. Morales then accepted RCA's lucrative offer to record.

RCA's A&R man, Herman Díaz Jr., convinced Noro he would sell thousands of records of American pop standards. For the following three years, Noro recorded tunes like "Sweet Sue, Just You," "Sheik of Araby," "Song from Moulin Rouge," "Fantasia Mexicana," "No Other Love," "The Terry Theme," "Am I Blue," "Me and My Shadow," and "Istanbul." These recordings lacked the fiery Morales swing and were responsible for his decline in popularity. To meet alimony demands, he made more bootleg recordings under pseudonyms. In 1958 he recorded "No Blues Noro" for Tico Records, which started him on the comeback trail.

In 1960 Morales returned to Puerto Rico to live. Ansonia Records recorded his quintet, and the tracks "Vitamina" and "Mi Guajira" sold the LP. During his peak years, Noro weighed 280 pounds, but by 1961 he had ballooned to over three hundred pounds. No one suspected he was going blind until he fell off a bandstand. On January 15, 1964, at age 53, he died of uremia at San Jorge Hospital in San Juan, Puerto Rico.

Originally published in Impacto *magazine.*

ELEVEN

JOE LOCO

"Loco," the Spanish word for crazy, became the name of a New York–born musician because he insisted that American pop classics like "Blue Moon," "Sweet and Lovely," "Little Brown Jug," and "Love for Sale" could be performed as mambos. Percussionist José Mangual added another reason: "The 'loco' tag was hung on him around the mid-1940s, after Verne Records recorded his tune 'Cada Loco Con Su Tema' for a Machito session." Loco's wife, Irma, said, "Joe suffered a head injury after being hit by a bus.... His friends began calling him loco."

Whatever the reasons for the name, Joe Loco was undoubtedly was one of Latin music's most revered musicians. More than half of his recordings after 1951 were Latinized American pop standards. Loco, a proficient orchestrator, added a typical Cuban mambo and *cha-cha-chá* feel to his arrangements of "Blues in the Night," "Serenade in Blue," "Too Marvelous for Words," "In the Still of the Night," "Gypsy in My Soul," and "How High the Moon."

He was one of the first musicians to follow Machito trumpeter Mario Bauzá in developing Latin jazz. He produced almost two hundred compositions and arranged hit tunes for the orchestras of Machito, Marcelino Guerra, Chano Pozo, Polito Galíndez, Pupi Campo, and Julio Andino. For over thirty years, beginning in the late 1930s, he was regarded a pianist's pianist, in recognition of his keyboard artistry with the bands of Montesino, Moncho Usera, Enric Madriguera, Bartolo Hernández, Machito, Polito Galíndez, Marcelino Guerra, Ramon Argueso, Fernando Alvarez, Armando Castro, Pupi Campo, Tito Puente, and Julio Andino.

Joe Loco was born José Estévez Jr. on March 26, 1921, to Puerto Rican parents who lived in the Hell's Kitchen section of Manhattan. He began violin and dance lessons at age eight while a participant in the Stars of the Future project run by Spanish Harlem's La Milagrosa Catholic Church. In 1934, he left school so he could tour and dance in vaudeville shows.

In 1937 a truant officer caught up with him and compelled him to attend Haaren High School, where he befriended Charles Pickells, a music teacher who taught him the rudiments of piano and trombone. During the same year, while living in Spanish Harlem, José was hit by a Madison Avenue bus. He was operated on and had a steel plate put in his head. He recovered and later married Puerto Rican beauty Irma Ledesma. Two years after the wedding, he became Montesino's pianist.

For the next three years, he played piano for many of New York City's most popular orchestras. In 1943, during the height of World War II, Machito's pianist Frank Gilberto Ayala was drafted and replaced by Luis Varona. Months later, Varona became the pianist for Machito's second Afro Cuban Orchestra, which Mario Bauzá had created for the newly arrived Cuban vocalist/songwriter Marcelino Guerra. Loco replaced Varona. "Immediately after Loco joined Machito," said percussionist José Mangual, "the band sounded different because of Loco's solos. They were hot. Dancers began calling us the Latin Count Basie Orchestra."

In December 1945, Loco was drafted and replaced by René Hernández, who had come from Cuba. In the air force, Loco taught himself to arrange music and wrote charts for Guerra, Vincent López, Noro Morales, and Xavier Cugat. Back in civilian life in early 1947, his first job was with the orchestra of Ramon Argueso. This is when he met Peter Gutiérrez, a Puerto Rican percussionist who years later would become a Latin music star using the name Pete Terrace. Loco completed several music courses with Juilliard professor Tom Timothy, and by mid-1947 he was recognized as one of Latin music's most creative composers and orchestrators. It was also in 1947 that Noro Morales's recording of "Tea for Two" sold thousands of 78s. At the same time, Loco and Tito Puente were sidemen in Fernando Alvarez's Copacabana Samba Band.

In October 1947, Loco left the Samba Band to organize the band of Jack López. A few months later, Puente also left to work for Pupi Campo's orchestra as a drummer, arranger, and business manager. One evening, Loco substituted for Campo pianist Al Escobar. It turned out to be a spur-of-the-moment, unrecorded historical event. Loco's piano solo was searing hot, and Puente's timbal and Johnny "La Vaca" Rodríguez's *cascara* work made for an exciting, exotic sound that created delirium. Loco and Puente stole the spotlight on the tunes "Earl Wilson Mambo," "How High the Moon," "Son de la Loma," "Mambo Rhapsody," "Pilarena," "Capullito de Alelí," and "Cuando Te Vea." Loco's and Puente's performances and their arrangements of these songs for Campo's 1948 Seeco recordings elevated the group to a spot among Latin music's top five bands.

On another front, Machito was dealing with a rebellion caused by a personality conflict between musical director Mario Bauzá and conga drummer Carlos Vidal. Vidal left the band and attempted to persuade other sidemen to follow him to Los Angeles. Bassist Julio Andino was the only one to go along, but lack of work forced him to return to New York months later. Loco, who had befriended Andino years earlier, organized the Julio Andino Orchestra, wrote new tunes, and challenged the Machito Orchestra to a music war at the Park Palace at 110th Street and Fifth Avenue.

Word about the war spread through El Barrio, and tickets for the Labor Day dance were sold out in advance. The Andino Orchestra, which had twenty Loco arrangements, was not expected to be a worthy opponent for Machito, who had a few hundred well-known charts. It was a David-and-Goliath battle, except that the giant Machito was not slain. But the Andino group fought valiantly, with libidinous ad-libs on "Plaza Stomp Mambo," "El Tubo," "Los Comimos La Paella," and "Fristi Popo." On December 1, 1949, the Andino Orchestra recorded these tunes for Gabriel Oller's SMC Label. Months later, the group disbanded.

In 1951, while Joe Loco was still Pupi Campo's pianist, the Joe Loco Trio made its first recordings, "Tu Plato" and "Yumbambé," for Tico Records. Months later, Loco was the pianist on a Tito Rodríguez recording session for Tico. Rodríguez, unable to sing because of laryngitis, convinced Tico president George Goldner to salvage the session by recording the Loco trio. Rodríguez was the fourth man on the session; he played claves. Loco recorded the pop tune "Tenderly." At Atlantic City, where the Campo orchestra was appearing, Loco received a phone call from Goldner, who told him that "Tenderly" was a hit and had sold close to a thousand records. Loco was offered a recording contract, which he accepted. One hour later, Campo, Loco, and their wives were in bathing suits enjoying the sun. Campo exploded when Loco told him he was leaving to direct his own group. Pianist Charlie Palmieri replaced him.

Most of Loco's Tico recordings sold in the hundreds, and instead of playing Latin ballrooms, he worked for top dollar in jazz clubs across the nation. The clubs included Chicago's Blue Note, Denver's Melody Lounge, and New York's Apollo Theatre. On March 23, 1953, a live radio broadcast from Birdland transmitted his recordings of "Locorama," "Blues in the Night," and "Bei Mir Bist Du Schoen," performed by Pete Terrace on vibes, Al Franklin on bass, Ray Rivera on timbales, Freddie López on congas, and Loco on piano. During the winter of 1954, George Goldner decided to increase record sales by unveiling the mambo rhythm in a tour of fifty-six cities. The Mambo USA tour sold out its Carnegie Hall concert. Loco wrote the tune "Mambo USA," which was another chart-buster. But in other venues across the country, the turnout was small. Consequently, the tour ended weeks later.

In 1955, when the Cuban *cha-cha-chá* was Latin music's most popular dance rhythm, Pérez Prado's hit "Cherry Pink and Apple Blossom White" sold over one million units, and Loco's cha-chas were in most New York City jukeboxes. After four years of receiving only a few dollars in royalties, Loco confronted Goldner about the "pennies" he was getting. Loco exploded when Goldner told him that his records did not sell, and Goldner agreed to let Loco record for Columbia in return for a percentage of sales. Columbia recorded two LPs for which Loco was paid well, received nationwide promotion, and got a contract. One of his gigs on a coast-to-coast tour was at a Las Vegas lounge. But the music director there fired the band for creating a "jungle" atmosphere. He resented how the group heated a can of wax to do maintenance on their bongo and conga skins.

In 1956, Tito Puente left Tico Records for RCA. Goldner now wanted a group with the vibraharp sound, and he offered Pete Terrace the chance to become a bandleader. Terrace told Loco he was leaving the group to become a Tico recording artist. Loco counseled him not to accept the offer and predicted that he would regret it if he took it. Loco and Terrace had been as close as brothers since they met in 1947 in Argueso's band. Now, they broke off their friendship.

Terrace organized a quintet, with Charlie Palmieri as pianist, for the LP *A Night in Mambo Jazzland*. Louie Ramírez, a cousin of Loco's wife, Irma, replaced Terrace on vibes. In 1957, Loco recorded *The Music of Rafael Hernández* for Ansonia Records. It was a masterpiece, and it would have sold well if it had been promoted. Two years later Ansonia recorded *The Music of Gonzalo Curiel*, another gem that also went unpromoted.

In 1959, Loco settled in Los Angeles with his wife and three children. Ramírez returned to New York and formed a group that included trumpeter/arranger Marty Sheller. The group was fronted by *conguero* Sabu Martinez for the 1961 Alegre LP *Jazz Espagnole*. In 1957, Morris Levy took over Tico Records. Terrace, no longer under contract, reconciled with Loco. In May 1960, Fantasy Records recorded *Going Loco* by the Pete Terrace Quintet, featuring Joe Loco on piano, Bobby Flash on bongos, Fred Aguilera on timbales, Julio Andino on bass, and Pete Terrace on vibes.

One year later, New York's interest in charanga gave way to the *pachanga* rhythm—a vogue that lasted less than three years. The Fantasy LP *Pachanga with Joe Loco* was released in February 1961, with Loco fronting the charanga orchestra of Mongo Santamaría. Loco continued to record music that sold very well for the Imperial, GNP (Gene Norman Presents), and Orfeon Labels. Loco was riding high will all kinds of audiences. While he was playing for a week at the Sahara Hotel in Las Vegas, movie actress Rita Hayworth (born Margarita Carmen Cansino in Brooklyn) caught all his performances. On his last night there, she approached him and asked him to play "Love for Sale."

But by 1967, the magic that had once made Joe Loco a living legend was gone. This was painfully evident on the album *Puerto Rico 67*, where it seemed that Loco's fiery piano solos were a thing of the past. Loco separated from his wife, moved to New York, and became a partner, along with Charlie Palmieri, Joe Loco, and Tito Puente, in the music-arranging services company Bandaide. Loco, Palmieri, and Puente wrote arrangements for anyone who wanted them. In 1968, Loco moved to Rio Piedras, Puerto Rico, founded the Loco Recording and Publishing companies, and started performing at San Juan's popular nightspots. By 1986, Loco was suffering from diabetes and had to have a leg amputated. During the second week of March 1988, he died in his sleep in San Juan, at age 67.

The vinyl evidence still exists to prove that José Estévez Jr., a k a Joe Loco, was one of Latin music's all-time great musicians. Yet if a truant officer had not compelled him to return to school in 1938, there never would have been a Joe Loco legend.

Originally published in Latin Beat *magazine, September 1996*

TWELVE

FEDERICO PAGANI

Although Latinos lived in New York at the turn of the century, the Latin music industry did not get started until 1930. It began after the Puerto Rican community became fed up with the lack of housing, with segregation into menial jobs and away from civil service positions, and with the lack of a voice in the affairs of city government. But in 1930, dances at the Golden Casino, on 111th Street and Fifth Avenue, and at the Park Palace, on 110th Street and Fifth Avenue, generated enough money to start an organization to advocate for New York's Puerto Ricans. Since those two sold-out events, the Latin music industry has grown into a multi-million-dollar entertainment business.

One of the major contributors to this lucrative industry was Arsenio Pagani-Santiago, popularly known as El Gran Federico. Often called the Father of Latin Dance Promotion, he began in 1940 to nurture and promote his brainchild through the financially difficult years of World War II, inventing wild promotional schemes that attracted people to dances in the way that magnets attract metal.

Pagani was also responsible for removing ethnic barriers at entertainment places that catered to American pop-music lovers. And whenever a theater, nightclub, or ballroom was financially anemic, the owner called Pagani for a transfusion. When bands needed exposure or work, Federico made it possible. Up to the late 1970s, he created employment for many musicians, artists, and others, and kept many entertainment venues financially solvent. Yet during these same years, whenever bad weather or uncontrollable acts of nature kept him from paying expenses, the same people he had helped often vilified and damned him. That was ironic, since without Pagani, many musicians would have had to find other employment to support themselves.

Pagani was a small man: he measured only five feet six inches and weighed 120 pounds. He spoke English with a thick Spanish accent and often ended up speaking the latter language after starting a conversation in the former.

He was born on January 12, 1907, to parents Andrea and Federico, in San Juan, Puerto Rico. As a youngster he worked as a printing apprentice, a carpenter, and a barber before relocating to New York in September 1925 to live with a friend of his family at Ninety-ninth Street and Third Avenue. He earned twenty-four dollars every two weeks at the Waldorf-Astoria Hotel as a kitchen utility man.

During the spring of 1926 he resided at 113th Street and Fifth Avenue. "Vicente Sigler, a Cuban-born trumpeter-bandleader, had the only Latin band in New York when I arrived from Puerto Rico," said Pagani, "Sigler worked the dances at midtown hotels....His repertoire consisted of Cuban *danzónes* and paso dobles."

During that era, Fifth Avenue between 110th and 116th Streets was an affluent area inhabited by wealthy Jewish professionals. On the corner of 110th Street and Fifth Avenue was the Park Palace, a Jewish catering hall where weddings were celebrated and the police, sanitation, and fire departments held their festivities. Around the corner on Fifth Avenue was Tatay's Spanish Music Center, owned by Puerto Rican Gabriel Oller, who sold guitars, sheet music, 78-rpm records, and pianola rolls. Separating the catering hall and Tatay's was the Photoplay Theater, which in 1931 became El Teatro San José, featuring Spanish movies and live stage shows of local talent. As Jewish residents moved away, the vacant apartments were increasingly occupied by Puerto Ricans and Cubans.

By 1935, Puerto Ricans outnumbered the remaining Jews. In subsequent years, as East Harlem became predominantly Puerto Rican, there was never a problem between the two ethnic groups. Jews often learned to speak Spanish and married Puerto Ricans. Anna Hersh, proprietress of the Park Palace, rented out her premises for Saturday night dances where men paid thirty-five cents and women entered free. One band would perform with a ten-minute break, and the musicians were paid eight dollars.

Pagani gave up the Waldorf job to work in a Brooklyn factory that manufactured rope; he also attended night school to learn English. In 1935 he left the rope factory to become Puerto Rican trumpeter Augusto Coen's band boy for fifty cents a night. He guarded the sheet music, transported it, set up music stands, and recovered them at the end of each dance. He listened attentively to all of Coen's negotiations with club owners and read all the contracts Coen asked him to file with the musicians' union. He asked hundreds of questions and learned the various wage scales. At the same time he was learning the rudiments of clave and bongo from Coen's pianist, Noro Morales.

After a year with Coen, Federico joined the American Federation of Musicians, Local 802. He formed the band Los Happy Boys, who became popular via their musical battles with the orchestras of Alberto Socarrás and Augusto Coen. In 1938, Cuban *timbalero* Montecino took over Los Happy Boys, and Federico formed La Guerilla. He played claves and bongos, Moncho Usera conducted, and the red-hot Joe Loco burned the piano keys.

In 1940 Pagani gave up the musician's role to promote Latin music wherever there was a large room and a bandstand. Asthma prevented him from serving in the United States armed forces. "To promote a Latin music dance in those days was difficult," said Pagani. *"La Prensa* published news from all over South America...I was unable to place an ad in it....There were no Latin music radio programs like there are today...radio stations claimed there wasn't a market for it."

For three years after World War II began, Pagani's stage shows at the Triboro Theatre at 125th Street near First Avenue were always sold out. He filled every seat in the theater by featuring the popular artists of several Spanish-speaking countries; for example, Mexico's Tito Guizar, Jorge Negrete, and Tonia La Negra, and Puerto Rico's Daniel Santos, Bobby Capó, and Myrta Silva. His success did not go unnoticed by other businessmen, and he was hired to produce similar shows in many East Harlem movie houses.

Wherever he promoted, New York Latinos heard the music of Alberto Socarrás, Juancito Sanabria, Alberto Iznaga, Noro Morales, and Machito, as well as vocalists Juan "El Boy" Torres, Marcelino Guerra, and Miguelito Valdés. In between theater engagements, he promoted dances. His outrageous contests attracted capacity crowds to the Park Palace, Golden Casino, Hunts Point Palace, and Odd Fellows Temple. Zoot suits—with wide shoulders, long pocket chains, and baggy pants tapered at the ankles—were in vogue for the hepcats of the early 1940s, and Pagani's zoot suit dance contest drew over five hundred competitors. The winner wearing the most outlandish suit won twenty-five dollars. Individual dances were tagged Peg Pants, Loudest Shirt, Best Looking Umbrella, Weirdest Looking Shoes, and many other zany gimmicks.

For *El Baile de los Cocos Pelaos* (The Dance of the Bald Heads) in 1943, half the men shaved their heads. For a Joe Louis dance he once held, Pagani sold every ticket within a week. Louis, the world heavyweight boxing champ known then as the Brown Bomber, was popular with Harlemites. During the evening of the dance, Pagani presented a man named José Luis—Joe Louis in Spanish—but of course, this guy was not the famous boxer. The packed ballroom broke out in uncontrollable laughter: the dancers were not annoyed by the scam, since they were totally engrossed in the fierce and swinging musical battle between Machito's Afro Cubans and Alberto Iznaga's La Siboney.

By 1944, Pagani's sold-out performances may have been the reason *La Prensa* newspaper began publishing ads about his dances. One ad showed an illustration of Xavier Cugat and Noro Morales squaring off with boxing gloves for their battle to become "King of the Rumba." In the mid-1940s, promoters Catalino Rolón, Art "Pancho" Raymond, and Gabriel Oller began crowding the dance promotion field. At the same time, musicians Machito and Mario Bauzá were promoting their own dances at the Plaza and Audubon Ballroom by hiring bands and paying them. In 1948, when very little of the dance promotion pie was left, Mario Bauzá got Pagani a job as promoter and ticket collector at the Alma Dance Studios at 53rd Street and Broadway. This dime-a-dance salon became the Palladium Ballroom in 1949, and with the help of a new Cuban dance rhythm, the mambo, Federico and the Palladium became famous.

In June 1956, Catalino Rolón replaced Federico as promoter of the Palladium. Pagani assumed the role of agent for international Latin music stars. The mambo was Latin music's most popular dance in the mid-1950s, and Pagani made an effort to introduce Antonio Arcaño y Sus Maravillas—the Cuban orchestra credited with the creation of the mambo in 1938 because of the brothers Cachao and Orestes López. But Pagani failed in the effort because of financial problems. He began promoting at the Bronx's Westchester Avenue Tropicana Club until December 1957. He returned to the Palladium in February 1958, then left a few months later to promote at the Embassy Ballroom, the Colgate Gardens, the Bronx Casino, the Caravana Club (where the *pachanga* dance craze started), and at lightweight world boxing champ Carlos Ortiz's Club Tropicoro.

On November 7, 1968, Hispanic New York honored Pagani with a tribute at the Hotel Americana in midtown Manhattan. Peter Rios, publisher of the original *Latin New York* magazine, presented him with a plaque in recognition of his contributions to the enhancement of New York's Latin music industry.

The final tribute to Pagani took place at Roseland on Friday, May 27, 1977. More than one thousand aficionados danced to the music of twelve orchestras, including Tito Puente's, Eddie Palmieri's, Machito's, Charlie Palmieri's, Conjunto Saoco, and Orquesta Broadway. In the *New York Times* two days later, critic Robert Palmer quoted Tito Puente noting that Pagani "has done more for our music than anyone during the 1940s, [when] black and other ethnic people were not allowed to have their dances downtown....Everything was in Harlem....Federico began promoting dances at the old Palladium at 53rd Street and Broadway....Machito got started with him then and I came along later in the 1950s."

During our interview at the Cheetah club in 1974, Pagani said, "I've heard every popular rhythm since 1925 to the present. First came *la conga*, and it was big. The next popular rhythm was *la rumba*, and it was more popular than the conga. Then Pérez Prado's mambo, Cuba's *cha-cha-chá* and the New York *pachanga*, which Charlie Palmieri and Johnny Pacheco created. Cuba's rhythms have always dominated the Latin dance scene.

"The most successful dance I promoted was Memorial Day, 1958, at the Saint Nicholas Arena. The sounds of Xavier Cugat, Machito, Marcelino Guerra, and Miguelito Valdés drew close to five thousand dancers. The second most successful dance was on Easter Sunday, 1958, at the Manhattan Center, when over four thousand people came to hear Pérez Prado, Tito Puente, and Cesar Concepción. I have no regrets about my career in the Latin music world....Latin music makes me feel young, and I always feel good."

Federico Pagani was married to Carmen for over fifty years; they had three children. His daughter Ana Pagani-Curley lives in Florida; his son Papi, who became a *timbalero* for the Tito Rodríguez band in 1960, passed away in 1970. Another son, Tito, died of rheumatic fever at age six. On December 21, 1987, Federico Pagani died of Parkinson's disease. He was buried at St. Michael's Cemetery in Astoria, Queens.

Originally published in Latin Beat *magazine, May 1994*

THIRTEEN

The Palladium

The Palladium Ballroom, once located at 1692 Broadway, off the corner of Fifty-third Street and Broadway in New York, closed its doors in May 1966. It had been open since 1947. The Palladium has always been and may always be the most talked-about nightspot in the annals of Latin music. It was the dancers' home away from home, a weekend escape from the everyday problems of life. It was a place where, for a dollar and twenty-five cents (and sometimes only seventy-five cents before 10 P.M.), people could meet and enjoy two bands, free dance lessons, a floor show, and a dance contest. In addition, the Palladium's libidinous mambo accomplished what social reformers for centuries could not do: by arousing people's passions and compelling them to the dance floor, it annihilated racial and religious barriers.

After Pérez Prado's "Mambo No. 5" hit the airwaves in 1949, ethnic and religious understanding improved, motivating many interracial marriages. By 1959, when the mambo peaked, it had been heard around the world. Its fame led non-Latino artists like Les Baxter, George Shearing, Les Brown, Woody Herman, and Cal Tjader to record mambos. The Palladium was a crucible. It melded Caucasians, African-Americans, and Asians in an atmosphere of trust and friendship, and helped dissolve stereotypes. Marlon Brando came to the Palladium, and so did Kim Novak, Sammy Davis Jr., Henry Fonda, Mel Ferrer, José Ferrer, Abbe Lane, Lena Horne, Shirley Booth, heavyweight boxing champ Ezzard Charles, Shelley Winters, George Shearing, Cal Tjader and other celebrities.

And yet very little has been written about the Palladium. I decided to change that situation, but I could not have done this article without the help of Vernon Boggs, sociologist, and David Carp, radio show host, Latin music historian, journalist, and investigator. Both unearthed information that is at the heart of this story.

The Palladium, of course, was a place for dancing, and one thing one finds when looking at Cuban music history is that blacks and white used to attend racially segregated dancehalls. During the 1920s, when Cuban dancehalls were called "academies," men bought five-cent tickets to dance with women. The academies with the best-sounding orchestras drew the largest crowds. White Cubans were moved by Afro-Cuban sounds, yet they would not patronize black dances because of the unwritten law, the unspoken *separación de las razas* (separation of the races).

Around 1940, that separation seemed to have been challenged by the arousing sounds of Arcaño y Sus Maravillas and Arsenio Rodríguez y Su Conjunto de Estrellas. White Cubans said, "To hell with the unwritten law," and began attending the Arcaño and Arsenio dances. In 1945, a standing-room-only crowd of white and black dancers packed a Havana dancehall. The draw was the Julio Cuevas orchestra, whose recording of "Agua de Tinajón" was being played from one end of Cuba to the other.

Alfredito Valdés, the brother of famed vocalist Vicentico Valdés and himself the vocalist for Ignacio Piñeiro's Septeto Nacional, was at that dance. "Everyone was there just to hear one tune, 'Agua de Tinajón,'" he recalled. "I was in front of the bandstand when the band began playing the René Hernández arrangement....Puntillita, who sang the lead, waved me up on stage and I began to sing chorus—*'Camagüey, agua de tinajón'*....No one was sitting down. Everyone was dancing." The swinging arrangement of "Tinajón" was one reason René Hernández was offered a job with the Machito orchestra, which he joined at the end of the year.

Meanwhile, in New York there were about fifteen "taxi dance" halls, where a dance hostess was given a ten-cent ticket for a dance. On January 23, 1942, the second-floor premises at 1692 Broadway, which was described as "three rooms, one unused room, two toilets, forty tables in each room, seats 125 people, bar twenty-by-five feet," became the Dreamland Dancing Academy, Inc. On June 3, 1944, its liquor license was lifted because of the arrests of two dance hostesses on charges of prostitution. On January 19, 1946, Louis Levine, Sylvia Cole, and Hyman Sigel filed their certificate of incorporation for the Palladium Ballroom, Inc. with their attorney, Louis J. Lefkowitz (who years later became Brooklyn's district attorney). The Palladium's license was approved on April 17, 1947.

Tommy Morton's name does not appear anywhere on the corporation papers. Nevertheless, he called the shots and ran the Palladium. The first thing he did was to contact Machito and offer him a job. Machito, who always included Mario Bauzá (his musical director) in the band's negotiations, spoke to Morton. The Machito orchestra was hired because it could perform the varied dance rhythms of Latin, tango, ballads, and swing music.

Ballrooms during those years were closing because they could not compete with Roseland and the Arcadia Ballroom. Morton believed he would attract dancers with a band that could play several dance rhythms, such as swing ("Don't Be That Way"), ballad ("Tabú"), rumba ("Tanga," "Ampárame"), and foxtrot ("Why Do I Love You"). One evening Morton invited Machito and Bauzá to his office. He told them the ballroom was not making money, that Roseland and Arcadia were getting all the business. Morton asked them why dancers from the Concord and Grossinger's resorts in the Catskills were supporting them. Bauzá responded with a question: "How do you feel about black people in your club?" Morton said he was only interested in the color green.

When Morton agreed to a one-shot Sunday matinee from 2 to 9 P.M., Bauzá and Machito engaged the experienced dance promoter Federico Pagani. Pagani suggested they form the Blen Blen Blen Club, and handed out publicity ads at Harlem's subway and bus stops. On the Sunday of the experiment, Bauzá was a block away from the ballroom when he saw hundreds of people in front of the club, along with police cars and officers. He thought a riot had occurred. But the police had simply been called to control the giant crowd.

Of the six bands hired to play this first Latin matinee in a downtown dancehall, Noro Morales's orchestra stole the evening as he overwhelmed dancers with his rumbas "Serenata Rítmica," "Noro in Rumbaland," "Rumbambola," "Tea for Two," and "Stop 21." Following Noro was the José Curbelo Orchestra, then Joseito Mateo's merengue band, the Marcelino Guerra orchestra, and an unknown pickup group. Machito finished off the experiment. The Palladium earned more money in this one evening than Morton had made since his license was granted. The once-a-week Latin dance matinee continued, and the number of attendees grew with each passing week. Then, one week before the New York State Liquor Authority granted Morton a liquor license, he was assaulted in the ticket booth.

In the *New York Times* of April 11, an article titled "Bandits Routed in Dance Holdup" reported that "one hundred couples were swinging and swaying to hot music....downstairs, Thomas Morton, 45, the ticket seller, looked up expectantly as four men approached his booth....one of the men produced a revolver and announced a stickup....another grabbed the gun and brought it crashing down on Mr. Morton's head." Although such incidents usually hold up licenses until a full investigation is completed, Morton quickly was granted his.

In 1948, Pagani caught the Pupi Campo orchestra at the midtown

Embassy Club. Campo's drummer, Tito Puente, was on the rise to stardom. Puente was experimenting with a tune he later called "Picadillo," which Pagani loved. Puente accepted a Sunday matinee with a pickup group Pagani introduced as the "Picadilly Boys." During this period, two bands used to play the entire matinee. Puente, with the aid of Campo's sidemen, won over the dancers with a jazz-oriented sound blended with *montunos*. The dancers loved the Puente sound and wanted to hear more. In March 1949, Puente left the Campo band. On July 4 of that year, he debuted with his seven-piece orchestra at El Patio Club in Atlantic Beach.

Meanwhile, before 1948 had ended, George Goldner and Art "Pancho" Raymond founded Tico Records and recorded Al Castellanos, Tito Puente, and Tito Rodríguez. The labels on these records had silver lettering on a black background. In 1950, Tico suspended recording sessions until a court battle enabled Goldner to become sole owner. Now the labels were red with silver lettering. Goldner had DJ Dick "Ricardo" Sugar promoting the Tico releases on a fifteen-minute nightly show, which years later grew to two hours or more.

On July 28, 1949, New York's State Liquor Authority (SLA) warned Morton about a disorderly conduct charge brought against two of the club's managers, Frank Mangrella and Michael Catalano. The SLA approved the license for the Palladium Enterprises on January 18, 1950. Then the ballroom closed for renovations. On Friday, March 17, 1950, the Palladium staged a grand reopening, featuring the bands of Julio Andino and Tito Puente. Months later, on September 19, the Palladium Ballroom became Morton Ballroom, Inc. Morton wanted credit for its success. The truth is, it didn't matter. The Palladium did not become the legend that it did because of its owner or even the club's atmosphere. Instead, its success was due to the orchestras of Tito Puente, Tito Rodríguez, and Machito. Their music—the excitement it created and the escape it provided for a few hours—made the Palladium famous. The big three could have attracted Latin New Yorkers to an empty lot or a cellar. Nostalgia is also inspired by Tico's recordings of the two Titos and the Machito orchestra at the dance hall.

In 1951, the Tico recordings of "Golpecito," "Up and Down Mambo," "El Arrebato," "Tony and Lucille Mambo," "Yambu," "Desert Dance," "Joe Lustig Mambo," "Bésame la Bembita," and "Mambo Mona (Mama Guella)" made the Tito Rodríguez orchestra sizzling hot. Puente's "Abaniquito," "Lo Dicen Todos," "Mambo la Roca," "Ran Kan Kan," "Guayaba," "Swinging the Mambo," "Picadillo," "Vibe Mambo," and "Babarabatiri" were hits.

One afternoon, Puente went to the ballroom to meet Max Hyman, president of the Palladium, to discuss business. As Puente approached the club, he saw Tito Rodríguez's name above his on the marquee. He told Hyman to change the billing or his band would not perform that night. The marquee was changed. That evening Tito Rodríguez arrived early, since his orchestra was slated to kick the evening off. He ordered the utility man to change the marquee and put Puente's name under his. When Puente arrived, he exploded and demanded that the marquee again be changed. It was, and both names were now on the same line, Puente's to the left and Rodríguez's to the right—indicating that Puente was getting top billing. When Rodríguez's first set was over that evening, he did not mention that Puente's band was the next one up, a courtesy bandleaders always extended to each other. Puente did not announce Rodríguez's name either. The childhood friendship of Puente and Rodríguez was at an end.

Someone then began circulating a rumor that Hyman's wife, Mona, was having an affair with Tito Rodríguez. The truth was that Mrs. Hyman had given Rodríguez an advance on his salary. Despite Rodríguez's denials of the affair, he was banished to the Park Plaza at 110th Street and Fifth Avenue, which became his home base. Rodríguez then proved that it was the music, not the allure of the ballroom, that attracted huge crowds. Hyman noticed the number of dancers had dropped off. He convinced himself that the rumor of an affair with his wife could not be true, and brought Rodríguez's band back to the Palladium.

The off-the-bandstand verbal war for top billing made the Dick "Ricardo" Sugar show the program to listen to for up-to-the-minute developments. Puente, who never mentioned Rodríguez by name, referred to him as "the pretty boy maraca player," then lauded his own composing and arranging skills. When Sugar grilled Rodríguez, the Puerto Rican vocalist shrugged his shoulders. He didn't know what Sugar was talking about and said he had no problem with anyone in the music world…that he had had many friends. Nevertheless, he would sing songs whose lyrics were double-entendres, allegedly directed at his rival. While the battle raged, Puente continued to score points with dancers for a year or so, when he backed Vicentico Valdés on vibes between midnight and 1 A.M., but only on ballads. During this period, the ballroom ticket booth was a few feet away from the sidewalk entrance. From there, it was another twenty-five steps to the ticket taker. Above the entrance to the ballroom was a montage of photos of musicians and dancers.

In 1952, Puente got his revenge when he recorded thirty-seven sides, all with hit potential. These sides catapulted Puente to Latin music's number-one spot, which he held until 1961, when the *pachanga* trend enabled Charlie Palmieri's and Johnny Pacheco's coronation as Kings of Latin

Music. Rodríguez continued to record. He continued to receive second billing wherever he and Puente appeared together. The vocalist switched to RCA in 1954. When Puente signed with RCA in 1956, Rodríguez returned to Tico; later he signed with UA Latino.

By 1954 the Palladium was known throughout the world. Every magazine of importance included an article about the Fifty-third Street dancehall. Under the headline "Touch of Jungle Madness," the New York *Daily News* of May 6, 1951, printed the following: "Jungle madness is rampant on Broadway....It is wild...it is sexy...it is mambo...but the craze is spreading to other halls, and there is no telling where it may stop." The December 1953 issue of *Ebony* magazine read: "Palladium mambo dancers are the most unrestrained north of Havana, Cuba....The wildest ballroom in New York today is Broadway's Palladium Ballroom...the secret of the success of the Palladium is the mambo."

In March, 1953, George Shearing's quintet was appearing at Birdland, one block south of the Palladium. One evening, bassist Al McKibbon invited vibist Cal Tjader to the Fifty-third Street ballroom. Both musicians entered on the Fifty-third Street side and leaned against a wall while listening to the music. Tjader said he couldn't believe what he was hearing—previously unheard of erotic sounds, soloists playing jazz, and a sexually arousing sound called *montuno*, provided by the Machito and Tito Puente orchestras. Tjader said he was "knocked flat" when he saw Puente utilize vibes in mambo. The following week Tjader, McKibbon, and Shearing were at the Palladium, where they were photographed with Tito Puente and Miguelito Valdés. Before the month was out, Fantasy Records recorded *Mambo with Tjader*. And in 1955, George Shearing embraced the Latin music world via his Capitol LP *The Shearing Spell*.

The first dance team to appear on the scene was the Mambo Aces—Joe Centeno and Anibal Vásquez—who not only performed on show nights but toured with bands. By the mid 1950s, the Palladium's Wednesday night shows and free mambo and cha-cha lessons by dance instructor Killer Joe Piro were the main magnets for the club. At 11 P.M., couples could compete for money in an amateur dance contest. This was followed by a show featuring professional dancers such as Augie and Margo, Byron and Tybee, Joe Lustig, Mike and Elita Terrace, Louie Manquina, Cuban Pete, Millie Donay, Carmen Cruz, Marilyn Winters, Cookie, Ralph Lew, and Ernie Ensley. There were also pie-eating contests and a "most beautiful legs" contest, in which gorgeous ladies lifted their dresses above the danger zone to deafening noise. And there was the "healthiest female chest" contest, which Tito Rodríguez truly enjoyed judging. There also were less lascivious activities. On the spur of the moment, the unexpected would occur, such as a timbales battle between Tito Puente and Willie Bobo, Al "Alfredito" Levy's timbales work, and dancing to a ten-minute version of Levy's "Chop Suey Mambo."

There was Tito Puente's twenty-ninth birthday celebration in 1953, when Noro Morales performed "Serenata Rítmica" and Puente ad-libbed on vibes; those ad-libs became the "Philadelphia Mambo." And then there was the evening in 1957 when an unknown Bronx *timbalero* (Orlando Marin's band consisting of vocalist Joe Quijano and pianist Eddie Palmieri, who was with Vicentico Valdés at the time) auditioned for a job. On the same evening, the Moncho Lena orchestra introduced vocalist Mon Rivera, who not only sang but also played piano and every instrument in the band. The next year, José Fajardo's charanga, featuring trumpeter Alfredo "Chocolate" Armenteros, blew everyone away when it sold out the Thanksgiving Eve dance. These and many more unexpected events made the Palladium the in place.

But the legendary ballroom was nearing the end of an era. On April 8, 1961, eight hundred dancers heard someone announcing in Spanish and English over a loudspeaker, "This is a raid." The club's lights went out as metallic objects banged against the floor. The police said they found knives, marijuana, heroin, and twenty-two-caliber pistols. As a result, twenty-five arrests were made and fifteen indictments brought. On the bandstand at the time was Cuban vocalist Rolando Laserie.

"I run a respectable establishment," said Max Hyman. He was handed three summonses for allegedly permitting known criminals, prostitutes, and narcotics pushers to frequent his premises. In September 1961, the Palladium lost its liquor license. It continued to operate as a dancehall, featuring outstanding bands, but the liquor sales restriction caused the club to lose piles of money. The Palladium's doors closed for good on May 1, 1966, after it featured the orchestras of Ricardo Ray, Eddie Palmieri, and Orquesta Broadway. Broadway's "Pare Cochero" was the last dance ever played at the most popular ballroom in modern Latin music history.

Originally published in Latin Beat *magazine, March 1995*

FOURTEEN

JOSÉ CURBELO

In 1959, the business-as-usual attitude of New York City's Latin music world changed when bandleader José Curbelo dissolved his orchestra and founded Alpha Artists, a booking agency for Latin musicians. What happened during the next twenty years was commendable or despicable, depending on who tells the story.

Prior to 1959, every Latin band had a manager—a band representative who would negotiate with club owners the amount of money the group would earn for an evening. The bands were at the mercy of ballroom proprietors, so if a band wanted a gig, it would have to agree to the less-than-musicians'-union scale demanded or not work at all.

In 1958, pianist-bandleader Charlie Palmieri directed a quintet that featured Johnny Pacheco on flute at the International Casino. The quintet was performing five hours a night for 180 dollars. When Curbelo offered Palmieri two hundred dollars for two hours work, Palmieri became the first of many Latin music artists to sign a three-year contract with Alpha Artists. Shortly thereafter, every music group of importance, including Tito Puente, Machito, Tito Rodríguez, La Playa Sextet, Pete Terrace, Orlando Marín, Ray Barretto, Noro Morales, Vicentico Valdés, and Orquesta Broadway, had Curbelo representing it. The club owners' take-it-or-leave-it attitude soon was a thing of the past. Either they agreed to Curbelo's demands or they wouldn't have any of the prominent bands. With Curbelo's help, musicians were now earning more money for an evening's performance than ever before.

In the mid-1960s, when the boogaloo was flourishing, Curbelo decided to stage dances to increase his cash flow and operate his agency. The young boogaloo bandleaders were hired and their groups were paid less than established bands were, even though boogaloo was the magnet that packed dance halls.

In 1969, the boogaloo bandleaders decided to unite and demand top billing and the same pay as established orchestra leaders were getting, given that the boogaloo was the drawing attraction. They rebelled against Curbelo and left Alpha Artists. By the end of 1969, not one boogaloo was being aired on any of New York City's Latin music stations, and the boogaloo was relegated to history.

Curbelo and I had an interview in 1977 at his office—then at Fifty-third Street and Broadway—in which I asked about his role in the late-1960s boogaloo mania. Curbelo said: "I started promoting dances and included groups which specialized in boogaloo. The boogaloo bandleaders turned on me; they wanted more money and billing over bands like Tito Puente. This confrontation was bad for business. As a dance promoter, I hired bands for the lowest possible prices. As an agent, I always tried to get the highest price possible. In doing both, I hurt the boogaloo bands, who should have been my first concern. When I realized I did them wrong, I stopped staging dances and booked bands only. I was going to make it up to them, when all of a sudden, the boogaloo had died out."

Curbelo has been vilified by some musicians for his belief that Tito Puente is Latin music's greatest musician and for allowing Puente to receive the best gigs at top dollar. Curbelo made sure that between 1960 and 1971 Puente received top billing over every artist except Celia Cruz. He was like a father protecting his son from harm. Curbelo has been the subject of many discussions, and I recall what my mentor, Machito, once told me. "Curbelo is the type of person you want representing you," he said. "He fights like a savage animal until he gets you what you've asked him for."

Over the years, I have held many opinions about Curbelo, and have mostly agreed with Izzy Sanabria, publisher of *Latin New York* magazine, who wrote in the September, 1978 issue:

> Highly successful men are either loved or hated; José Curbelo has been highly successful in music, both as a performer and a businessman. Many promoters have resented him through the years. His crime: demanding respect and top dollar for the talent he represented. In a business filled with small time hustlers, habitually mounting promotions on con jobs, and bad checks, Curbelo was a power to reckon with—even more powerful than the musicians' union. The mentality of promoters has always been to pay talent as little as possible, while lining their pockets with maximum profit. While the musicians' union couldn't stop a promoter from underpaying bands (or not at all), José was able to literally freeze top talent until a promoter made good his debts. At one time, he almost had every major attraction under contract. While most people identify the title "King of Latin Music" with Tito Puente, few realize who is the power behind the throne...the person is José Curbelo. Although Puente has fought with all his

musical genius and drive to retain his title, it was Curbelo behind the scene, wheeling and dealing to secure it. As a booking agent, Curbelo ruled with an iron hand, demanding top billing for Puente on every poster and advertisement, creating an image and demanding top dollar for his talent. Throughout his professional career, José Curbelo has been and continues to be a fierce competitor, a fighter, a doer, a gentleman in the Spanish tradition who commands "Respeto."

José Curbelo was destined to be a musician from the day he was born in 1919. From the time he became alert to the world around him, he heard music and stories about *los Bravos de Cuba* (Cuba's best musicians).

In 1898, his grandfather joined the Americans fighting in Cuba during the Spanish-American War. After the war ended, he married and relocated to the United States, where his wife gave birth to José's father. José was born in Cuba and registered at the American consulate as an American with a Cuban mother and an American father. The most popular musicians in Cuba at this time were pianist Antonio María Romeu; flutists El Morro, Belisario López, Panchito "Flauta Mágica," and Alfredo Brito; and flutist/vocalist Paulina Alvarez (who directed her own charanga). Fully steeped in a musical environment, José began his studies of piano and composition under the tutelage of Pedro Menéndez.

A few years later, this child prodigy enrolled at the Molinas conservatory, from which he graduated at age fifteen. Thereafter, he gained experience with Los Hermanos Lebartard, flutist-composer Gilberto Valdés, and Orquesta Havana-Riverside before leaving Cuba for New York City on May 17, 1939.

"The first thing I did," said Curbelo, "was to get a musicians' [union] card so I could work. After I paid for it, I was told that a union regulation prevented me from working until after three months. My first job was at La Martinique at Fifty-seventh Street and Sixth Avenue. Months later, in December, I was at the union hall when I met a sixteen-year-old musician named Ernest "Tito" Puente. We were hired for the same gig, and it was then I noticed what a great drummer he was. That same week I was offered a job at Miami's Book Club. I recommended Tito for the drummer's spot; Tito accepted and we headed for Miami in my car. We roomed in a bungalow for five dollars a week. Our septet played Latin, American pop, waltzes, and foxtrots. After three months we returned to New York. Tito went his way; I went mine."

Curbelo went on to perform with the orchestras of Xavier Cugat, Juancito Sanabria, and Oscar de la Hoya before organizing his own nine-piece group in 1942. His orchestra, along with Machito's, supplied music for La Conga Club's diners and dancers. At this time, the bands of Xavier Cugat, Anselmo Sacasas, Noro Morales, and Machito earned twice as much as other Latin bands, even though their repertoire at the downtown clubs consisted of bland, Americanized Latin tunes. Curbelo followed suit and played bland charts at the Havana-Madrid, Zanzibar, and Latin Quarter, as well as at Catskill resorts. His recordings for RCA Victor were melodic and rife with great piano solos, yet lacking the typical Cuban feel. One of his bestsellers was a 1947 recording of "Managua, Nicaragua," which was on the popular *Hit Parade* radio show for weeks.

Before 1942 ended, the Curbelo image began to change, from someone whose work was bland to a performer of fiery Cuban rumbas. After all, he had to compete with Machito's "Nague," "Chacumbele," and "La Paella." The true Curbelo sound emerged when he cut loose with piano *montunos*. Curbelo, as well as Sacasas and Noro Morales, learned that non-Hispanics liked the Afro-Cuban sound much more than watered-down Latin American pop. His arousing rumbas were mentioned by the columnists of New York dailies.

Occasionally, Curbelo's photograph appeared in newspapers, along with stories about his love affairs with some of society's most gorgeous ladies. By 1946, his band was among Latin music's top ten orchestras and was a pioneer of the then-developing Latin New York sound. His recordings for Coda Records—"Llora," "Tú Come Pellejo," "Canelina," and "Que No, Que No"—featured vocalist Tito Rodríguez, who in 1962, during a musicians' grievance hearing, was unable to prove that Curbelo had a monopoly on New York's Latin music industry.

"Let's set the record straight," said Curbelo during our interview. "I never resented or tried to hurt Tito Rodríguez. I respected him as a man and as a great musician. He had this thing about Tito Puente: he was jealous of him and wanted billing over Puente. I did not agree to that, since Tito Puente is a composer, a music arranger, and a record producer, and plays several instruments. What angered me most was his lack of respect of Tito's music credentials. Yes, I protected Tito Puente, the same way I protected everyone under contract to me, and if you want to know why Puente got the best gigs or top dollar, just listen to his recordings and then you'll know why."

Curbelo's own 1946 and 1947 RCA recordings feature the two Titos as Curbelo sidemen. Tito Puente and vocalist Vicentico Valdés became overnight sensations with the Curbelo–Bobby Escoto composition "Abaniquito." In 1952, Tico Records recorded two of Curbelo's most exciting mambos, "Paula" and "El Jibarito." Then, in the mid-1950s, Curbelo's group included *conguero* Sabu Martínez, trombonist/vibraharpist

Jack Hitchcock, tenor saxophonist Al Cohn, *timbalero* Jimmy Santiago, and Latin music's best vocalists—Mechita (the sole female singer), Bobby Escoto, Gilberto Monroig, Santitos Colón, Mon Rivera, Tony Molina, and Willie Torres. Curbelo's Fiesta recordings of "Cha Cha Cha in Blue," "Que Se Funan," and "La Familia" were in every jukebox in Hispanic communities across the United States.

In 1971, Curbelo left New York for a career in Miami real estate. He returned in 1976, signed all of the charangas on the scene, and included special attractions like La Lupe, Santos Colón, Vitín Aviles, Linda Leyda, and Willie Millan's up-and-coming trumpet *conjunto* Saoco. By the beginning of the 1980s, however, new powers were emerging to control New York's Latin-music world.

These days, José Curbelo lives in Miami. He has accomplished much in life, but what he is most proud of is how he improved the livelihood of Latin musicians and got them the respect they deserved.

Originally published in Latin Beat *magazine, July 1997*

FIFTEEN

Monchito Muñoz

New York City's *son*, *guaracha*, and rumba aficionados of the Depression era had their first chance to appreciate Cuban percussionists in the early 1940s, when Chino (not Chano) Pozo came on the scene. Pozo, born in Havana April 10, 1915, arrived in New York City in 1937 (Chano Pozo arrived a decade later).

Subsequently, Chino performed on bongos, congas, and timbales for the orchestras of Machito, José Curbelo, Noro Morales, Tito Puente, Tito Rodríguez, Enric Madriguera, Pérez Prado, Stan Kenton, Herbie Mann, Xavier Cugat, René Touzet, and Billy Taylor, as well as the Jack Cole Dancers. During the 1940s, his unique percussion skills made him an invaluable sideman, a bandleaders' favorite for dances and recordings. Pozo was so in-demand that he worked only with bands that offered him top dollar.

Pozo's popularity began to decline in 1952, when New Yorkers first heard the unprecedented conga drumming of Ramón "Mongo" Santamaría. Tito Puente's timbal and vibraharp artistry focused public attention on other outstanding percussionists, including Santamaría, Candido Camero, Willie Bobo, Ray Barretto, José Mangual, Francisco Aguabella, Carlos "Patato" Valdés, Carlos Vidal, Sabú Martínez, Orestes Vilató, Armando Peraza, Nicky Marrero, Orlando Marín, and Giovanni Hidalgo. For more than fifty years now, many deserving percussionists have enjoyed the spotlight. Yet one has remained in obscurity.

That master musician has drummed for the bands of Pérez Prado, Alfredito Levy, Xavier Cugat, Miguelito Valdés, Johnny Conquet, César Concepción, Emilio Reyes, Bartolo Hernández, Charlie Palmieri, Rafael Cortijo, Tito Puente, Tito Rodríguez, Eddie Palmieri, and Rafael Muñoz. I am referring to Monchito Muñoz, a soft-spoken gentleman who boasts, "I never had a day job. I've always supported my wife and children from work as a musician."

He was born Ramón Muñoz-Rodríguez to parents Rafael and Carmen on June 6, 1932, in San Juan, Puerto Rico. During the 1920s, his father played bass for theater orchestras that accompanied silent movies. In 1935, Rafael directed an orchestra at El Escambrón Beach Club that included Noro Morales on piano. At age seven, Monchito attended Catholic school and took piano lessons from Noro Morales's sister Alicia. At that time, percussion students in Puerto Rico learned by performing on trap drums—the type of drum sets used by North American jazz and pop bands. Tony Sánchez, Rafael's drummer, tutored young Monchito until Sánchez was called to serve in World War II. Candido Segarra replaced Sánchez and became Monchito's teacher until Segarra was drafted. At age ten, Monchito was the drummer when his father's orchestra played for the opening of San Juan's Hotel Normandy.

In 1943 the popular bands in Puerto Rico were those of Rafael Muñoz, Mario Dumont, César Concepción, Moncho Usera, Miguelito Miranda, Panchito Minguella, Pepito Torres, and Armando Castro. In addition to Latin music, they all played the swing music of North American jazz orchestras such as those of Glenn Miller, Tommy Dorsey, Harry James, Gene Krupa, and Artie Shaw. Muñoz had been a devotee of Gene Krupa—at the time the most popular big-band jazz drummer—since he first heard Krupa on "Sing, Sing, Sing" (with Benny Goodman's band) and "Drum Boogie." He learned to read music and could drum to all the American pop charts. After drumming for his father for over a year, the young Muñoz passed the sticks to Candido Segarra, who had been honorably discharged from the army and returned to the band.

In 1944, at age twelve, Muñoz moved with his family to New York City, where they settled in an apartment at 164 West 108th Street, near Manhattan Avenue. In the immediate vicinity lived Latin musicians Mario Bauzá, Alberto Iznaga, Steve Berrios, Chuck Duchesne, Tony Escoiles, Papi Pagani, Frankie Colón, and Roberto "Chinky" Olivencia. At PS 165, Monchito fell in love with a beautiful Puerto Rican girl whom he married years later.

In 1945, there was a club on the East Side of Manhattan where the bands of Harry James, Charlie Barnet, Tommy Dorsey, Stan Kenton, and other American jazz icons appeared for two weeks at a time. "One Sunday, my father took me to the club," said Monchito. "Backstage I saw a bongo and I began to play it. Gene Krupa, whose band was the featured act, heard me and urged his manager to convince my father to let me tour with his band. My father declined the offer because I was only fifteen, still attending school, and I spoke very poor English. Mr. Krupa posed for a photo with my father and me. Months later, I went to the Strand Theatre in midtown Manhattan to see the Gene Krupa orchestra. Krupa offered me a recording date. I was recorded playing bongo on the tune 'Chiquita Banana.' When I left Puerto Rico for New York in 1944, I played trap drums only. I learned to play timbal while I was in Bartolo Hernández's band."

Throughout 1945, Muñoz worked with several "rumba" bands—all club dates he got from musicians' union local 802. In 1947, the newly formed Rafael Muñoz orchestra debuted at the Bronx Tropicana Club. Luis Barreto played the bass, Charlie Palmieri was on piano, and Monchito Muñoz, Rafael's son, handled the drums. Music impresarios Federico Pagani, Catalino Rolón, and Willie Chevalier booked the Muñoz band in all the theaters of Spanish Harlem.

In 1949, Rafael Muñoz disbanded his group and returned to Puerto Rico. Monchito remained in New York as Catalino Rolón's drummer. A year later, Muñoz replaced Humberto Morales in his brother Noro Morales's band and participated in the Decca recordings of "The Up and Down Mambo," "Sha-Wan-Ga Mambo," and "Cuban Mambo," which featured jazz trumpeter Doc Severinsen. During his three-year tenure with Noro Morales, Muñoz drummed on his days off for the bands of Miguelito Valdés, Emilio Reyes, Bartolo Hernández, and Tito Puente. By the summer of 1952, Muñoz had joined Tito Rodríguez's band and recorded the tunes "Zambele," "El Rinconcito," "Luna de Miel," and "Levántate Manuel" for Tico Records.

"When the *cha-cha-chá* caught fire in 1954," Monchito remembered, "I, along with a few musicians in the band, got annoyed when we had to play six *cha-cha-chás* in a row. For two years, beginning in 1953, I am on all the RCA recording sessions."

On October 24, 1955, Monchito Muñoz was Tito Rodríguez's drummer in a twenty-minute Universal motion picture called *Mambo Madness*. It was filmed at the Palm Gardens, then located at Fiftieth Street and Eighth Avenue.

"After two years with Tito Rodríguez," Muñoz continued, "my wife and I moved to Puerto Rico. After a few months we returned to New York and rented an apartment in Flushing, Queens. Just before the summer of 1954, my uncle Willie [Willie Rodríguez, a popular New York City *timbalero*] secured a job for me as a replacement for Jimmy 'La Vaca' Santiago in the José Curbelo orchestra. My first gig was at El Patio Club in Atlantic Beach, Long Island, until Labor Day. Before the year ended I recorded four tunes with Curbelo, which were released as 78s on the Fiesta label. I remember recording 'Que Se Funan' and a timbal solo on 'Sun Sun Babae.'

"In 1954, I was at a wedding in which pianist-bandleader Johnny

Conquet was playing. On conga drum was the then-unknown Ray Barretto. A few weeks later, I convinced Curbelo to hire Barretto. In November 1957, Mongo Santamaría and Willie Bobo left Tito Puente's orchestra to join Cal Tjader's group. I got Bobo's spot and I persuaded Puente to hire Barretto. The following week Ray Barretto and I participated in Puente's RCA recording of *Dance Mania, Volume 1*. For the three sessions to finish the album I am listed as Ray Rodríguez [Rodríguez is Monchito's mother's maiden name]. In 1959, Papi Pagani left Tito Rodríguez's band and I asked for his spot. Tito Puente became annoyed and tried to talk me out of leaving....I told Tito that I was a drummer and I preferred to play timbal, not bongo. I joined Rodríguez's orchestra, went on tour to Puerto Rico, and then drummed for Rodríguez's quintet [which included Eddie Palmieri] for a Las Vegas gig."

In 1959, when his father's orchestra opened at San Juan's La Concha Club, Monchito and his family moved to Puerto Rico. One evening, while Monchito was drumming for Rafael's orchestra, Charles Fisk, the music director at the San Juan Hotel, learned of his trap drumming skills and that he could read music. Monchito accepted Fisk's offer to play stage shows and backed artists such as Tony Bennett, Perry Como, and Carmen McRae. After three years, Fisk's contract terminated, and Monchito formed a quartet that included trumpeter Juancito Torres.

In January 1980, when Charlie Palmieri and his family moved to Puerto Rico, Palmieri formed a new group, and the first musician he contacted was Monchito Muñoz. Since then, Monchito has always found work as a drummer. His virtuosity was finally recognized when the well-known percussionist Alex Acuña was quoted in the May 1982 issue of *Modern Drummer* magazine: "I found another excellent drummer, named Monchito Muñoz, who played with Tito Rodríguez in the 1950s," Acuña said. "He showed me clave: when a tune starts a certain way, you automatically have to know which clave to use. For example, take 'The Peanut Vendor.' I used to start [on] three, and he said, 'Start on two, which goes with the melody; the other way is like you and the melody are having a fight.' And I said, 'Wow! [I've] been playing wrong all my life.' So I started to find out. I don't want to say anything bad about them, but there are a lot of drummers here in Los Angeles now who do not play in clave and do not play...correctly. I was lucky to meet Monchito."

Originally published in Latin Beat *magazine, December/January 2000*

SIXTEEN

JOHN "BIG DADDY" RODRÍGUEZ

"I never held a day job....I lived off music, nothing else...there was always work for me." These are the words of John Rodríguez, a k a La Vaca—"The Cow"—a nickname given to him by trumpeter Mario Bauzá in 1943 because the six-foot thirteen-year-old was tall and overweight. Also known as Big Daddy, Rodríguez was the father of John "Dandy" Rodríguez, Tito Puente's percussionist and business manager.

Since 1945, Big Daddy has performed and recorded with some fifty orchestras, including those of Noro Morales, Xavier Cugat, José Curbelo, Tito Puente, Esy Morales, Desi Arnaz, Miguelito Valdés, Pupi Campo, La Playa Sextet, Alfredito Levy, René Touzet, Chico O'Farrill, Machito, Pete Terrace, Joe Quijano, Louie Ramírez, Gilberto Valdés, Lou Pérez, Orlando Marín, and the Los Angeles bands of Stan Kenton, Terry Gibbs, Eddie Talamante, Manny López, and Johnny Martínez. He has almost one hundred eight-by-ten-inch photos of these orchestras, which picture him with congas or bongos. During the course of his career, Rodríguez got to know Chano Pozo, Willie Bobo, Joe Loco, René Hernández, and Los Angeles trumpeter Paul López.

"When I started in the music industry, jobs were plentiful," Big Daddy said. "There were about thirty bands, ballrooms all over the city, theaters, cabarets, vaudeville, and church dances. I remember working two weeks with Noro Morales at the Copa. When the job ended I worked with another orchestra the following day. I worked every day of the week substituting for a musician who had to have the night off....I was never without work....I earned over three hundred dollars a week while the average working man was earning twenty-five dollars."

John Rodríguez was born on April 4, 1930, to Cheno and Providencia Rodríguez, who were originally from Toa Alta and Bayamón, Puerto Rico, respectively. But by 1930 they were living at 771 Madison Avenue, near 116th Street, in New York City. John and his neighborhood friends Willie

Bobo, Pupi Torres, and Victor Pantoja attended PS 57 at 115th Street and Lexington Avenue. Following are John "Big Daddy" Rodríguez's comments about his life as a musician, made during a two-hour interview with this writer that was conducted in March 1984.

"In 1940, at age ten, I attended house parties just to hear musicians like Polito Galíndez, René Martínez, and Gilberto 'Tico Tico' Cotto perform. Two years later I attended my first nightclub dance at the Park Palace Ballroom, where Machito and the Afro Cubans were featured. It was Chino Pozo's bongo solo on Machito's Decca label recordings of 'Nague' which inspired me to learn to play the bongo. My first job was with La Sensamaya Kids, an orchestra of Spanish Harlem teenage musicians that included Ray Dávila on bass and Bobby Rodríguez [from the Machito and Tito Puente orchestras] on *tres* guitar.

"Being a musician enabled me to hang out with other musicians in front of Piquito Marcano's photo shop on the corner of 111th Street and Fifth Avenue. There was also a daily visit to the musicians' billiard parlor at 113th Street and Madison Avenue to check a bulletin board that listed gigs for musicians. One day in 1943, while musicians congregated in front of Marcano's photo shop, I heard the newly arrived Marcelino Guerra say, 'Last week Federico Pagani paid me ten dollars for my first dance at the Odd Fellows' Temple [on East 106th Street between Park and Lexington Avenues]. Last month when I played my last dance in Cuba I was paid $1.25 for six hours work.'

"During November 1945, conga drummer Pedro 'Pulidor' Valiente told me that Noro Morales was searching for a bongo player. I was given the job. For the following twenty years I performed with Noro's band on and off. I recorded several Seeco label 78s [including] the 'Walter Winchell Rhumba,' 'Tu Regreso,' and 'La Reina,' sung by Tito Rodríguez. At the beginning of 1946, I traveled to Miami with José Curbelo's band and after a few months returned to New York and landed a conga drummer's job in Xavier Cugat's thirty-two-piece band.

"After performing at New York City's Capitol Theatre, Cugat reduced the size of the band. His vocalist, Luis Del Campo, formed his orchestra and I became his *bongocero*. At this time I was living at 35 East 109th Street. I was treated like a neighborhood celebrity. Willie Bobo was one of the neighborhood kids who carried my bongos to avoid paying an entrance fee. During this time period, La Conga Club closed, reopened as Club London, then became the China Doll in September 1946.

"By the beginning of the summer of 1946, the Del Campo musicians had uniforms, Joe Loco arrangements, and a contract to appear at Young's Gap in the Catskills. On the same bill was vocalist Miguelito Valdés as a special attraction. At this time he was the most popular Latin artist, having appeared in movies.

"One evening, while on stage, Valdés praised Del Campo's teenage pianist Gil López [who was later pianist for the Tito Rodríguez and Tito Puente orchestras]. 'Ladies and gentlemen,' said Valdés, 'would you believe that this brilliant pianist is only fifteen years old?' The following day, representatives of the summer resort fired Gil López for being underage. Weeks later, López was back at the piano while Del Campo appeared at Saratoga during the racing season.

"Noro Morales was broadcasting from the China Doll every Sunday at 4 P.M. So was José Curbelo and Anselmo Sacasas from wherever they were appearing. Marcelino Guerra's orchestra packed the ballrooms at the Lincoln Square Center and St. Nicholas Arena [Guerra's home base]. The in place was midtown Manhattan. Carlos Valera's band was steady at the Havana-Madrid with Alberto Iznaga's La Siboney. In El Barrio, the popular places were the Park Palace at 110th Street and Fifth Avenue, and the American Legion at 112th Street, where Federico Pagani featured Joe Loco's La Guerilla, Montecino y Sus Happy Boys featuring vocalist Doroteo, the Bartolo Hernández orchestra, José Budet, and other local bands.

"In late 1947, I joined Tito Rodríguez's quintet at Grossinger's. Gil López was his pianist, with Jimmy 'La Vaca' Santiago on timbales, Luis Barretto on bass, Nilo Curbelo on trumpet, Tito on vocals, and me on bongos. During 1946 I met Pérez Prado for the first time. We met at the LaSalle Cafeteria, where musicians hung out after they left the Local 802 musicians' union hall. It was winter and Prado didn't have a coat. So I got him one. At the time he was selling his big band arrangements for two dollars. Cugat was recording at least once a month and needed new charts. Getting an audience with the pope would have been easier than one with Cugat. When Cugat gave me five minutes I persuaded him to buy Prado's arrangements...he bought a stack of them.

"In 1948, I was in Pupi Campo's orchestra when Joe Loco was the pianist and Tito Puente was the *timbalero*, music arranger, and business manager. Tito's and Joe Loco's arrangements placed Campo's band among the top five. Tito wrote and arranged a swinging mambo he called the 'Earl Wilson Mambo' for Seeco Records. On it I play *cascara* [by hitting the bongos' wooden sides with timbal sticks].

"It was after Labor Day that Federico Pagani advised Tito to organize a *vente tú*—a pickup group—to play a Sunday matinee at the Palladium. Pagani promoted the group as the Picadilly Boys, a three-trumpet *conjunto* which included Charlie Palmieri on piano, Luis Miranda on congas,

Manuel Patot on bass, Angel Rosa on vocals, the trumpets of Jimmy Frisaura [and] Al and Tony DeRisi, me on bongos, and Tito on timbales. The Picadilly Boys lasted less than six months. Every week the personnel would change because of other commitments. For instance, if Charlie Palmieri was not available, Luis Varona, Joe Loco, or Al Escobar would be at the piano. Chino Pozo would replace me on bongo. Tito began building his repertoire with charts of 'Abaniquito,' 'Pilarena,' 'Cuando Te Vas,' and 'Picadillo,' just to name a few. During this time the hottest bands were Noro Morales and Machito. Whenever musicians were not working, they would go to the China Doll just to hear Noro, or to wherever Machito was appearing. Noro's and Macho's bands were the only bands with five saxes, and they were always introducing new sounds.

"In early 1949, Pupi's orchestra was at the China Doll when Tito Puente decided to leave and form his own group. Pupi was devastated...he depended on Tito for new tunes and arrangements. On June 1, 1949, the Picadilly Boys, which consisted of Jimmy Frisaura, Bobby Woodlen, Chino González, and Nilo Curbelo on trumpets, Luis Varona on piano, Tito on timbales, and me on bongo, were at the WOR studios for a Spanish Music Center recording session to back vocalist Alfredito Valdés [Vicentico's brother].

"We recorded four numbers whose Spanish titles were changed...to attract non-Hispanics. 'El Mambo Se Ha Puesto Duro' was changed to 'El Mambo en Broadway.' 'Taraeo' became 'Encanto Cubano.' 'Drume Negro' became 'Afro Cuban Serenade,' and 'Picadillo' became the 'Arthur Murray Rhumba.' The following month, Tito Puente and his Mambo Boys debuted at Atlantic Beach.

"My next recording with Puente was in 1950 for RCA, when Vitín Aviles sang 'Ran Kan Kan.' It was one of the year's top hits and made Aviles very popular. Six years later Tito utilized me for the RCA LP *Cuban Carnival*. In mid-1949, I met Mexican trumpeter Paul López, a brilliant composer and music arranger. Paul wrote and arranged '110th Street and Fifth Avenue' while he was in Noro's band and never received credit for it. His mistake was not copyrighting the tune. Noro used to buy tunes from composers and take credit as the composer. Ruben Berrios, who wrote 'Ponce,' sold it to Noro for one hundred dollars.

"The late 1940s and early 1950s were peak years. Of all the recordings I did, the Pupi Campo Seeco sessions stand out. It was 1948 in a studio above the Ed Sullivan Theater on Broadway across from the Palladium Ballroom. It was a rinky-dink studio with one microphone. The recordings were outstanding because of Joe Loco's and Tito Puente's arrangements. I went on to work for the orchestras of Esy Morales, Chico O'Farrill, Desi

Arnaz, Rafael Font, Anselmo Sacasas, and Xavier Cugat. Whenever Maria Alicea [the wife of Paul Alicea, director of La Playa Sextet] lost her voice, I was always called to sit in.

"I recorded with Alfredito Levy in 1952. Willie Bobo was on timbales, Mongo Santamaria on congas, Tony Molina and Pellín Rodríguez were vocalists, Ziggy Schatz and Levio Fuentes were on trumpets, and Charlie Palmieri played piano. Sitting in on piano on some tracks were Ray Coen and Chick Corea. I remained with Alfredito on and off for three years.

"My next job was with Noro Morales. Noro seemed to be an avid gambler. He always needed money to pay to monthly alimony to three ex-wives. It was 1952 and Noro's band was scheduled to perform at El Montmartre Casino in Havana, Cuba. Pellín Rodríguez and I were in the casino when Noro walked in. He exchanged ten one-hundred-dollar bills for chips. We saw Noro lose a hundred dollars a minute for ten minutes at roulette. Pellín remarked, 'Do you think we will get paid tonight?' We were paid back in New York.

"My next job was with Tito Rodríguez. During the two years in Tito's orchestra we became good friends. I was living at 109th Street when he visited me almost daily to play poker. Yes, there was a rivalry between the two Titos. I remember the time Puente added two saxophonists for the first time…Rodríguez did the same one week later.

"One evening, while both Titos' orchestras appeared at the Audubon Ballroom, the dancers acted wild when they heard Puente's vibraphone sound. Rodríguez learned to play vibes and played it at a few gigs. They weren't speaking to each other at the time because of a top-billing problem. When the big three appeared at the ballroom, the marquee always had Machito on the top line alone. Under Macho's name was Puente, and under his was the name of Rodríguez. Rodríguez suggested to Puente that they alternate billing on the second line, but Puente said no.

"The top-billing war brought out the best in both Titos. They were outstanding in trying to outdo each other. When the dancers realized what was happening, instead of dancing they would stand in front of the bandstand and watch this great show of 'who was better than who.' I love both Titos…their bandstand wars were showstoppers, something great to behold.

"I left Rodríguez in 1954 and freelanced. In 1956, Puente was going to finish the RCA LP *Cuban Carnival*. One of the cuts, titled 'Cuban Fantasy,' required Tito on vibes. Willie Bobo, who would switch to timbales, recommended me to replace him on the bongo. One of the tunes to be recorded was an instrumental *cha-cha-chá*. Tito mentioned he wanted lyrics, and sat down at a piano and played the melody. He urged his vocalists to invent lyrics. Machuco sang *'Que será.'* Then Mongo Santamaría sang *'mi china.'* Then Yayo El Indio sang *'que será.'* Willie Bobo added *'mulata.'* Mongo added *'qué será mi prieta.'* Then Tony Molina sang *'qué lo que tiene mi cha-cha-chá.'* Tito was smiling and continued on piano. All the vocalists offered lyrics and so did Tito. To complete the lyrics was *'China, prieta, mulata qué será…china, prieta, me baila cha-cha-chá.'* Tito, all excited, summoned Jerry Sanfino to listen and ad-lib flute riffs. The tune was titled 'Qué Será Mi China,' one of Tito's most-often-requested tunes.

"In 1958, I, along with José Mangual, recorded the *Machito at the Concord* album. Two years later I met Louie Ramírez at Brooklyn's Silhouette Club, and he gave me a job. I am on his Alegre LP *Vibes Galore*. I've been a musician for more than half a century. I've lived off music…the Latin music world has been good to me. Times have changed, and in this time and age there's not enough work for all musicians. I agree…that a musician should have other skills in the event a music career is cut short."

John 'Big Daddy' Rodríguez's last job was with Tito Puente's orchestra in 1990 at the Bronx's Orchard Beach, when he sat alongside his son, John Jr. Ten years later, at 8 A.M. on November 25, 2000, he died after going into cardiac arrest at his Bronx apartment. On Sunday, December 3, Rodríguez's body was viewed at La Paz Funeral Home at 285 East 149th Street in the Bronx. The following day, after a mass at the Immaculate Conception Catholic Church at 150th Street and Melrose Avenue in the Bronx, he was buried at St. Charles Cemetery in Farmingdale, New York.

My 1984 interview with John "Big Daddy" Rodríguez was limited to two hours because I did not have a second cassette. But his memory was filled with hundreds more hours of Latin music history covering a half-century. He knew the way it was, because he had lived it all.

Originally published in Latin Beat *magazine, March 1998*

SEVENTEEN

TITO RODRÍGUEZ

Not until after Tito Rodríguez's death did I become aware of his worldwide importance and huge following in North and South America. Reports of his demise were repeated hourly on every English-speaking radio station. He was written up in the obituary columns of all the New York newspapers and in *Time* magazine. All the Spanish-language New York City radio programs were dedicated to the life of the singer and his music. Stories about him ran for a week after his death and revealed much bitterness among family members.

Rodríguez's wife, Tobi, wanted his body cremated and the ashes taken to her native Japan. Bobby Capó (the popular Puerto Rican vocalist of the 1940s and 1950s), the Rodríguez family, and prominent Puerto Ricans insisted that the body be buried in Puerto Rico. Rodríguez family members and close friends tried to persuade Tobi to have the body buried in a cemetery in San Juan. When they failed to sway her, they were quoted as saying they would ask the governor of Puerto Rico and the State of New York to intervene.

Bandleader Tito Puente, whose musical rivalry with Rodríguez has become legendary, said: "The Latin music world has lost a grand person, a serious and responsible professional. I remember the nights we played the Palladium Ballroom....I had to play my best, as he was a tough competitor who always gave the public his best."

Thousands of fans viewed the body at the Frank E. Campbell Funeral Home on East Eighty-first Street in Manhattan. On the evening of Friday, March 2, 1973, the body was flown to Puerto Rico, but only for a public viewing. Thousands of people from all over the island paid their respects. The magazine *Panorama* sold a memorial booklet for fifty cents with many photos and as many inaccurate stories and statements about the musician's life. Despite the many close friends Rodríguez had, only Mariano Artau, Angel René, Rodríguez's brother Johnny, and his wife, Tobi, could supply correct details of his life.

Izzy Sanabria, the publisher of the popular *Latín New York* magazine, assigned me to research the singer's life for the second issue of the publication. I was fortunate to interview dance promoter Federico Pagani, Rodríguez's accountant Bernie Krane, musicians Machito, Tito Puente, Joe Loco, José Curbelo, Angel René, and Rodríguez's sister Nevia. All supplied firsthand information, but the best interview came from Rodríguez's wife, Tobi. On November 19, 1975, she was in New York, scheduled to leave for Florida the following day. Our interview took place at the cafeteria of Gimbel's department store at Eighty-sixth Street and Lexington Avenue. I turned on my tape recorder and placed it between us on a small table. As the interview proceeded, the machine picked up her sudden bursts of emotional crying, mixed with the department store's bells and human hustle-bustle. Recalling life with her husband at times made her choke up and weep uncontrollably. She was deeply in love with her husband and her recollections were painful, yet she refused to postpone our conversation. Thanks to Tobi and the others I interviewed, we now have an accurate account of Tito Rodríguez's life.

According to Tito's sister Nevia Camacho, José Rodríguez-Fuentes, a musician born in San Pedro de Macorís, Dominican Republic, married Nina Lozado of Holguín, Cuba. She gave birth to Pablo "Tito" Rodríguez on January 4, 1923, while the family lived near Stop 18 in Santurce, Puerto Rico. In 1932, after the birth of her tenth child, she died. Her husband passed away six months later.

In 1939, at age sixteen, Tito was the maraca player and vocalist for his brother Johnny's Conjunto Siboney, for whom he made his first recording, "Oye Mi Bajo," on February 8, 1940. A few years later, Johnny became Enric Madriguera's vocalist when he got a job as a bongo player. One day Johnny had a heated argument with Madriguera and walked off the bandstand. Young Tito offered to take his brother's place and was given the job. On March 28, 1941, Tito sang "Acércate Más" and "Se Fue la Comparsa" for Madriguera's RCA Victor recordings.

He left the violinist-bandleader's group in March 1942 to replace vocalist Miguelito Valdés in the Xavier Cugat orchestra. His first recording with Cugat was "Bim Bam Bum," made for Columbia Records on July 20, 1942. He spent the next year in a U.S. Army uniform, and upon his discharge in 1943, he began singing for pianist-bandleader Noro Morales. His Seeco recordings with Morales include "Tu Regreso," "Vámanos Ya," "Ya Empezó," and "La Reina." After that, Rodríguez worked for Eddie LaBarron, then with José Curbelo in 1946.

Months after Rodríguez joined Curbelo, Lee Mortimer wrote in his *Daily*

Mirror column that a new night club, the China Doll, would soon open at Fifty-first Street and Broadway where La Conga club had once stood. A talent scout searched the big cities for Chinese artists and dancers for the club. Takeku Kunimatzu, an attractive young Japanese-American woman born on January 23, 1925, in Washington state, changed her name to Tobi Kei and passed herself off as Chinese in order to gain employment. She was hired as a dancer.

Playing the music for the stage shows was the José Curbelo orchestra. The club's management insisted that musicians stay away from chorus girls. Tito Rodríguez ignored the warnings. Once he made a date with Tobi and asked her to meet him at 1 P.M. in front of Roseland Ballroom, where Local 802, the musicians union hall, was located. Under a torrential rain, she waited two hours. When he didn't appear, she went home. That evening at the China Doll, she saw him and asked, "What happened to you today?" With a serious look he answered, "Didn't you notice it was raining...did you want me to get wet?"

On February 7, 1947, Tito Rodríguez recorded four 78-rpm sides for the Chano Pozo orchestra, which in reality was the Machito band. Pozo drummed, Arsenio Rodríguez played *tres* and Rodríguez sang "Rumba en Swing," "Porqué Tu Sufres," "Cómetelo Tu," and "Pasó en Tampa" for Gabriel Oller's Coda label.

After months of courting Tobi, Rodríguez married her. A year later, on August 23, 1948, their daughter Cindy was born. One month later, Tobi went back to work at the China Doll because José Curbelo had fired Tito. Rodríguez had been given a day off to care for Tobi, who was ill. Another musician told Curbelo that Tito was not at home but at a bar drinking. "The situation became rough," Tobi remembered. "We had a baby daughter and Tito was without work." Rodríguez found singing jobs, mostly one-nighters. He recorded "Wha' Happen" with the Don Rivero orchestra.

It was during the winter of 1947 that Tito organized a quintet featuring Gil López on piano, Luis Barreto on bass, Chino Gonzalez on trumpet, and Freddie Reyes on percussion. After months of work the group disbanded in 1948. By the middle of that year, Tito had an eight-piece *conjunto*. Tobi recalled, "He begged for music from composers and arrangers. Lenny Green, a booking agent for Mercury Artists, got him low-paying jobs in Brooklyn dives." At year's end, the Tito Rodríguez orchestra recorded the René Hernández arrangements of "Merengue Pa' Tí," "Palo Tiene Jutía," "Cero Tú," and "Jacobo Basura" for Oller's SMC (Spanish Music Center) label.

Months later, Pérez Prado's "Mambo No. 5" exploded, kicking off the mambo era. On August 31, 1949, Tito Rodríguez and the Mambo Devils congregated at the Beltone studios to record the Tito Puente arrangements of "Un Yeremico," "Frisao," "Mango del Monte," and "Guarare." Shortly afterward, the Tico record company of George Goldner and Art Raymond recorded Tito Rodríguez y Sus Lobos del Mambo because an angry Gabe Oller would not let Tito use the name Mambo Devils. Thanks to DJ Dick "Ricardo" Sugar's nightly airing of "La Renta," Rodríguez was in demand. Sugar's exposure of Tito Puente's "Abaniquito" many months later gave Puente an instant hit. The Tico releases, which sent their careers soaring, put them on a collision course. Although the Machito, Noro Morales, and Pupi Campo orchestras were battling then for the number-one spot, the talk in Spanish Harlem put the two Titos into the competition.

Bernie Krane, a certified public accountant, became Rodríguez's mentor and was responsible for developing the vocalist's business acumen. Turnover in personnel was handled in a professional manner. Each musician bought his uniform, and Rodríguez would buy it back upon his departure from the group. His musicians, all Local 802 members, were paid union wages. After each performance, whether for a dance or a recording session, a check was ready the following day at the union hall. The "Mambo Wolves" looked like a class act on the bandstand. Thanks to music arrangements by Gil López, René Hernández, and Harold Wegbreit, Rodríguez's sound was exciting and danceable. His good looks and grooming, his friendliness off the bandstand, and his swinging mambos made him an idol.

In January 1951, the first issue of *Latin Talk* magazine sold for ten cents. It featured photos of Rodríguez and Puente with bold black lettering: "Two Titos Tops in Mambo." Rodríguez trumped Puente, since his photo was on the left and Puente's was to the right. Rodríguez then tried for top billing on the Palladium Ballroom marquee, which gave proprietor Max Hyman a headache. Puente, who was watching the marquee being set one day, saw the Rodríguez name being placed over his and blew his top. The utility man switched names a few times; eventually, both ended up on the same line, with Puente's on the left. That night at the Palladium, only a few observant people noticed that the bands were not afforded the customary courtesy of being announced as they took the stand. Neither bandleader introduced the other.

Rodríguez, who had been denied a salary advance by Hyman, received the money from Hyman's wife as a loan to be repaid. Rodríguez mentioned the loan to a musician, who told another musician, who told another. By the time the gossip got back to Hyman, a musician who did not like

Rodríguez had transmuted the loan into a love affair with Mrs. Hyman. Her husband then barred the Rodríguez orchestra from the Palladium.

Tito's home base became the Park Palace Ballroom at 110th Street and Fifth Avenue. The Tico releases of "Jose Lustig Mambo," "Bésame la Bembita," "El Arrebato," "The Desert Dance," "Golpecito," "Tony & Lucille Mambo," "La Toalla" and "Mambo Mona (Mama Guela)" made dancers' feet reverberate at the packed Park Palace and Audubon Ballrooms. Hyman soon realized that his wife had been faithful, and he reopened the Palladium doors to the Rodríguez orchestra.

Although a war was not officially declared, it was obvious to all who were not deaf or blind that the two Titos were engaged in an intense rivalry. Puente's vibraphone tunes of "Por Tu Amor," "The Donkey Serenade," "Cuban Cutie," and "Vibe Mambo" filled the Palladium floor. Rodríguez learned to play vibes and was featured doing so on some of his recordings. Top bands usually recorded four times a year, producing four 78-rpm singles in each session so they could be released every two months. Before 1952 ended, Puente had recorded thirty-seven tunes, and each had hit potential. He became so sizzling hot that other bands on the scene got very little attention. The only other bandleader receiving acclaim was Joe Loco, who rose from sideman to bandleader the same year because of his mambo rendition of the American pop standard "Tenderly."

Rodríguez signed with RCA in 1954, since Tico seemed to be catering more to Puente. Rodríguez's recording of "Me Lo Dijo Adele" sold very well. The Rodríguez family was living at 953 Rogers Place in the Bronx when Tobi gave birth to their son Tito Jr. at the Polyclinic Hospital on February 20, 1955. Tobi remembered the event as one of the happiest days in her husband's life. "Tears were in his eyes as he watched me cradle Tito Jr. in my arms….He tenderly touched my hand and said, 'Thank you honey, now Tito will carry my name.'"

In 1956, long-playing albums began appearing in record stores. Pérez Prado's "Cherry Pink and Apple Blossom White" became a million-seller because of RCA's international distribution. Puente was lured to RCA by Morris Levy, and Rodríguez returned to Tico and recorded *The Wa-Pa-Cha (El Guapacha)*, introducing a new rhythm that did not catch on. For unknown reasons, his request to be filmed at the Palladium for a movie short was denied by Hyman. The twenty-minute movie was filmed at the Palm Gardens and was seen at every RKO movie theater in New York City. Work offers poured in, and he was booked solidly for months in advance. RCA released his *Three Loves Have I* in 1957, and in 1958 Tico released *Señor Tito Rodríguez*, the last album Rodríguez did for the label.

During this period, pianist Eddie Palmieri joined the band. "Tito had been working on a review he was going to take to Las Vegas," Palmieri remembered. "In December 1958, the band opened up at the Hotel Riviera with a weak act. Tito wore a cowboy hat and guns and sang 'Hopalong Tito.' Tobi sang 'Poor Butterfly' in a Japanese kimono, and Martha, the vocalist, sang 'Flower Drum Song.' The only positive response was for the septet when we played 'Faggot's World' and 'Satin and Lace.' We bombed, and in January 1959 we were back in New York."

After an Ansonia recording session, Rodríguez did not record again until after Puente returned to Tico in 1959. Toward the end of that year, José Curbelo disbanded his orchestra, opened the Alpha Artists booking agency, and signed every band of importance, including Puente's and Rodríguez's. During the same time, Rodríguez signed with United Artists; his contract stipulated that he would be the only Latin bandleader to record for UA. "He had a headache with Puente's competition," Tobi remembered. "He no longer would play second fiddle, and he was going to make sure his recordings wouldn't be buried again." The contract stipulation hurt Charlie Palmieri (Eddie's older brother), whose *Charanga* album was on UA. United Artists' A&R man suspected that Palmieri would refuse to record Hawaiian music; Palmieri was let out of his UA contract and months later signed with Al Santiago's newly formed Alegre Records.

Rodríguez's United Artists album *Live at the Palladium* enjoyed tremendous sales. His orchestra was as close to perfection as any orchestra could get. That enabled him to ask for and receive "over the scale" wages at the Palladium. During the summer of 1962, Rodríguez's recording of "Cara de Payaso" became his third smash hit since the beginning of the year.

He showed Hyman the record-sales charts of Puerto Rico and South America, which time and time again listed "Payaso," "Cuándo, Cuándo," and "Vuela la Paloma" at number one. He asked for equal billing with Puente in all ads and on the marquee. Puente refused, and the issue was put before Local 802, which ordered equal billing. Puente quit the union. José Curbelo tore up Rodríguez's contract. Rodríguez could not even buy a job in New York, and he worked mostly out-of-town gigs. He filed a grievance with the musicians' union alleging that Alpha Artists was a monopoly because he could not get work in New York City. He was unable to prove it.

Popular disc jockey and dance hall promoter Chico Sesma offered Rodríguez a well-paying gig in Los Angeles. When Rodríguez learned the other bands would be Tito Puente's and Joe Cuba's, he was given verbal assurance that he would have equal billing with Puente. When Curbelo learned that Rodríguez would be on the same bill, he warned Sesma about giving the top line solely to Puente. On the evening of Sesma's Latin

Holiday Festival at the Hollywood Palladium, Rodríguez's limousine pulled up to the Palladium. He got out, looked up at the marquee, and saw Puente's name over his. After glaring at it for a moment, he realized there was nothing he could do to change the situation. His band performed; he said nothing to Sesma. After this incident, Rodríguez made sure that he and Puente would never perform again on the same bill.

In 1963, his prolific talent was hailed throughout Latin America, thanks to his monster hit recording "Inolvidable" on a South American record label. The sales of over one and a half million copies made screaming headlines. It no longer mattered to Tito if he was locked out of dance halls in the United States. He was now wanted all over Latin America, and no one could change that.

"From this point on," Tobi said, "he included in his contracts that he would first approve the other bands on the same bill with him...he became a first class businessman. He had to in order to survive in this business." But like most successful businessmen, Tito could not foresee all the bad deals. He was paid with checks that bounced. In 1964 a Venezuelan boxing promoter failed to pay him for two weeks of work; the sidemen were paid with Rodríguez's private funds. Two years later another Venezuelan offer came; this time Rodríguez demanded and received a fifty percent advance. When his musicians learned what he was paid, they asked for more money. It was this confrontation with his sidemen that prompted Rodríguez to break up his big band.

In the spring of 1966, vibraharpist Oscar García received a phone call from Rodríguez with an offer to join his octet. García, almost delirious, agreed to meet the bolero king the following day on Southern Boulevard in the Bronx. On May 2, 1966, at 2:45 P.M., the emotionally drained and tired García stood in front of Mel Green's clothing store and was joined shortly afterward by *timbalero* Mike Collazo, tenor saxophonist Ray Santos, *bongocero* John "Dandy" Rodríguez, and pianist René Hernández. At precisely three o'clock, a large, white Cadillac El Dorado driven by Rodríguez pulled up, picked up the musicians, then headed for the vocalist's lavishly furnished home in Little Neck, Long Island.

Shortly after the rehearsal began in the exquisite, wood-paneled basement, Rodríguez noticed that García was having trouble transposing music written in difficult keys for another instrument. A few hours later, the octet debuted at the Chateau Renaissance in North Bergen, New Jersey. At the end of an evening six weeks later, Rodríguez spoke to García alone in the parking lot and told him he was dropping the vibes because the instrument was not the sound he wanted. On his way back to the Bronx, the subdued García stared out the automobile window and vowed to someday get revenge on Rodríguez.

"Tito decided to relocate to Puerto Rico," Tobi continued. "He concentrated on working in television as a solo. He thought he wanted to live in San Juan until he learned how New York Puerto Ricans are treated there...he couldn't penetrate the television field...all doors were closed to him."

Despite the obstacles, the tenacious Rodríguez broke into television when the parent company of United Artists, Transamerica, bought one of the island's channels. He bought a real estate parcel and built a home designed like a Far East pagoda. His workday began at 10 A.M. and sometimes lasted until the following morning. For thirty weeks, Puerto Rico's channel seven presented *El Show de Tito Rodríguez*, featuring guests such as Sammy Davis Jr., Shirley Bassey, Tony Bennett, Sarah Vaughan, José Ferrer, Xavier Cugat, Joe Loco, Vitín Aviles, and a host of international celebrities. The show was seen in New York City, Los Angeles, Mexico, Panama, and throughout South and Central America.

When the industry handed out annual awards, program director Onix Baez received one. Rodríguez was overlooked. He became furious when he learned that a well-known television producer corrected a German journalist by saying that Tito Rodríguez should not be considered the island's most popular artist because the vocalist was not considered by the natives to be Puerto Rican. "When he didn't win an award," said Tobi, "he believed it was because he was considered a New Yorquino."

Oscar García got his revenge in 1968, when he replaced Louie Ramírez in Joe Cuba's sextet. The sextet was in Puerto Rico and followed Rodríguez into the Coco Lobo Room at the Flamboyan Hotel. One evening, while Rodríguez was among the capacity crowd, García felt vindicated when the vocalist and others rose to their feet to give him a standing ovation. He floored them with his fiery vibes solo during "Joe Cuba's Madness."

Cuba's group was invited to Rodríguez's home the following day. García, who had been in an accident a few weeks before, made the visit hobbling on crutches. "Five minutes after I was in his home," said García, "Tito melted the ice between us with his warm and friendly nature....He gave me the cane he used after his car accident in Argentina the year before and said, 'Remember, I made it possible for you to get around.' We both broke out in smiles, he put his arm around me, and whatever resentment I felt toward him disappeared rapidly."

A few weeks later, while on a sightseeing tour near Carolina, García and his wife were stranded and looking for transportation. A blue Chevrolet Camaro stopped and offered them a ride. It was Tito Rodríguez, dressed in white tennis shorts, a polo shirt, and sneakers. During the ride García realized that Rodríguez was not an icy businessman every minute of the day but a person who was also concerned with the livelihood of his fellow musicians. He had given up the role of bandleader to become a television personality, yet he bemoaned the demolition of New York's Palladium Ballroom, which would put eight bands out of work. "Do you understand where he was coming from?" García said. "He had nothing more to do with dance halls, yet he thought about the musicians that were unemployed."

It was the snub by the Puerto Rican media that motivated Rodríguez's move to Coral Gables, Florida. He wanted nothing more to do with television. Although he was no longer recording, his Musicor label recordings, which were aired on the radio, made it seem as though he was never away. "Mio," a 1967 hit, maintained him among the most romantic singers on the scene. In 1968 he reentered the music wars again with his UA Latino LP *Estoy Como Nunca*.

From this point on, his health deteriorated. The first time he showed signs of illness was in Puerto Rico during the taping of one of his last shows. Before it began he mentioned that he felt very tired. Halfway through a song, his voice cracked. That alarmed him.

In late 1969 he decided to establish his record company, the TR label. While formulating his plans, he decided to undergo a medical examination. The doctor detected an extra heartbeat. A heart specialist examined him, found nothing wrong, and referred him to an internist. After a thorough examination, the doctor shocked him. The normal blood count of white corpuscles needed to fight off infections is nine thousand to ten thousand. Rodríguez's test showed a count of seven hundred thousand.

He flew to England for a renowned specialist's opinion. He registered at the exclusive Dorchester Hotel and waited to submit to more tests. While awaiting the results, he contracted British musicians to record the music for his first TR album, *Inolvidable*. Then the shocking results came: he was suffering from leukemia that was slowly progressing. It was still in the chronic stage, meaning he could live many more years with it. But once it reached the acute stage, the white blood cells would multiply uncontrollably and lead to death. Medication was prescribed; it successfully slowed the creation of white blood cells. But it would be a matter of time before the drug's toxic side effects would damage his kidney and heart.

Tito returned to the United States, informed his wife and family of the doctor's findings, and urged them not to tell anyone. He inaugurated the TR Record Company in August 1971. Its office was on the twelfth floor at 1650 Broadway, at the corner of Fiftieth Street. He mixed the master tape of *Inolvidable* and had RCA press the recordings. Months after his hot-selling LP *Palladium Memories* was released, he was in Peru, where his performance in a nightclub was recorded. This became the music for his *25th Anniversary Performance* LP, which was released one month before he died.

To date, *25th Anniversary Performance* has caused much speculation about whether or not Rodríguez meant it as his farewell album. According to Chico Alvarez, the artist who designed the cover, it was his idea to do the layout—a "four ages of man" arrangement of photographs of Rodríguez as a small child, a youth, a young man, and an older man. Alvarez remembers choosing the four pictures "from a collection of two hundred rare photos, and Tito liked my format."

I have no doubt that the photo layout was Alvarez's idea and not Tito's. Nevertheless, the music and lyrics of one tune make me suspect that Tito meant this to be his last recording. For one thing, many of the tunes had already been recorded on other labels. For another, he also sang a medley of tunes of his favorite composer, Rafael Hernández. Then, there is the enigma in the finale on side B, which ends the recording. Rodríguez bids the listeners farewell in Spanish with "The time has arrived...how sad my heart is....The time has arrived...I have to go....This is my destiny...I've always lived with it....I hear it as it gets closer...it tells me it is time to leave....Ciao [goodbye]."

Angel René, a musician and close friend said, "Tito never thought about dying...he was going to live." But René also speculated that "he may have known at one time that the end was near....A few weeks before the Madison Square Garden concert I saw him reading the Bible."

His will to live is verified by Tobi. "When he informed me that he was told he had a few more years to live, he said to me with a grinning smile, 'I'm going to stick around and give Tito Puente hell for a few more years.'" And indeed, Richard Nader, the salsa concert impresario, signed him for a February 2, 1973, appearance, with top billing. But again, Nader failed to do what many other promoters had been unsuccessful at since the Titos' feud erupted in 1951: he could not get the two men on the same stage.

Nader called Rodríguez a few times in Florida and stressed that he didn't believe the vocalist alone could draw a crowd. He suggested that Puente's orchestra play Rodríguez's music. Rodríguez kept saying no, and a few weeks before the concert he told Nader, "If you don't think I can draw with my name, then cancel me and get someone else." Rodríguez wanted the Machito orchestra to back him. They got the assignment.

On the morning of the concert, a freezing rain cast a gloom over New York City. Rodríguez registered at the Statler-Hilton Hotel, one block away from Madison Square Garden. "During the afternoon," said Tobi, "Tito called me in Miami. He said, 'The weather has me hoarse....I hope the rain doesn't keep the people away....You know how hard I fought Nader for this.'"

Later on, toward evening, Tito was visited by Angel René, by his daughter Cindy and her husband Phil Di Carlo, and by Rodríguez's sister Nevia with her husband, Billy Camacho. At the Garden, all his family members were seated except for René and Camacho, who remained in the dressing room with him.

Amid the noisily cheering, packed house, Rodríguez opened up with "Mamá Güela," his theme song, and created bedlam. At times he coughed uncontrollably. René kept giving him glasses of water. The thirty minutes he spent singing on stage was probably the most grueling half-hour the vocalist ever endured in his career. His face began to blanch, and he was covered with sweat. Nader remarked, "After fifteen minutes of singing, Tito wiped his heavily perspiring forehead and said, 'I don't know if I can continue.'" By 11 P.M. he was resting at the apartment of his sister Nevia in Flushing, Queens.

Two days later, on Sunday, he started out for New Jersey to visit his daughter Cindy. Excruciating abdominal pains caused by a bleeding ulcer compelled him to return to his sister's apartment. A doctor examined him and made an appointment for treatment on Tuesday morning, February 6, at the New York University Medical Center. Minutes before leaving Nevia's apartment for the appointment, he began bleeding from the mouth. When the bleeding stopped, he hailed a cab. En route to the NYU hospital, he began to hemorrhage from the nose and mouth. The cab driver, alarmed at seeing the steady flow of blood drench Rodríguez's gray tweed coat, drove him to the emergency room of Bellevue Hospital.

That same afternoon, Tobi learned from her son what had happened. "I arrived in New York the following day and I went to see him....I was told he was in critical condition....When I first saw him he was lying quietly...thin clear plastic tubes extended from his nose, and needles attached to the thin brown tubes which fed him glucose intravenously protruded from his arm....I was the first to speak....I told him I heard he was a smash at the Garden....He spoke in a low, halting speech...he told me to return the advance money he received for a Panama engagement....He said, 'When I get out of here, let's go to Panama....I don't want to stand them up.'"

Five days later, when the doctor stopped the internal bleeding, Tito was transferred to the NYU hospital, where a doctor named Jones told Tobi that the leukemia had progressed to the acute stage. "I was by his bedside during the last week of his life...I slept near him on the cot. The Puerto

Rican hospital employees sneaked into the room....He hadn't eaten food for weeks...neither did I."

On the morning of February 28, 1972, Tito got out of bed, took a bath, and shaved with Tobi's help. His sunken eyes and drawn cheeks were evidence of the weight he had lost. Dr. Jones ordered Tobi to leave the hospital. "I returned to the hospital about 7:30 P.M....a nurse said he had asked for me....I passed his sisters on the way into his room....He was lying quietly staring at the ceiling...when he saw me he said he couldn't bear the terrible pain. A bit after 9 P.M. a doctor entered the room and asked me to help sit up Tito so he could listen to his heart. We sat Tito up and I had my arms around him while the doctor's stethoscope moved up and down. Then all of a sudden Tito's body became limp and he slumped forward....I knew he was gone....I told the doctor but he didn't hear me....I nudged the doctor's arm and he realized Tito had died....His call for help was the alarm which brought doctors and nurses rushing into the room. I looked at Tito...the pained expression was gone from his face....He looked as if he were sleeping. As I started to walk out of the room, the hospital staff rushed by me with equipment to revive him...but it was too late."

By 8 A.M. on Thursday, March 1, most Latin New Yorkers had already felt shock waves on hearing the news of his death. Every English- and Spanish-language radio station repeated the words no one wanted to hear. From where I stood (near the door of the Lexington Avenue local train), I saw many people glaring at their newspapers and looking shocked. Tears streamed down some young women's cheeks.

"Tito Murió" (Tito Died) read the bold black letters of *El Tiempo*, whose front page was covered by a picture of Rodríguez's handsome face. "Sepultarán en San Juan a Tito Rodríguez" (Tito Rodríguez to be Buried in San Juan) was the headline in *El Diario-La Prensa*. The *New York Times* wrote a lengthy obituary of the sort VIPs merit. When I read the fifty-five-word notice in the *Daily News*, I got angry. For twenty-five years Tito had created employment for musicians, disc jockeys, bartenders, waiters, ushers, and guards. He earned large sums of money, the lion's share of which was withheld and split between recording companies and taxes. A fifty-five-word testimonial for the man who helped make this city the capital of the Latin-music world—that was criminally insensitive.

During the days following his death, until he was put to rest, the Spanish-language media startled the Hispanic population of New York and Puerto Rico with mysterious information about his illness and about a bitter quarrel among the family over his purported wish to be cremated. Speculation about his nationality caused heated discussions. Some people insisted he was Dominican; others claimed he was Cuban. And many vociferously decreed, "He's Puerto Rican." For a week after his death, Rodríguez's recordings dominated the airwaves, and stories about his life ran in all the Spanish-language newspapers. But questions about Tito's cremation and his nationality were the public's main concerns.

Those who knew Tito Rodríguez will tell you he would have been saddened over the importance given his ethnic background. To him, the individual—not nationality or religion—was what mattered. Bernie Krane, his close friend, mentor, and accountant, is Jewish. Tobi, his lovely wife, is Japanese. Members of the Rodríguez bands were of several nationalities and religions. All that mattered was their proficiency and how well they read music.

Tito was a special kind of man. He was also a model of courage. He kept his terminal illness a secret, for he hated pity. In retrospect, however, one discovers clues pointing to the fact that he was dying. Six months before he died, Rodríguez and his orchestra played at a dance, promoted by Leo Vasquez, Bobbie Rodríguez, and Eddie Colón, that took place in New York at the Statler-Hilton on Saturday, September 9, 1972. Tito usually worked with fourteen sidemen, but that evening he had twenty-five of his favorite musicians on the stage. A few of them came from out of town, some from other orchestras. Did they feel any special significance about this reunion? Or was it just another dance to them?

After Rodríguez appealed to the dancers to crowd near the bandstand so photographers could snap photos from the balcony, he made a brief speech. The handsome, impeccably dressed vocalist thanked the people in Spanish for the huge turnout. Tito Puente and his wife were among the crowd. Then Rodríguez faced his sensuous vocalist, Martha, held both her hands, kissed her cheek, and thanked her for leaving her family in California to attend this event. Later he introduced all of his musicians by name and thanked them for making "this night unforgettable." "Inolvidable," his biggest hit, followed.

The day after his death, radio hosts Polito Vega of WBNX and Paquito Navarro of WHOM captured Latin New Yorkers' attention during their daytime shows with old, scratchy 78-rpm recordings and stories. Vega opened his show with Willie Pastrana's recording of "Fiesta en el Cielo," sung by a Puerto Rican vocalist of Italian descent, Mike Guagenti.

Details of Tito's life were recounted by Machito, Vitín Aviles, Vicentico Valdés, and Johnny Albino, to name a few, via telephone conversations held on Vega's show. Machito came to Vega's program and helped him answer hundreds of calls from listeners. Paquito Navarro's show was equally interesting and informative, as his guests mentioned things not noted by Vega, and Navarro played rare recordings. Radio hosts Dick "Ricardo"

Sugar and Joe Gains also dedicated their shows to Tito.

ABC television's 7 P.M. newscast showed film of a long line of people waiting to enter the funeral parlor at Eighty-first Street and Madison Avenue. A conversation between Richard Nader and reporter Geraldo Rivera revealed that Rodríguez showed signs of illness at the Garden concert.

On Friday, March 2, the body arrived in San Juan at 12:15 P.M. on American Airlines flight number 677. The San Juan paper *El Mundo* reported that the remains would be on view at the Ehret Funeral Home in Hato Rey until 10 A.M. Saturday, March 3. After the rites were finished, Tito's wife ordered the body taken to an undisclosed location.

The March 7, 1973 issue of *El Diario* reported in bold black letters, "Tito Rodríguez Cremated in Florida," and continued with the news that "the body of Tito Rodríguez was cremated Monday, March 5, 1973, during the afternoon in the Slad Care Funeral Home in Hialeah, Florida. His ashes were placed in a gold metal box and given to his wife....The bereaved Mrs. Rodríguez told reporters in a sobbing voice that she just couldn't throw her husband's ashes to the wind, as he wished. Angel René corroborated Tobi's claim, stating that Tito once told him about his wish to be cremated and have his ashes thrown in the wind. Tito did not say where this was to take place.

Although he was treated shabbily in Puerto Rico because he was a "Newyorican," he loved the country of his birth, and I believe he left a clue indicating his desire to rest in Borinquén. In the 1968 recording of "San Juan" on the UA Latino album *Este es Mi Mundo*, he emotionally signs the words in an uptempo Sinatra-like song: "On a Caribbean island...there is a place I can't forget....I go all alone...dreaming of San Juan...wondrous memories I can't forget....San Juan...where romance blooms in the sun...that's where my heart found the one...who became the one for me....And now in every dream I see...San Juan...where we would stroll holding hands...there on the warm tropical sand...we found paradise for two....San Juan...where I let love slip away...but I'll go back there someday...oh my fine, my love lost, until then, I'll keep dreaming of...San Juan...I'll keep dreaming of...San Juan...I'll keep dreaming of...San Juan."

Originally published in Latin Beat *magazine, September and October 1991*

EIGHTEEN

TITO PUENTE

The Tito Puente legend began on April 20, 1923, when Tito was born at Harlem Hospital to Ercilla and Ernest Puente—Puerto Ricans who then lived at 1850 Madison Avenue in Manhattan. In 1928, Tito's sister Anna was born. Young Tito attended PS 43, Cooper Junior High School, and Galvani Junior High School. Later he dropped out of Central Commercial High School. His mother encouraged him and Anna to enter show business careers. They joined Stars of the Future, a youth community group organized by the director of the funeral parlor Funeraria Monge, located between 115th and 116th Streets on Madison Avenue.

In 1935, when Tito was twelve and Anna was seven, both were active participants in the Stars of the Future, whose meetings were held at La Milagrosa Catholic Church at 115th Street and Lenox Avenue. Tito made his first communion and confirmation at La Milagrosa. The church sponsored a yearly coronation of its two most talented children, who were crowned king and queen to reward their artistic ability and popularity. A surviving photo snapped in 1935 at La Milagrosa shows young Tito in a blue soldier's uniform and cap. Also in the photo are Anna and her girlfriend Olga San Juan, who years later became a movie actress. Tito was crowned king four times because of his dancing skills.

In 1937, at age fourteen, Tito was a Boy Scout; his troop met weekly at the American Legion on Fifth Avenue and 116th Street. He was attending Central Commercial High School then, but all he thought about was music. During his lunch break, Tito could be found in the auditorium surrounded by a crowd as he played "Boogie Woogie" on the piano. During the day, Tito was part of a vocal trio or quartet who gathered on a school stairway or a street corner to sing "Sweet Sue, Just You," "Am I Blue," and other songs the Ink Spots had made popular. By this time, Tito and his sister were being tutored by a pianist named Blue Mountain. The lessons had begun after Tito heard Cuban pianist Anselmo Sacasas's solo for

Orquesta Casino de la Playa's RCA recording of "Dolor Cobarde." Months later, Tito added trap drums to his studies after he was amazed by Gene Krupa's drumming on Benny Goodman's rendition of "Sing Sing Sing." He learned alto sax when his parents rented a room to a music teacher now remembered only as Professor Millian.

In 1939, at age sixteen, Tito dropped out of school to become a full-time musician. Not old enough to apply for musicians' union membership in Local 802, he still qualified for a New Jersey card. He was now living at 53 East 110th Street, between Madison and Park Avenues. During the same year, he met another sixteen-year-old named Pablo Rodríguez, who had left Puerto Rico to live in New York. Pablo lived with his brother Johnny at 65 East 110th Street. Pablo, who years later became famous in the Latin Music world as Tito Rodríguez, met Puente at La Casita María, a teenage hangout on the block where they lived. Both were on the same baseball team. They were close buddies, partly because they were proud Puerto Ricans but mainly because of their interest in music.

In December 1939, Puente went to the musicians' union office, then located at Fiftieth Street and Sixth Avenue, and got a job drumming with a Latin band. On the same gig was the newly arrived Cuban pianist José Curbelo, who was impressed with Tito's drumming skills. When Curbelo was offered a three-month gig in Miami, he recommended Puente for the drummer's job. Curbelo remembers thinking that "I had seen the best drummers in Cuba…until I saw Tito perform." For three months they were roommates, each paying half of the ten-dollar-a-week rent.

Three months later, Puente was drumming for the Stork Club Orchestra of Johnny Rodríguez (Pablo's brother). Then he joined Anselmo Sacasas's band at Chicago's Colony Club. On January 27, 1941, Tito recorded "Los Hijos de Buda," "Yumba," "La Conga," and "Cachita" with Vincent López's Suave Swing Orchestra. During the next year and a half, Tito ended up drumming for pianist Noro Morales, playing Decca recording dates and appearing in four Morales's music-film shorts: *The Gay Ranchero* (December 14, 1941), *Cuban Pete* (February 9, 1942), *Ella* (April 20, 1942), and *Mexican Jumping Bean* (May 18, 1942).

In June 1942, Tito replaced Tony Escolies in the Machito orchestra and recorded "Oye Negra," "El Botellero," and "Eco." After this Decca session, Chino Pozo and Tito left Machito to join the Jack Cole Dancers. The following month, Tito returned to Machito and was drafted into the United States Navy. After boot camp he was assigned to the U.S.S. *Santee*, an aircraft carrier that escorted merchant supply ships. The chaplain organized a ship's band, and "Ernie" Puente played alto sax. It was from pilots who were musicians in civilian life that Tito learned to compose and arrange music. During the evening, on the hangar deck, the band entertained the crew with "Sunny Side of the Street," "Sweet Georgia Brown," "Green Eyes," "Just Friends," and the much-requested "How High the Moon?" and "One O'Clock Jump."

While out at sea, Tito was informed that his sister Anna had died of spinal meningitis. He was given an emergency furlough. During his one week at home, he escorted his parents to La Perla del Sur, a Puerto Rican social club at 116th Street and Madison Avenue. At the urging of the audience, he sat down at a piano and performed "Mis Amores" (a Puerto Rican *danza*), which he dedicated to his mother, and Debussy's "Clair de Lune," in memory of his sister.

Puente's first Latin music arrangement was "El Bajo de Chapotín," which he sent to Machito. For the remainder of his enlistment, Tito was involved in nine naval battles that spanned the Pacific and Atlantic Oceans. Upon his 1945 honorable discharge on the West Coast, he visited his childhood friend, the movie actress Olga San Juan, in Los Angeles. A federal law required that all returning World War II servicemen get their old jobs back. Puente approached Machito for his. Machito told him, "Uba [Nieto] supports five kids and a wife." Tito Puente got the message and landed work with Frank Martí's Copacabana band. This was followed by stints with the José Curbelo orchestra and the Fernando Alvarez Brazilian band before Tito become the drummer, contractor, and musical director of the Pupi Campo orchestra in September 1947. From the time of his first gig with Martí to his job with Campo, Tito had been taking classes with professors at the Juilliard School.

The accomplished pianist, composer, and music arranger José Estévez Jr.—better known as Joe Loco—replaced Al Escobar in Campo's band in 1948. Loco's and Puente's orchestrations put Pupi Campo's orchestra among Latin music's five most popular bands. On each recording they arranged, they made sure their names appeared on the label. Some of Puente's arrangements were: "Pilarena," "How High the Moon," Son de la Loma," "Está Frizao," "Piérdete," "Cuando Te Vea," and "The Earl Wilson Mambo."

During the late summer of 1948, the dance promoter Federico Pagani visited the Embassy Club to hear the Campo orchestra. After a tune ended, Puente huddled with Loco and played a phrase on the piano. Tito then sang out a melody he wanted duplicated by bassist Manuel Patot and trumpeter Chino González. What followed was one of those rare moments in Latin music, as the haunting melody raised goose bumps in listeners. "The music was so arousing," Pagani said, "that it made my blood turn." After the tune ended, Pagani asked Puente for the name of the tune. "I haven't titled it yet," Puente said. *"Es un picadillo"*—it's a mishmash.

Years later, at his office at 1674 Broadway, Tito Puente said, "I was going to give the tune an Oriental title because of the strongly Oriental feel of the melody." In 1949 he recorded it as "Picadillo." A year later, Miguelito Valdés recorded it as "Chang."

Pagani offered Puente a Sunday matinee dance at the Alma Dance Studios (which the following year became the Palladium Ballroom) with a pickup band. After Tito agreed to play, Pagani said, "I'll present your group as the Picadilly Boys." The Boys, most of whom were Campo sidemen, were Jimmy Frisaura, Al DeRisi, and Tony DeRisi on trumpets; Manuel Patot on bass; Angel Rosa vocals; Chino Pozo on bongos; and Al Escobar, Luis Varona, and Charlie Palmieri alternating as pianists, with Puente on timbales and vibes.

"Tito was incredibly good," recalled Pagani. "He had a fresh sound with a jazz influence. For weeks thereafter his name kept popping up…dancers wanted to hear more of his music." During the week before Alfredito Valdés's recording session at the Spanish Music Center on June 1, 1949, Tito wrote the arrangements for "El Mambo de Broadway," "Enchanted Cubano," "Afro Cuban Serenade," and "Picadillo" (the last song was retitled "The Arthur Murray Rhumba" by SMC owner Gabriel Oller).

Tito was enjoying the adulation that bandleaders garner. In March 1949, he told Campo he would be leaving to organize his own group. The original Puente band congregated at the Luis Varona music studios, at 116th Street between Park and Madison Avenues, for its first rehearsal. Varona was on piano, Jimmy Frisaura and Gabriel "Chino" González were on trumpets, Angel Rosa did vocals, Manuel Patot played bass, and Frankie Colón took charge of congas, along with Tito Puente. Most of the tunes were American pop instrumentals, on which Colón did not play.

On July 4, 1949, the seven-piece Tito Puente orchestra debuted at El Patio Club at Atlantic Beach. The few Latin charts played were toned down. The following month Tito Rodríguez approached his childhood pal Tito Puente and hired him to arrange the music charts of "Un Yeremico," "Frisao con Gusto," "Guararé," and "Mango del Monte" for the August 31, 1949, SMC recording session. One week after the Atlantic Beach gig ended on Labor Day, Tito Puente added a third trumpeter, Tony DeRisi, and *bongocero* Chino Pozo.

One day, while eating lunch with Cuban vocalist Vicentico Valdés at the LaSalle Cafeteria next door to Local 802, Pozo introduced Valdés to Puente. According to Frankie Colón, "The first time I saw Vicentico was late September 1949, when he was invited on the Palladium bandstand to sing. He sang the bolero "Tus Ojos." He was so good we had to repeat it.

Tito told him to stay, so Vicentico ended the night singing chorus to our lead vocalist Paquito Sosa. That same week, Sosa left and Vicentico replaced him.

"It was in either October or November of 1949," Colón continued, "that Puente utilized three trombones, four trumpets, four saxes, and a full rhythm section at the WOR studios on Forty-eighth Street and Seventh Avenue. After recording 'Un Corazón,' 'Solo Tú y Yo' and 'Mambo Macoco' in three hours, Tito surprised us by dismissing the trombonists and saxophonists and passing out his charts of 'Abaniquito' to the remaining musicians, who were Pozo, Varona on piano, and four trumpeters—Frisaura, DeRisi, González, and Mario Bauzá—vocalists Graciela [Machito's sister], Vicentico, and me. This version was incredible. Vicentico was outta sight ad-libbing, and Mario blew his ass off on the solo. After the take we listened to it, and Tito wanted a second take. He changed his mind when Mario convinced him…that another take wouldn't come out as fiery." Disc jockey Dick "Ricardo" Sugar, hired by Tico Records to host a fifteen-minute program, played "Abaniquito" nightly and brought Puente and Valdés instant recognition.

The first sidemen changes occurred in 1952, during the Korean War. Pianist Gil López was replaced by Charlie Palmieri. The next year, Mongo Santamaria replaced Frankie Colón. It was during this period that the childhood friendship of Tito Rodríguez and Tito Puente began to deteriorate because of the custom of top billing on marquees and posters. Both wanted to be listed first on the Palladium marquee, and a music war ensued. Rodríguez won the first round in 1951, with his outstanding Tico recordings.

The following year Puente all but annihilated the competition, with thirty-seven brilliant Tico Recordings. He had someone sending him new material every week—new songs that were sold in Havana as stock arrangements. He would add the magic Puente touch to change them and make them sound even better. Although Tito Puente had introduced the vibraharp to Latin music in 1950 (on "Por Tu Amor"), its impact was not really felt until after "Vibe Mambo" was recorded in 1951.

On Dick Sugar's show, Tito Puente referred to "the other guy" without even mentioning Rodríguez's name. When Rodríguez appeared on Sugar's program, he acted as though there was no problem, no war, but he could not explain why he and Puente had stopped announcing each other's names as the bandleader performing next. Puente was relentless, introducing a new recording every week, as well as some tunes that were played a few times and never recorded. More exposure followed. During this time, Cubop, a hybrid of Cuban music and bebop, was at its height of popularity, and Tito Puente had jazzy Afro-Cuban charts that were broadcast from Birdland on September 22, 1952. On that evening, Puente conquered New York with "Babarabatiri," "Cal Miller Mambo," "Ran Kan Kan," "Mambo Inn," "Mambo City," and "Esy."

The biggest and saddest news of 1953 was the split between Puente and Vicentico Valdés after the band returned from its first trip to Los Angeles. Another top-billing problem was the crux of the breakup, through no fault of Valdés. Los Angeles, whose Hispanic community is predominantly Mexican-American, was more aware of Valdés, since he had lived and performed in Mexico for years. A Los Angeles promoter placed Valdés's name over Puente's, and the war of wars broke out between the bandleader and his vocalist. On their return to New York, Valdés left the band.

Percussionist Willie Bobo also became Puente's antagonist: a rivalry had existed even before they were introduced. Bobo, like Puente, knew the value of publicity, good or bad, and did anything to get noticed. As undisputed timbales champ, Puente heard about this young contender, who was becoming a legend by way of Bronx and Spanish Harlem *bembés*— impromptu street parties—and who was battling his way to the top of the music world with spectacular knockouts. Because of his admiration for Mongo Santamaría, Puente reluctantly hired Bobo as Manny Oquendo's replacement; still, he found ways to put him down. One evening, for example, on a live remote from Birdland, Puente pronounced all the soloing musicians' names correctly—all, that is, except for the percussionist's. "On bongos," he said, "Willie Boborosa."

Annoyed with Valdés's departure, Tito Puente would not hire a singer for almost a year; meanwhile, on Sugar's program, he said his *cha-cha-chás* did not require a singer. Before 1955 ended, Puerto Rican singer Gilberto Monroig was doing the lead vocals. Six months later, Monroig was gone, and Tito Puente and Bobo took over the vocal duties. With each passing year, the Puente orchestra grew in popularity.

From 1955 to 1960 there were many personnel changes. Singer Santos Colón left José Curbelo and began his illustrious career with Tito Puente in 1956. In November 1957, Santamaría and Bobo left Puente to join Cal Tjader. By mid 1958, Puente's best-selling LP, *Dance Mania, Vol. 1*, afforded him international recognition. For two years, *Dance Mania* was the number-one Latin album.

Since the 1960s, Tito Puente has survived the new rhythm trends of *pachanga*, boogaloo, Latin soul, and disco—genres whose hits have crowned new kings of Latin music such as Johnny Pacheco, Charlie Palmieri, Joe Cuba, Johnny Colón, Eddie Palmieri, Ray Barretto, and Larry Harlow.

Other Puente feats include the TV show *El Mundo de Tito Puente*, which began in 1969; the Tito Puente Scholarship Fund, started in 1979; honorary doctor of music degrees awarded to him in 1987 by the State University of New York in Old Westbury and in 1999 by Columbia University and the New England Conservatory of Music; and four Grammy Awards. Low points in his career have been the rise in the early 1970s of Fania Records, whose artists have received ten times more airplay than Puente; and the unfavorable critique of Tito Puente's 1974 Tico LP *Tito Unlimited* by two DJs and writer John Storm Roberts.

But then came 1977 and the beginning of Puente's comeback to the apex of the music world. It was fueled by the combined efforts of Fania president Jerry Masucci, *Latin Times* magazine publisher David Maldonado, Latin Percussion instrument company owner Martin Cohen, music arrangers Marty Sheller and Louie Ramirez, radio station WKCR's *The Latin Musicians Show*, and reissue producer Domingo Echevarria's RCA projects. As a result, every Puente RCA recording was released on CD, and so was the best and highest-fidelity Tito Puente orchestra material available on the Concord Jazz Picante label. By the time of his death on June 1, 2000, during a heart operation at New York University Medical Center, Tito Puente was almost certainly the best known Latin musician in the United States.

Originally published in Latin Beat *magazine, February 1991*

NINETEEN

JIMMY FRISAURA

For more than four decades, beginning in 1949, the Tito Puente orchestra was a successful music group for two reasons. The first, of course, was Tito Puente—bandleader, composer, arranger, and master of the timbales, vibraharp, marimba, alto sax, and keyboards. The second was Jimmy Frisaura, the band's trumpeter and business manager, who handled the everyday business affairs of the Puente organization. Not only was Frisaura Puente's executive assistant, he also sang chorus, hired and fired musicians, made out their payrolls, informed them of upcoming gigs and what uniform to wear, assigned the music charts and collected them at evening's end, handled hotel and plane reservations, listened to and settled grievances, and was always on the phone notifying a substitute that a job was available. Frisaura kept a list of substitute trumpeters, saxophonists, pianists, and so on. Whenever a regular left the orchestra, he would offer the name at the top of the list a steady job with the band.

While I was marshaling information for this story, not one of the many musicians I spoke to had anything but praise for Frisaura. One recalled an evening when he was incapacitated and Frisaura sent him home with a night's pay. Another sideman said, "Jimmy was the backbone, really the boss of the orchestra; Tito went along with everything Jimmy said ninety-nine percent of the time.... Jimmy was the father of the orchestra."

Vincent "Jimmy" Frisaura was born to Sarah and Michael Frisaura, an Italian-American couple, on October 2, 1924, in McKeesport, Pennsylvania. Reared in the Gun Hill section of the Bronx, he began his musical career at age eleven as a bugler for the Our Lady of Grace Church. Two years later he was studying the trumpet. In 1941 he played his first dance with his high school band before organizing his own group, Jimmy Frazier and the Sapphire Blues Orchestra.

Frisaura's neighborhood buddy, trumpeter Gene Rapetti, a k a BG, recalled the time they played hooky from school just to hear the Harry

James orchestra at a Broadway theater. "Jimmy was an altar boy in 1941. His reputation as the Bronx's Harry James got him jobs with local bands at the Chester Palace, which subsequently became the Stardust Ballroom. I played trumpet for Tito between 1950 and 1960; it was Jimmy who taught me the *típico* feel of Latin trumpet. One of my unforgettable memories on the Palladium bandstand was the night Dizzy Gillespie's orchestra was appearing one block away at Birdland. During a break, Dizzy joined us on stage and riffed on 'Mambo Birdland.' Another memory was the day the orchestra was in a studio to record four sides for Tico Records. It was the first time I saw Mongo Santamaría, who sat in on congas. I believe we recorded 'Monterrey,' 'La Güira,' and the bolero 'La Gloria Eres Tú,' on which I blew the trumpet solo. We didn't have a fourth tune. Tito sat down at a piano and played a melody he was making up and wrote the music on paper. Within five minutes, he completed it and sang it out to the band. We recorded it, and he named it 'Mambo Diablo.' I also remember the many nights bandleaders Stan Kenton and Woody Herman visited the Palladium and just listened to us playing mambos. Jimmy made this all possible for me…he always helped musicians in need."

Frisaura was also a trumpet instructor. One evening in 1948 he dropped by the Latin Quarter nightclub, where one of his students was appearing with the Pupi Campo orchestra. "I was tired of the out-of-town one-nighters," said Frisaura, "I wanted to stay in the city.…When I heard Campo's music I was fascinated by the Latin sounds. My first Latin-music recording was Tito Puente's arrangement of "How High the Moon" for Pupi Campo. In the band was Joe Loco on piano, Johnny 'La Vaca' Rodríguez on bongos, and Chino González on trumpet. When we went on the road, Tito was my roommate; we became inseparable. It was at Miami Beach's Saxony Hotel that we discussed the formation of our orchestra."

During the fall of 1948, Latin music impresario Federico Pagani caught the Pupi Campo orchestra at the Club Embassy in midtown Manhattan. At the request of Pagani, Puente organized a pickup group, the Picadilly Boys, to perform at the Palladium Ballroom's Sunday matinee. One of the trumpeters of the now-legendary Picadilly Boys was Jimmy Frisaura. For the following six months, the Picadilly Boys consisted of musicians who were available on a week-to-week basis. A few of the trumpeters were Tony Russo, Al DeRisi, Tony DeRisi, and Nilo Curbelo. The pianists were Charlie Palmieri, Joe Loco, Luis Varona, and Al Escobar.

In March 1949, while appearing with Campo at the China Doll Club, Puente split from the Campo orchestra to form his own band. "We debuted," said Frisaura, "at El Patio Club's Atlantic Beach on July 4, 1949. We had the job before we had the band. We had a *conjunto* [with] Luis

Varona on piano, Manuel Patot on bass, Frankie Colón on conga, and Angel Rosa on vocals. Our first hit was 'Abaniquito,' then 'Ran Kan Kan' in 1950. We played the Palladium Ballroom for fifteen years, and the *conjunto* was enlarged in 1950 to a big band, which included trombones and saxes. Since 1949, the most requested tunes have been 'Babarabatiri,' 'Cayuco,' and 'Cua Cua.' When the orchestra played its first date at the Palladium in September 1949, there were three trumpeters. Four months later, another trumpeter was added to the section, which consisted of Frank Lopinto, Sammy Scavone, Gene Rapetti, and I [on bass trumpet]. Shortly thereafter, a baritone and alto sax were added. Six months later, the trombones of Kai Winding and Eddie Bert were added for the RCA recordings of 'Tuxedo Junction' and 'Take the "A" Train.' These two outstanding recordings were never performed at dances; neither were the tunes in the 1960 RCA LP *Tambo*, which included Alberto Socarrás on flute and Doc Severinson, Bernie Glow, and Ernie Royal on trumpets.

When vocalist Vicentico Valdés left the Puente orchestra in 1953 to launch his bandleading career, the Cuban *cha-cha-chá* rhythm was in the infant stage of its popularity. According to Puente, he and Willie Bobo sang chorus, since a lead vocalist was not required. Almost a year passed before Puerto Rican singer Gilberto Monroig became the band's vocalist in 1954. Less than a year later Monroig was gone and replaced by Santos Colón.

By the end of the decade, the Tito Puente orchestra was Latin music's number-one attraction and was earning top dollar. The new music trends charanga (1961) and boogaloo (1966) became Latin music's most popular rhythms. The boogaloo drastically reduced employment for non-boogaloo bands. But it did not affect the Puente, Machito, and Tito Rodríguez orchestras, since the Palladium dancers of the 1960s had obtained better-paying jobs compared to their former salaries in the 1950s, and they continued to support the Titos and Machito.

The 1970s saw the Puente band's lowest point in popularity, for various reasons. One was the emergence of the artists on Fania Records, whose proprietor, Jerry Masucci, bought airtime in cities with large Hispanic populations. In addition, Fania made two movies about the company's artists and their brand of salsa. There was also competition from Latin-soul music—the Latin hustle—and from Fania All Stars concerts in foreign countries and Madison Square Garden. Finally, Polito Vega's five-day-a-week, three-hour WBNX program, *Salsa*, aired the recordings of Fania artists exclusively. The greed of New York City landlords must also be blamed for Tito Puente's decline, since large ballrooms were forced to close after Governor Nelson Rockefeller permitted the building owners to double and triple their monthly rents. Orchestras that had once earned more than a thousand dollars for a gig were now compelled to work at lounges, which greatly reduced their pay.

Puente's popularity reached an all-time low in the mid-1970s, when Morris Levy, who owned the Tico and Roulette labels, would not buy airtime for his artists, one whom was Puente. Puente's 1974 Tico LP *Tito Unlimited* was badly critiqued, and his standing plummeted. But Masucci launched Puente's comeback in 1976 by making it possible for the Puente orchestra to be seen coast to coast on two popular TV programs of the period—the Dinah Shore and Marie Osmond shows. Masucci also recorded Puente's *Tribute to Beny Moré* in 1978, for which Tito won his first Grammy Award. After that, Puente won three additional Grammys.

In 1981, this writer interviewed Jimmy Frisaura. "My biggest thrill," he said, "occurred in 1970 when Richard Nader presented a Latin music concert at Madison Square Garden....When the Puente orchestra came on stage, the noise was deafening...over eighteen thousand people cheering us....It was a great feeling to know we were appreciated....Up to 1961 Latin music had progressed with the addition of jazz...then when the *pachanga* became popular, the creativity was lost....The creativity was not regained with the boogaloo....These two rhythms were simplified forms of music....Surviving became a difficult task...the number of bands far exceed the number of jobs available....The recently formed bands were working four gigs in one day, always below scale....Latin musicians have never united to discourage the abuses we faced....In the 1950s we earned a salary for one gig for which in the 1970s we had to work two gigs on the same evening....For each performance each sideman has two hundred charts in his book....Tito has a preference...he would rather play jazz....During the early 1950s most Latin musicians were always in studios. We were always recording....I have recorded with all of the top bands in New York City....For the 1955 RCA recording of 'Por Tu Amor,' I am blowing the trumpet solo....With every passing decade, the music gets better...for instance, for the music of the 1950s, we learned and improved upon the music of the 1940s....It was the same for the musicians of the 1940s...they drew from the music of the 1930s....Today's musicians draw from the music of the preceding decade, so it could only get better."

In 1989, while en route to a gig, Frisaura suffered a heart attack and was rushed to St. Luke's Hospital, where he remained for two months after heart bypass surgery. He rested another two months, then informed Puente that he was ready to return to work. He blew the first set at Sweetwater's, near Lincoln Center. During a break outside on the sidewalk, he reportedly closed his eyes and slumped against a car. He was rushed to St. Clare's Hospital a few blocks away where he was diagnosed with a blood clot in his brain that resulted in aphasia—the loss of power to use or understand words. On February 9, 1993, while WBAI DJ Nancy Rodríguez was airing a Tito Puente tribute at 2 P.M., Bill Cosby leaned over and spoke into a microphone, "For you, Jimmy, get better."

With Jimmy Frisaura incapacitated, the job of business manager for the Tito Puente orchestra was inherited by percussionist John "Dandy" Rodríguez. The release of the movie *The Mambo Kings* in 1992 enabled the group to perform in many countries outside the United States for the money Puente demanded. Tenor saxist Mitch Frohman said, "Now we are going to places like Australia, Hong Kong, New Zealand, Japan, and Israel...places that you would not think of wanting to hear a Latin jazz band....Tito has been knocking down doors, and it is a tragedy that Jimmy is not around to reap the fruits of his work....Tito would be the first to tell you that he misses him immensely."

On Thursday, February 19, 1998, Frisaura suffered his fourth heart attack. He was placed in the intensive care unit at a Perth Amboy, New Jersey, hospital. The following Monday, February 23, his lungs collapsed and he expired at 1:30 P.M. His childhood friend Gene Rapetti made the funeral arrangements. The wake was held at the East End Funeral Home in the Bronx on Gun Hill Road. During the evening of February 24 and 25, hundreds, including Tito Puente himself, paid their respects. Among the Puente alumni were Gil López, Ray Barretto, Frankie Colón, Mike Collazo, Andy Senatore, Puchi Bulog, Marty Holmes, Dave Kurtzer, Mitch Frohman, and Orlando Marín. A condolence phone call came from an old friend, Los Angeles trumpeter Paul López, who said, "Every time I was in New York, Jimmy got me gigs." On Thursday, February 26, Jimmy Frisaura was laid to rest at the Bronx's St. Raymond's cemetery.

Originally published in Latin Beat *magazine, June/July 1998*

TWENTY

FRANKIE COLÓN

Percussionist Frankie Colón's orchestration of the tunes "Qué Pena Me Da" and "Africanerías" for the 1963 LP *Reunion: Miguelito Valdés with Machito and his Orchestra* made him a much-sought-after arranger. For more than fifty years, he has played conga, timbales, and bongos for the orchestras of Chico O'Farrill, Luis Barreto, Noro Morales, Vicentico Valdés, Machito, and Argueso, whom he was with for more than a quarter century at Roseland.

What makes Frankie Colón noteworthy is his eyewitness role to Latin music history as it unfolded in New York after 1949. For fifty years, salsa aficionados wondered about the creation of the Tito Puente orchestra. How did it start? Why? Where? And when? Puente does not remember; trumpeter Jimmy Frisaura (who has been with him since the group's formation) is not sure of the facts; pianist Luis Varona passed away. Now, for the first time, we have Colón's eyewitness account, reinforced by his elephantine memory.

Paco Colón was born in the 1930s to a Colombian mother and Puerto Rican father. He was reared in Spanish Harlem when the vendors in *la marqueta* were solely Jewish, Italian, and Greek. His and his brothers' favorite music was the swinging jazz of the popular big bands. His appreciation for Latin music began in 1942, when Decca Records released Machito's recordings of "Nague," "Tingo Talango," and "El Muerto Se Fue de Rumba."

Three years later, at Robert E. Simon Junior High School, he met Robert "Chinky" Olivencia and Papi Pagani, whose influences would point him toward a musical career. "When Papi told me his father managed the Machito orchestra, I became interested," said Colón. "I must have been in Papi's apartment a hundred times and I never got to speak to Federico except to say hello and goodbye. He was always rushing somewhere."

Before the year ended, Colón and Olivencia began the first of three years of percussion studies under the tutelage of Papi Pagani. Through Pagani, Colón met Chano Pozo when the great Cuban *conguero* made a guest appearance with the Miguelito Valdés orchestra at the Triboro Theater in 1948. *Bongocero* Johnny "La Vaca" Rodríguez introduced Colón to Tito Puente, who was the *timbalero* and contractor for the Pupi Campo orchestra when it appeared at the Carnival Room in the Hotel Capitol, at the corner of Forty-ninth Street and Eight Avenue.

"One night, after the Campo band finished playing a tune, Johnny invited me to sit in," recalled Colón. "I remember Johnny looking at Tito, who nodded approval of my playing. Around March 1949, Johnny mentioned that Tito was going to leave Pupi to form a band that would open that summer at El Patio Club in Atlantic Beach, Long Island. Johnny had a commitment, so he recommended me.

"Tito and I discussed the job at LaSalle Cafeteria. He suggested I attend the first rehearsal the following week at Louie Varona's mother's music school, the Marguerite LeCompte Music Studio, at 116th Street between Park and Lexington. At this rehearsal was the original Tito Puente band, which consisted of Jimmy Frisaura and Chino González on trumpets, Angel Rosa as the vocalist, Luis Varona on piano, Manuel Patot on bass, Puente on timbales, and me on congas. They didn't rehearse Latin music, just American pop tunes. The following week I sat in on conga. Whenever Tito switched to vibes I felt terrified…he left me alone to carry the rhythm section.

"On July 4, 1949, the seven-piece Tito Puente orchestra made its debut at El Patio. Puente did not use the arrangements he had written for Campo, because they were for three trumpets and saxes. Instead, he used the arrangements he had written for the Picadilly Boys, plus other tunes with two trumpets added. We played more American pop music than Latin."

One week after the Patio gig ended on Labor Day, the Puente orchestra was enlarged for a Palladium appearance. Trumpeter Tony DeRisi and *bongocero* Chino Pozo were added. Weeks later, on the Palladium bandstand, Colón remembered seeing Vicentico Valdés for the first time. "He climbed on stage with maracas," said Colón. "He sang a bolero—"Tus Ojos." He was so good we had to repeat it. Tito told him to stay, so Vicentico ended the night singing *coro* to our lead vocalist, Paquito Sosa. That same week Sosa left the band to fill other commitments, and Vicentico became Puente's vocalist."

In October or November 1949, Puente used three trombones, four trumpets, four saxes, and a full rhythm section for a Tico recording session at the WOR studios at Forty-eighth Street and Seventh Avenue. "After recording three sides in three hours," said Colón, "Tito surprised us by dismissing the trombonists and saxophonists and passing out his charts of 'Abaniquito' to the remaining musicians—Chino Pozo on bongos, Manuel Patot on bass, Luis Varona on piano, trumpeters Jimmy Frisaura, Tony DeRisi, Chino González, and Mario Bauzá, and vocalists Graciela [Machito's sister], Vicentico, and me. We played it once so the engineer could get a balance level. We were familiar with the number since it was part of our repertoire, but this version was incredible. Vicentico was outstanding with his ad-libs and Mario blew his ass off on the solo. After the take, we listened to it and Tito wanted a second take. He changed his mind when Mario convinced him not to, that another take would not come out as fiery."

From Frankie Colón I learned the exact dates Manny Oquendo, Gil López, Mango Santamaría, and Charlie Palmieri joined the Puente band. I learned about the behind-the-scenes Puente–Tito Rodríguez top-billing feud on the Palladium bandstand, the secret intrigue of the Latin music industry, the genius of Chico O'Farrill, and much more. Frankie Colón is not only a seasoned percussionist and a top-notch arranger, he is an invaluable source of Latin New York's music history.

Originally published in Latin Beat *magazine, October 1998*

TWENTY-ONE

Vicentico Valdés

Ask any Latin music aficionado over forty what the name Vicentico Valdés suggests, and you will probably get responses like "romance," "love," "tenderness," and "the Latin Frank Sinatra." For thirty years, beginning in 1949, Valdés was among Latin America's most popular vocalists, at times considered number one. He was one of a handful of performers who could sing ballads as well as up-tempo salsa.

In 1950, when the Machito and Noro Morales orchestras were engaged in their musical battles over who was numero uno, Valdés's mambos drew attention to Tito Puente's band and enabled it to make the leap from obscurity to a secure position among the five most popular Latin orchestras. Valdés's voice was a vein of gold for Tico Records and was responsible for Puente's meteoric rise to the top of the Latin music world in 1952.

On January 10, 1921, Vicentico was born to Ramon and Amparo Valdés in the Cayo Hueso district of Havana, Cuba. His musical influences were his older brother Alfredo, vocalists Cheo Marquetti and Abelardo Barroso, and the Sexteto Cauto. In 1930, Alfredo became Sexteto Nacional's lead vocalist after Cheo Jiménez died of pneumonia in New York Harbor, on a ship preparing to sail to the world's fair in Barcelona, Spain.

Five years later, Alfredo made it possible for his fifteen-year-old brother to sing "Flor de Ausencia" with Cheo Belén Puig's orchestra at Havana radio station CMQ. After this, Vicente gained experience with a number of *conjuntos*, always singing *guarachas*. In 1942 he gave up his lead vocalist spot with Orquesta Cosmopólita for a move to Mexico City. Alfredo, already in Mexico, lined up Vicentico's first job.

Even before 1948, Valdés was known throughout Mexico. His live radio performances with the popular Mexican bands of Arturo Núñez, Rafael de la Paz, and Chucho Rodríguez (with whom he recorded "Tumbaito" and "Obsesión") received much airplay over station XEW.

In September 1948, Valdés was in Los Angeles. West Coast Mexican-Americans loved him and gave him their adulation. Before the year ended, he returned to Mexico and gathered his clothing. By February 1949, he was in New York City. Marcelino Guerra, a top vocalist/bandleader at the time, gave his countryman a job singing. Months later while at musicians' union local 802, then located inside Roseland Ballroom at West 52nd Street, Valdés ran into an old friend, percussionist Chino Pozo. Pozo invited him for coffee at the nearly LaSalle Cafeteria.

Inside the cafeteria was Tito Puente, who recalled their first encounter: "Vicentico was dressed in a black pinstriped suit and had a cigar in his mouth." Pozo made the introductions and had Puente invite the vocalist to a rehearsal for a Verne recording session. That night at the rehearsal, vocalist Paquito Sosa was having difficulty singing the ballad "Tus Ojos." Pozo suggested to Puente that Valdés be allowed to sing it. Puente, hunched over his vibes, his mallets tapping the keys, looked up and heard Valdés croon, *"Hoy día miro tus ojos / tus ojos tan tristes / tus ojos tan verdes / tan verdes como el mar."* In Pozo's words, "It was a unique, romantic sound…unheard of before in Latin music." Valdés ended up recording "Tus Ojos" and "Camaguey."

In October 1949, the Tito Puente *conjunto*, which consisted of Luis Varona on piano; Mario Bauzá, Jimmy Frisaura, Tony DeRisi, and Gabriel "Chino" González on trumpets; Chino Pozo on bongos; Manuel Patot on bass; Frankie Colón on congas; Tito Puente on timbales; and Vicentico Valdés as vocalist, congregated at the WOR studios at Forty-eighth Street and Seventh Avenue. There they did the Tico recording session that produced "Mambo Macoco" and "Abaniquito." Via the Dick "Ricardo" Sugar radio show, Latin New York was treated to "Abaniquito" nightly, and the airplay resulted in instant recognition for Puente. Valdés's fiery ad-libs and Mario Bauzá's thrilling trumpet solos made the adrenaline flow and turned "Abaniquito" into the song most identified with the Palladium Ballroom.

Pozo left Puente in 1951 and was replaced by Manny Oquendo on bongos. Valdés's arousing delivery on the tune "Babarabatiri" made this Tico 78 a bestseller and added thrust to the soaring Puente orchestra. In 1951 a top-billing war erupted between Tito Puente and Tito Rodríguez— a battle between the two bandleaders for listing on the top line of a marquee or poster.

Nineteen-fifty-one was Tito Rodríguez's year. His recordings of "The Desert Dance," "Mambo Mona," "Golpecito," and "Tony and Lucille Mambo" were just a few of the songs that drew dancers away from the Palladium and over to the Park Palace Ballroom at the corner of 110th

Street and Fifth Avenue. The following year, the Puente orchestra nearly annihilated its competition with thirty-seven Tico 78s, all of which were potential hits. Some of the music charts were Cuban stock arrangements, and some were from ballads written by Cuba's José Antonio Méndez. Contributing to Puente's popularity were Valdés's renditions of "Mambo Con Puente," "Baile Mi Mambo," "Tatilibaba," "Quiéreme y Verás," "Camina Camarón," "Marijuana," "La Güira," "La Gloria Eres Tú," "Aprieta el Pollo," "Penjamo," "Guaguancó en Tropicana," "Wampó," and "Batanga."

Pianist Gil López was drafted into service for the Korean War in 1952 and was replaced by Charlie Palmieri. The following month, Frankie Colón was drafted and replaced by Mongo Santamaría. With the exception of the Machito and Noro Morales orchestras, Latin bands during this period were known only in places where their recordings were distributed. For Tico, that meant New York, New Jersey, Miami, and San Juan.

Then the sizzling Puente band was contracted to play its first West Coast gig. Upon their arrival in Los Angeles, Puente saw a poster reading "Vicentico Valdés con la Orquesta de Tito Puente." Puente exploded, and in a fit of anger reprimanded Valdés for having his name read first. Puente's heated words offended Valdés, whose name was more familiar to Los Angeles Hispanics than Puente's was. Valdés gave Puente notice that after returning to New York he would no longer be a band member.

The Vicentico Valdés Orchestra was thus formed in late 1953. It included Manny Oquendo on bongos, Joe Cain on trumpet, and the Puerto Rican Ray Coen-Concepción as pianist and arranger. The following year, Valdés's Seeco recordings of "Derroche de Felicidad," "Como Fue," "Plazos Tracioneros," "Tenderly," and "Si Te Dicen," placed him among Latin music's top bandleaders. Most of his Seeco recordings were of René Hernández arrangements, and for the next five years they were bestsellers.

In 1956 Valdés was honored with an invitation to record with Cuba's venerable La Sonora Matancera, who had no problem giving him top billing on one of their Seeco LPs. From this meeting came the hit tunes "Los Aretes de la Luna," "Una Aventura Más," and "Añoro."

Valdés gained international superstar status in 1959 with his Seeco recording "La Montaña." At that point he broke up the band and continued as a solo act. Like another romantic balladeer of the day, Lucho Gatica, he was contracted to sing throughout Latin America. At around the same time, Seeco released its Tropical label album of 1950 Puente recordings, including Valdes's hit vocals on "El Yoyo" and "Arrollando." The collection was titled *Tito Puente and Friends*.

On April 18, 1975, a standing-room-only crowd jammed the Corso Ballroom at 86th Street near Third Avenue to witness the midnight reunion of Valdés and Puente. It was a memorable occasion. Valdés, attired in a tan leisure suit, sang the hits he and Puente had recorded. The next reunion occurred on April 6, 1984, when Valdés was honored by the Willie Bobo Committee at Club Broadway; he sang his repertoire and was backed by the Puente orchestra. A plaque handed to him by Angel René read, "Vicentico Valdés: For enriching our lives with romance, love and unforgettable moments through your unique vocal style."

Valdés recorded more than thirty great albums on labels such as Tico, Seeco, and United Artists. Two of my favorites are his 1982 and 1986 Bronco label LPs with the orchestra of Bobby Valentín, whose orchestrations are of Grammy Award quality. Vicentico Valdés is truly a Latin American treasure. [Editor's note: Vicentico Valdés died on June 26, 1995, in New York City.]

Originally published in Latin Beat *magazine, June 1993*

TWENTY-TWO

VITÍN AVILES

For decades, the talent of vocalist Vitín Aviles went unnoticed, even though he was among Latin music's five most popular singers during the 1940s and 1950s. He is one of a few vocalists who can sing up-tempo salsa as well as romantic ballads. For a half century, whenever a seasoned vocalist was needed, Aviles was always one of the few chosen. Yet during all that time, no one ever publicly said thank you to Aviles. This neglect was rectified on the evening of February 4, 2000, at the Point Community Development Center, located at Garrison Avenue and Manida Street in the Hunts Point Section of the Bronx. An overflow crowd of over 250 people turned out for this overdue night of recognition. The event was promoted on three of New York City's most popular Latin-music programs—Vicki Sola's *Que Viva la Música* on Saturdays from 12 to 4 P.M., German Santana and Carlos Rosario's *Caribe Latino* show on WKCR on Mondays from 10 P.M. to 1 A.M., and Nancy Rodríguez's *Ritmo Con Ache* show on WBAI on Sundays from 2 to 4 P.M.

Among the musicians in the audience were vocalists Frankie Figueroa, Willie Torres, and Miguel Quintana; percussionists Frankie Colón, Ray Mantilla, Rudy Romero, Anibal Texeira, Benny Bonilla, and Luis Mangual; flutist Dave Valentín; bassist Leo Flemming; guitarist Juan Irene Pérez; and vibist Steve Pouchie. Sponsors of this event were Latin-music historians Henry Medina and René López, along with Bob Sancho of the Bronx Lebanon Hospital.

Vitín Aviles was born September 30, 1924, in Mayaguez, Puerto Rico, to José and Gregoria Aviles. As a teenager Vitín was trained by his father to cut hair; meanwhile, he learned to sing by listening to the recordings of Orlando "Cascarita" Guerra of Cuba's Casino de la Playa orchestra. Young Aviles was a barber Monday through Friday; weekends, he sang with Mayaguez's Orquesta Hatuey and later on with La Anacaona.

In 1945, when Vitín was twenty-one, the Aviles family moved to San

Juan. After telling his father he wanted to be a singer, Vitín received the following advice: "The average musician cannot retire—he has no future—but a barber will always have employment, because men need haircuts every three weeks." Aviles learned to play guitar and bass and sang with Orquesta Serenata Tropical at the Copacabana Club in Santurce.

One evening bandleader Miguelito Miranda dropped by the Copa. "Miguelito heard me sing and offered me a recording date," said Aviles. "I accepted his offer and recorded the tune 'La Televisión' for the then newly formed Verne Records." The tune, composed by the Cuban José Carbo Menéndez and arranged by Pérez Prado, was a stock arrangement Miranda bought for a dollar. "La Televisión" was recorded at the WIC studios in San Juan. After the recording Aviles formed a sextet that worked at the Escambrón cabaret. In mid-1946 an acetate disc of "La Televisión" was made and mailed to Verne's New York office in Spanish Harlem. Before 1946 ended, Aviles received a phone call from Mariano Artau, a popular New York Latin-music disc jockey, who told him "La Televisión" was a smash hit. Artau said he could have a Saturday and Sunday at the Park Plaza Ballroom at 110th Street and Fifth Avenue. "I paid Pérez Prado to play piano and select an eleven-man pickup group. Prado rehearsed the group, we sailed through 'La Televisión,' and we sounded good. After this Prado went to Mexico and on to stardom."

Following the Plaza gig, Artau and Aviles dropped by La Conga Club at Fifty-third Street and Broadway, where Miguelito Valdés, the featured act, was backed by the Pupi Campo orchestra. Artau introduced Aviles to Campo, who was aware of the success of "La Televisión" and offered him a job. When Campo quoted a salary of $175 a week, compared to the $65 a week awaiting him in San Juan, Aviles joined the Campo band and recorded some memorable tunes. There were other jobs when Campo's orchestra was not working, and many recording dates. In late 1949 Aviles replaced vocalist Angel Rosa in Tito Puente's Picadilly Boys at the Palladium Ballroom. Aviles sang lead vocal on Puente's "Ran Kan Kan" for an RCA session; it became a huge hit in 1950. Then, Aviles said, "Bandleader Armando Castro [who co-wrote the hit 'Jack, Jack, Jack'] offered me a salary I just could not refuse, so I joined his band at San Juan's Hotel New Yorker....Angel Rosa was going to rejoin Puente again but the lead vocal job went to Vicentico Valdés."

In early 1950 Aviles was back in New York, and back singing with Pupi Campo. An incomplete discography of Aviles's recordings includes "Champú de Cariño" with Carlos Varela (1946); "Negra Consentida," "Capullito de Alelí," "Hi, Hi, Hi," "Tú No Sabes Nada," and "Despacito" with Pupi Campo (1947–48); "Ran Kan Kan" with Tito Puente (1949);

"Yumbambé" and "Tu Plato" with Joe Loco (1951); and the monster La Playa Sextet tracks "Coco Seco," "La Basura," "Los Marcianos," "Preludio en Ritmo," "Marijuana," "Salta Perico," and "Guieta Caiman" (1955–57), which were heard every day on Dick "Ricardo" Sugar's radio show. Vitín also recorded songs for a 1959 Ansonia session—among them "Perdiendo la Cabeza," "Echale Taquito," and the bolero "Nina"—with the Aviles Orchestra, which included arranger and pianist René Hernández, pianist Ray Coen, trumpeters Jimmy Frisaura, Bernie Glow, and Joe Cain, bassist Eddie Gómez, *timbalero* Willie Bobo, and conga and bongo player Johnny "La Vaca" Rodríguez. The union of Charlie Palmieri and Aviles for Palmieri's 1972 Alegre label album *El Gigante del Teclado* produced "La Hija de Lola," "Mi Vecina," "Coco," and "El Pan Sobao."

At the homage at the Point, Aviles accepted a plaque and a raucous ten-minute standing ovation. He said he was pleased that the tribute happened while he was alive. "I came to New York for a weekend," he said, "and remained for fifty-four years."

Aviles has experienced many memorable moments, including some painful ones. He was once mugged outside a Queens club and his hands were stomped, which prevented him from ever playing a guitar again. In 1958 his wife of forty-three years died; he grieved and did not sing for years. Then there was the loss of a quarter-million dollars in a real estate deal.

The increasing cost of employing live musicians compelled Aviles to sing along with tape-recorded instrumental music. At the Point, he sang many of his popular hits to such "TV track" accompaniments. But at one point during the evening, the sizzling Demetrios Katsaris Orchestra backed him on "Hija de Lola," and the flute riffs suddenly induced the audience erupt in mass euphoria. A spotlight caught Dave Valentín riffing and blowing hitherto unheard-of "Lola" ad-libs on flute. Valentín had the crowd on its feet, and the Point was rocked to its foundation. The event had begun at 7:30 P.M. and was scheduled to end at ten. But the euphoria pushed it to 11:30. The evening ended with the guest of honor singing "Por Qué Ahora." The Vitín Aviles tribute was videotaped for posterity.

Originally published in Impacto *magazine, 2000*

TWENTY-THREE

GILBERTO MONROIG

On Friday, May 3, 1996, Gilberto Monroig, one of Puerto Rico's most popular artists, died after a long illness. Like Tito Rodríguez, Ismael Rivera, Cheo Feliciano, Hector Lavoe, and Vitín Aviles, he was internationally known as a vocalist who could sing ballads and up-tempo salsa and do it well.

Born in Santurce on July 2, 1930, he was attracted to music and was tutored at the age of ten by Luis, an older brother, on guitar and vocals. For the next ten years Gilberto sang at parties, weddings, and social gatherings. He made his professional debut with the orchestra of Guillermo Manzano. He sang ballads with the orchestra, and Mon Rivera sang the up-tempo tunes.

During the mid- to late 1940s, Bobby Capó was Puerto Rico's most popular vocalist. Right behind him were Vitín Aviles and Gilberto Monroig. Monroig relocated to New York during the early 1950s and sang with a few of the city most popular orchestras. Al "Alfredito" Levy was an up-and-coming bandleader in 1952 who—like his idol Tito Puente—played timbales and vibes. "When I first heard Gilberto at an upstate resort, I wanted him," Levy recalled. "He was what I needed." Pianist/bandleader José Curbelo ended up with Monroig, who was one of the reasons Curbelo's orchestra was among Latin music's top five in the early 1950s.

In the spring of 1953, the Tito Puente orchestra had just returned from a California tour when the dancers at New York City's Palladium Ballroom heard the shocking news that vocalist Vicentico Valdés had split with Puente over a top-billing misunderstanding. The Puente-Valdés split was very depressing for many Latin New Yorkers. For five years, beginning in 1949, the two musicians had recorded over one hundred Tico label 78s, making Puente a serious contender against Machito and Noro Morales for the number-one spot among Latin bandleaders. Now many people remarked that no one could ever replace Valdés. Puente's close friend José Curbelo offered him Gilberto Monroig, and in mid-1953 a new chapter in the Tito Puente legend began.

Monroig established himself immediately via the Tico 78 "Picao y Tostao," which got universal play in Latin New York. In one year, Monroig recorded fourteen great sides with Puente, including "Bambaram Bam Bam," "Ya Lo Puedes Decir," and "El Diablo de Esa Mujer." The Palladium and the exclusive summer resorts gave gigs to Puente's twelve-piece orchestra, which included Jimmy Frisaura, Al DeRisi, Gene Rapetti, and Harold Wegbreit on trumpets, Rafael "Tat" Palau on tenor saxophone, Shep Pullman on baritone saxophone, Charlie Palmieri on piano, Mongo Santamaría on congas, Willie Bobo on bongos and cowbell, Manuel Patot on bass, Puente on timbales and vibes, and Monroig on vocals.

Monroig's last recording with Puente was "Malcriada," a bolero that was his biggest hit. Soon afterward, however, personal problems developed that prevented Monroig from leaving Puerto Rico. His inability to return to the United States left Puente without a vocalist. Once again, Curbelo came to Puente's aid by giving him his vocalist—Santitos Colón, from Mayaguez, Puerto Rico. Monroig resumed his singing career in Puerto Rico, and it improved with each passing year. At times he was the island's number-one vocalist, and he was dubbed "the Puerto Rican Frank Sinatra." He couldn't give up cigarettes and was always seen smoking on stage and during television performances.

In 1982, a crowd of 2,500 people witnessed the concert Dos Tiempos de Monroig at the Luis A. Ferré Performing Arts Center, featuring Monroig and his son Glenn. All of Puerto Rico was aware of the significance of this reunion of father and son, who had not seen or spoken to each other in years. During a moment when the musicians were taking a breather, Gilberto put the microphone close to his mouth and said what a great feeling it was to be reunited with his son. He looked at Glenn and said, "Son, you are honest." The son grabbed a mike, looked at his father, and said, "Dad, you are difficult." Both smiled, embraced, and began singing "Vivo Orgulloso de Tí" (I Am Proud of You), a duet written by Glenn. The audience was blown away. No one expected this moment of emotion to manifest itself after years of bitterness. The people stood up and responded with thunderous applause as tears streamed down their faces.

In 1994, Monroig recorded his last album, *Hechos No Palabras*, with the tune "Confesiones," a song about faith, rebirth, renewal, and acceptance of the realities of life. He left a legacy of hit recordings—"Simplemente Una Ilusión," "Egoísmo," "Qué Sabes Tú," "Mi Loca Tentación," "Cenizas," and "Mi Jaragual." After he died, his wake was held at the Institute of

Puerto Rican Culture, and he was buried at the San Juan Municipal Cemetery on May 4, 1996. He is gone, but in New York, Miami, and Los Angeles, "Picao y Tostao" and "Malcriada" make it seem as though Gilberto Monroig is still among us.

Originally published in Latin Beat *magazine, August 1996*

TWENTY-FOUR

SANTITOS COLÓN

On Saturday, February 21, 1998, the renowned balladeer Santos Colón, known as Santitos, died in Puerto Rico. The five-foot-six-inch, 140-pound vocalist had been suffering with prostate cancer. The beginning of the end had come the evening before in a recording studio as he was preparing to record two boleros with vocalist Carmen Delia Depiní. He complained of stomach pains, then left the studio for his apartment in Laguna Gardens. Next morning, while lying in bed, he was stroking his dog, Nina, and talking with his wife, Judy, when suddenly he began bleeding from his nose and mouth. He was rushed to the emergency room of a hospital in the city of Carolina, where he slipped into a coma. He was taken to the intensive care unit and placed on a life support system, but at 7:10 P.M., he died from a cerebral hemorrhage.

More than five hundred people attended Colón's wake at the Institute of Puerto Rican Culture in Old San Juan. Among the mourners were vocalist Ismael Miranda, Junior Laredo, Mary Pacheco, and Ruth Fernández, who joined others in singing such Colón hits as "Horas y Minutos," "La Vida Es Un Sueño," "Apóyate En Mi Alma," "Tus Ojos," and "Noche de Ronda." Tito Puente was unable to attend the wake, as he was in New York attending the funeral of his business manager and lead trumpeter of forty-one years, Jimmy Frisaura. On Tuesday, February 24, Colón was cremated, and his ashes were placed alongside his mother's at the municipal cemetery in Mayaguez, Puerto Rico.

Born Angel Santos Vega Colón in Mayaguez on November 1, 1922, he began singing with the orchestra of Frank Madera in San Juan during his teen years. (Frank Madera was a brother of José "Pin" Madera, a tenor saxophonist and music arranger for the Machito orchestra during the 1940s and 1950s.) After seven years with Madera, Colón joined the band of trumpeter Miguelito Miranda in the late 1930s, then switched to La Orquesta Tropicana and finally to the orchestra of Pedro Flores.

In 1950, Colón relocated to New York and sang with the orchestra of trumpeters Jorge López and Tony Novos before joining the José Curbelo orchestra. "Santitos joined my band during the summer of 1953," said Curbelo. "He replaced Gilberto Monroig, who I recommended to Tito Puente as a replacement for Vicentico Valdés. His first recording for me was a bolero he composed, titled 'Rendezvous,' in 1953. In 1954 I recorded the album *Wine, Women, and Cha Cha Cha* for Fiesta Records. In it Santitos sang 'Telaraña' and 'Que Se Fuñan.'…As I am speaking to you [by phone], I am looking at my photo album. I see a Cleveland newspaper advertisement in which I featured Santitos. I was on the same bill with Dizzy Gillespie at a jazz club, the Loop Lounge, in December 1953. In 1954, Gilberto Monroig left the Puente orchestra. After Tito recorded the RCA LP *Cuban Carnival* in 1956, I recommended Santitos to Tito. I replaced him with Willie Torres."

Colón's first recording with the Puente orchestra was the blockbuster *Dance Mania, Vol. 1*, which for years was Puente's best-selling album. Completed after three visits to RCA's studio in midtown Manhattan, the album includes the tunes "El Cayuco," "Mambo Gozón," "Complicación," and "Saca Tu Mujer," recorded November 21, 1957. The tracks "Llego Mijan," "Cuando Te Vea," "Agua Limpia Todo," and "Mi Chiquita Quiere Bembe" were recorded on December 5, with "3-D Mambo," "Varsity Drag Mambo," "Estoy Siempre Junto a Tí," and "Hong Kong Mambo" following two days later. The album was released in early 1958.

For the next ten years, Colón's popularity increased with the recordings of "Caramelos" *(Pachanga Con Puente*, Tico, 1961); "Ay Cariño," "Te Desafio," "Tus Ojos," and "Mi Bomba Sono" *(Exitante Ritmo*, Tico, 1963); "Cua Cua" and "Sepárala También" (*Dance Mania, Vol. 2*, RCA [recorded in 1960 and released in 1963]); "Babarabatiri" and "El Que Usted Conoce" *(Tito Puente in Puerto Rico*, Tico, 1963); "Apóyate En Mi Alma," "Imágenes," and "Llora Timbero" *(De Mí Para Tí*, Tico, 1964); "Mírame Más," "Cuando Caliente el Sol," and "Cómo Está Miguel" *(Carnaval En Harlem*, Tico, 1966); and "Guanguancó Margarito" *(The King*, Tico,1968).

Domingo Echevarría, who co-produced the CD reissues of Puente's RCA recordings, recalled his conversations with Colón while the Puente orchestra appeared weekly at the Pan American Lounge in Queens during 1971. "Santitos told me he was influenced by vocalists Elena Burke, Beny Moré, Vicentico Valdés, Omara Portuondo, Marco Antonio Muñiz, Miguelito Valdés, and Daniel Santos," Echevarría said.

In 1970, after fourteen years as Puente's lead vocalist, Colón was persuaded by Jerry Masucci, president of Fania Records, to launch his solo career. The Fania LP *Portrait of Santos Colón* was followed by the mega-hits "Fiel" and "Triste Navidad." Shortly thereafter, Colón became a member of the Fania All Stars.

In 1971, Colón recorded the Tico LP *Pa'Lante*, his seventeenth and last album as Puente's lead vocalist. He sang chorus for recordings by Louie Ramírez, Chico O'Farrill, Miguelito Valdés, Ray Barretto, the Tico and Fania All Stars, La Lupe, Meñique, and Celia Cruz. He also did ten albums under his own name for Fania Records. Two weeks before his death Colón recorded ten boleros, scheduled for release in March 1998.

On Sunday, February 23, 1997, Colón participated in the celebration at El Museo del Barrio in New York City of Tito Puente's fiftieth anniversary as a bandleader. When Colón began singing "Ay Cariño," he waved to Puente to join him on stage. Puente climbed the podium, and for the next three minutes El Museo was in a time warp. People who used to dance to this tune in the 1960s seemed mentally transported into the past. It was nostalgia, cultural pride, a reminder of one's youth, and it felt great! Through the magic of music, Santos and Tito made time stand still. The audience rose to its feet, bellowing its approval.

On December 15, 1997, Tito Puente celebrated his fiftieth anniversary again, at the Luis Muñoz Marin Amphitheater in Hato Rey, Puerto Rico. Thousands cheered, stomped their feet, and roared after Tito and Santitos performed the song that had gained them an audience throughout Latin America. One witness said he would always remember Puente, his left arm extended across Santitos's shoulders, singing "Mírame Más." This was the last time the two great musicians ever appeared on stage together, and the memory of their collaboration is unforgettable.

Originally published in Latin Beat *magazine, April 1998*

TWENTY-FIVE

TONY MOLINA

It was 9 A.M. on Thursday, May 25, 2000. The lobby of the Crowne Plaza Hotel, near Los Angeles International Airport, was crowded with people whom promoter Albert Torres had invited to the second Bacardi Salsa Congress celebration. Television and video cameras rolled and bulbs flashed while questions were asked of the legendary Palladium Ballroom dancers Pedro "Cuban Pete" Aguilar, Freddie Rios, and Mike Ramos. After fifty years of performing on stage across the United States, the trio was finally given the recognition they had earned. In the crowd surrounding the dancers, I saw a man waving his hands and yelling, "Max, it's me, Tony!" After a few seconds I realized it was Tony Molina, one of Latin music's most popular New York vocalists of the 1950s and 1960s, who had sung and recorded for the orchestras of Joseíto Román, Fausto Curbelo, José Curbelo, Tito Puente, Alfredito, and Ramon Argueso.

The 1950s were Molina's best years. Latin New Yorkers became accustomed to his unique sound on the Curbelo and Alfredito recordings heard daily on the popular WEVD radio program hosted by Dick "Ricardo" Sugar. While eating breakfast at the hotel's cafeteria, Molina spoke about periods of his life that I was not previously aware of. While we spoke, he allowed me to tape our conversation.

Antonio Molina, of Puerto Rican and Venezuelan heritage, was born on December 11, 1927, in Mayaguez, Puerto Rico. Months after his birth, his parents moved to a Brooklyn tenement on Columbia Street off Atlantic Avenue. Molina's musical education consisted of listening and singing along with the recordings of Miguelito Valdés, Machito, Piquito Marcano, Johnny Rodríguez, Doroteo, Davilita, Johnny López, and Bobby Capó. At age fifteen he attended dances with his father and would not move from the bandstand as he listened to vocalists Polito Galíndez and Panchito Riset. On Saturday nights he listened to the popular radio program *Your Hit Parade*. On Sunday mornings he listened to *Battle of the Baritones*, which aired the recordings of Frank Sinatra, Dick Haymes, Perry Como, Andy Russell, the brothers Bob and Ray Eberly, and Bing Crosby. After a few hundred hours of singing to recordings and the radio, he debuted with the septet Alma Boricua, which performed at bars and lounges in Brooklyn's Hispanic neighborhoods. The group's repertoire consisted of a few original tunes, plus popular boleros sung by a lead and a second voice.

In 1944, Molina sang boleros and *guarachas* with a guitar trio whose lead guitarist was Carlos Maldonado (Ricardo Ray's father). Brooklyn Latinos flocked to the neighborhood lounge to dance, socialize, and enjoy a few hours away from the everyday problems of life. Although there was no cover charge, dancers enjoyed chunks of free cheese and a ten-cent glass of beer, and the musicians earned a few dollars.

During the mid 1940s, Noro Morales, Machito, Marcelino Guerra, José Curbelo, Pupi Campo, Carlos Varela, José Budet y Sus Tropicales, Alberto Iznaga's La Siboney, Moncho Usera, and the Sensamaya Kids were the pride of Latin New York. In every store that had a jukebox one could hear Vitín Aviles's "La Televisión," Noro Morales's "Bangin' the Bongo" and "Rhumba Rhapsody," Machito's "Ampárame" and "Ban Ban Queré," Carmen Cavallero's "Voodoo Moon," and Xavier Cugat's "Linda Mujer."

During the next two years, Molina had steady gigs with Los Hermanos Mercado until he began singing with a popular big band at the Don Julio Club in Greenwich Village. Molina joined Local 802 of the musicians' union and ran into Johnny Conquet, a childhood buddy who was the pianist and music arranger for Joseíto Román's Orquesta Quisqueya. Molina joined Román's orchestra in 1947. The group was one of the six bands that participated in the "subway dance" that opened the doors of the Palladium Ballroom to Latin-music orchestras. Mario Bauzá, Machito's musical director, spoke to Tom Morton, manager of the Palladium Ballroom (then a dime-a-dance ballroom) about experimenting and taking a chance with Latin music. The dance was a financial success, and the sounds of rumba, *guaracha, son,* and merengue kicked off the era of the mambo and the Palladium Ballroom.

Speaking about this period of his life, Molina said, "To me, it was just another dance....I remember some of the big guys—Noro Morales, José Curbelo, Marcelino Guerra, and Machito—played that night. I had no idea until now the importance of that dance. I remember the large crowd in front of the ballroom waiting to get in. I remember the crowded dance floor. Joseíto played an hour of merengues and people loved it. Wow! I was part of a historical event, the beginning of the Palladium Ballroom's legend."

Quisqueya's home base was the Bronx's Tropicana Club. In 1950, the band dissolved. Molina kept employed with Local 802 gigs. In 1954, pianist/bandleader Fausto Curbelo liked Molina's vocal delivery and urged him to contract his nephew José for a steady job. "After I called José, I auditioned at his apartment at Fiftieth Street and Eighth Avenue. I sang three mambos and three boleros. I was instructed to listen to Curbelo's singer Gilberto Monroig's phrasing. Monroig was about to leave to join Tito Puente's orchestra and I was his replacement. Santitos Colón and I sang the lead vocals. After a few months, the orchestra recorded four 78s on which I sang lead on 'Poco Pelo,' 'La-La-La,' 'Sun Sun Babae,' and 'Guaguancó en Nueva York.' Before the year ended, I replaced Pellín Rodríguez in Alfredito's band. My first job was in Grossinger's [an upstate New York resort]. Ray Coen-Concepción was on piano; Al Beck, Stan Mollick, and Don Leight were the trumpeters; and Lydio Fuentes was on bass. While appearing at Atlantic Beach's El Patio Club, the Alfredito orchestra backed Diahann Carroll, a vocalist who later became a movie actress.

"In 1956," continued Molina, "Alfredito was experiencing serious personal problems and he just disappeared. I rejoined Curbelo; I recorded "Guayaba," "Bandolera," and a duet with Santitos Colón, "Eque Tumbao." Curbelo was offered a Las Vegas date. The Curbelo sextet followed Louie Prima in the Sands Hotel lounge. I played conga on the American pop standards, and after three months I was back in New York. I hooked up again with Alfredito and recorded the Tico LP *Cha Cha Cha Goes Modern*, and it became a hot-selling album. The album is for dancers. The musicians on this session were Ray Coen on piano, Ziggy Schatz and Don Leight on trumpets, Evaristo 'Guajarón' Baró on bass, Monchito Muñoz on timbal, Johnny 'La Vaca' Rodríguez on conga, Julio 'El Vaquero' on bongó, Alfredito on vibes and chorus, and me on the lead vocals."

On January 9 and April 6, 1956, the twenty-three-piece Tito Puente orchestra was at New York City's RCA studios to record the LP *Cuban Carnival* (reportedly Puente's second-best-selling album). Singing chorus were Willie Bobo, Yayo El Indio, and Tony Molina. "Tito was aware of me," said Molina. "He had heard my recordings with Curbelo and Alfredito, and during this session Tito had written an instrumental *cha-cha-chá* that needed lyrics and a title. Mongo Santamaría, Willie Bobo, Yayo, and I invented lyrics, and Tito titled the tune 'Que Será Mi China.'

"On one occasion before the session, Tito's band was booked to play the Palladium and the Manhattan Center on the same evening. Tito, with half of his regular sidemen and substitutes, played the Palladium, and I sang lead at the Manhattan Center with Tito's band directed by Jimmy Frisaura.

Back in the studio, I was able to learn the tunes we were going to record, all except 'Guaguancó Margarito,' which Machucho sang."

The tremendous sales of Alfredito's *Cha Cha Cha Goes Modern* prompted Fiesta Records president José Morand to sign Molina as an exclusive artist. Morand wanted Molina backed by a La Playa Sextet type of sound. Molina agreed with Morand's decision as long as he could continue to sing and record with Alfredito's orchestra. The first musician contacted for this Fiesta session was the highly regarded pianist and arranger Ray Coen-Concepción. Frank "Paquito" Dávila was on trumpet, and Mario Cora and Luis Ortiz were on *tres* guitar. Of the four recordings released as singles in 1957, "La Peluca" and "Ya No Te Puedo Querer" became best-selling hits.

In 1959, Curbelo gave up music and organized Alpha Artists, a booking agency for New York's Latin-music orchestras. Alfredito was still missing, and Molina sang with Ramon Argueso's Roseland Ballroom Orchestra, a popular New York band Tony had worked with on and off since the early 1950s. In 1966, after a long absence, Alfredito reappeared and persuaded Molina to record the LP *Guajira con Boogaloo* for Cotique Records. The tracks "Situation in F Minor" and "Quivican," with Molina on vocals, were instrumental in making the album a success.

Molina remained with Alfredito for ten years. In 1974, Hector Lavoe, Yayo El Indio, and Meñique (from Panama) sang chorus while backing Molina's lead vocals for Hector Rivera's Tico LP *Lo Máximo*. The album, which featured Cachao on bass, was never released.

Two years later, Alfredito founded Alfredito Weddings, a Latin-music booking agency with fifteen bands that supplied music for wedding receptions. Alfredito's business venture became a financial success, but after five years he again disappeared from the music scene and was never heard of again. "During all of the years I was with Alfredito, I can honestly say he respected his musicians," said Molina. "The guys loved him. He treated me as if I was a member of his family. He is the only bandleader who paid me more than the union scale."

In September 1992, when Ramon Argueso retired, Molina left the music scene and relocated with his wife and children to Lancaster, California, outside of Los Angeles. Albert Torres's second Bacardi Salsa Congress celebration in Los Angeles was a joyous, exciting four days of salsa dance exhibitions by some two thousand dancers from all over the world. The salsa congress was a highlight of my life. I was able to see and enjoy the dance legends Cuban Pete, Freddie Rios, and Mike Ramos. But most importantly, I was reunited with Tony Molina, one of New York's most popular vocalists, and a friend.

Originally published in Latin Beat *magazine, February 2001*

TWENTY-SIX

ORLANDO MARÍN

During the last fifty years, many bandleaders have disappeared from public view. Their orchestras could not add new tunes to their books, they could not perform rhythms reflecting new musical trends, and their recordings no longer received radio exposure. Orlando Marín, a slender, five-foot-ten-inch-tall musician and one of the 1960s' top ten bandleaders, faded from the New York Latin-music scene—but not for any of these reasons. Instead, he was done in by the pains and disappointments that every Latin musician experiences.

Ollie Marín's musical influence came in steps. As a youngster he was tremendously impressed by Buddy Rich and Gene Krupa, who during the 1940s were considered the world's best drummers. Later, Ollie danced for hours to 78-rpm recordings. His neighborhood buddies Eddie and Charlie Palmieri, Sabú Martínez, Chicky Pérez, Tommy García, Lou Goicochea, and Hector Rivera also affected his development. They studied together at the High School of Industrial Arts (now the High School of Art and Design), and all went on to become musicians.

"Going to school was enjoyable," said Marín. "I ate my lunch in five minutes and spent fifty-five minutes listening to mambo music in a large room where teachers' meetings were held." In that same room he met Mike Collazo, who later became a percussionist for the orchestras of Tito Rodríguez and Tito Puente and for Orquesta Broadway. He also met Joe Quijano, the future vocalist and bandleader. Marín, a conga drum hanging from a strap on his back, followed Collazo around the school asking questions. In the process he learned the different cowbell beats and several drumming techniques.

In 1951, Carlos Palmieri, a well-known neighborhood musician, took Ollie with him to New York City's Hotel Diplomat, where Palmieri's *conjunto* performed for the baptismal party of world welterweight boxing champion Kid Gavilán's daughter. The thrill of being a musician that night inspired a musical career. Carlos Palmieri—who later became Charlie Palmieri—"was the most popular person in our neighborhood," said Marín. "Whenever Charlie walked along Longwood Avenue, people on the street and looking out of windows would greet him as if he was a celebrity."

One afternoon during 1952, Ollie was drumming to the Tito Puente recording "Tito Timbero" when he heard a knock on his door. He opened it and saw a well-dressed salesman who said he was also a musician looking for a drummer for a group he was about to form. Ollie told the salesman, Gil Calderón, that he already had a group. Calderón, who three years later would become Joe Cuba, wished Ollie well and left.

Marín's professional debut was with Coco, a guitar trio. After a few months of drumming with Chino Gueits y sus Almas Tropicales, a band led by Charlie and Eddie Palmieri's uncle, Ollie and Eddie Palmieri organized a band. Palmieri, then fourteen years old, was not permitted to go out at night unless he was accompanied by a guardian. Marín, who was two years older, became the guardian. The band, whose vocalist was Joe Quijano, rehearsed at the Bronx's PS 52 on Kelly Street. The first four tunes in the repertoire were Cuban stock arrangements that sold for one dollar apiece. The group's first recordings were of "Abaniquito" and "Sun Sun Babae."

In 1953, Marín left the band after a misunderstanding with Palmieri. Months later, he was back directing the group after Palmieri joined Johnny Segui's *conjunto*. The Marín orchestra gigged at the Sunnyside Garden, Hunts Point Palace, Tropicana, and Stardust ballrooms. Quijano, who left Marín to join Alfredito's Levy's band, was replaced by Armando "Mandín" Vega. The latter did the vocals on "Mi Mambo" for the Plus label—Ollie's first recording.

In 1956, Fiesta label president José Morand recorded the Marín orchestra, and "La Mesa" was heard throughout Latin New York. At this time, the mambo and *cha-cha-chá* were at the peak of popularity. Federico Pagani, promoter for the Palladium Ballroom, was searching for bands to fill in for the big-three house bands while Tito Puente, Tito Rodríguez, and Machito were on tour. This reporter was at the Palladium on the evening when the orchestras of Moncho Leña and Orlando Marín auditioned. Thanks to the versatility of vocalist Mon Rivera, who performed on every instrument that night, Leña's band landed gigs. Marín's fiery drumming on "Mi Mambo" and vocalist Joe Quijano's rendition of the ballad "La Gloria Eres Tú" were enough to convince Pagani of the band's potential. Quijano left again and was replaced by Mandín. For months thereafter, the Marín orchestra was on the Palladium bandstand performing its Fiesta recordings of "Oye Mi Son Cha-Cha-Cha," "El Guyabero," "Wildfire," and "La Mesa."

In May 1958, while his band was a hot attraction, Ollie was drafted into the U.S. Army. After two months of basic training at Fort Dix, New Jersey, and nine months at Fort Smith, Arkansas, he did thirteen months of soldiering in Korea. By the time he finished, two years had gone by, and Ollie was unaware of the new charanga fad. He came back into civilian life in May 1960, when the charanga of Charlie Palmieri was gaining attention. Marín formed a Latin-jazz septet with vocalist Victor Velásquez, flutist Bobby Nelson, *conguero* Nick Ramos, bassist Izzy Feliu, pianist Paquito Pastor, and *coro* singer and cowbell player Tito Jiménez. They played every rhythm, including the *pachanga*, which was the rage at the time, and utilized the scat-singing vocal riffs of Marín, Velásquez, and Jiménez. At this time Francisco Fellove, a Cuban vocalist living in Veracruz, Mexico, had already infected a number of musicians with his Afro-Cuban bebop vocal riffs—most notably the Mexican group Lobo y Melón. Marín's was the only New York orchestra utilizing Fellove's "Chua Chua" scat riffs. Marín's scat sound caught fire and opened the doors to popular ballrooms and the two "in" places in Bayside, Queens—the Manor and the Limbo Lounge.

During the summer of 1961, the owner of the Alhambra Lounge at 163rd Street and Southern Boulevard in the Bronx had been trying to attract people to his cabaret. Most Bronx dancers patronized the Hunts Point Palace and the newly opened Triton Club just up the block. It was the Marín band that filled the Alhambra on Wednesdays, then Fridays and Saturdays, before the gigs were given to Mongo Santamaría's charanga. This reporter saw spontaneous jam sessions in which Charlie and Eddie Palmieri would sit in on piano, Davy Montagne or Oscar García played vibes, Walter Jefferson alternated between sax and flute, and vocalist Chivirico Dávila overwhelmed everyone with stunning *guaguancós*.

At this time, Ollie met Nora Rodríguez, a sultry Puerto Rican nicknamed China because of her almond-shaped eyes. He fell hopelessly in love, and wherever his band played, China was there. In 1962, after his successful Alegre LP *Se Te Quemó La Casa*, from which "La Casa" and "Ritmo Bembé" received much airplay, he directed a big band with twelve sidemen. His future in Latin music appeared bright, and in 1964 he married China. During the same year, his second Alegre LP, *Que Chevere*, kept him in the limelight but away from China. *Chevere* became a hot-selling LP and Marín was in demand.

His dream of a lifetime came true when his orchestra, along with Tito Puente's, was contracted to perform at Virginia's in Los Angeles for two weeks in June 1965. One evening, Ollie invited Puente to participate in a drumming duet (à la Buddy Rich and Gene Krupa) to the tune "Llegué." It was an unexpected thrill to see and hear these two master *timbaleros* rock the foundations of the club. When it ended, the listeners were on their feet applauding.

In 1967, Marín's orchestra was a hot attraction. He spent more time away from home, and this eventually caused him and China to separate. Their breakup grew out of the misunderstandings and loneliness that most musicians' wives endure when they are left alone week after week. Musicians are a unique species. Their day begins at nine in the evening and continues until the wee hours of the morning. They utilize every bit of their creative genius to please a public that often takes a musician's artistry for granted. After his day is over and the rest of the world is sleeping, the emotionally wired musician tries to unwind. If he is tired or sleepy, he goes home to bed. But sometimes he is wide-awake, with a lust to socialize. He has adopted the habits of a night owl. To some women, Latin musicians are shameless male bees who fly from flower to flower, enjoying all the honey they can taste. Other women understand the fans' adulation, the tension that needs an outlet, and the demands made upon an artist. There are also women who can no longer tolerate the weekend loneliness and feel compelled to seek another life. China was one of those women.

Ollie began to neglect his livelihood and devoted most of his time to trying to reconcile with his wife. His name started disappearing from marquees, posters, ads, and dance halls. "It is so difficult to explain the pain I felt when I lost China," said Marín in a dispirited tone. "Dying would have been easier for me at the time....Nothing mattered...all I thought about was her....I just wanted her back."

During the year of their parting, Ollie's hit recordings of the tunes "Mi Jevita" and "Aprende a Querer" (from his Fiesta LP *Está en Algo*) kept his band among the top ten. But by the end of the year, his problems had become so intense that his popularity simply dissolved. China and Ollie were divorced in 1970.

In 1972, Al Santiago (of Alegre Records fame) had an idea that resulted in La Saxofónica, a group of five saxophones and a rhythm section, led by Marín. The group recorded an LP, *Saxofobia, Vol. 1*, whose outstanding tracks—"Louie's Saxofobia," "Orlando's Saxofobia," and "La Mesa"—make it one of the most exciting Latin-jazz albums ever recorded. On May 22, 1997, the Orlando Marín orchestra was feted for being the third-oldest active orchestra, after Tito Puente's and Machito's. Tony Rodríguez, the promoter of the club La Maganette, honored Marín with a plaque that read: "In recognition of a musical legend. You started in 1951, making it forty-six years and still counting. A *timbalero*, composer, and bandleader. We have benefited from your contribution to Latin music. On behalf of your friends and fellow musicians, from the bottom of our hearts, we wish to say, Thank You."

For almost half a century the Orlando Marín orchestra has brightened the lives of New York City's salsa dancers. At this writing, he was appearing at Tito Puente's Bronx restaurant once a month and his band was still swinging. Just recently his sextet, with Connie Grossman on flute, blew a lot of mental fuses with a fiery "Peanut Vendor" at Willie's Steakhouse in the Bronx. It is widely believed that Buddy Rich's skills were just a bit better than Gene Krupa's. For those who witnessed the Puente-Marín timbal exhibitions at Virginia's and the Hollywood Palladium in June 1965, Puente was Buddy Rich. And Orlando Marín proved that he was Gene Krupa.

Originally published in Latin Beat *magazine, September 1998*

TWENTY-SEVEN

LA LUPE

During the 1960s, Tito Puente recorded a number of significant LPs with two important female vocalists—Celia Cruz and La Lupe. Among the Tico recordings with La Lupe were *Tito Puente Swings—The Exciting La Lupe Sings* (1965), *Tú y Yo* (1965), *Homenaje a Rafael Hernández* (1966), and *El Rey y Yo* (1967). La Lupe actually became the featured vocalist and performer. She was highly instrumental in enhancing the role of women, not only in Puente's orchestra but also in Latin music generally. Although Celia Cruz has been a more dominant personification of this aspect of Latin music, La Lupe's contribution to the arts should not be underestimated.

—from *Tito Puente and the Making of Latin Music*, by Steven Loza

During her career, La Lupe was not just another female vocalist living the shadow of Celia Cruz. She was her own press agent. Sometimes she sounded like the legendary French vocalist Edith Piaf. She was uninhibited: on stage she would remove clothing and display her voluptuous body, to the delight of her mostly male audiences. She spoke broken English on the popular TV talk shows of David Frost, Mike Douglas, Dick Cavett, and Merv Griffin. She was written about in every Spanish-language newspaper and magazine.

In 1964, the Santería candles she habitually lit burned her house down. The same thing happened to her apartment twenty years later. During the 1970s she won the lead female role in the Broadway musical adaptation of Shakespeare's *Two Gentlemen of Verona*, playing opposite Raul Julia. La Lupe's tenure on the Latin music scene lasted fourteen years, from 1963 to 1977, and she produced twenty-five best-selling albums. Her mega-hits were "Qué Te Pedí" and "Oriente." She got my attention in 1966 with her rousing rendition of "Los Carreteros," found on Tito Puente's Tico LP *Homenaje a Rafael Hernández*. Her delivery of this Hernández tune is so emotional that it can raise blood pressure and induce tears in Puerto Ricans.

Of partial French descent, Guadalupe Victoria Yoli Raymond was born on December 23, 1942, in San Pedrito, Oriente, Cuba. Listening as a child to the recordings of Olga Guillot and Celia Cruz, she made up her mind to be a vocalist. After winning a singing contest at age twelve, she traveled to Havana for tutoring. Four years later she landed a job singing with a trio directed by Eulogio Reyes, whom she married. By the end of 1958, she had separated from Reyes and was singing as a soloist at Cabaret La Red. She was paid twenty-eight dollars per week for singing ten sets a day, with each set lasting forty-five minutes. Her repertoire consisted mostly of Spanish translations of American pop hits sung by Nat "King" Cole, Frank Sinatra, Tony Bennett, and Elvis Presley.

Lupe arrived in New York City in 1962 and immediately began singing at the Cuban cabaret La Barraca in midtown Manhattan. Months later, while leafing through the Cuban magazine *Bohemia*, Cuban *conguero* and bandleader Mongo Santamaría read about a Cuban female vocalist who would get possessed by the devil while on stage. Curiosity led Santamaría to La Barraca, where Lupe spotted him and introduced herself.

On December 17, 1962, Riverside Records recorded *Mongo Introduces La Lupe*. The album's liner notes, written by Dr. Eligio Valera read: "In this album Mongo has had an opportunity to do something that always gives him the greatest satisfaction—to introduce new talent. This time it is La Lupe! I would describe her as an untamed but sincere musical artist. This fortunate addition to Mongo's group was born in San Pedrito (Oriente province), a town so small that before La Lupe's debut in show business it was unknown even to most Cubans. Lupe comes from a very poor family [and] was for a time a school teacher but felt more attracted to music than by the classroom. When I hear her sing on this album, I have to feel the change was for the best."

The tracks "Besitos Pa' Ti," "Canta Bajo," and "This Is My Mambo" won La Lupe instant national recognition. When Santamaría's band performed at the Apollo Theatre, Club Triton, the Palladium Ballroom, and other prominent venues, Lupe was a featured star. Before a tour of Puerto Rico began, she told Mongo she could not go because she was pregnant by Puerto Rican vocalist Willy García (whom she later married), and she signed an exclusive contract with Tito Puente.

In 1964 Lupe debuted with the Puente orchestra at Loews Boulevard Theater in the Bronx. Months later she visited El Torero, a Cuban cabaret-restaurant located on Broadway between 162nd and 163rd Streets in the Washington Heights section of Manhattan. Entertaining the diners was the Julio Gutiérrez Quintet, with tenor saxophonist José "Chombo" Silva, conga player Marcelino Valdés, bassist Izzy Feliu, pianist Julio Gutiérrez, and vocalists Hector Fernando, Robertico Lozano, Willy Chirino, and Carlos Oliva, who alternated weekly. At one moment during the evening, Gutiérrez's pianissimo introduction of a lush ballad was joined by the soothing wails of Chombo Silva's tenor sax. Hector Fernando, a tall, handsome Cuban vocalist, contributed to the sensuality by cooing the lyrics of "Jugué y Perdí," a song about love lost through an error in judgment. The music and lyrics, composed by pianist-flutist-bandleader Lou Pérez, depict one of Pérez's own experiences. About one minute into the tune, the chatter and din had subsided and the place was quiet. Lupe stopped speaking and fixed her eyes on vocalist Fernando. When the tune ended, she walked over to the singer and said something to him, then spoke to Gutiérrez.

During a break, Fernando gave Lupe a piece of paper. She sat down, read it, and said, "I'm going to record this." At the beginning of the following set, Gutiérrez told the audience that Lupe was going to sing a duet with Hector Fernando. While she was singing, she kept looking down at the lyrics on the paper as she harmonized to "Jugué y Perdí." It was a memorable performance, a moment in Latin music history that went unrecorded and unmentioned until now. Fernando ended up recording "Jugué y Perdí" for the Pop Art label in 1965. For reasons unknown, Lupe never did. Instead, she recorded a melodic "Jugué y Perdí" sound-alike, "Qué Te Pedí," with Tito Puente. It would eventually be her best-selling record.

After a few successful Tico recordings with La Lupe, Puente could no longer tolerate her antics and unpredictable temper tantrums. In 1968 he canned her. The firing was perpetuated on vinyl during their recording of the tune "Oriente," in which she sang *"Ay ay ay, Tito Puente me botó."* In an effort to keep her in the limelight, Tico President Morris Levy had the Machito orchestra back her on November 16, 1968, the night Levy crowned her Queen of Salsa. But after the dance, Lupe faded into obscurity.

Nine years later, she returned to the New York entertainment world and learned she was still a favorite among record buyers. This writer attended her comeback, and following are my notes about her performance.

"On Sunday, January 30, 1977, four thousand Lupe fans ignored the freezing, five-degree weather, paid four dollars each, and filled every seat at the Bronx's Puerto Rico Theater—which was only about twenty degrees warmer inside than outside. From the second La Lupe appeared on stage until the moment she ended her act, the crowd was hers. Shortly after Machito and his orchestra had the people swaying in their seats to his vocals on 'Buena Noche Cha Cha,' Lupe was introduced as the Queen of Latin Soul. Out of the wings she strutted, in a regal white gown and queen's tiara. For the next forty-five minutes her performance warmed up people who had been so cold they would not remove their coats, hats, and gloves. She sang Latin-rock tunes in English, as well as 'Qué Te Pedí' and 'A Beny Moré'; she ad-libbed jokes (especially about the cold temperatures in the theater); she changed clothes on stage and lifted the skirt of her expensive black, backless gown to show she was keeping warm with wool gray knee socks. To the tunes 'Oriente' and 'Virgen del Cobre,' she *bembé*'d all over the stage.

"Lupe showed class when she sincerely praised Machito's son Mario Grillo (who directed the orchestra) for the excellent job he was doing. She lauded 'El Gran Machito' for his pioneering efforts to popularize Latin music in New York, and Bobby Rodríguez y La Compañia for warming up the audience with an outstanding set.

"Toward the end of the show, Tito Puente made an unexpected guest appearance and brought the audience to its feet with a thunderous ovation. Lupe looked surprised, then began crying uncontrollably when Puente embraced her in a bear hug. Bedlam prevailed for several minutes. Two musicians who'd had a falling out, who hadn't spoken to each other for years, put aside their differences and gave Latin New Yorkers a happy moment. Puente took over the timbales from Mario Grillo and played along to 'Oriente' with La Lupe. They smiled at each other as she sang *'Ay ay ay, Tito Puente me botó.'*"

In the February 4, 1973, edition of the *New York Times*, reporter Don Dove wrote:

> The housewife in Englewood, New Jersey, who shops the local supermarket with her mother is also the official "Queen of Latin Song" with partisan audiences that stretch from New York's "barrio" to Venezuela and beyond. She also has no agent and she answers her own phone. She is Lupe García, known as La Lupe to her fans, and she was one of the headliners Friday night at the second Festival of Latin Music at Madison Square Garden. In 1962, Lupe visited Mexico. After two weeks she relocated to Miami and bought a car that transported her to New York City. New York was not better at first, and part of La Lupe's metropolitan experience was living on welfare. But eventually she was offered a job singing and recording with Tito Puente. It was the start of a lucrative partnership for both. On stage Lupe is nothing if not energetic. She will pull her hair…stamp her feet until they are swollen and even scratch her face in the emotion of the moment. Lupe calls the moment "espíritu santo"! She said, "When I sing I get goose bumps.…In Cuba they called me crazy…they didn't understand at first—that

was part of the trouble…but now with this Latin festival, with all these new clubs opening…this is a chance we've never had before in America.…It makes me very proud."

Months later, on June 18, 1977, another Latin music concert was staged at Madison Square Garden. Here is a fragment of what reporter Pete Hamill wrote for the June 20 edition of the *Daily News*, under the headline "Lean, Mean La Lupe Is Back…Electrifies Aficionados":

> Here she comes across the stage: dressed from chin to toe in orange chiffon, glittering with gold rings and glass baubles, her skin the color of cappuccino coffee. She begins to sing, and fifteen thousand people in Madison Square Garden on a Saturday night rise as one. After many years away, La Lupe was back in town. "I was scared to death," she said. "This is a comeback for me.…I been away…I not know how they like me anymore." She was 125 pounds now, lean and mean. On the final number, she pulled out all the stops: moaning, making a chattering sound with her voice, her right hand kneading her breast, whipping the dress around her, tearing at her hair, the sound orgasmic and huge as the band moved to the end and the song stopped and she was gone."

Three years before this concert, in 1974, Jerry Masucci, president of Fania Records, had assumed control of Tico, Alegre, and Mardi Gras artists such as Tito Puente and Ricardo Ray. He was not interested in La Lupe but recorded her to avoid a lawsuit. Her album *One of a Kind*, released in 1977, was not promoted and received very little airplay. By early 1980 she was living with her children in an apartment on Manhattan's Upper West Side. She was under a doctor's care for depression. She was tormented by overweight, poverty, drug abuse, and the pain of losing her niche in the Latin music world.

La Lupe died on February 28, 1992, at peace, some say, because she had turned to Christianity. Thousands of mourners lined up behind police barricades, waiting for a chance to view the open casket at La Iglesia de Dios at 138th Street and Cypress Avenue in the Bronx. On Friday, November 26, 1999, Puerto Rican artists La India, Eddie Palmieri, Cheo Feliciano, Andy Montañez, and Roberto Avellanet came together for Homenaje A La Lupe (Homage to La Lupe). The tribute, staged at the Roberto Clemente Coliseum in Hato Rey, reverberated for hours with unforgettable Lupe recordings. Her diehard fans hope there will be more tributes in the future.

Originally published in Latin Beat *magazine, May 2000*

TWENTY-EIGHT

TWO CENTURIES OF CHARANGA

I. Beginnings

The origins of popular Latin dance music such as the *son*, rumba, *guaracha*, mambo, and *guaguancó* are mostly African. The *danzón*, Cuba's national dance, was created by musicians who extracted specific elements from the African, Spanish, French, Haitian, and Chinese cultures in Cuba during the nineteenth century.

The roots of the *danzón* are inextricably tied to the *charanga francesa* (an orchestra of strings and flutes), and Cuban music historian Alejo Carpentier has traced the charanga to France. During the sixteenth, seventeenth, and eighteenth centuries, when the Spaniards occupied Cuba, they competed with other European nations for the world market in tobacco and sugar. Africans were transported to the Caribbean as slaves to provide labor. In Haiti, Frenchmen enjoyed their culture, food, and music—the minuet and contredanse—provided by a charanga consisting of a five-key ebony flute, violins, a piano, and a contrabass. As sugar production increased, so did the population of African slaves. Eventually the slaves outnumbered French whites.

In 1791, Haiti's blacks revolted. During the war for independence that followed, many French planters fled with their slaves to New Orleans and to Cuba, where the French contredanse was introduced in Santiago de Cuba. In 1803, the contredanse began its first stage of evolution with the composition "San Pascual Bailón." Havana during this era was picturesque, with two- and three-story white, Spanish-style houses, horses and carriages, cobblestone streets, and the breathtaking sight of sails inflating on tall schooners that crawled through the blue waters of Havana Bay.

It was an era in which white Cubans were full of grandiose ideas. Lovely women wore long dresses and bustles, and waved hand fans. Men strutted in elegant waistcoats, tapered trousers, fluffy white shirts, and boots. During the 1860s, the European bluebloods of Matanzas congregated nightly at El Liceo Artístico y Literario to watch dancers perform the minuet, rigaudon, quadrille, contredanse, and *contradanza española*. The *contradanza* was especially enjoyable because two of the four parts were *"vivo y picante"*—lively and spicy.

In June 1877, Miguel Failde-Pérez, a Cuban mulatto of French and Spanish heritage, improvised on the French contredanse, thereby creating the *danzón*. Failde-Pérez was a resident of the town of Simpson, which is situated in the mountains overlooking Matanzas. Of the four *danzónes* he wrote, "Las Alturas de Simpson" (The Heights of Simpson) was the one he chose to introduce to the public two years later at the Liceo de Matanzas. On this historic occasion, twenty elegantly dressed couples—each including a woman holding a bouquet of flowers—danced to Failde-Pérez's orchestra, which consisted of a tuba, trombone and clarinet, two violins, two tympani drums, and a cornet for the lead parts.

Within months, Failde-Pérez's *danzón* had taken many Cuban cities by storm. But success would have meant nothing to Failde-Pérez if people in Havana—including music professor Raimundo Valenzuela, the city's most popular musician—had not accepted the new music. At the end of a Failde-Pérez concert, however, Valenzuela sprang to his feet and enthusiastically applauded. A newspaper later quoted him calling *danzón* "the typical music of Cuba...it will be our national dance."

Valenzuela wrote *danzónes* for his brass concert band and included parts for saxophones, bass, and bassoon. By 1900, the *danzón* featured the clarinet and cornet for solos. In his book *The Music of Cuba*, published in Mexico in 1946, Alejo Carpentier wrote, "It is said that [Failde-Pérez] invented the *danzón* without realizing that it was not new, that it was always the *contradanza*, which was around many years before." Carpentier implied that the *danzón*'s origins are French. Some books about Cuban music contain documentary evidence that Failde's *danzón* is an extension of the French-derived *contradanza*. Yet the latter never had an Afro-Cuban feel until Failde-Pérez added it, making the music livelier, happier, and more enjoyable.

By the turn of the century, Cuba had more *danzón* orchestras than any other kind. By then, the danzón had experienced only one innovation. Previously, it had contained only two tempo changes, *el paseo* and *la comparsa*. Now, it had three, four, and more. Following Cuba's independence in 1902, the island was increasingly influenced by music and fashion from the United States, as well as the English language. Thomas Edison's invention of the phonograph made it possible in 1909 to record the *danzónes* "María Teresa" and "El Garrotín," by Orquesta Pablo Valenzuela, in the United States. The next *danzón* innovation occurred the following year, when José Urfe, an Afro-Cuban, wrote "El Bombín de Barretto" (Barretto's Derby). "Bombín" was performed by Enrique Peña's orchestra and included a *montuno*, which created another part in the *danzón*. While the first part of the *danzón* sounded like marching music at a parade, Urfe's *montuno* was played at a fast, syncopated tempo and enriched the last part of the tune.

By this time, a new charanga sound had already existed for eleven years, but few people were paying attention. Pianist-composer Antonio Maria Romeu (1876–1955), a white musician of French descent, formed a *charanga francesa* and Africanized it with Afro-Cuban musicians and instruments. Most important, he introduced the piano to this type of orchestra. After a few years he replaced the tympani drum with *pailas* (timbales) and *güiro*. It is been written that when Romeu's *charanga francesa* performed at La Diana, a Havana café, on July 22, 1899, it was the first band of its kind to have done so. Because of the blaring sounds of the tuba, trombone, bass drum, and cornet, many Cubans preferred outdoor concerts over the confinement of a dance hall, and wealthy Cubans avoided entertaining in their homes for the same reason.

In 1923, the soft sounds of Romeu's charanga put Failde-Peréz's *danzón* into the history books to the tune of "El Danzón Antigua." The *charanga francesa* made stars of flutists El Morro, Panchito "Flauta Mágica," and Belisario López. Their stimulating flute *montunos* in Romeu's 1926 arrangement of "Tres Lindas Cubanas" played to packed clubs.

In 1929, Aniceto Díaz (1887-1904), an alumnus of Failde-Pérez's band, combined the *danzón* and the *son* and introduced the *danzonette* via his composition "Rompiendo la Rutina" (Breaking the Habit). The *danzonette* differed little from the *danzón* except that it featured vocalists such as Paulina Alvarez, Abelardo Barroso, Fernando Collazo, Dominica Verges, Joseito Fernández, Pablo Quevedo, and Barbarito Díez.

The following year, Gilberto Valdés, a white musician greatly admired by black Cubans, successfully integrated the African drum into classical music. Valdés, who was recognized for his flute virtuosity and philharmonic compositions, wrote a score that includes music for *batá* drummers. Problems arose at first, because the drummers could not read music. Valdés patiently played the score, signaling where he wanted the drums to enter and where to stop. The result was a sensual, erotic sound that the critics applauded.

In late 1936, bassist Israel "Cachao" López was introduced to Antonio Arcaño, a flutist from Armando Valdés Torres's Orquesta Gris. The following year, Orquesta Gris became La Maravilla del Siglo, a charanga directed by vocalist Fernando Collazo. By now, Cachao was composing and arranging music. The idea for the mambo was audible in his bass lines; "Reza del Meletón" is a good example. The next year, Cachao's brother Orestes López capitalized on the concept by creating the *danzón*-mambo. Until recently, Cachao was not given credit as a contributor to the creation of the mambo. It is an honor he shares with Antonio Arcaño, since Orestes has been quoted as saying he never could have made the mambo without Arcaño's flute riffs.

In 1957 the Arcaño orchestra recorded "Meletón" for the Gema label under the title "Chanchullo." (In 1963, Tito Puente built on the tune's introduction to compose "Oye Como Va"). More evidence of Cachao's contribution to the mambo is provided by 1950s-era Cuban pianist-composer-bandleader Bebo Valdés. "Before Orestes wrote 'Mambo,'" Valdés said, "Cachao wrote and arranged the *danzón* 'Gloria Maceo' for Arcaño...it was every bit as exciting as Orestes's mambo. It was a hit with the dancers. Cachao was the first to write music for piano in a charanga orchestra....Until the time he did it, pianists would read and play violin parts."

In 1938, Collazo's musicians abandoned him to form a cooperative in which each member would receive an equal share of the money earned. Arcaño became the director and changed the orchestra's name to La Primera Maravilla del Siglo.

Until 1937, the Cuban danzón had three parts: the introduction, *el paseo* (meaning "the walk"), and *la comparsa*—the main theme. One summer evening while Orestes sat in on piano, the new sound—*"el ritmo nuevo"*—replaced *la comparsa* in the third part. When the tune ended, Arcaño's sidemen congratulated Orestes. They knew something new had happened, that a new sound had been created. At first the dancers were not impressed; they preferred the *comparsa*. "From now on," said Arcaño, "we will include *esa sabrosura*"—that funky sound—"in all our *danzónes*."

In 1938, according to Cuban musicologist Leonardo Acosta's book *From the Drum to the Synthesizer*, Orestes's 'Mambo' was played for the first time by the Arcaño orchestra over the Mil Diez radio station. Two years later, after witnessing the introduction of the conga drum to Cuban dance music by Arsenio Rodríguez, Arcaño paid Arsenio's brother Quique to teach his band boy, El Colorao, to play congas. Within weeks, El Colorao was thumping a *tumbadora* in Arcaño's band. The new sound of mambo, pianist Jesus López's *guajeos*, Arcaño's rousing flute riffs, and the conga drum sound made Arcaño y Sus Maravillas Cuba's most popular orchestra.

II. From Mambo to *Cha-Cha-Chá*

Flutist-bandleader José Fajardo is a witness that the Arcaño orchestra was the first to play the *danzón*-mambo. He said, "I first heard Arcaño over the radio in 1939 while I was in the Cuban army, stationed at El Rancho Bollero. I immediately became an admirer of his. In 1940 or 1941 he was playing a modern *danzón*."

Another charanga legend had its beginning on September 30, 1939, in the town of Cienfuegos in the province of Las Villas. Four of the eight musicians who debuted as La Rítmica Aragón were Orestes Aragón (musical director), Efrán Loyola (flute), René González (violin), and Orestes Varona (*pailas*).

In 1947, Aragón became ill and named violinist Rafael Lay as musical director. Nineteen-year-old Rolando Lozano replaced Loyola on flute in 1950. Orquesta Aragón broke away from the traditional charanga-*danzón* sound in 1953 by picking up the tempos of mambos, *sones*, and *cha-cha-chás*. Arcaño's group limited itself to playing *danzónes* only, so Aragón's versatility made them more popular. Responsible for Aragón's rise to the number-one spot were the 1953–54 RCA recordings of "El Agua del Clavelito," "Mambo Inspiración," "Tres Lindas Cubanas," "Mentiras Criollas," "Pare Cochero," "Baila Vicente," and "Cero Codazos, Cero Cabezazos."

Between 1954 and 1989, Aragón's music became a favorite in remote parts of the world. Richard Egües, who replaced Lozano on flute in 1954, was the spark plug who fired the Aragón to global popularity. In 1982, Rafael Lay was killed in an automobile accident. Egües replaced him as musical director until he left the orchestra in 1984. Lay's son has been Aragón's musical director since then.

In 1946, Arcaño started experiencing daily stomach pains, which prevented him from playing the flute. He convinced José Fajardo to replace him on Saturdays and Sundays. José Antonio Cruz, a cousin, filled in Mondays through Fridays. "Arcaño's band was hot," said Fajardo. "It is no exaggeration when I tell you it performed 365 days a year.…When dancers heard me blow *montunos*, they screamed, 'Bravo Arcaño!' Arcaño was annoyed by this and would let the people know he was Arcaño, not I. On the evening of March 16, 1949, I had a heated argument with Arcaño and I quit while we were on stage.…Antonio Sánchez, a violinist, ended the evening playing flute.…Our friendship was at an end…I never wanted to see or speak to him again."

Fajardo formed his charanga on September 15, 1949. Radio stations didn't want charangas, outside of Belisario López and Arcaño, on Mil Diez—radio station 1010 AM. On September 29, Fajardo's gig at Club Juan Alberto Gómez de Regla was cancelled. He was told that Arcaño had threatened not to let his band play if Fajardo's did. "In Cuba during the 1940s, all the well known bandleaders didn't like new bands," said Fajardo. "They didn't want competition…they did anything they could to prevent the new bands from working." The newly formed orchestras of Fajardo and Orquesta América got around restrictions by building a respectable reputation among Havana's many societies, such as Los Jóvenes de Atorche, Jóvenes del Silencio, and Los Jóvenes del Muelle.

By 1950, Fajardo was well known in Cuba, even though he was never on radio. Record companies refused to record charangas, since *danzónes* were not selling. Even Arcaño was not selling. Panart Records wanted only trumpet *conjuntos*. When Panart decided to record four *danzónes*, Fajardo's violinist Enrique Jorrín suggested "El Silver Star," "La Engañadora," "Qué Bonita Es," and "Angoa." Then, in 1950, Jesús Goris of Puchito Records recorded Fajardo's "Tengo Una Novia," "Ritmo de Pollos," and two other songs. With each passing year, Fajardo grew in popularity. In 1958 his Panart recording of "El Aguardiente" made him a favorite with New York Latinos. Months later his Panart LP *Ritmo de Pollos* packed the Palladium on Thanksgiving Eve 1958. Hundreds of dancers crowded Broadway and Fifty-second Street, waiting to get in. From the second-floor ballroom one could hear "El Aguardiente," "Ritmo de Pollos," "Hermosa Ofelia," "A Mí Qué," "Fajardo Está de Bala," "Ay Qué Frío"—one swinging tune after another.

For the last three years of the 1950s, Fajardo and Aragón were sizzling hot. In Cuba the demand for Fajardo resulted in three Fajardo orchestras. The charanga "Fajardo" performed in Santiago de Cuba, "Fajardo y Sus

Estrellas" played in Cienfuegos, and "José Fajardo" appeared in Havana. The bands worked morning, noon, and evening, and Fajardo played alongside other flutists for one hour.

In 1961, when the orchestra filled engagements in Japan, Fajardo decided he could not live under Cuba's new political regime. After a three-day engagement in New York, he remained in the city with *güiro* player Osvaldo "Chihuahua" Martínez while the band returned to Cuba. Fajardo and Chihuahua lived in Miami, where Fajardo organized two bands—the second one was in New York. When he decided to live in New York, he took pianist Sonny Bravo and *timbalero* Orestes Vilató with him. During the mid-1970s to early 1980s, Fajardo was a top-billed act. His Sunday-afternoon music battles with Orquesta Broadway are legendary.

It is written that violinist-composer Enrique Jorrín was inspired by Cachao and Orestes López's mambo to create a new rhythm. Jorrín, born December 25, 1926, at Candelario, Pinar del Río, Cuba, was studying violin, harmony, and counterpoint at a Havana conservatory in 1941, at the age of fifteen. Later he performed for Los Hermanos Contreras, La Ideal, Los Hermanos Penalver, and Arcaño y Sus Maravillas before joining Orquesta América in 1954. His experimentation resulted in a change in the third part of the *danzón* in 1949, when he composed "El Silver Star." The song was named after an Afro-Cuban social club whose members were mostly young people. The new sound was not fiery like the mambo; it was laid back, with a one-two-three cadence—a sound produced by the sliding of dancers' feet. He called the sound *cha-cha-chá* and introduced it at a dance salon at the corner of Prado and Neptune while he was a member of Orquesta América.

In 1953 Jorrín's "La Engañadora" became a monster hit in Cuba and began the *cha-cha-chá* era. The following year Jorrín formed his charanga and took off for Mexico. Via Mexican motion pictures, his *cha-cha-chá* sound was enjoyed throughout Latin America. For the last five years of the 1950s, the Cuban charangas of Aragón, Cheo Belén Puig, Orquesta América del 55, Sensación de Barroso, Melodías del 40, Pancho el Bravo, Rosendo Ruiz, Sublime, Felix Reyna, Neno González, Estrellas Cubana, and José Fajardo were in demand because of their *cha-cha-chás*.

In 1957, Cachao's Panart LP *Descargas: Cuban Jam Sessions* exploded in Cuba and set off a tremor that was felt around the world. Cachao, now recognized as the King of the Bass, used his popularity to reveal his Orquesta Típica in two outstanding Kubaney LPs, *Con el Ritmo de Cachao*

(1957) and *El Gran Cachao* (October 1959). Via these recordings he proved that the *danzón*-mambo was very much alive and capable of competing with the *cha-cha-chá*. The outstanding tracks are: "Cuarenta Que Son Uno," "La Cayuga," "Jóvenes de la Defensa Pueblo Nuevo," "Julito y Sus Flautas," "América Club," and "El Príncipe Niño."

In 1963 Cachao left Cuba to live in Miami. In October he was playing bass for Charlie Palmieri's charanga, La Duboney. Following this stint, he worked with the orchestras of Machito, Johnny Pacheco, Tito Rodríguez, Joe Quijano, Eddie Palmieri, Julio Gutierrez, Lou Pérez, and Orquesta Broadway; he also worked with the George Hernández orchestra in Las Vegas for a short time, before settling in Miami. In 1977 Cachao peaked again via two outstanding Salsoul label recordings—*Cachao y Su Descarga 77, Volumes I and II*.

For unexplained reasons, Cachao seemed to go into hibernation in the 1980s. Movie actor Andy Garcia revived Cachao's career on July 31, 1992, with a rousing concert staged in Miami's James L. King Center. The ageless legend is now back on top of the Latin music world, thanks to Garcia's movie production *Como Su Ritmo No Hay Dos*. Since the 1959 Cuban revolution, Orquesta Alimen, Orquesta Revé, and Original de Manzanillo are the only other Cuban-based charangas that have become popular outside Cuba.

III. The American Charangas
Orquesta Gilberto Valdés was the first charanga based in the United States. It was formed in New York in 1952 and included Willie Bobo on congas, Papi Pagani on timbales, Rogelio Valdés on bass, Machucho on vocals, and Alberto Iznaga on one of the three violins. Organizer Valdés was a Cuban-born flutist whose home base was the Bronx Tropicana Club. Although his repertoire was every bit as exciting as Antonio Arcaño's, New York Latinos were not interested in dancing *danzónes* the entire night. So Valdés's charanga lasted less than one year, after which Valdés left the orchestra to Alberto Iznaga.

Iznaga added brass, but the band just didn't catch fire. By the end of the summer of 1954, two out of three recordings in New York were *cha-cha-chás*. Disc jockeys Dick "Ricardo" Sugar and Bob "Pedro" Harris plugged La Playa Sextet's "El Jamaiquino," and it became the first recognized *cha-cha-chá* hit in New York City. The Palladium's big three—Machito, Tito Puente, and Tito Rodríguez—recorded *cha-cha-chá* hits. Puente's "Rico

Rafael Hernández

Gabriel Oller, 1976

Conjunto Caney, 1939. Left to right: (top) Elio Osácar, Rubén Berrios, Ana Marquez, Fernando Storch, René Martínez, (bottom) Tony Negret, Alfonso Reyes.

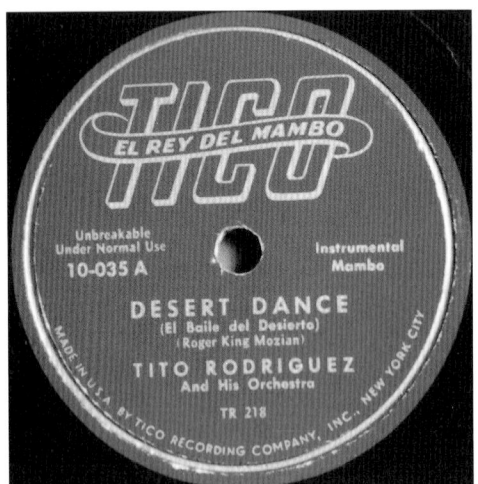

Alberto Socarrás

Augusto Coen, 1940

Vicente Sigler, 1940

Xavier Cugat

Machito, Miguelito Valdés, Graciela, and Mario Bauzá, 1974

La Lupe

Anselmo Sacasas, 1941

Marcelino "Rapindey" Guerra, 1945

Noro Morales, 1946

Joe Loco

Ana Pagani and her father, Federico Pagani, mid-1950s

Tito Rodríguez, early 1950s

José Curbelo, 1947

Frankie Colón

Miguelito Valdés, Juan "El Boy" Torres, and Federico Pagani, 1958

Charlie Palmieri

Tito Puente Orchestra, 1951. Left to right: Gil López, piano; Tito Puente, vibraharp; Amado Vísoso, bass; Vicentico Valdés, vocals; Frank Lopinto, trumpet; Frankie Colón, conga; Jimmy Frisaura, trumpet; Gene Rapetti, trumpet; Manny Oquendo, bongos.

Orquesta Alberto Socarrás, Club Cubanacan, 1934

Charlie Palmieri's conjunto, 1955. Left to right: Charlie Palmieri, piano; Manuel Patot, bass; Pepi Pagani, timbales; Vitín Avilés, vocals; Joe Abbot, trumpet; Joe Cain, trumpet; Aníbal Texeira, bongos.

Joe Quijano Orchestra, 1961

Vicentico Valdés

Santitos Colón

Orlando Marín, Tito Puente, and Jimmy Sabater, 1998

Tony Pabón, 1970

Maria Alicea and Willie Torres with the La Playa Sextet

Joe Cuba

Jerry Masucci

Willie Rosario

Orlando Marín, 1961

Hector Lavoe

Joe Bataan

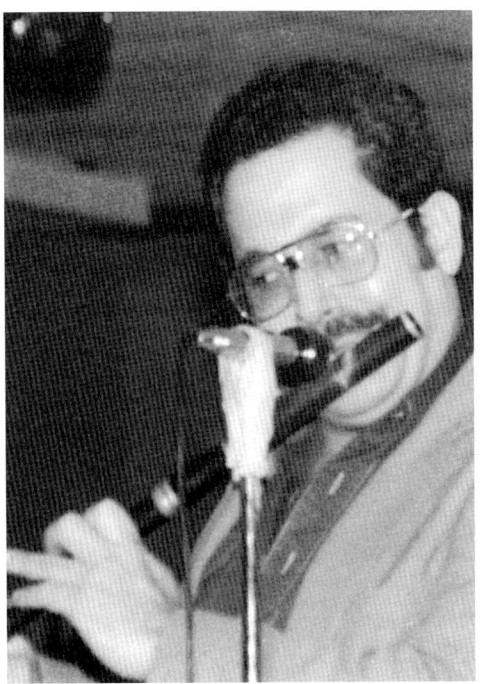
Eddy Zervigón, late 1980s

José Fajardo, 1996

Cheo Feliciano

Vacilón," Rodríguez's "Me Lo Dijo Adela," and Machito's "El Niche" were the songs most often requested. Cuban charangas performed at New York dance halls but failed to turn dancers on because they played a "jumpy" *cha-cha-chá* that lacked the *montuno*'s typical Cuban feel.

Pérez Prado's 1955 million-seller, "Cherry Pink and Apple Blossom White," may have convinced bandleaders that the public liked *cha-cha-chás* without *montunos*. Some of the worst *cha-cha-chás* ever made were recorded in Cuba and the United States during this period; they did not sell. A year later, another Prado *cha-cha-chá*, "Patricia," sold over four million records worldwide.

In 1946, a Cuban conga drummer, Armando Sánchez, left Havana to live in the United States. He formed the second American charanga on March 15, 1956, while in Chicago. Orquesta Nuevo Ritmo consisted of René "El Látigo" Hernández on piano, Cuco Martínez on timbales, Julian Cabrera on *güiro*, Elizardo Aroche and Pupi Legarreta on violins, Victor Venegas on bass, Rolando Lozano on flute, and Rudy Calzado, Leonel Bravet, and Pellín Rodríguez on vocals. In June, Nuevo Ritmo debuted at the Windy City's Petit Lounge. The group conquered Chicago and recorded a 45, "Tumba la Caña," which propelled them to a performance at New York's Palladium on July 15, 1959. Their album *Heart of Cuba*, on the GNP label, was recorded at the Capitol Records studios in New York on August 31, 1959. It seemed that Nuevo Ritmo was on its way to stardom. But suddenly, with no explanation, Armando Sánchez left the group and moved from Chicago to New York.

Meanwhile, Charlie Palmieri had been leading a quintet at Chicago's Ambassador West Hotel. One evening, Palmieri caught Orquesta Nuevo Ritmo at a lounge. "I had no desire to play charanga music until I heard Armando's group," he said. "They sounded great....My contract was going to terminate toward the end of 1958....I thought about returning to New York and forming a charanga in the Aragón mode [but] I couldn't find a flute player."

Back in New York, Palmieri encountered Dominican flutist/percussionist Johnny Pacheco, who was then working with Dioris Valladares's orchestra at the Monte Carlo club on 137th Street and Broadway in Manhattan. Palmieri first hired Pacheco as a drummer, but Pacheco began playing lead solos on flute when trumpeter Mario Cora left for Puerto Rico. Before 1958 ended, Palmieri's charanga, La Duboney, began its quest for recognition. The band had ten musicians on flute, vocals, and strings. By 1961, Palmieri was wearing half the crown of King of Latin Music.

The other half of the crown was on the head of Johnny Pacheco, who had left Palmieri's band to form his own charanga in September 1959. His "Oyeme Mulata" was heard for months throughout Latin New York. After Pacheco's second LP was released, with his rendition of "Caramelos," he and Charlie Palmieri became Latin New York's most popular musicians. The third most popular musician at the time was vocalist Joe Quijano, who stayed right on Palmieri's and Pacheco's heels with great charanga and *pachanga* recordings.

In 1961, Mongo Santamaría assumed the musical director's role for Nuevo Ritmo and included a couple of new faces—percussionist Willie Bobo and saxophonist/violinist José "Chombo" Silva. Mongo recorded five charanga LPs, as well as *Pachanga with Joe Loco*, for Fantasy Records. At the beginning of the charanga-*pachanga* era, only a few flute players in New York were competent enough to blow danceable *montuno* riffs. Flutists Rod Luis Sánchez, José Canoura, George Castro, Pupi Legarreta, Bobby Nelson, Eddy Zervigón, Rolando Lozano, Alfredo López, and Panama's brilliant Mauricio Smith—all were overworked but happy about it. They inspired other flute players like Felix Wilkins, Frank "El Yucateco" Sánchez, Mike García, Danny Hinton Ramos, and a tall, handsome, blond Irishman named Kevin Sweeny, whose *montunos* brought attention to Orquesta Novel in the 1960s.

Lou Pérez, a pianist, flutist, composer, and arranger of mixed Cuban and Puerto Rican heritage, is one of Latin music's legendary musicians. He is an imaginative genius whose recordings are masterpieces. In 1961, his charanga was among New York City's best. Two years later, while performing at a club in Washington, D.C., Pérez was overwhelmed one evening by the virtuosity of an African-American violinist named Eddie Drennon. At Pérez's behest, Drennon moved to New York and fiddled for Pérez until he was lured away by other charangas. In 1969, Pérez recorded *Of Latin Extraction* for the Chateau Madrid label—one of the best recordings of all time. Especially noteworthy is Pérez's arrangement of "Guantanamera," with a piano solo by Irishman Roberto Foley that makes this the most inspiring "Guantanamera" ever recorded.

Perez's creative genius became obvious in 1976 via his Tico LP *Nuestra Herencia*, which depicts the history of Afro-Cuban music. The album cover has a photograph of Pérez, and underneath it he hints about the title track: "Somewhere in a distant time, entwined in the concept of creation, lies our beginning, and that beginning lies in the splendor of Our Heritage."

The recording begins with the sound of thunder, as a way of invoking the beginning of life. African music follows, including *batá* drumming. Then come the Spanish melodies that, blended with African rhythms, resulted in Cuban music. Pérez invented the rhythms of "Tamboleo," "Ritmo Melón," and "El Bom Bon." In the 1987 movie *Dirty Dancing*, actors Patrick Swayze and Jennifer Grey danced to Perez's tune "De Todo un Poco."

From 1961 to 1965, Ray Barretto directed one of New York's most popular charangas and recorded five outstanding albums. Barretto was one of the few Latin musicians to record a crossover hit—"El Watusi," which made the American pop charts in 1962. Meanwhile, when Eddy Zervigón's Orquesta Broadway emerged on the scene in 1963, no one suspected it would be another Arcaño y Sus Maravillas. But Charlie Palmieri knew it. "The last charanga on the scene was Orquesta Broadway....The minute I heard Broadway I loved it....I analyzed it as a group that would not stay unknown for long."

In 1977, Broadway was working fifteen dances a week. Its music battles with José Fajardo and Típica Novel at the Roundtable in midtown Manhattan made that club the place to be on Sunday afternoons. Broadway's popularity made flutist and musical director Eddy Zervigón the King of Latin Music in 1977. Another charanga that got started the same year as Broadway did was Típica Novel. Novel was among New York's top five groups from the mid-1970s until well into the 1980s.

In August 1974, Broadway disbanded, and half of its members moved to Miami. The remaining five musicians formed Típica Ideal, directed by pianist/arranger Gil Suárez. Within one year, Ideal was among the top five bands in New York. Broadway's return to New York in 1975 was the reason Ideal split up. But then, yet another group emerged: on January 7, 1977, the husband and wife team of George and Margie Maysonet debuted their Charanga America at a Brooklyn after-hours club. They were so good that the following week they were performing at the elite Casablanca in the Hotel Riverside. The tune "Ayúdame San Antonio," from their debut LP on the El Sonido label, opened doors to other clubs.

Today, Charanga America is still in demand. One evening during a WBAI fundraiser, popular DJ Al Angeloro was unable to cajole his listeners to make a donation. When he aired America's "Light My Fire," the phone lines started lighting up, and within minutes WBAI was six hundred dollars richer. "Light My Fire" is one of the best recordings of all time, because of Jorge Maldonado's English vocals, Gustavo Cruz's erotic flute riffs, and Eddie Drennon's hip arrangement.

Other great U.S. charangas include Charanga 76, Latin Dimensions, Rolando Lozano's Orquesta Antillana, Chihuahua Martínez's Orquesta Metropolitana, Charanga Casino, Bongo Logic, Charanga De La 4, Hector Serrano's Charanson, and the groups of Rudy Calzado, Susie Hansen, and Alfredito Valdés Jr. For stimulating flute-and-string sounds listen to Charlie Fox's *Just for Fun* (Gema, 1963), George Shearing's *Mood Latino* and *Latin Rendezvous* (Capitol, 1961 and 1962), Eddie Drennon's *Charanga Soul* (Kim, 1980), *Labah Sosseh with Orquesta Aragón* (Disco-Stork, 1980s), all the SAR label recordings, Rudy Calzado's *Rica Charanga* (Caiman, 1986), *Son Primero* (Montuno 1987), Típica Novel's *A Touch of Brass* (TR 1976), Charanga 76's *Manhattan Groove* (US Music, 1984), Orquesta Broadway's *Estrellas del Ritmo* (Guajiro, 1980), *Charanga Colonial* (Neon, 1982), Bongo Logic's *Cha-Cha-Charanga* (Rocky Peak, 1988), Susie Hansen's *Solo Flight* (Jazz Caliente, 1993), and *Africando, Vol. 1: Trovador* (Stern's Africa, 1993).

Above all, the exceptional musicians—those who keep the charanga tradition going strong—include Cachao, violinists Eddie Drennon, Harry Scorzo, Alfredo De La Fé, Ricardo Whittington Jr., Lewis Kahn, Susie Hansen, and Karen Briggs, and flutists Lou Pérez, Eddy Zervigón, Artie Webb, Nestor Torres, Gustavo Cruz, Dave Valentín, Mauricio Smith, Andrea Brachfeld, Connie Grossman, and Karen Joseph. Maybe the charanga was created in France. But its history has been made possible by musicians in Cuba and the United States.

Originally published in Latin Beat *magazine, August, October, and November 1994*

TWENTY-NINE

José Fajardo

In 1972, vocalist Roberto Torres went to New York's JFK airport to meet the flight that was delivering José Fajardo from Miami. Both musicians then rode to a midtown recording studio, where Fajardo's assignment was to improve the flute riffs on an already recorded album. After all the tracks were overdubbed, the musicians eagerly listened to the playback. The flute solos were stunning and typically Cuban; there was no doubt that the Mericana label LP *Latin Dimensions* would be a bestseller. And it was, thanks not just to Fajardo but to Roberto Torres and A&R man Ralph Lew, who knew the Fajardo legend and were sure he could add what was missing.

There was a time during the mid- to late 1950s when Cuba's music world recognized José Fajardo as "La Flauta de Cuba." What makes this story noteworthy is that Fajardo's rivals—Richard Egües, Juan Pablo Miranda, José Antonio Cruz, Joseito Valdés, and Rolando Lozano—were world-class flutists, just like the top Cuban flute players before Fajardo—Panchito "Flauta Mágica," El Morro, and Belisario López, for example. Fajardo's leap from mediocre unknown to Cuba's most popular flutist is a lesson in never giving up, no matter what the obstacles might be.

On October 18, 1919, José was born to Alberto Fajardo and his wife, the former Inez Ramos, in the town of Banes, Pinar del Rio. Papa Fajardo was a clarinetist and the musical director of a woodwind orchestra that only played *danzónes*. He tutored his children—Albert Jr. on violin, daughter Ilda on piano, and José on piano and clarinet. On September 20, 1933, José and his father went to Havana. Young José was going to select a birthday gift but did not know what he wanted. On the way to a Havana department store, they passed a pawnshop and José stopped. His father saw his son's eyes fixed on a five-key ebony flute and immediately knew what José wanted. "After my father bought the flute," said Fajardo, "we headed home on a train. Back home, the first person we went to see was Fernando

Sánchez, a barber who also played flute and clarinet. On a yellow piece of paper torn from a bag, Sánchez drew the positions of the fingers for each note in the scale." At the end of three months, José was blowing scales with the speed of a jet flight. In March 1934, his sister formed La Orquesta Ilda, a juvenile band that included José on clarinet and flute, brother Alberto on violin, Laso on bass, Luis Cuni (Miguelito's brother) on timbales, and Marengo (Cuni's cousin) on vocals.

In 1936 the Fajardos moved to Havana. "Havana was full of talented musicians, and there wasn't work for the majority of them," recalled José. "My cousins were high officials in the Havana police department and the Cuban army, so I put my flute away and became a police officer. From regular patrol duty I rose to a high rank, an assistant to Joaquin Pedraza, whose brother was the chief of police. I was not cut out for police work, so after two years I left the police department to join the army. While stationed at El Rancho Cuhuero, I heard the charanga orchestra of Antonio Arcaño over the radio. He introduced a new sound for that time, *el ritmo nuevo*, which he called "mambo." I immediately became an admirer of his. For the following two years I lived in soldiers' barracks and guarded government buildings, and I was discharged in early 1940. I decided on a music career, so I headed for the La Concha beach resorts of Marianao. I decided I was going to learn from the musicians at the cabarets. I was starting out as a novice and had not touched the flute in three years....I couldn't blow a scale."

After listening to the bands at La Concha, Fajardo approached Oro Mesa, a flutist at the Casanova cabaret, and prevailed on him for instruction. "Night after night, unashamed, I begged the musicians of all the cabaret bands to let me sit in," said Fajardo. "There were bands that wouldn't let me sit in because I sounded horrible. They would say, *'Aquí viene el blanquito, no deje que se siente'* (Here comes that white guy, don't let him sit in). Afterwards, musicians gave me tips on technique, which helped improve my performance. I never got to sleep anytime before 4 A.M. I drove myself because it became more than a challenge to earn my livelihood; it became a question of honor. I vowed I would show those musicians who humiliated me that I could learn to play well. For two years I begged to sit in. I studied and I tolerated the humiliation. I just lived to learn my flute."

One day in 1942, Fajardo was sitting in with Oro Mesa's charanga when the resort owner stopped and listened to Fajardo's solo. It sounded like Arcaño's. Fajardo was scheduled to play two *danzónes* a night for seventy-five cents. He was now in demand and invited to sit in with whomever he pleased, including Oro Mesa, Carlos del Castillo, René Alvarez, Paulina Alvarez, and Orquesta Ideal. By the end of 1946, Antonio Arcaño could no longer play flute on a day-to-day basis. Severe stomach pains plagued him, and his cousin José Antonio Cruz had to substitute from Monday through Friday. José Fajardo played Saturday and Sunday. Arcaño continued to play flute, at times twice on the same evening. But in 1949 he quit. "To this day," said Fajardo, "no orchestra has accomplished what Arcaño's band has. It performed 365 days a year for a few years and many times two and three engagements during the same day. There were recordings, radio Mil Diez daily shows. They visited many towns in Cuba's six provinces. I was the flutist for auditions for radio Sala and Mil Diez."

At the beginning of 1947, pianist Jesús López had a verbal confrontation with Arcaño and decided to leave the band. He urged Fajardo and bassist Cachao to join him. Arcaño found out and talked them out of leaving. One evening, Fajardo lit a fire with his flute improvisations and the dancers behaved as if they were possessed. They applauded and screamed, "Bravo Arcaño!" This annoyed the real Arcaño, who grabbed the microphone and let the dancers know that *he* was Arcaño, even as he failed to acknowledge Fajardo. "On March 16, 1949," said Fajardo, "my *floreos* to Cachao's "Pueblo Nuevo" that incited an explosion of applause and the words 'bravo Arcaño'—which caused Arcaño's heated words and indeed offended me—caused me to quit the orchestra on stage." Antonio Sánchez, a violinist, ended the evening playing flute. The following day, Arcaño visited Fajardo and apologized but could not talk him out of leaving his band. Eulogio Ortiz replaced Fajardo.

"After I left Arcaño, I didn't work steadily," Fajardo remembered. "I worked with Orquesta Neno González before I formed my orchestra on September 15, 1949." That is when Fajardo learned that Arcaño's musicians had left him. "I inherited pianist René 'El Látigo' Hernández, Cachao's nephew Orlando on bass, Chihuahua Martínez on *güiro*, [and] violinists Felix Reyna and Elio Valdés. We debuted September 23…the radio stations didn't want charangas except Belisario López and Arcaño."

On September 29, Fajardo's orchestra was at the Juan Alberto de Regla Hall ready to perform. "I'm sorry, José," said the organization's president. "I am canceling your appearance….Arcaño said he wouldn't play if your band did…and we need Arcaño—he sells out dances."

"In Cuba during the 1940s, all the well-known bandleaders didn't like anyone to form a new group; they didn't want competition," continued Fajardo. "Everything was done to prevent new bands from working. Unfortunately, Cuba had two societies, black and white. Arcaño was adored by both, and newly formed orchestras were not hired on Arcaño's say-so."

The Fajardo orchestra, whose personnel was entirely Afro-Cuban, built a reputation with a stimulating sound that reminded dancers of the modern Arcaño sound. By 1950, Fajardo's radio remotes made him well known throughout Cuba. But despite his newfound popularity, record companies would not record charangas or *danzónes* because they no longer sold—not even Arcaño's. Nevertheless, Panart Records recorded four Fajardo *danzónes*—"El Silver Star," "La Engañadora," Qué Bonito Es," and "Angoa," on the recommendation of violinist Enrique Jorrín. These and other Panart recordings became 45-rpm singles in 1954 and subsequently were included in Fajardo's first twelve-inch LP, *Cha Cha Cha in Havana*.

In 1955, Fajardo visited New York for the first time. He went to the Chateau Madrid to hear the Vicentico Valdés orchestra. He was introduced to Charlie Palmieri, who introduced him to Tito Puente, who introduced him to Count Basie at Birdland. One year later, the Fajardo parade of hits began with the tune "Kikirikí" on the Panart LP *Una Noche en Montmartre*; then came three *danzón* albums on the Puchito label whose passionate music paved the way for a 1957 invitation to appear at New York's Waldorf-Astoria.

The next year, Fajardo's orchestra sent a tremor through North America with his Panart LP *Ritmo de Pollos*. Along with Tito Puente's *Dance Mania, Vol. 1*, *The Best of Beny Moré*, and Rolando Laserie's *Sabor*, this was one of 1958's top-selling albums. Palladium Ballroom promoter Catalino Rolón imported Fajardo's orchestra for the 1958 Thanksgiving Eve dance. This writer and his wife were two of hundreds of people unable to get into the Palladium that night. Responsible for this incredible turnout were the LP's tunes "El Aguardiente," "Ritmos de Pollos," "Hermosa Ofelia," "A Mí Qué," "Fajardo Está de Bala," and "Ay, Qué Frío."

In 1959, flutist Gilberto Valdés returned to Cuba, ran into Fajardo, and told him he had read about the hundreds of dancers stranded outside the Palladium on Thanksgiving Eve. Fajardo remarked that it reminded him of Arcaño's sold-out dances. "Speaking of Arcaño," said Valdés, "what is the problem between you and him? He's an admirer of yours. The other day he said you are one of the best flutists in the world. He's Cuban. He's a brother. How about forgetting the past?" That same week, Valdés and Arcaño made a reservation for dinner at the Havana Hilton. When Arcaño saw Fajardo walk into the dining room, he rose from his chair, smiled, and shook Fajardo's hand firmly. Both musicians embraced each other like brothers who were reunited after a long absence. "During dinner," said Fajardo, "we never brought up the past. We buried it, and to this day Arcaño and I are the best of friends."

Before the year ended, Cuba's new political regime would cause many Cubans to leave Cuba. Meanwhile, Panart released *Saludos from Fajardo*, an album that anointed the bandleader as Cuba's King of Latin Music with its tunes "No Te Quedes Con Las Ganas," "El Relojito Travieso," "La Sallita," "Mi Tonada," "Bonito y Sabroso," and "El Aguardiente", featuring Fajardo on flute and vibraphone.

In 1961, Panart released *Sabrosa Pachanga*. Fajardo's flute riffs to "La Charanga" and "Pa' Coco Solo" were so overwhelming that no one paid attention to another tune on the LP, "Sayonara." The word is Japanese for goodbye, and indeed the song was a message from Fajardo about his plan to leave for Tokyo, Madrid, and New York and never return to Cuba. In 1961, while playing a three-day gig in New York City, his remark about settling in New York alarmed his musicians, who demanded their money and flight tickets back to Cuba. Fajardo remained in New York with Osvaldo "Chihuahua" Martínez. However, he got homesick for the Cuban culture, the sounds of *"oye chico"* and *"oye mi socio,"* and Cuban food. So he moved to Miami in 1963, where Sirena Records released his LP *Fajardo Llegó a Miami*. Again four outstanding tracks—"Fajardo y Su Flauta," "Flor de Amor," "Barco Sin Puerto," and "Año 1963"—made his orchestra one of the most sought after. In 1964, when Columbia released *Sabor Guajiro*, the Panart company in Miami recorded Fajardo's "Guajirando," "Goza el Montuno," "Vamos a Gozar," and "La Flauta de José" for the LP *Cuban Jam Session, Volume 5*, which included "La Charanga," "Busco Una Chinita," "Juaniquita" and "Pa' Coco Solo," four tunes recorded in Havana during 1957 that had not been released. This sizzling-hot album won Fajardo gigs in Puerto Rico during 1965. He told people he was going there to live.

But a year later, he was back in New York performing at La Barraca Lounge in midtown Manhattan for one third of the receipts. Six months later, he and his family moved to Miami and remained there until March 1976, when he returned to New York and participated, along with Orquesta Broadway and Típica Novel, in the charanga spectaculars held at La Maganette, Basin Street East, and the Roundtable. He signed with Coco Records in 1975 and in 1977 recorded *Selecciones Clásicas*, his best selling album to date.

Because of the album's sales, Fajardo's orchestra was invited to perform for Hispanic inmates at the Fishkill Correctional Facility in Beacon, New York, on September 23, 1978. The facility, eighty miles from New York City, received over two hundred visitors for the El Grito de Lares Festival celebrated by Hispanic inmates. For two hours, beginning at 2 P.M., the inmates forgot about the thirty-foot fence that enclosed them on a grass lawn and danced with mothers, wives, and girlfriends to Fajardo's hits. An award was presented to Fajardo because, as a spokesperson for the prisoners said, "He cares about us."

When Coco Records folded, Fajardo signed with Fania. Although his heart and thoughts were in Miami with his countrymen, the work was not. He has remained in the New York area and is never without a job. He lives in Union City, New Jersey, with his family and is a Cuban-American hero. In 1994, for unexplained reasons, his hands began to shake uncontrollably, and he started having difficulty playing flute. An X-ray revealed two colon polyps, which have since been treated with chemotherapy. After recovering, Fajardo was a guest on Chico Alvarez's WBAI radio program *Third World Gallery*. There, Fajardo listened to Alvarez read Eliseo Cardona's words from the April 28, 1995, *Miami Herald*. Cardona quoted Guillermo Rubalcaba, a seventy-year-old pianist and composer living in the Vedado section of Havana (and the father of Latin-jazz pianist Gonzalo Rubalcaba). Guillermo Rubalcaba praised Fajardo and his orchestra for performing the dance rhythms of Havana. *"Dale José un abrazo y dile que lo queremos"* (Embrace José and tell him we love him), he wrote. Fajardo broke down, wept, and could not speak.

Later, promoter Tony "Hardware" Rodríguez organized a tribute for Fajardo at La Maganette, scheduled for February 11, 1996. That day, a blizzard paralyzed New York City, and the mayor urged everyone to stay home until the snow could be removed. Even so, four hundred of Fajardo's friends and fans attended La Maganette to hear his orchestra and Orquesta Broadway. A jam session ensued that included pianist Alfredo Valdés, *timbalero* Nicky Marrero, vocalist Rudy Calzado, and flutists Connie Grossman, Karen Joseph, and Mauricio Smith. Eddy Zervigón, Chico Alvarez, and Rudy Calzado honored Fajardo with testimonials, and he was awarded a plaque by promoter Rodríguez. Fajardo was given the mike, and in his raspy voice he said in Spanish: "I can play this flute, but when it comes to speaking, I cannot. Thank you for this honor while I'm alive. Eddy Zervigón was the only one who visited me and called me. Thank you for this night." [Editor's note: José Fajardo died December 19, 2001.]

Originally published in Latin Beat *magazine, May 1996*

THIRTY

CHARLIE PALMIERI

In the September 13, 1988, *New York Times* obituaries, reporter Jon Pareles wrote:

> Charlie Palmieri, one of the most important pianists in salsa, died of a heart attack yesterday at Jacobi Hospital in the Bronx. He was 60 years old. Mr. Palmieri, the older brother of the pianist Eddie Palmieri, was born in New York City. He worked his way up the circuit of Latin dance orchestras and hotel bands in the 1950s, and led groups in the popular conjunto format, with trumpets in the foreground. On New Year's Eve of 1959, Mr. Palmieri introduced the band Charanga Duboney—a Cuban-style charanga with flute and four violins in the front line—which would change Latin music in New York. Charanga Duboney, featuring Johnny Pacheco on flute, was hugely popular in the early 1960s, sometimes playing as many as four dances a night; it revived the sound of Cuba's Orquesta Aragon and brought a new, streamlined kind of swing to Latin music in New York. While reviving the charanga, however, Mr. Palmieri also helped create forward-looking jazz hybrids. In 1961, he became the musical director for the Alegre All-Stars, a group of Cuban, Puerto Rican and New York Latin musicians who merged mambos with extended jazz solos on albums for Alegre Records. In *The Latin Tinge*, a history of Latin music in the United States, John Storm Roberts calls his sessions "an almost perfect balance of jazz and Latin elements," and says the half-dozen recording sessions spurred "a hundred imitations." Charanga Duboney and the Alegre All-Stars established Mr. Palmieri as a leader in Latin music. He performed with his own groups, as a guest with such jazz musicians as Cal Tjader, and in all-star "piano summit" concerts with his brother. In the 1970s and early 1980s, he divided his time between Puerto Rico and New York, but after moving to the Bronx again he formed El Combo Gigante, a Latin-jazz ensemble featuring vocalist Jimmy Sabater. After a heart attack, Mr. Palmieri was told he would not regain full use of his hands, but he returned to regular performing and recording. His most recent album was *A*

Giant Step. He is survived by his mother Isabel, his wife Esther, his children, Charles Jr., Nina and Karen, and one grandchild, all of New York.

Charlie Palmieri was more than simply one of Latin music's most accomplished pianists or top music arrangers. In the body of the stout, five-foot-eight-inch musician was a heart that always had a love affair with mankind. For years, while this reporter gathered information for stories from many musicians, Palmieri's countless good deeds and warm personality were always mentioned.

"Charlie's beautiful," said vocalist Manny Roman three weeks before he died in 1974. "Working with him was one of my few happy experiences."

"He's the greatest cat in the world," said bassist Eddie "Gua Gua" Rivera, adding, "and he always paid me well." Percussionist Pablito Rosario said that "working in Charlie's band was like learning in college...he was always teaching us things." Vocalist Willie Torres said, "I owe much to Charlie...he made me aware of recording tips which improved my technique."

Israel "Cachao" López, the renowned bass player said, "Charlie gave me my first job in New York at a time I needed it most." Indeed, in 1963 Palmieri asked his bassist Roy Colindres to allow Cachao, then a newly arrived Cuban refugee, to take his place for a few weeks so that Cachao could have pocket money. Colindres, a Cachao aficionado, did so gladly.

A few hours with the warm-natured pianist was enough for me to understand why people loved him as a person as well as a musician. It was a Friday afternoon, May 23, 1975. I had just parked in front of Palmieri's family home on Miles Avenue in the Bronx. The warm sun and the chirping birds flying from tree to tree enhanced the beautiful scene on the Bronx side of the Throgs Neck Bridge. Upon spotting me from a window, Palmieri, dressed in white pants, T-shirt and sneakers, met me with a handshake outside his home and suggested, "How about some lunch?" On the way to the kitchen he stopped, bent down, and patted his dog Bandit, whose stomach was upset. We talked while munching on sandwiches and coffee, stopping occasionally so he could answer the phone. When his wife, Esther, came into the kitchen, Palmieri's words of praise about his brother Eddie trailed off; he got up quickly, took a package from Esther's hands, then warmly kissed her. With his right arm around her, he introduced me to his "favorite girl."

"We met," said Charlie, smiling, "when she crashed my thirteenth birthday party....I impressed her by playing the piano. I knew immediately she was stuck on me."

In 1948, Palmieri waited until October 2 rolled around to marry the former Esther Bartholomey at La Milagrosa Catholic Church in Harlem. Whatever important events took place in his life, he tried to schedule them on October 2, the day he had made his professional debut as a musician.

His own debut in the world occurred on November 21, 1927, at Bellevue Hospital. The previous year, Carlos Palmieri Manuel Villanueva and Isabel Maldonado-Palmieri had left Ponce, Puerto Rico, to live in a tenement at 110th Street and Madison Avenue. By the time Carlos Jr. was six, the Palmieris had moved around Spanish Harlem quite a bit. The family finally settled at 68 East 112th Street, near the corner of Park Avenue. It was here that Charlie first got his taste of music. He would stand on the side of a piano facing his cousin Elsie and watch her perform her exercises. After a few weeks, he played everything Elsie played without omitting a note—and he didn't know how to read music!

One afternoon during 1934, as piano tutor Ramón García was approaching Elsie's apartment, he thought he heard her practicing. When he entered the apartment and saw a boy in short pants sitting on books and pounding out notes, he told the Palmieris about their prodigy. The lessons began, but as Charlie grew older, they began to interfere with the young man's social life. "I was fascinated by the piano," said Charlie, "but I hated to study. I wanted to be with the guys; there is nothing more frustrating than stepping up to the plate in a stickball game, then have your mother call you away for a piano lesson."

When brother Eddie was born in 1936, Charlie was well into his studies of classical music. Every day for a week after Eddie was born, Charlie would leave PS 101 at 111th Street, walk to the hospital, and wait to wave to his mother, who stood by the fourth floor window. He had to see his mother every day to be sure that she and his baby brother were all right. Five years later, he and Eddie were winning prizes in amateur talent shows held at the El San Jose and Campoamor theaters. Eddie sang in an alto voice while rattling maracas, accompanied by Charlie on the piano.

In 1941, the Palmieris moved to 830 Kelly Street, at the corner of Longwood Avenue, in the Bronx. "For six months, I kept riding the subway to Harlem every day," remembered Charlie. "I missed my friends, the games, and the block....Before the year was over, most of my friends joined me in the Bronx and I stopped going to Harlem."

This is when he first heard the recordings of Noro Morales, Anselmo Sacasas, and Gilberto Ayala, and he did a good job simulating their styles. Charlie began attending the big band dances with a guardian. "I cannot explain the thrill I felt when I first saw Machito sing 'Sopa de Pichón' at the Park Plaza. I became a Machito fan for life. Macho, Noro Morales, and Miguelito Valdés were my influences.

"Valdés is the one responsible for elevating Afro-Cuban music to respectability," continued Palmieri. "Prior to his exhibiting it in Cuba, the music was not permitted in hotels or resorts. Miguelito removed the racist barriers by making the music sound exciting with his innovations; his contribution to Latin music may never be equaled."

Wherever José Budet y Sus Tropicales appeared, Charlie would also be present. Johnny Soler, Budet's pianist, always let the youngster play the then-popular tunes "Los Dandys" and "El Carbonero."

On October 2, 1943, Charlie, a cowboy-movie fanatic, was spotted by a taxi driver while waiting in line to buy a ticket at the Prospect Theater. The driver, who was also a musician, told Palmieri that the bands of Budet and Osario Selasie at the Park Palace were short of pianists. Together they drove to the ballroom, where Palmieri was introduced to bandleader Selasie as "the savior of the night." Selasie, eyebrow arched, shook hands with the short teenaged musician and looked as though he thought someone was playing a joke on him. He tested the youth by having him play the well known ballads "Vieja Luna" and "Desconfianza." Afterward, Selasie-smiled and told his men, "We have a piano player."

The next day, news about the teenaged pianist circulated by word of mouth. The following week, after finishing their gigs, pianists from other bands visited the Park Palace to satisfy their curiosity about this reportedly phenomenal event.

In recalling the incident, Palmieri says that "Luis Varona was the first pianist to appear, saying to me, 'Move over kid!' as he pushed me aside. After him came Howie Pagan, then Gilberto Ayala, Rafael Audinot, Noro Morales, and others. I was mad as hell. It turned out to be a piano players' festival. What they did was show me up as a fresh kid."

The seven-month gig with Selasie was followed by a one-and-a-half-year job with Orquesta Ritmo Tropical. In 1946, Charlie graduated from Samuel Gompers High School. He then gave up the steady gig with Ritmo Tropical to freelance with bands that "swung the hip music." He tickled the eighty-eights for Moncho Usera, Polito Galíndez, Bartolo Hernández, and La Playa Sextet, and made his first recording, "Se Va la Rumba," with Rafael Muñoz's band. When pianist Joe Loco decided to leave Fernando Alvarez's Copacabana Samba Band in October 1947 to organize vocalist Jack López's big band, Tito Puente, Alvarez's musical director, began searching for his replacement.

Anibal "Big Tex" Texeira set up an afternoon meeting for Palmieri to meet Puente at Local 802's Union Exchange, a hall on Fiftieth Street between Sixth and Seventh Avenues where musicians congregated daily to get gigs. Puente played with the Copa band until May 1948, when he became Pupi Campo's contractor and musical director.

For Palmieri, 1948 was a memorable year. He married his childhood sweetheart, Esther; his first band, El Conjunto Pin Pin, recorded for the Alba label; and he began his studies of harmony, composition, and arrangement with Otto Chesna. Whatever other mysteries the piano contained, he learned about them from Margaret Bonds, an African-American Baptist-church organist whom he credits for making him a complete pianist.

Palmieri left the Copa in 1951 to do one-nighters with several bands. For three months he toured with the Xavier Cugat band, which was showcasing the very sensuous singer Abbe Lane. During the summer of that year, while a war raged in Korea, Tito Puente's pianist, Gil López, was drafted into the Army. Palmieri replaced him while the sizzling Puente orchestra appeared at the Playhouse of the President Hotel in Swan Lake, New York. Palmieri was Puente's pianist for the Tico recordings of "Mambo Diablo," "Rainfall," and "The Vibe Quintet." He also played instrumentals and did an appearance at Birdland. In December 1953, he left the Puente Band. Within three months, Palmieri joined Jack Paar's *Today* show on CBS as the pianist for the television band of Pupi Campo. Eight months later, when Campo left Paar's show, Palmieri also left to organize a band whose debut at the Palladium Ballroom featured vocalist Vitín Aviles. When the group failed to get work, he became a sideman for the bands of Pete Terrace, Johnny Segui, and Vicentico Valdés.

In December 1956, an offer of steady work at the Buttery Room of the Ambassador West Hotel in Chicago enabled him to form a quintet whose personnel would all sing. The idea arose from Orquesta Aragón's recording of "Tres Lindas Cubanas." Toward the end of September 1958, the Chicago gig was over and Palmieri returned to New York. He worked with Tito Rodríguez's orchestra for a while but just couldn't accept being a sideman again.

"Once you're sergeant, you just don't want to be a private again," he said. One night during October 1958, while Palmieri's small group was working opposite the Dioris Valladares orchestra at the Monte Carlo Ballroom at 137 Street and Broadway, he followed some piercing flute sounds to a room. There he found a tall, thin musician doing the piping. Palmieri watched and listened for a few minutes, then approached the flutist and said, "Hi, I'm Charlie Palmieri."

"I'm Johnny Pacheco," said the other musician, shaking his hand. With these words the beginning of a new musical era was born. Pacheco, a New York City resident of Dominican descent, became Charlie Palmieri's *timbalero*. When trumpeter Mario Cora left the band to live in Puerto Rico,

Pacheco began playing lead solos on flute.

Jack Lewis of United Artists Records realized the commercial potential of this band's appealing sound and persuaded Palmieri to record pop favorites like "Mack the Knife," "The Gaucho Serenade," and "Close Your Eyes." But the tunes that became popular throughout Latin New York were "Chun-Ko," "Bruca Maniguá," and "Yo Tengo un Mate." During the summer of 1959, this red-hot charanga band was in great demand. The name Duboney began to appear on posters for two or three dances on the same evening, since both Palmieri and Pacheco were doing the booking, in different parts of town. The dancers let Palmieri know they felt robbed—that the high price of tickets entitled them to dance to his band for an entire evening. When Palmieri decided that he alone would book the band, Pacheco left to form his own charanga in September 1959.

In 1960, United Artists signed vocalist Tito Rodríguez after the company agreed to Rodríguez's demand that his orchestra be the only one to record Latin music for the label. Rodríguez had nothing personal against Palmieri. After years of rivalry and top-billing feuds with Tito Puente while both Titos were with Tico Records, Rodríguez wanted avoid hassles. Palmieri, unaware of Rodríguez's contract stipulation, was forced to break his contract with United Artists when he refused to record Hawaiian music. "No!" he screamed angrily. He thought United Artists president Jack Lewis and the rest of the world was going nuts. "If the music cannot have the typical Cuban sound, I don't want to record," he insisted. Later, Palmieri was sorry he did not record Hawaiian music. "I may have started another music trend," he speculated.

In 1961, two monster hit tunes from his first Alegre LP, *Pachanga at the Caravana Club,* allowed Palmieri to share the charanga limelight with Johnny Pacheco, who at the time was smoldering hot. "The tunes 'Son de Pachanga' and 'La Pachanga Se Baila Así' are the ones that put us in business," said a smiling Palmieri. At a Bronx dancehall, the Caravana Club on 149th Street between Third and Brook Avenues, the dancers' favorite step was the *pachanga*. A sort of Latin Charleston, this dance had dancers hopping and yelling *"a caballo!"* while waving a handkerchief around their heads.

Some dancers called it the *pachanga,* while others called it charanga. Adding to the confusion were those who called the orchestras *"pachanga* bands." This prompted Joe Quijano and Charlie Palmieri to write "La Pachanga Se Baila Así."

The lyrics told the story: "There's a lot of discussion in Latin communities, where everyone is dancing pachanga. / They say a charanga is the orchestra that plays it / And that what everyone dances is *pachanga,* the rage of the day." After this, all speculations about the dance and the orchestras ended.

In the fall of 1961, Alegre's president, Al Santiago, gathered his musicians at the Bronx Triton Social Club for a jam session. Within a month, New York Latinos had heard about the club on Southern Boulevard, between 163rd Street and Westchester Avenue. From the packed Tuesday night jam sessions came the Alegre All Stars, whose first album, *El Manicero,* was directed by Charlie Palmieri. During their years with La Duboney, flutist Rod Luis Sánchez, violinist José "Chombo" Silva, and vocalists Willie Torres, Felo Brito, and Victor Velásquez contributed to four very good Palmieri albums for Alegre.

In 1965, as the *pachanga*'s popularity started waning, La Duboney's sound changed with the addition of Mark Weinstein's trombone. The alteration didn't go over well during the band's first evening in Venezuela. Dancers let Palmieri know that they wanted the charanga sound back. So before his band performed on the second night, Palmieri wrote six *pachanga* arrangements for three trumpets and two trombones—and for the Venezuelan flutist he hired to appease the dancers.

But mere months after Palmieri tightened up his *pachanga* brass sound, Pete Rodríguez, Joe Cuba, Ricardo Ray, and Johnny Colón started a trend toward the boogaloo and shing-a-ling. For next two years, Palmieri watched as steady work and recording contracts were given to established bandleaders with connections and to young bandleaders whose groups specialized in these new rhythms. Reluctantly, he recorded boogaloos for a 1967 Alegre LP, *Either You Have It or You Don't.* "A recording is a calling card," he said. "It tells the public you are still around. I didn't care for the boogaloo, but I've learned that if you do not follow a popular trend, you're dead."

To the melody of Frank Sinatra's 1965 hit "It Was a Very Good Year," Palmieri sang, "1969, it was a very dead year," then burst out laughing. His band didn't receive one offer to play in 1969. On the brink of a nervous breakdown that year, a dispirited Palmieri confided to Tito Puente that he could no longer tolerate the long periods of unemployment. Puente dissuaded him from moving to Puerto Rico by making him musical conductor for the television show *El Mundo de Tito Puente.* "Tito's proposal was a lifesaver," Palmieri said. "It kept me busy writing and arranging for the show." When the television series ended, a three-year teaching job with Community School District No. 7 of the New York City Board of Education paved the way for Palmieri to teach Puerto Rican Studies and Latin Folkloric Musical Heritage at the City College of New York.

During the early 1970s, the Cheetah was the in place for dancers. But very few people knew what was going on behind the scenes, where the war for top billing was smoldering. To appease the bandleaders, dance promoter Ralph Mercado allowed the Fania Records artists to rotate the billing. Anyone outside the Fania family had to take second billing or not work at all. The quest for the top line of an advertisement or marquee was described in the July 1973 issue of Izzy Sanabria's *Latin New York* magazine. Popular bandleaders were asked, "Is top billing really important?" Charlie Palmieri replied, "It is necessary because it means financial success. Whoever has a hit record should get top money and top billing. Rotating the billing will not help me. If a club hires me once, it will hire some other band twenty times. I'm not in the clique. Understand that this practice is not personal. It's business. I see no solution because there are too many bands and very few clubs to work at. Interest must be created in many cities outside of New York so bands can travel, keep employed and get top dollar. Our city should sponsor a two-week carnival in Harlem or the Bronx every year like those in South America, Panama, Cuba—you know, a Latin Woodstock. Top billing means money to me, and I look forward to the day I knock Puente and my brother Eddie off the top line. If I can't do it on merit, I am not going to cry about it."

Charlie Palmieri's life was marked by many highlights. One of the biggest happened at the *Lo Dice Todo* concert held at New York's Avery Fisher Hall on March 7, 1977. The outstanding, virtuoso performances of Cachao, Charlie Palmieri, and flutist Gonzalo Fernández brought tumultuous standing ovations. It was a once-in-a-lifetime concert; you had to have been there to see it, hear it, feel it—and even then I'm not certain you would have believed it. It began when ten violinists, including Alfredo De La Fé, Eddie Drennon, and Pupi Legarreta, walked to their seats and sat down. Master of ceremonies Roger Dawson's voice boomed as he announced the arrival of Charlie Palmieri. The white spotlight caught him standing near the piano, smiling and waving to the applauding crowd. After Cachao was introduced, the renowned bassist nodded to Gonzalo Fernández, whose flute began the introduction to the *danzón* "Jóvenes del Ritmo." At a break in the piece, the violinists began swinging a syncopated mambo phrase. At this, bodies swayed and the musicians looked ecstatic, with eyes closed in euphoric concentration. In front of me, Cachao, the composer and arranger of the tune, hunched slightly, plucking strings on his bass, smiling and glancing occasionally toward Charlie Palmieri, who was playing with the gusto of the Phantom of the Opera plotting revenge. When the tune ended, zealous fans stood up and offered thunderous applause.

"Adelante," another Cachao tune and arrangement, followed. It grew more and more exciting, beginning with the melody, returning to the introduction, then introducing a second melody and finally a mambo. The spotlight caught Palmieri leaning forward on his stool, his fingers moving in a blur on the keys. After his fiery solo there was a break, followed by pizzicato strings and flute *montunos*. The concert hall was in a furor. When the tune ended, feverish fans rocked the auditorium. Backstage, Palmieri was in a jolly mood. "It was a gas," he said. "I love this type of music and I admire Cachao. It was a labor of love." Following the concert, the Salsoul LP *Cachao 77* was released.

Palmieri moved to Puerto in early 1980, for many reasons. "The most important was that I just could not tolerate the frigid temperatures of New York," he said. "The New York Casino was my home base. My band worked three and sometimes four times a week. But we were not fully compensated for our efforts. Agents and club owners do not like to hear about traveling expenses, uniforms, the band boy who lugs the music and instruments, and the cost of living. I lost many talented sidemen because I could not meet their salary demands. Well, that all changed for me in Puerto Rico. I earned the same money for a Saturday night in PR that I earned in four New York gigs."

On February 24, 1983, Palmieri was in New York to speak to his brother Eddie about a concert in an outdoor stadium in Puerto Rico that Winston cigarettes was going to sponsor. It was 11 P.M., and Charlie was sitting in the kitchen playing chess with his son Charlie Jr. All of a sudden, Charlie was gasping for air. His son's quick thinking saved his life; he rushed his father to Jacobi Hospital in the family car. An EKG showed that Charlie had suffered a mild heart attack, and he was released. Father and son were back at their chess game when new pains made Charlie feel as though he was choking.

"I felt an instant pain on the top of my chest," he said. "Then I got a terrible pain under my arms. I tried to use my hands and arms. I was unable to do so. I collapsed. I tried to stand, to lie down. No matter what I did, the terrible pain would not go away. I was sweating profusely. My son's quick thinking saved my life a second time in the same night. Eight days of the six weeks I was in the hospital were spent in the intensive care unit.

"The heart attack changed my outlook on life. During the last three years, I have improved my music skills in Puerto Rico. I do not want to play the nightclub circuits anymore. I want to live at a slower pace, become involved in recordings, become a producer, teach, write, be more of an arranger. But not a bandleader; being a bandleader is tough. Many times I would be the fourth band on the bill, and we started at 2 A.M. I do not want to double up [play two dances on the same night] anymore."

Charlie Palmieri began to live in a more relaxed way. He performed with the orchestras of Joe Quijano, Orlando Marín, and El Combo Gigante, which he co-led with vocalist Jimmy Sabater. On Friday evening, January 6, 1984, Palmieri was honored by New York's Latin music industry in an event staged by the Angel René Committee at the Club Broadway. It was one of his best moments. Over two thousand Palmieri aficionados spent a night recognizing one of Latin music's most beloved musicians.

In May 1988, Palmieri received a phone call from the proprietor of the Bass Clef, a jazz club in London, England. "What a break!" he said. "I took thirty charts, which included 'Picadillo,' 'María Cervantes,' and 'Mambo Show.' During the first two days of my seven-day stay, I rehearsed the band of King Salsa, headed by *conguero* Robin Jones. I took in all the sights. [The London performance] was a success that will allow more musicians to go there to play salsa and Latin jazz." While Palmieri appeared on Al Angeloro's Saturday night radio program *Montuno*, he was told in Robin Jones's presence that Palmieri, Johnny Pacheco, and Louie Ramírez would be going the Bass Clef in October.

At 1 P.M. on September 12, 1988, I received the first of many phone calls at my job, informing me that Charlie Palmieri had died of a heart attack that morning at Jacobi Hospital. Hours later, I opened my mail. One letter was an invitation that read, "Charlie Jr., Karen and Nina Palmieri invite you to a surprise ceremony as their parents Esther and Charlie renew the vows of marriage in celebration of their 40th Wedding Anniversary Sunday, October 2, 1988."

When Charlie Palmieri was born, life became a bit happier. Many people's lives were a little richer because they crossed Charlie's path. More important than his fame were his warm personality and his love affair with mankind. Nature has a mysterious way of rewarding people who merit it. I believe it rewards people whose concern for others' well-being rings with sincerity. This concern was evident throughout Charlie's life. It was there when he stood outside the hospital to await his mother's wave, signaling that she and Charlie's brother Eddie were OK. It was there when he asked me if I'd had lunch, when he thought about his dog's upset stomach, in the tenderness and love he expressed toward his wife and children, in the recording tips and advice for better ways to do things that he gave his young sidemen, in his constant attempts to create happy endings. But Charlie would never brag about his wonderful character. During our one-and-a-half-hour interview, he spoke at length about his sidemen and music colleagues, but not once did he mention the many musicians he had helped. They had to tell me themselves.

A week after his death, Palmieri's childhood friend Joe Quijano organized a tribute, scheduled for November 6, whose proceeds would ease Esther Palmieri's monetary obligations. An eight-by-ten-inch ad circulated through dance halls all over New York City:

> A performance by bandleaders, musicians, colleagues and friends of the late Charlie Palmieri to benefit Charlie's widow will be performed at the Puerto Rico Theater. I, Joe Quijano, as coordinator of this memorial event, undertake this project for the sole purpose of seeing that Charlie's name is not taken commercially by others, and that the moneys received go directly to his widow, Mrs. Esther Palmieri, as a show of gratitude for all that Charlie gave to us—both as a musician and a great human being. The expenses of the rental of the Puerto Rico Theater, the lights and sound will be paid by your contribution. The fee at the ticket booth will be $10.00 per person. In addition, I'm asking for all musicians we know to bring their instruments so we can play together—as a loving message to our great friend in heaven. Make your donation by check or money order made payable to: Mrs. Esther Palmieri.

For four hours, more than one thousand people enjoyed music provided by the cream of New York Latin musicians. Esther Palmieri was handed a check for a generous sum to cover her immediate expenses. Her beloved husband was buried at the Bronx's St. Raymond's Cemetery.

For years, bold letters on Charlie Palmieri's LP covers had screamed *El Gigante del Teclado, Vuelve el Gigante,* and *Adelante Gigante.* He was indeed a giant of the keyboard, drawing applause from everyone—fans, critics, and fellow musicians. Listen to Palmieri's recordings of "Coco," "El Pan Sobao," "El Guaya Catalina," and "El Tema de María Cervantes," and you, too, will never forget this man with outsized talent and enormous heart.

Originally published in Latin Beat *magazine, August and September 1999*

THIRTY-ONE

JOE QUIJANO

In 1961, a flute-and-violin sound created in Cuba enabled American bandleaders Johnny Pacheco and Charlie Palmieri to become Latin music's most popular musicians. Aficionados called this type of orchestra a charanga, while others referred to it as a *pachanga*—a word coined by Cuban vocalist Eduardo Davidson. Davidson's recording "La Pachanga" became a hit in Cuba. Meanwhile, in the Bronx, Pacheco's orchestra was packing the Triton Ballroom and Hunts Point Palace on Southern Boulevard with its renditions of the tunes "El Güiro de Macorina" and "Oyeme Mulata." Reportedly, it was at the Triton that dancers created steps to the *pachanga*. The new moves were unique: they required people to act as though they were skating, while hopping, twirling handkerchiefs above their heads, and crying *"a caballo!"* The *pachanga* became all the rage.

In 1961, Puerto Rican vocalist/bandleader Tito Rodríguez's United Artists LP *Let's Dance the Charanga* was released and resulted in the dance step known as charanga.

During the summer of 1961, Joe Quijano, in his second year as a bandleader, was in the basement of Charlie Palmieri's Bronx home composing new tunes. Quijano would utter words, and Palmieri put them to melodies. As Palmieri sat at a piano listening, Quijano sang out:

> *Hay una discusión en el barrio*
> *de como se baila la pachanga.*
> *Hay una confusión en el barrio.*
> *Se creen que charanga es pachanga.*
> *Una charanga es la orquesta que está de moda.*
> *Y una pachanga es el baile que se baila ahora.*
> *Ahora no hay discusión en el barrio.*
> *Se sabe lo que es charanga.*
> *Ahora ho hay confusión en el barrio.*

Se baila lo que es una pachanga.

There's an argument in the neighborhood
about how to dance the *pachanga*.
There is confusion in the neighborhood.
People think charanga is *pachanga*.
But charanga is an orchestra.
And *pachanga* right now is the dance.
Now there's no more arguing in the neighborhood.
Now people know what charanga is.
Now there's no confusion in the neighborhood
Dancers dance the *pachanga*.

Weeks later, Quijano's Conjunto Cachana—with Charlie Palmieri and Hector Rivera on piano, Lou Goicochea on congas, Joe Rivera on bass, Luis "Chicky" Pérez on bongos, the trumpets of Fania All Stars members Herman González and Bobby Valentín, and the chorus of Willie Torres, Paquito Guzmán, and Quijano—recorded "La Pachanga Se Baila Así" for Columbia.

After the popular DJ Dick "Ricardo" Sugar aired the song during his Saturday afternoon show, Conjunto Cachana soared to popularity almost overnight. The five most popular bandleaders then were Johnny Pacheco, Charlie Palmieri, Joe Quijano, Tito Puente, and Tito Rodríguez. Quijano's *conjunto* was performing at all of New York's and Puerto Rico's popular ballrooms. Quijano and Palmieri were credited with clearing up the confusion about charanga versus *pachanga*. Their contribution aided the development of Latin music in New York City.

For the last forty years, dancers have enjoyed Joe Quijano's music. What many do not know is that as a social activist, he has been one of the rare musicians to organize and coordinate tributes for musicians in their twilight years who are in need of funds. Although he has never had problems with liquor or drugs, he has directed programs that helped abusers. And in 1983, Quijano proposed and coordinated *The Tito Puente Roast*, seen on a New York City Spanish-language TV channel. The film introduced the Tito Puente Scholarship Fund.

Quijano has been the proprietor of his own recording company, Cesta Records, and the owner of an elite supper club in Puerto Rico. In Colombia he is a star attraction, and currently his recordings are aired daily throughout that country.

Despite all his individual accomplishments, the thing that has made him proudest is his Puerto Rican heritage. Quijano, like his hero Noro Morales, has recorded tunes whose titles are a tribute to Puerto Rican culture—for example, "Mayaguez," "Cataño," "Barrio Obrero," "Bayamón," "En Mi Viejo San Juan," "Puerta de Tierra," as well as his Puerto Rican Christmas album, which contains the *seis con décima* "Un Jíbaro en Nueva York."

Joe Quijano's life began on September 27, 1935, at Puerta de Tierra, Puerto Rico. "My hometown," he said, "had the hippest jukeboxes....Every day I heard Panchito Riset, Beny Moré, and the recordings of Cuban and Mexican artists."

In October 1941, he and his mother relocated to New York to live with an uncle at 1016 Simpson Street. In 1948, at age thirteen, Quijano attended PS 52, a junior high school where he befriended Orlando Marín and Eddie Palmieri, two Puerto Ricans who years later would become famous musicians. The three youngsters were already listening to the music of Noro Morales, Machito, Marcelino Guerra, Antonio Arcaño, and Arsenio Rodríguez.

By 1950, the trio of friends had become a quintet. Within two years after that, the group began calling itself the Orlando Marín Conjunto. Its first four charts were "Abaniquito," "La Toalla," "Sun Sun Babae," and "El Cumbanchero." With the addition of other stock arrangements, the Marín Conjunto debuted at the Bronx's Hunts Points Palace, where each musician earned one dollar after five hours of work.

In 1952, Marín and Quijano met Mike Collazo, the drummer for Tito Puente and Tito Rodríguez, at the High School of Industrial Arts. Collazo's percussion tips helped them to drum. The following year, Eddie Palmieri directed the group for four months until he left to join Johnny Seguí's *conjunto*. Marín resumed his bandleader role, and the group started performing at St. Athanius Church, Sunnyside Gardens, the Stardust Ballroom, and La Tropicana.

In 1956, Quijano was employed by the Trans-Lux Corporation, which created displays for the fronts of theaters using cutouts of movies. During his lunch hour, Quijano would eat next door at the Palladium Ballroom, where he saw the bands of Tito Puente and Tito Rodríguez rehearsing.

"Before the year ended, I was in Cuba for two weeks," said Quijano. "I was overwhelmed by the Senen Suarez sound, which consisted of one trumpet, a flute, and a rhythm section....Back in New York, I approached Charlie Palmieri and told him of my idea of utilizing a combination of two trumpets and a rhythm section playing a charanga feel, with singers in unison, similar to the Orquesta Aragón sound."

In early 1957, the Marín Conjunto auditioned at the Palladium Ballroom. One tune they performed was the bolero "La Gloria Eres Tú," sung by Quijano. Palladium promoter Catalino Rolón liked the sound of the group and gave it gigs. When July rolled around, Quijano left Marín's band to join the orchestra of Alfredito Levy at a resort in New York State's Catskill Mountains. Levy, who was proficient on timbales and vibes like his idol Tito Puente, was sizzling hot then. Marín acquired vocalist Armando "Mandin" Vega, who recorded "Mi Mambo" for the Plus label. Quijano landed a job with Tico Records, the label that had Tito Rodríguez, Machito, Pete Terrace, and Noro Morales under contract.

"Ralph Seijo, Tico's A&R man, recorded me," said Quijano. "My sound did not appeal to him, and the recording was never released....Then, in 1959, United Artists released Charlie Palmieri's album, which kicked off the charanga-*pachanga* era....I went to work for Good One-Stop, a wholesale distributor servicing retail stores and jukeboxes....I convinced the owners to bankroll the recordings of 'Rumba en Navidad' and 'Descarga Charanga,' which were released on the AQA label...then things started to happen for me....I owe Charlie Palmieri my success as a Latin music artist...his melodic arrangements sold my recordings....I supplied lyrics like 'Pachanga 'n Changa,' some silly things....None of the lyrics told a story...they were just *coros*. I remember the day Charlie and I were discussing the difference between *pachanga* and charanga....Tito Rodríguez's album *Para Bailar la Charanga*...this is why we composed 'La Pachanga Se Baila Así' and ended the confusion."

After that summer day in 1961, Quijano recorded thirty-seven more albums, using top arrangers such as Charlie Palmieri, Hector Rivera, Bobby Valentín, Johnny Conquet, Paquito Pastor, Luis "Perico" Ortiz, Charlie Fox, and René Hernández. The work puts one in mind of La Sonora Matancera, and of Orquesta Aragón's chorus. They remind listeners that the Joe Quijano orchestra created one of the popular sounds of the 1960s.

Originally published in Latin Beat *magazine, August 1998*

THIRTY-TWO

EDDY ZERVIGÓN

There is one musician in New York whose orchestra has never failed to pack dance halls since the early 1970s. Though his photo has appeared in magazines fewer than ten times in the last three decades, he is recognized wherever he goes and is always accorded the adulation that superstars receive. His name is Eddy Zervigón. For thirty years he has stood at center stage, blowing rousing flute *montunos* that time after time have left dancers in a state of euphoria.

Not since the early 1940s, which saw the legendary Antonio Arcaño, or the 1950s, when Rolando Lozano, Richard Egües, and José Fajardo thrilled Cubans, has there been a flutist capable of arousing so many passions with such libidinous music. With his flute perched on his lips, he bends, stands erect, occasionally closes his eyes, and wobbles, while his ebony flute emits high, staccato but melodic phrases. For Cubans, his music evokes pleasant memories of the swank cocktail lounge at the Hotel Nacional, the saltwater aroma of El Malecón, the palm trees on the gray sandy beaches of La Concha and Varadero, *danzón* and *guajira* music floating from the cantinas along El Paseo del Prado, and the flickering neon lights of the Havana skyline.

The group responsible for these vicarious feelings is Zervigón's Orquesta Broadway. "Como Camina María," "Año 1965," "Yo Sí Como Candela," "Tú No Me Quieres," "Guaguancó a Todos Los Barrios," "Pa' Africa," "Moanga," "Isla del Encanto," and "Fefita," as well as the emotional cry of vocalist Roberto Torres on "La Sitiera," are just some of a long list of Broadway recordings that have provided mental journeys to Cuba. The first step toward the creation of Orquesta Broadway occurred on July 7, 1940, in Güines, Cuba, when twin sons Eddy and Rudy were born to Pedro Zervigón and his wife, Carmen Ayala-Zervigón.

In 1954, when Eddy was thirteen, he gave up a three-year study of the trumpet for the piccolo "because it was smaller and easier to carry." A priest at a Catholic monastery taught him to play the instrument. One year later, when Orquesta Aragón played a dance in Güines, Monterito, a drummer for Orquesta Melodías del 40, introduced young Zervigón to Richard Egües. Following Egües's advice to learn the flute, Zervigón engaged Mulatón, a seventy-year-old retired flutist, who taught him the rudiments of the instrument. Two years later in Havana, Eduardo Egües (Richard's father) began polishing up Zervigón's performances with advanced flute instruction.

In 1958, Eddy and his twin, Rudy, a violinist, co-led La Ideal. When José Fajardo left Cuba in 1960 to live in Miami, violinist-composer Felix Reyna inherited his band. He renamed the group Las Estrellas Cubanas, and Zervigón filled Fajardo's role. During the next two years, Fidel Castro's policies propelled the exodus of thousands of Cubans to other countries. Zervigón also decided to leave. Not even top-dollar offers to play with Orquesta Sensación or Neno Gonzalez Jr. were enough to change his mind. In April 1962, he left Havana for the United States, worked four months in Miami with his band Ritmo de Estrellas, then left for New York City on July 29, 1962. He roomed as a boarder in a first-floor apartment at 535 West 135th Street, near the corner of Broadway. In the same building lived Roberto Torres and Gil Suárez, two musicians who would later play important roles in his musical life.

Zervigón's first New York job was with Johnny Pacheco's band at the Palladium Ballroom in August 1962. One-nighters with the orchestras of Arsenio Rodríguez, Joe Valle, Lou Pérez, Pupi Legarreta, Alfredito Valdés, and others convinced him to form his own band. A search for sidemen did not extend far from his apartment. Within a three-block span lived vocalist Monguito "El Único" Quian, bassist-vocalist Adalberto Santiago, *timbalero* Kike Vélez, *conguero* José Valiente, violinists José Andreu and Rudy Zervigón, pianist René "El Látigo" Hernández, and the co-leader of the group, vocalist Roberto Torres. Torres's proposal to name the band El Conjunto Güines was not accepted, since most of the musicians were not from that Cuban town.

All-day rehearsals in Zervigón's room made the apartment building a popular spot in the neighborhood. At times, small crowds would mill around the first-floor window just to listen to the overwhelming flute and violin riffs accompanying the rousing Torres incantations. "Eddy and the boys sounded good," recalled pianist Gil Suárez, who was working with Johnny Pacheco at the time. "That little room was the birthplace of his band." Unable to agree on a name for the band, they debuted as La Charanga at the Bronx's Colgate Gardens. The in place at the time was Max Hyman's Palladium Ballroom. To work there, a band that was unknown had to sell five hundred tickets for its dance. On the evening Torres and Zervigón picked up the tickets, promoter Catalino Rolón suggested that they call their group Orquesta Broadway, since most of the band's personnel lived near the avenue. During the same evening, the co-leaders met two brothers who were working with another band on the bill. Ira and David Herscher, two musicians from Brooklyn, filled the vacant piano and bass spots.

In early 1963, the following musicians played the Palladium Ballroom as the original Orquesta Broadway: Eddy Zervigón (flute), Roberto Torres and Edmundo Koppe (vocalists), Hector Zeno (timbales), Johnny Palomo (conga), Mike Martínez (*güiro*); Rudy Zervigón and Abraham Norman (violins), David Herscher (bass), and Ira Herscher (piano and *tres* guitar). The legend of Broadway began with the 1964 Gema label album *Dengue*, in which the tune "Como Camina María" established them as the saviors of the waning flute-strings-and-vocal sound. For three years, beginning in 1965, this red-hot charanga made Basin Street East, an East 48th Street nightclub, the place to be on Sunday afternoons.

During that thirty-six-month span, Broadway's Musicor label albums *Arrímate Pa' Ca, Tiqui, Tiqui,* and *Do Their Thing* solidified the group's standing as one of New York's ten best orchestras. Speaking about why he changed his charanga sound in 1965, Charlie Palmieri said: "I counted fifteen charangas in the city. The last charanga on the scene was Orquesta Broadway. Now I was getting so much money. Here came a brand new charanga that sounded excellent. The minute I heard Broadway, I loved it. I think they were on the right track. They had good numbers, they were sincere in what they were doing, and they were working for little money. It was a just-starting band. So I was getting a thousand dollars, and they were getting three hundred because they were unknown. I analyzed it as a group that would not stay unknown for long. I thought that La Duboney [Palmieri's charanga] had [had] its day, and Orquesta Broadway was influential in my decision to disband."

Something unexpected happened during Broadway's 1968 recording of the album *Do Their Thing* that made it a popular seller. Prior to recording the boogaloo "Black is Black," Ira Herscher instructed vocalists Roberto Torres and Elliot Romero for weeks in the pronunciation of the song's English lyrics. On the day of the recording, Romero and Torres faced each other and, in a markedly Spanish accent, sang the following words into the overhead microphone: "Blok ees blok, I wan my jeva bock. / Eef gray ees gray, sin she wen a way, yea men. / Wha ken I do, cuz I-I-I-h-h-h...." At this point, Romero broke into an uncontrollable laughing fit, which compelled Torres and Ira Herscher to break up also. The unexpected spontaneous laughter was what producer Al Santiago banked on to sell the record. He was right.

In 1970, Ira Herscher temporarily relocated to Los Angeles, where his brother David was living. Gil Suárez replaced him. In 1972, Ira was back in New York and was contacted by an African friend, who proposed a trip to Africa. With the upcoming trip on his mind, Zervigón changed the title of Pedro Espinosa's tune "Oye Mi Son" to "Pa' Africa." The bandleader agreed with Norman Abraham's suggestion that pianist Paquito Pastor arrange the tune. Espinosa sang the melody and lyrics for a cassette recording that Abraham delivered to Pastor. "Norman and I sat down at my piano," recalled Pastor, "and I began writing out ideas and background music, like what the flute and violins were going to sound like....Norman gave me violin cues....The whole idea was to keep the composer's concept and build a crescendo of excitement up to the *montuno*....The guitar and *coro* were figured out at the studio....Ira's suggestion that he come in with *el tres* after the break was a stroke of genius." The tune, from the All Art label LP *Como Me Gusta*, was one of the most listened to throughout 1972 and 1973.

At 6 P.M. one Saturday in September 1973, Orquesta Broadway boarded an Air Afrique flight at New York's Kennedy Airport and arrived in Abidjan, the principal city of the Ivory Coast, ten hours later. At the airport a television camera crew caught each musician leaving the plane. The musicians formed a semicircle, and vocalist Vicente Consuegra led the others in singing "Pa' Africa"; a videotape of the performance was shown on television hours later. Then they boarded a bus and headed for the plush Hotel Ivoire. During an open-air concert, Suarez's Beethoven's Fifth Symphony introduction of "Quinta Guajira" elicited a tumultuous roar of applause and shouts. Mike Amitin, the tall, slender, blond bass player, said "It's a trip to hear Orquesta Aragón's and Orquesta Broadway's recordings over African radio....The people treated us as if we were the Beatles or James Brown." While reminiscing about the first African trip, Amitin broke into a smile when he mentioned how Broadway's musicians communicated with the French-speaking Africans. "Most French words end in the pronunciation of *ay*, as in *Française* [frahn-say], *enchanté* [on-shahn-tay], et cetera," said Amitin. "Well, the guys were saying to the Africans, 'You like musicay Cubanay? Me live near Ocean Parkway, me drive Chevrolet coupé, you like 'Quinta Guajira,' OK?" While the Africans looked at the musicians as if they were crazy, the French-speaking Amitin, doubled over from laughing, could not control the tears that streamed from his eyes. Two months later the band played in Paris, France, for one week.

After the trip, Eddy Zervigón relocated to Florida. "The warm climate,"

Zervigón said, "was the reason for moving to Miami." His answer was partially true. But the real reason was something he tried to push out of his mind—a horrifying experience in New York City that took place in early 1974. From a reliable source, this reporter learned that the bandleader had almost been killed by two muggers on the day of New Year's Eve, 1972, when he was attacked in the elevator of his apartment building at 36 Laurel Terrace in upper Manhattan. He valiantly fought off the muggers, who were trying to rob him, and was slashed on his wrist while fending off a knife thrust. The assailants escaped. That evening, a shaken Zervigón played a dance at the Riverside Plaza Hotel and welcomed in the New Year with a bandaged wrist. Although he mentioned a few times after the incident that he wanted to leave New York, he did not.

Then, in February 1974, he experienced a tremendous shock when he learned that his three-year-old son was almost killed by an apartment robber. One day, an elderly woman who had been his son's babysitter since his birth took the child to her home. She answered a knock on her door, and a young man pointing a gun at her forced his way into her apartment. When she told the robber she didn't have any money, he battered her savagely. After he pointed the gun to the child's head and threatened to shoot him, the bloodied babysitter gave the thug all her valuables. When Zervigón learned of the horrifying incident that evening, he decided it was time to leave Fun City.

On Wednesday, August 14, 1974, Orquesta Broadway played its last New York gig at the Corso nightclub. The well-publicized dance began for me at 9:05 P.M., when the dance salon looked desolate except for a few people having a taste at the long bar. Red-jacketed waiters moved briskly from table to table, spreading red cloths and laying out ashtrays. Suspended from the middle of the ceiling, a slowly turning mirrored globe reflected the colorful bulbs around it. Thin rays of blue, green, and red polka-dot colors showered the empty, dimly lit dance floor. Pianist Gil López's introduction of a peppery *descarga* spurred master of ceremonies Marty Arrett into action. Arrett kicked out his left foot and began to mambo to the music of Ray Barretto's band, and another Wednesday-night show was underway.

During the intermission that followed Barretto's performance, Ernie Ensley, a collector of live-performance tape recordings, finished setting up his fourth microphone on the bandstand. For eight of the fifteen minutes that the *danzón* "Fefita" lasted, Orquesta Broadway reminded me how much it was going to be missed. Zervigón's overwhelming flute riffs during the mambo parts made my flesh swell with goose bumps. After Broadway's first set ended, the flutist walked with Gil Suárez to the kitchen, where

Machito shook his hand and said, "*Oye*, we are going to miss you." Off to the side of the kitchen, out of the way of the hustling waiters, Zervigón helped Suárez write the flute parts for the tunes "Pare Cochero" and "Oye Mi Bajo." Suárez had already organized Típica Ideal, a *charanga* that would try to fill the void created by Broadway's departure.

At 1:15 A.M., Broadway finished playing. Twenty minutes earlier, a silent crowd had attentively listened as Marty Arrett read a moving tribute inscribed on a plaque. The plaque was presented to Orquesta Broadway by Arrett on behalf of the Corso's management. Then the wall-to-wall floor of dancers stomped, whistled, and applauded vigorously during a two-minute standing ovation and refused to allow the band to leave without an encore. Broadway swung on "Me Voy Pa' Morón." Behind the four rows of people staring up at the bandstand, dancers swayed and spun like tops. Up on the raised platform, ten musicians labored feverishly. As they steamed through the up-tempo tune, some heads bobbed, Zervigón's and Amitin's shoulders shrugged for emphasis, and the violinists mamboed in unison with the two vocalists. Eddy Zervigón, feet slightly apart, jerked his head and shoulders every once in a while, while his exciting flute riffs raised the hair on the back of my neck.

After the encore, the heavily breathing dancers bade the orchestra farewell. To the melody of "Goodnight Ladies," the majority of the sardine-packed ballroom vociferously sang out, "Goodbye Broadway, goodbye Broadway, goodbye Broadway, we hate to see you go." With glossy eyes and a toothy grin, Zervigón stepped up to the microphone and said in his bass voice, "Thank you. We love you. Excoose de oxcent." Minutes later, five members of the band warmly shook hands and embraced the five who were moving to Miami. All had lumpy throats and tears in their eyes. While a cluster of people formed to the right facing the bandstand to say farewell, the dance floor became brightly lit.

The unusually long periods of unemployment in Miami were the reason for Broadway's return to New York in 1975. A packed Casablanca ballroom reacted to the musicians as if they were heroes who had returned from outer space. Coco Records contracted the band for its LP *Salvaje*. In 1977, eight outstanding tunes from the Coco LP *Pasaporte* made Orquesta Broadway one of the most popular Latin orchestras in New York City. Although "Barrio del Pilar" and "El Material" were overwhelming tunes, the one heard most often, "Isla del Encanto," seemed almost certain to win Orchestra Broadway *Latin New York* magazine's awards for Band of the Year, Best Charanga, Best Flutist, and Best Song of the Year. But it did not happen. The band was not included in the magazine's poll, because as publisher Izzy Sanabria said, "No one nominated Broadway." The following month, *Latin New York* magazine published a photo in which Zervigón stood over a prone Sanabria at a nightclub, hours after the awards presentations.

On the back of Orquesta Broadway's Coco LP *New York City Salsa*, released in 1978, white lettering on a black background reads "First prize: King of Salsa [signed] *El Diario–La Prensa*, Schlitz Beer, 1997." For Zervigón, 1977 was good and bad. It saw Broadway working more than any other band—fifteen dances a week, five each Saturday. The flutist developed a herniated esophagus, which prompted the seasoned flutist Bobby Nelson to fill in for Zervigón while he recovered from an operation. Cuban-born trumpeter Roberto Rodríguez was added to solo on half of the flute parts.

Coco Records dissolved in 1978. Orquesta Broadway's next recordings were *Estrellas del Ritmo* (Guajiro Records, 1980), *Charanga Colonial* (Neon Records, 1981), and *Orquesta Broadway Loves New York* (Broadway Records, 1982). It was during 1982 that the band's international appeal surfaced at the Festival de Orquestas in Cali, Colombia. This festival is a competition among the Latin-music world's most popular orchestras, and the winner is selected by counting white handkerchiefs waving in the air: the band that gets the most hankerchiefs wins. On Sunday, December 26, 1982, El Gran Combo de Puerto Rico faced Orquesta Broadway in the finals. The moment arrived to select a winner, and thousands of white handkerchiefs hit the air when Broadway was announced. The December 29 issues of three Cali newspapers headlined: "White Handkerchiefs for Orq. Broadway of New York," "White Handkerchiefs for Broadway," and "Winner of the Most Excellent Charanga."

Although it did not record for five years, Orquesta Broadway continued to be heard in New York because live performances at local clubs were aired on Al Angeloro's Saturday night WBAI show, *Montuno*, and on WKCR's *The Latin Musicians Show*. "At the moment," said Zervigón in February 1988, "I have enough music for three new albums. I will not record because it would be a waste of good music. The Latin AM stations are playing little salsa...the FM stations that do play it give it away because mostly everyone is taping the new recordings and not buying the albums....The public has the final say...they should let the radio stations know what type of music they want to hear."

A letter dated February 14, 1987, from journalist and Latin music DJ Pere Luhtala (Finland's number-one authority on salsa music) responded to the six one-hour shows on cassettes I sent him about Eddy Zervigón and Broadway. "Dear Max," it began. "La Orquesta Broadway is the *best* charanga in the world...much better than La Aragón...better rhythm, better melodies, it swings more mightily....After Antonio Arcaño y Sus Maravillas, Broadway is *the* best charanga group."

The moment of recognition for Broadway finally arrived on Saturday, October 14, 1989, when Anna Arraya, Tony "Hardware" Rodríguez, Tony Cruz, and Gilberto García staged a tribute at the Bronx's Club Tapestry. At 11 P.M., this reporter was honored with the invitation to speak and present the award while being videotaped. Before the presentation, I read what millions of people read in the October 13, 1989, edition of the New York *Daily News*, in Miguel Perez's popular column, "Qué Pasa": "Even in the music world where a new star shines practically every day, there are unsung heroes. And in the Latin music industry, where it is much harder to achieve stardom, some people spend a lifetime making beautiful sounds without getting adequate recognition. Such is the case of Cuban flutist Eddy Zervigón, who will be the subject of a much deserved tribute tomorrow night at Club Tapestry. For the last 26 years, Zervigón has been the flutist and musical director of Orquesta Broadway, New York's most popular dance orchestra. But somehow he has been missed by the spotlight."

But not on this night. I started the presentation this way: "Today is another day in the history of New York's Latin music, because the artist we honor is alive to enjoy it. For many years now, a number of musicians have died and gone unnoticed. During the '30s and early '40s, whenever a musician died, his colleagues played their instruments while they followed the hearse carrying his body. The funeral procession zigzagged the streets of Spanish Harlem until it ended in front of the building where the deceased had resided. This is all the recognition the majority of musicians received during this time period....This apathetic view of Latin musicians changed in 1967 when Peter Rios, a Puerto Rican commercial artist, founded the original *Latin New York* magazine and published stories about Latin music's finest. In 1973, under the direction of Izzy Sanabria, *Latin New York* writers began unearthing the buried facts of New York's Latin music past and documenting what English- and Spanish-language newspapers considered unimportant. Since then, many great moments of Latin music, and biographies, have been published. The magazine folded in 1985. But more important than the history or the bios is the spotlight of recognition...that magic moment when the spotlight is on the individuals for the world to see. Eddy Zervigón will have his moment of recognition tonight because Anna Arraya, Tony Rodríguez, Tony Cruz, and Gilbert García have made it possible....They knew this was long overdue. Since 1963, when Broadway debuted, Anna was part of the wall-to-wall dancers who crowded ballrooms just to hear its music. She danced to it at the

Palladium, Chateau Madrid, Club Cubano, Basin Street East, the Roundtable, Chez José, Casablanca, and the Corso. In 1958, Eddy was a student of meteorology...he wanted to be a weatherman at the Havana airport. A year later he decided to be a musician. Think about this now....Whenever you listen to all those great Broadway recordings, aren't you happy he decided to become a musician?"

Eddy Zervigón accepted his plaque, which read "Presented to Eddy Zervigón. Your music for the last 26 years has made New York the Havana of North America. Along with Orquesta Broadway you have made New York's night life more enjoyable for its listening and dancing pleasure...." The visibly overwhelmed Zervigón stepped up to the microphone and said, "I am not a man of many words; however, I appreciate this, especially you the public...and the Puerto Rican people who have supported us....The Puerto Ricans and I are one...I will always have them here in my heart."

On October 14, 1992, popular DJ Al Angeloro of WNYE hosted a tribute to Orquesta Broadway in celebration of its thirtieth anniversary at S.O.B.'s (Sounds of Brazil). After thirty years, Orquesta Broadway is among Latin music's most popular orchestras. As Charlie Palmieri predicted, Eddy Zervigón and Broadway did not remain unknown for long.

Originally published in Latin Beat *magazine, March 1993*

THIRTY-THREE

HECTOR RIVERA

It was 1961, and I was at Club Triton in the Bronx, where Johnny Pacheco held Tuesday-night jam sessions. During the first break, records were played. As I was watching Pacheco, he suddenly walked away from a group of people so that he could stand under a speaker and listen to the newly released Hector Rivera recording of "Tumba Que Tumba," from his Epic album *Pachanga y Charanga!* It was arousing. It stimulated. It raised one's blood pressure. Pacheco sensed all this, but he did not know that when the recording was made, Rivera was conducting the orchestra, which consisted of Vicentico Valdés, Santos Colón, and Rudy Calzado on chorus; Marcelino Valdés on conga; Walfredo de los Reyes on timbales; Manny Oquendo on bongos; René "El Látigo" Hernández on piano; Rod Luis Sánchez on flute; and Bobby Rodríguez on bass. Any time a tune edged out a beautiful Latina in Pacheco's mind, the song had to be something special.

Four months later, Epic Records recorded *Viva Rivera,* and Rivera's composition and arrangement of "Ya Se Formó" proved that his first Epic LP was no fluke. He had finally achieved his supreme moment of recognition, after four years of paying dues by writing and arranging for Elmo García, Joe Cuba, Orlando Marín, Moncho Lena, Yayo El Indio, Rey Caney, Ray Barretto, Johnny Pacheco, the Tico All-Stars, the Alegre All Stars, and of course, for his own band.

Rivera was born to Candida and Pablo Rivera of Guayama, Puerto Rico, on January 26, 1933, while the couple lived at 62 East Ninety-ninth Street in Spanish Harlem. Five years later, young Hector was turned on to Cuban *danzónes,* which he heard daily on the radio. In 1943 the Riveras moved to an apartment on Fox and Tinton Avenues in the Bronx. It was here that he first heard Machito's "Sopa de Pichón" and decided to study music. He became a student of pianist Luis Varona (of Machito's and Tito Puente's orchestras); he continued to learn by listening to the recordings of Noro Morales, Varona, and Machito's René Hernández. In time this area of the Bronx would become an incubator for future Latin music stars such as Tito Rodríguez, Ray Barretto, Manny Oquendo, Charlie and Eddie Palmieri, Chicky Pérez, Orlando Marín, Joe Quijano, René "El Látigo" Hernández, Tommy García (of the Tito Rodríguez orchestra), Ray Coen (from Tito Puente's band), and Arsenio Rodríguez. But Noro Morales's recordings were Rivera's true inspiration.

In 1947, Machito's Continental label recording of "Me Dejan Solito" blew Rivera's mind. A year later he began his orchestration studies with trumpeter Eddie Forestier, who gave him the piano job in his band. Off the bandstand, Rivera spent his leisure time dancing at the Palladium. When he wasn't dancing, he could always be found behind the piano, watching Joe Loco, René Hernández, Al Escobar, and Luisito Benjamín. He always made time to visit the China Doll, and no matter how many times Noro Morales's group played "110th Street and Fifth Avenue" or "Ponce," Rivera never tired of listening to them. He joined Elmo García's band in 1951, then left the next year to lead his own group, which debuted at Hunts Point Palace in the Bronx. The other band on the bill was the newly organized orchestra of Orlando Marín, with pianist Eddie Palmieri and vocalist Joe Quijano.

Then Rivera was called up to serve in the Korean War. The day before he left for basic training, he was one of many invited guests at a Machito recording session that Columbia Records had arranged in order to create a live session atmosphere. Rivera saw the band record "Mambo Inn," "Sambia," "Beeree Bee Cum Bee," and "Sí Sí, No No." While stationed in Guam, he met Ignacio "Nacho" Sanabria, a Puerto Rican whom he encouraged and helped to become a vocalist. At the time, the *cha-cha-chá* was fast becoming the new dance rage, and not being able to hear or get a *cha-cha-chá* recording was driving Rivera crazy. He thought that if it was good enough to replace the mambo, it had to be something special.

In late 1954, Rivera was on leave. While climbing the steps to the Palladium Ballroom, he heard strange music—a flute and chorus. Inside the ballroom, Tito Puente and Willie Bobo were singing chorus to "El Jamaiquino" in a cha-cha tempo. Not even Machito's *cha-cha-chá* turned him on. "I was expecting something special—hot, very swinging like the mambo. I expected it to be better than the mambo, but it wasn't." Rivera was discharged from the military on March 2, 1955.

Alfredito Levy, Latin music's Jewish star of the time, was just as hot as Puente, Tito Rodríguez, Joe Loco, and the La Playa Sextet. After six months with Alfredito, Rivera played his 78s for Moncho Lena and got arranging assignments for Orlando Marín's "Mi Mambo," "Wildfire," "Carmela," and the hit "La Mesa." The cha-cha craze had yet not peaked when Mercury Records contracted Elmo García to record. García, who played only claves and no other instrument, asked Rivera to write and arrange four tunes; he also asked someone else to do the same thing. When the second arranger failed to come up with four tunes, Gil Fuller, Mercury's A&R man, gave the assignment to Rivera. The 1957 recording of *Let's Cha Cha Cha with Hector Rivera* used the Machito orchestra minus the saxophones. Rivera will never forget this recording session. He saved a sheet of music from the event that still has his bloodstains on it. They were caused by a sucker punch to the nose delivered by Elmo García. Subsequently, the Hector Rivera Quintet was formed. Then Rivera spent a year with Arsenio Rodríguez before replacing Eddie Palmieri in Vicentico Valdés's orchestra in 1958.

Three years later, when *pachanga* and charanga were the rage, Ray Barretto, who had just left the Tito Puente band, was given the chance to record an LP. Barretto asked his neighborhood buddy Rivera to write and arrange all of the music for the 1961 Riverside LP *Pachanga with Barretto*. Three tunes, "Pachanga Oriental," "Pachanga Suavecito," and "Oye Heck," were outstanding because of Barretto's personal selection of Hector Rivera on piano; Rod Luis Sánchez on flute; Willie Rodríguez on timbales; a chorus consisting of Tito Rodríguez, Elliot Romero, and Rudy Calzado; and the violins of Daniel González, José Andreu, and Chombo Silva. Shortly afterward, Rivera won Latin America's attention with his thrilling Epic label LPs. One of the Epic tracks, "Petite," became the Joe Cuba hit "Mujer Divina." Although Rivera was a recording star, he was still Vicentico Valdés's pianist. After Valdés, he played piano from 1964 to 1966 for the red-hot Johnny Pacheco *conjunto*, and continued writing and arranging music. Rivera is pianist and arranger for the 1967 Tico LP *Joe Cuba Presents the Velvet Voice of Jimmy Sabater*, which includes "Caress Me," "Pensar," "Los Dos," and "No Te Olvides De Mí."

In the late 1960s, when the boogaloo was causing a stir, Rivera's tune "At the Party" made the Top 40 charts. He refused to describe the rhythm as boogaloo; instead, he labeled it "Latin soul." Thus, another rhythm joined the family of Latin music. The *At the Party* LP also contains Rivera's version of "Asia Minor," truly one of the best recordings of the year. If there was any doubt about what Latin soul is, Rivera's 1969 Four Points label album *Hecto-Mania* defined it. Dick Sugar was the only Latin DJ to play it regularly. Even so, the R&B and jazz programs gave it well-deserved exposure. Rivera did other great recordings for United Artists and Tico Records. His imagination has added to many great salsa recordings. Of those, none compare with his composition and arrangement of "Bobby: Bajo y Clarinete" for the Alegre All Stars 1977 album *Perdido*. Listen to it and you will understand why bandleaders during the late 1950s used to say, "Get me Hector Rivera!"

Originally published in Latin Beat *magazine, November 1991*

THIRTY-FOUR

TONY PABÓN

At the time, no one knew that a limb was about to sprout on the tree of Latin music. The year was 1966. The fertile ground was the Palm Gardens Ballroom at Fifty-second Street and Eighth Avenue, where New York African-Americans gathered to hear bands whose music made them calypso, samba, twist, wobble, hully-gully, limbo, frug, monkey, jerk, and grind. Eddie Palmieri's recording of "Azúcar" was the reason why Joe Cuba's, Ricardo Ray's, and Pete Rodríguez's bands were contracted to play the same dances.

Most black dancers remained unmoved by the Cuban dance rhythms, mainly because they didn't know how to mambo. One evening, several dancers urged pianist-bandleader Pete Rodríguez to add "soul" to his music. Rodríguez consulted his English-speaking trumpeter, Tony Pabón, who suggested they fake the pop-soul tunes of the moment. It worked, and a new era in Latin music began.

"In early 1966, we kept getting repeated requests from dancers to add a little soul to the music." said Pabón. "At the time, nothing similar to the boogaloo was being played by a Latin band, nor was the word 'boogaloo' used. Pete [Rodríguez] asked me to write music that would please the dance promoters. A week later, I heard Peggy Lee sing 'Fever.' I wrote a tune inspired by the bass lines of 'Fever' and called it 'Pete's Boogaloo.'" Thus the Latin boogaloo was created and became Latin music's most popular dance rhythm until 1969.

When Antonio "Tony" Pabón was born to José and Rosa-Colón Pabón on March 6, 1941, in Santurce, Puerto Rico, *jíbaro*, *bomba*, and *plena* were the background music of his life. Three years later, the Pabóns relocated to New York, where they settled in an apartment at 103rd Street and Third Avenue. His memories of El Barrio are pleasant: he had many friends, loving parents, and Latin music. At PS 121 he befriended Tony Cofresi, Papy Roman, and Elias López, who would all make their mark years later as Latin music trumpeters. He also befriended Hector Castro, a tuba player at the time, who became Johnny Pacheco's pianist and arranger in the 1960s and directed Conjunto Candela in the 1970s. But it was Harry James, America's most popular bandleader in the 1940s, who inspired Pabón to study trumpet at Harlem's Patrick Henry School.

In 1956, when the Pabóns moved to Fox Street in the Bronx, Tony began studying musical composition and orchestration with a Juilliard professor. Months later, he made his professional debut with the band of Bolivar Vidal. He moved on to the Randy Carlos group (with whom he recorded "Smoke") and later to the La Playa Sextet (where he recorded "Coco Seco"). Subsequently he went to Orlando Marín's group and then to Quique Monsanto's band before joining the Pete Rodríguez orchestra as co-leader.

Founded in 1956, the band consisted of Pabón on trumpet, Frankie Marín on timbales, David Pérez on bass, Pete "El Conde" Rodríguez on bongos, and Pete Rodríguez on piano. "El Conde" left within months and was replaced Benny Bonilla. "It took us seven years of struggling before we hit," said Pabón. "We clicked in 1964 with our first LP, *At Last—La Magnífica* [Remo Records]."

Via his composition and arrangement of the ballad "La Carta," from the 1965 Remo LP *La Reencarnación*, Latin America became aware of Tony Pabón. Inspired by the universal dilemma of the lovers' quarrel, Pabón gained the limelight with a melody whose lyrics put lumps in listeners' throats. His words described a man madly in love, waiting by his mailbox for a letter that might never arrive. The song included the man's words of apology and elaborated on how much he missed his sweetheart. The situation simply could not have been fiction: it must have been taken from real life, probably from a moment in Pabón's life that he put to music.

It was Tony Pabón's compositions, arrangements, and English vocals on "Micaela," "El Hueso," "I Like It Like That," "Bobby," and "Fango" that made them bestsellers and propelled the Rodríguez orchestra to the top.

In November 1969, an angry Pabón left Rodríguez's orchestra to direct a cooperative band named La Protesta, which debuted at Le Abalon Ballroom in the Bronx on November 21, 1969. Eight musicians, dressed in powder blue jackets, white ties, navy blue shirts, and navy trousers, climbed the bandstand and set up. At the edge of the bandstand were promoters Ralph Mercado, Leo Vásquez, Eddie Colón, and Ciso Vizcaino, and musicians Ray Barretto and Joey and Willie Pastrana.

The mambo "Averigua" quickly filled the dance floor. By the evening's end, La Protesta had signed a recording contract with Alegre Records. For the next six years, La Protesta and its vocalist, Nestor Sanchez, attracted a large following. In 1971 Pabón met Rico Records' Ralfi Cartagena and signed a long-term contract. Nestor Sanchez's rendition of "Nana Seré," from the first LP, was the beginning of Pabón's climb to stardom.

The Pabón charisma continued to spread in February 1974, when he began to co-host the Channel 41 television show *Esto Es Lo Nuestro* with the attractive Hilda Mirros. Every week Pabón and Mirros presented live music and interviewed widely known Latin music personalities such as Larry Harlow, Pellín Rodríguez, Roberto Roena, members of La Típica Novel, and Puerto Rican superstar vocalist Vitín Aviles.

"Vocalist Ismael Rivera was a musician who made a tremendous hit with the young people on the show," said Pabón. "He spoke about his tough life, his drug problems and how they almost ruined his life, his love for his mother and her love for him....He really came across...they gave him a standing ovation."

On New Year's Day 1976, Tony Pabón almost died. The incident occurred a few minutes after midnight. The dancers at St. Joseph's Hall in New Jersey noisily welcomed in the new year. Pabón, trumpet in hand, faced the dancers on the crowded dance floor and waited for the din to subside before tapping off the mambo "El Capitán." His mouthpiece slowly found its way to his lips and he began to blow. Immediately after hitting a high note, he felt a piercing pinch in his stomach and doubled up in pain. After a minute or so, he regained his composure and resumed playing. At 4 A.M. he left for his home in Ramapo, New York. Two hours later, he awoke in his bed because his face felt wet. His fingers touched his mouth and he realized that the moisture was blood. The dark red fluid was streaming from his nose and mouth, soaking his white T-shirt.

In a panic, he rushed to the town's hospital and learned that his pancreas had exploded from strain, rupturing a vessel and causing internal bleeding. Hospital orderlies hurriedly escorted him to the emergency room and helped him onto a bed. Although his stomach hurt and he was gagging on his own blood, his wide-open eyes followed the doctors' and nurses' every movement as his heart beat like a tom-tom. A doctor located the problem, closed the ruptured artery, and averted Pabón's death by pumping blood out of his stomach. For the next two weeks, Pabón had to lie quietly on his back while a thin plastic tube, threaded through his nose, transported blood from his stomach into a gallon-sized bottle under his bed. Three months passed, and nature did its healing. Meanwhile, Pabón dared not sneeze for fear the bleeding would resume.

A week after the surgery, Pabón made a vow to abstain from liquor. His health improved, he left the hospital, and he retired as an active musician. He credits his survival to a strong belief in God and an unrelenting determination to live. Since January 1977, he and his wife Rachel have been distributors for Ritmo Records, which distributes albums recorded in South America and the Caribbean that have no representation in the United States.

Before ending our interview, I was pleasantly surprised to learn more about the tune "La Carta." I asked Pabón what the happiest moment in his life was. Smiling, he answered, "When I received Rachel's letter."

Originally published in Latin Beat *magazine, April 1992*

THIRTY-FIVE

JOE CUBA

This story is about six Latin musicians from Spanish Harlem. Joe Cuba is a self-taught percussionist who rose to become the most popular Latin bandleader in New York City (along with Eddie Palmieri) for three years, beginning in 1967. Cuba accomplished this feat because his path and those of Jimmy Sabater, Tommy Berrios, Willie Torres, Nick Jiménez, and Cheo Feliciano were destined to cross. This is how it happened.

Jaime "Jimmy" Sabater was born on April 11, 1936, to parents Ernesto and Theresa Sabater, originally from Ponce, Puerto Rico, while they were living on the first-floor of a tenement at 2 East 112th Street. In 1945, Jimmy was a member of the Viceroys, who spent their days playing stickball, listening to the sounds of Machito, Noro Morales, Marcelino Guerra, and Polito Galindez, and hanging out on a stoop to sing songs made famous by Nat "King" Cole. Willie Bobo, a fellow Viceroy who lived on the first floor of the adjoining building, would wake Jimmy up every Saturday morning. Bobo, whose window faced Sabater's, would pop his rapidly moving fingers on top of an oatmeal box—pa-ku-tuku-pa—and say, "You better get with it!"

Bobo introduced Sabater to Willie Rodríguez, and the drum tutoring began in 1950. As Jimmy learned the secrets of percussion from drummers Uba Nieto, Papi Pagani, Monchito Muñoz, and Bobo, he repeated them by playing along to Tito Puente's recording "El Timbal." That same year, the Viceroys visited 115th Street between Madison and Park Avenues and failed to wrest the stickball championship of El Barrio from the highly touted Devils, who beat them by ten runs. At this game, Jimmy met Gilberto Miguel Calderón, known as Sonny. Later that night the Viceroys were invited to a party by girls who lived on 115th Street. As the nattily dressed Viceroys approached the building, they were bombarded with balloons full of water by someone with a unique, throaty laugh. At the party, Calderón gave each Viceroy a stick of Feenamint gum. After a few hours, the Viceroys, desperately waiting to use the bathroom, learned that the gum was a laxative. And they could not get to the toilet, since someone with a deep, throaty laugh was inside, forcing the door shut.

Sabater's first gig was in 1953 with the five-piece Hector Castro group at the Hotel Lucerne, for which he was paid five dollars. In the summer of 1954, he joined the José Panama Quintet. Shortly thereafter, Sonny Calderón became Panama's conga player. Months later, Panama abandoned the group to start another one. Calderón held the group together and became its musical director.

Calderón, who in the mid-1950s became Joe Cuba, was born on April 22, 1931, to Puerto Rican parents Miguel, from Santurce, and Gloria, from the town of Sebastián. Since he was a boy, Sonny had a sense of humor and always laughed lustily after committing one of his pranks. "Music," he said, "interested me in my late teens. I attended Cooper Junior High School until 1946. I was a good baseball and basketball player....Latin music meant nothing to me....Cooper was an all Afro-American school. All my friends were black, and Louis Jordan's 'Nobody Here but Us Chickens' was the type of music I jitterbugged to."

In the early 1940s, when his father owned a candy store at 115th Street, Calderón became a member of the Devils stickball team. After the water-balloon bombardment of the Viceroys, the soaked kids from 111th Street rushed into the building and encountered the Devils, who denied they had been on the roof. Sabater, eyes closed, cheek to cheek with a girl, removed his jacket and placed it on a couch. At the end of the evening he found his jacket pockets stuffed with lettuce and tomatoes by a prankster whose throaty laughter was heard drifting away from the apartment.

Months later, after listening to Tito Puente's "Abaniquito," Sonny Calderón dropped out of college to pursue a musical career. His first conga teacher was Victor "El Negrito" Pantoja. Santos Miranda, Pupi Torres, and Wilfredo "Chonguito" Vicente taught him also. Sonny debuted with El Conjunto Alfarona X when Sabu Martínez left unexpectedly for Los Angeles. Then he joined pianist Noro Morales's quartet. "During the early 1950s," he said, "the *New York Post* listed the weekend dances of 'Noro Morales and his fourteen-piece orchestra.' With two congas I took a train to Brooklyn. I was the first to arrive at the Hollywood Terrace. Then came the drummer and bass player with Noro. The club's spokesman announced that ten musicians missed their flight in South America and that refunds were available. I learned that this ruse was used every week and that no one dared ask for a refund....It was operated by underworld people...it was done to save money."

Percussionists Willie Bobo, Pupi Torres, Chonguito, Patato Valdés, Negrito Pantoja, Santos Miranda, and Calderón hung out on *"congueros' corner"*—114th Street and Fifth Avenue. It was here that Sonny met bassist Roy Rosa, who was searching for a conga drummer to join the Joe Panama group, which patterned itself after Joe Loco's quintet. The Panama quintet, which was featured at Club Los Muchachos on 104th Street and Madison Avenue, was rivaled by pianist Nick Jiménez's group at the San Juan Club two blocks away, on 102nd Street. When Panama's father succeeded in convincing his son to form another group, Calderón took over and founded a band consisting of Roy Rosa, Tommy Berrios, Jimmy Sabater, and Victor Pantoja. The search for a vocalist ended one night when Calderon heard Willie Torres sing "I've Got You under My Skin" in English.

Willie Torres was born to Puerto Rican parents on October 30, 1929, while they resided at 107th Street between Lexington and Park Avenue in Spanish Harlem. Torres believes he was born to sing, and as a preteen he won prizes for his vocals. As he aged he became one of the many Latinos who were influenced by Bing Crosby; later he was influenced by Mel Tormé. In 1945, Torres became the vocalist for Pappy y Sus Rumberos. One evening in early 1952, Torres visited an after-hours club, El San Juan, where he met a tall, thin pianist-composer and crackerjack arranger named Nick Jiménez.

Jiménez was born in Santurce, Puerto Rico, on June 15, 1929, and was living in Spanish Harlem the following year. In 1942, he began piano studies under the tutelage of Luis Varona (of Machito and Tito Puente fame). By the time Nick had reached his eighteenth birthday, he was still undecided about whether he wanted to be a maritime radio operator or a musician. The Korean War turned him into a soldier. After his honorable discharge in 1952, his five-piece group was featured at the San Juan Club. It was here that Jiménez met his future wife, Irene, married her, and discovered Willie Torres. Years later he accepted Calderón's offer and replaced Joe Panama on piano.

In 1956 Roy Rosa died, and his bass spot was taken over by three bassists before Jules "Slim" Cordero occupied the position. Cordero was born on December 16, 1925, to Puerto Rican parents. He graduated from Chelsea High School before being drafted into the Marine Corps in February 1946. Upon returning to civilian life, he displayed his stickball skills for the 114th Street Falcons and studied bass with Professor Baselman of Juilliard. In 1949, Slim began his professional career with the Ricky Gardel Orchestra. He gained valuable experience with the bands of Juanito Sanabria, Xavier Cugat, the Lecuona Cuban Boys, Carlos Varela, Polito Galíndez, La Playa Sextet, Vicentico Valdés, and

Tito Puente before joining the Joe Cuba Sextet.

Cordero also became a songwriter and vocalist. "After Willie left, I was given a chance to sing "To Be with You." When I refused to sing into the mike, José asked Jimmy to do it." Slim is on every Joe Cuba recording released from 1958 until he retired twelve years later, in 1970.

Tommy Berrios of Ponce, Puerto Rico, came into the world on December 23, 1932. His vibraharp is what gave the Joe Cuba group its unique sound. In 1933, the Berrios family settled at an apartment on 110th Street and Madison Avenue. Like most American kids Tommy's age, he was mesmerized by the drumming skills of Gene Krupa on Benny Goodman's "Sing, Sing, Sing." After completing two years at Benjamin Franklin High School, he began his drum studies with a Mr. Jilinksi. The Berrios children, Tommy and his two older sisters, were proud Puerto Ricans, but their favorite music was the jazz, pop, and R&B that their radio supplied daily. After Tommy heard the Stan Kenton orchestra in the mid-1940s, he knew that music was for him. In 1950, he was knocked flat after hearing Tito Puente's vibraharp work on the ballad "Por Tu Amor."

In 1951, Berrios was drafted; he served in an army band in Munich, Germany, where he learned to play bells, vibes, and marimba. The first thing he did after his January 1953 discharge was to buy all the Tito Puente 78s he could get his hands on. For hours every day, anyone passing 110th Street and Madison could hear Tommy out of the open window on the second floor, playing along to "Vibe Mambo," "Mambolino," "Mambo Diablo," and "Philadelphia Mambo." One day he answered a knock on his door. The young man in the hallway shook his hand and said, "Hi, I'm Jimmy Sabater. The Joe Panama group needs you."

"The American pop repertoire," said Berrios, "and [the absence of] Latin tunes annoyed us, and a confrontation with Panama resulted in us losing our jobs. Sonny took over as director, Nicky [Jiménez] inherited the pianist's chair, and when Willie [Torres] joined us, we were on our way." Tommy's musical genius became evident when he ad-libbed the parts that were not written out for him. But in 1967, he developed personal problems and resigned from the sextet.

In 1953, the former Panama group debuted at El San Juan Club as the Cha-Cha Boys. "I was given a gig at the Bronx's Starlight Ballroom," said Calderón, "and the promoter, Catalino Rolón, convinced me to rename the group Gilberto Calderón. I didn't know the ballroom owner didn't like the new name, so Rolón told him, 'Let's call it the Joe Cuba Sextet.' When I read in the *New York Post* that Joe Cuba was the Starlight's attraction, I got pissed and called Rolón and said 'Who the fuck is Joe Cuba?' And Rolón said, *'You're* Joe Cuba.'" Thus, one of Latin music's most popular dance and romantic music bands since 1955 began its reign.

English lyrics from a vocalist backed by a Latin band were first recorded by Xavier Cugat in the late 1930s (Cugat used vocalists Dinah Shore and Buddy Clark). But such recordings were never accepted as Latin music. Recognition for the first success goes to Pupi Campo's 1947 Seeco recording of the watered-down *guaracha* "Mary Ann." Then came the DeCastro Sisters on Tito Puente's 1952 Tico recording of "Tonight I Am in Heaven," followed by José Curbelo's 1956 Fiesta recording of "Cha Cha Chá in Blue." There is evidence, however, that Nick Jiménez and Willie Torres introduced English lyrics in the up-tempo mambo earlier, in 1952. Joe Cuba successfully used mambos and ballads with English lyrics at Jewish and Italian dances at the Bronx's Stardust Ballroom. That success won him a two-year stint at the Pines, a Jewish resort in South Fallsburg, New York. It was here that Jiménez composed "Mambo of the Pines," which later became the monster hit "Mambo of the Times," one of the group's four Rainbow label recordings in 1956. With the help of popular DJ Dick "Ricardo" Sugar, the tune, the sextet, and Willie Torres made a tremendous impact. More importantly, the group's vibraharp-piano-and-percussion sound dispelled the myth that only brass ensembles would please dancers. "We were on a roll," recalled Joe Cuba. "We were performing at the best clubs, opposite names like Harry James and Harry Belafonte. In 1956, we appeared on the only Latin show on TV, the Don Pasante show, for eighteen weeks in a row."

"When Nicky joined the group," said Sabater, "we began to play original tunes, many of them written and arranged by Nicky."

"In 1955," said Cuba, "I had been pestering agent Sid Sayre for gigs. While [I was] in his office, Marty Franklin, whose trio played the pop and Latin music at the Pines, called him to say he quit for a better job offer. Sid turned to me: 'I have a job…it's room, board, food, and fifty dollars a man every week.' I took it."

Puerto Rican pianist-bandleader Johnny Conquet convinced Eddie Heller to record the Cuba sextet on his Rainbow label. The tune to promote the resort, "Mambo of the Pines," was changed to "Mambo of the Times" to avoid a legal hassle. Bobbie Lunn, a young, attractive Jewish girl, was the group's bassist until 1957. Though the fact has generally been unknown until now, Cuba's recordings included the bongo playing of Willie Bobo, José Mangual Sr., and Johnny "Dandy" Rodríguez. Dandy was on every LP after *Diggin' the Most*.

"We also became the first orchestra to dance on stage while performing," said Cuba. "In addition to our original tunes, we had arrangements of Tito Rodríguez's hits. One night we played them all in our first set. Tito then climbed the bandstand and asked me, 'What do you suggest we play?' This was around 1956, when Willie and Nicky wrote 'Núnca,' which subsequently became a tune with English lyrics, named 'To Be with You.'

"Just before the Grossinger's gig in 1957," continued Cuba, "Willie told me he was leaving the group to replace Santos Colón in José Curbelo's band. We all took this hard...he was a star act...his English vocals made him a featured act....I became pissed...I was fuming....At this sad time Tito Puente had experienced a vocalist problem....Vicentico [Valdés] left him in 1954 and was replaced by Gilberto Monroig, and months later Monroig had to return to Puerto Rico. Jimmy Frisaura, Puente's trumpeter said, 'Singers are incidental....Tito and Willie Bobo sing chorus on most of the tunes...you and Jimmy should do the same.' One night in 1958, Tito Rodríguez counseled me at the Palladium....He told me to forget about Willie Torres, to wish him well and replace him with his band boy, a musician who could sing. He introduced me to José 'Cheo' Feliciano, whom I auditioned at El Club San Juan. Not only did Cheo come late, he couldn't sing our English-lyric tunes. Cheo showed great promise...I could hear it...he won me over wit his warm personality. He knew all the Tito Rodríguez tunes. He started out banging a cowbell. As we added Rodríguez charts, he began to sing them."

"In the shake of the dice, we came out all right," said Sabater, "because it was Cheo who made the Joe Cuba Sextet. He put us on the map."

José Luis Angel Feliciano-Vega, a k a Cheo, was born in Ponce, Puerto Rico, on July 3, 1935. His musical influences were his father and the Colombian baritone Carlos Ramírez. In 1952, at age seventeen, he relocated to New York's Spanish Harlem. He frequented nightclubs that featured popular Cuban rhythms performed by the orchestras of Machito, Tito Puente, and Tito Rodríguez. Cheo befriended Frank "Machito" Grillo, who became his adviser. He learned to thump a conga in street jam sessions, which resulted in jobs with groups that were just starting out. One evening in 1956, Cheo's friends urged Tito Rodríguez to give Cheo a chance to sing. Cheo, who knew all of Rodríguez's repertoire, was given Tito's maracas as he climbed the Palladium Ballroom's bandstand. He sailed through "Changó Tá Vení."

"I looked for Tito in the crowd....I was dying to hear what he thought," said Cheo. "Tito walked toward me smiling, raised both arms in the air, and urged the dancers to applaud more. He said to me, 'You want to sing...so sing.' I sang 'Barito.' It was the first time I sang before an audience...nothing I've done has ever matched that thrill."

Months later, Cheo learned from Spanish Harlem's musical grapevine that Joe Cuba was searching for a vocalist. "I'll never forget the day I started with the sextet," said Cheo. "It was October 5, 1957, my wedding day [Cheo married Socorro 'Coco' Prieto]. From the ceremony, I rushed to the dance hall, doubled up [played a second gig] until 5 A.M., then left for my honeymoon."

Willie Torres's departure from the sextet upset many aficionados in the same way as when Vicentico Valdés split from the Tito Puente Orchestra in 1954. Many of Cuba's fans were convinced that Torres's uniquely fiery delivery in English could never be replaced. His live performances of "Mambo of the Times," "I Talk to the Trees," "Alegre Mambo," and "Joe Cuba's Mambo" were infectious. I also doubted that any vocalist could do the job Torres did. One evening during early 1959, I caught the Cuba sextet at Brooklyn's Airport Lounge. I became a believer. Cheo was incredibly good. His delivery on "El Agua No," "Muñequita Linda," "Cara Suica," "El Botecito," and "Con Mi Mambo" won him many admirers. Outside the lounge during a break, he was smiling and shaking the hands of Italian and Jewish dancers who were showering him with praise. However, his heavy Spanish accent while singing English lyrics was noticeable. "Cheo's English was not too good," said Sabater, "so Sonny decided to let me sing the English-lyric tunes."

"Because of the budget," said Cuba, "Cheo didn't make it to Grossinger's with us. On weekends Cheo and two trumpeters were added and we sounded like a big band. Our Mardi Gras label recordings served as publicity notices. Between 1960 and 1962 we accumulated the hits 'To Be with You,' 'A Las Seis,' and 'Cómo Ríen.' One day Catalino Rolón introduced me to Sidney Siegel of Seeco Records. Mr. Siegel said to me, 'I hear you didn't make money with your Mardi Gras recordings. Well, you aren't going to make money here either. However, I'm going to put you on the map, I promise you.' We hit it off well…he was straight with me. I told him about the reactions to 'To Be with You.' He said Spanish people will never accept an English-lyric tune, not to record it. Two days before we recorded the *Steppin' Out* album, I called Willie Torres and told him I decided that Jimmy would record 'To Be with You' and that he was in the band. At the studio, Joe Cain, the A&R man who produced the album, refused to record it. After he listened to it, he recorded it."

Willie Torres's budding career was stifled. He did not record with Curbelo. In 1961, he left Curbelo to join the then smoldering-hot Charlie Palmieri charanga La Duboney and recorded Arsenio Rodríguez's ballad "La Vida Es Un Sueño." From then on, whenever Torres sang in the chorus for a recording, he would let the world know he was there by yelling one of his signature cries, *"¡A comer!"* or *"¡Y dice!"* "When I left Cuba's group," said Torres, "it was understood that I would record ['To Be with

You'], since it was Nick Jiménez's music and my lyrics. We all knew it was going to be a big hit and would make the singer popular."

Thanks to Joe Cuba, Jimmy Sabater got to record "To Be with You." During the Seeco *Steppin' Out* recording session at the Beltone Studios in 1962, Sabater was given his chance for immortality. "It was about 1 P.M.," said Sabater, "and Cheo had just finished recording 'Cómo Ríen.' There was a short silence, then we enthusiastically applauded him...he gassed us. Then Sonny told me to get in the vocalist's booth to record. Hector Rivera, who arranged the music, sat in on celeste."

"There was a problem in the studio that day," recalled Tommy Berrios. "'To Be with You' was a sure hit...it couldn't miss, and we all knew it. When Sonny told Jimmy to record it, Cheo blew up and said he was the lead singer and should do it. Joe and Cheo exchanged heated words....Even Jimmy's and Cheo's wives got into the argument. Jimmy won the assignment and I had to ad-lib because Nicky or Hector didn't write...parts for me."

"When the recording was released on 45s," said Sabater, "it was put in jukeboxes all over town. During a break I visited the Starlight Bar, which was directly under the Palladium Ballroom. When I walked in, Willie Bobo and conga drummers Tommy López and Patato Valdés said, *'Aquí viene el famoso cantante'*—here comes the famous singer. They kidded the hell out of me."

"Cómo Ríen" elevated Cheo Feliciano to the elite group of vocalists that included Lucho Gatica, Tito Rodríguez, Vicentico Valdés, Graciela (Machito's sister), and Vitín Aviles. When Feliciano's "Aunque Tú," a ballad from the 1964 Seeco LP *Diggin' the Most*, was released, Latin music had another Frank Sinatra. "The *Steppin' Out* LP placed us among the top ten," said Cuba. "One day at the Village Gate, Symphony Sid and Jack Hooke told me I was wasting my time with Seeco, that Morris Levy of Tico Records would treat me much better. When I got out of my Seeco contract, I owed Mr. Siegel an album. We recorded *Hangin' Out* [1963], *The Soul of Spanish Harlem* [1964], *Qué Problema*, and *Derecho Y Virao* for Tico. [We did] *Songs Mama Never Taught Me*; the Tico All Stars 1965 Village Gate concert in which Jimmy and I participated in; the last Seeco LP, *Comin' at You* [1965]; and *Bailadores* [1965] until 1966, when the boogaloo scene arrived."

If record sales and standing-room-only crowds at ballrooms are good indicators, then the orchestras of Joe Cuba and Eddie Palmieri were the kings of Latin music in 1966. Right on their heels were the orchestras of Ricardo Ray, Pete Rodríguez, and Johnny Colón. "It is not true," said Cuba, "that Eddie and I had a billing problem...he and I were close friends. Whenever we worked together we rotated the billing. I never cared who got top billing...I never asked for billing over any band. Whenever I appeared on the same bill with the two Titos, I was always told I could not have top line or equal billing with them. I would appear angry and hurt, threaten not to play unless I received more money. This ploy never failed. People do not pay attention to billing. It doesn't matter where a band's name is....If it has a hot record, it is the draw."

Cheo's last album with Cuba was *We Must Be Doing Something Right!*, recorded in 1965 and released in 1966. "Ever since I thought about singing," said Cheo, "I wanted to be a star. [But] with Cuba I didn't feel I was getting all the recognition due me." By now it was 1965, and Cheo had personal problems to deal with. He and the Cuba sextet parted, and Willie Torres replaced him. Four years later, Jerry Masucci, president of Fania Records, gave Cheo his passport back to life in the Latin music world when Masucci released the Vaya label recording of *La Voz Sensual de Cheo* in September 1972.

Cuba's peak years were 1966 to 1969. The boogaloo was in, and every recording was a bestseller. The Cuba sextet landed the best jobs, top pay, and tours to Mexico, Holland, Los Angeles, and the Caribbean.

"Cheo lifted the group to a high level of popularity," said Cuba, "but had he been the lead vocalist during the boogaloo era, I doubt we could have exploded the way we did. Willie Torres was tailor-made for the new rhythm, and along with the help of Jimmy, Nicky, and Hector Rivera, the sextet reached new heights of popularity."

Sabater, who wrote "El Pito" with Nick Jiménez, remembered, "I was listening to a Dizzy Gillespie recording of 'Manteca.' During a bass riff, Gillespie sang, 'I'll never go back to Georgia, I'll never go back.' Nicky and I sat down at a piano and we wrote the tune." The song "Pruébalo" was the one that was supposed to hit, but WLIB DJ Dale Shields liked "El Pito," played it, and put it on the R&B charts. Years later, during a telephone conversation with Tito Puente, Cuba learned that the recording of "El Pito" was out of clave. Cuba told Puente in a serious tone, "You know, Tito, now that the record has passed a million in sales, it being off clave bothers me."

One afternoon while Cuba was in the Tico offices, label president Morris Levy received a phone call from a man with a heavy Southern accent who asked for Joe Cuba. Cuba took the call. "Mistah Kew-bah, this is the office of the governor of Georgia...what does it mean, you'll never go back to Georgia?" Cuba, sensing he might be blowing a gig, replied, "Oh, it's my girlfriend Georgia, she broke my heart....I'll never go back to her."

In mid-1966, Tico released *Wanted Dead or Alive*. "The ideas for the boogaloos 'Bang Bang,' 'Oh Yeah,' and 'Push Push Push' were inspired by the black teenage dancers at the Palm Gardens, which years later became the Cheetah," said Sabater.

Tommy Berrios remembered the creation of "Bang Bang." "It came into being one night at the Riverside Plaza. No matter what we played, a few brothers sang "bang, bang" to every tune. Jimmy and Nicky started it with a piano vamp, then all of us contributed to its creation. Someone added 'beep beep,' another 'uh-huh,'…another 'umgawa, black power.'…At a rehearsal we worked it all out in less than a half-hour."

"When we started to play the tunes and sang 'black power!'" said Cuba, "we began to notice the black clenched firsts above heads. When Morris Levy heard it for the first time, he jumped out of his chair and said, 'What's that?' He didn't like the words, so we changed them."

Willie Torres's contribution to making *Wanted*, the most successful Cuba LP, must be lauded. His renditions of "Que Son Uno" and the sensuous ballad "Triste" would have received my vote for a Grammy nomination in 1966 if Latin music had had a category in the Grammys at the time. The Cuba whirlwind continued in subsequent years. In 1967, the Cuba sextet and the Eddie Palmieri band seemed more in demand than ever; they were also top record sellers. Jimmy Sabater became the Latin Nat "King" Cole via his recordings of "Caress Me," "Pensar," "Funny," "Los Dos," and "The More I See You" for the Tico LP *La Voz Sensual de Jimmy Sabater.*

Compared with other bands, the Joe Cuba Sextet had very few sideman changes. Its bass players have been Roy Rosa (1955), Cito Martinez (1957), Luis Barreto (1958). Jules "Slim" Cordero, Tommy Berrios, Louise Ramírez, Oscar García, and Phil Díaz were the vibraphonists. The vocalists have been Cheo Feliciano, Willie Torres, Jimmy Sabater, Willie García, and Mike "Pasquale Caputo" Guagenti, while Nicky Jiménez, Alfredo Rodríguez, and Charlie Palmieri have played keyboards.

In 1967, vibraharpist Oscar García wrote me from the Flamboyan Hotel in San Juan, Puerto Rico, while the sextet was there for a two-week engagement. Part of his letter reads, "I still can't believe all that's happening.…We are mentioned in all the newspapers and magazines. We are respected as if we were movie stars. After this [comes] six weeks in Mexico, then South America." In a private conversation with me in 1975, García said, "With Joe Cuba there was never a worry about unemployment. Sonny never entered the top billing war in New York…he was too busy making money and traveling throughout Latin America. Because of the hit tune 'El Pito,' Sonny always traveled with a few cardboard cartons filled with flat plastic whistles with his name inscribed on them. He would throw them to the people."

"All that glitters is not all glamour" is García's way of saying that a musician's life has its high and low moments. The highs are the pleasant memories of traveling to different countries, the football-like pep talks in the kitchen by coach Cuba before an event, the goofing and laughs the sextet shared. The lows are the unpleasant memories of being stranded for days in Argentina, the theft of García's vibraharp at boxing champ Carlos Ortiz's Bronx Tropicoro Club, the parting from the group of dear friends like Nick Jiménez and roommate Willie Torres, and the constant need to be on the road, which made García lonely for his wife and children. In 1971, García left the Cuba sextet. Currently he is a highly paid computer specialist during the day and plays with a jazz group at night. Willie Torres also left in 1971. In January 1992, he retired as a New York City bus driver and now collects a pension. Since he left Joe Cuba, he has not stopped recording; he is still one of the best singers in the industry.

Nick Jiménez earned a bachelor's degree in music and is now teaching at the Musical Conservatory of Puerto Rico. Tommy Berrios is a new man. Whatever problems he faced in 1968 no longer haunt him. He and his octet, Fantasy, are looking for gigs. Slim Cordero is itching to get back on a bandstand. He hopes that the sextet will unite in response to numerous requests by people to once again see the Joe Cuba group. Jimmy Sabater parted from the group in 1975 and hasn't had a day off since; he sings with the best groups. He and Charlie Palmieri co-led El Combo Gigante until Palmieri's death in 1989. Sabater, without doubt, is identified with the song "To Be with You." Cheo Feliciano is a superstar, a little gray around the temples, but a much wiser and happier man. In 1988, he reunited with Jimmy Sabater for Coche Records to record *El Sexteto Otra Vez.* Joe Cuba is a licensed paralegal. He has had a total hip replacement and is rounding up sidemen for a comeback.

The success of the Joe Cuba Sextet was a result of several elements: six musicians (four of them self-taught), original songs, quality arrangements and their successful execution, and good promotion. The group also got a boost from the Latin music grapevine, which passed along approval by word of mouth from one community to another. "To Be with Them" as all this unfolded would have been to enjoy every event the group experienced—especially those that were accompanied by a deep, throaty, mischievous laugh.

Originally published in Latin Beat *magazine, July 1992*

THIRTY-SIX

WILLIE TORRES

A popular Latin music vocalist during the 1950s and 1960s, Willie Torres is among a small number of Latin musicians who has enjoyed retirement only because he developed other skills besides musicianship.

New York City's Latin-music industry began flourishing in the 1930s, and by the end of the decade there were about fifteen orchestras. In the 1940s, that number doubled. During that period, when Latin musicians belonged to Local 802 of the American Federation of Musicians, bandleaders filed contracts with the union for recording, theater, and ballroom jobs. On the contracts were the names of the musicians and their social security numbers. The union had two pay scales: Broadway theaters and hotels such as the Waldorf-Astoria were "class A" locations and paid top dollar. Ballrooms such as the Park Plaza or the dime-a-dance clubs in midtown Manhattan were "class B" and paid less. Both union pay scales were subject to withholding taxes and deductions for social security and pension benefits. This system continued until the early 1950s, when the owners of newly formed recording companies persuaded Latin musicians not to file contracts so that they could keep the money the union deducted.

Major labels such as RCA and Columbia continued to file contracts for recording sessions of the Machito, Noro Morales, Tito Puente, and Tito Rodríguez orchestras. Union musicians all wanted to work the class A venues, and very few Hispanic musicians got the jobs. The Roseland Ballroom's dances were always packed on weekends. Roseland's "Latin Tuesdays" were also crowded to capacity, but musicians were paid fifteen dollars less than the weekend musicians because Latin music played on an off night was considered class B. El Caborojeño and Broadway Casino, two popular dance halls on the West Side of Manhattan, paid sidemen ninety dollars for three one-hour sets on Fridays, Saturdays, and Sundays. Latin musicians complained, and union delegates confronted the club owners, who promised to pay a scale of $120 for the weekend.

A few months later, Latin musicians abandoned the union when it was revealed that the club owners were still paying ninety dollars for a weekend. The owners' take-it-or-leave-it attitude led several bandleaders to accept the jobs. Many of the musicians working these clubs were not union members, and this angered the union. Membership declined, along with contracts for class B jobs, and deductions for taxes, social security, and pension benefits were not withheld. Eventually some bandleaders were investigated for not withholding taxes and for owing the federal government substantial amounts of money. Because of these under-the-table practices, musicians who reached retirement age without a savings account were in trouble, since many had no pension benefits. By the late 1990s, some of the best Latin musicians had passed their sixty-fifth birthdays. Yet they have been compelled to keep gigging: the other option is to become homeless.

Willie Torres is a typical Latin musician, a self-taught vocalist who learned from other musicians' experiences not to make the same errors of judgment they had. He has made certain he would not have to endure the no-pension fate.

Torres was born on October 30, 1929, while his Puerto Rican parents lived at 103rd Street in East Harlem. At age seven he was a member of the Union Settlement, a recreation center for the children of Spanish Harlem. One summer day, when the Coca-Cola company invited the settlement's children to tour their plant, Torres won a prize for his rendition of "Goody Goody" in a singing contest. From then on he was always singing—on the street, in building hallways, and in school. He hung out on 103rd Street, where Puerto Rican actor Henry Silva and blind guitarist José Feliciano were reared. During his teenage years, Torres was influenced by the recordings of Mel Tormé and Frank Sinatra. He became a Latin music aficionado after being tremendously moved by Orquesta Casino de la Playa's recording of "Las Ferias de las Flores."

Like many Puerto Rican kids in Spanish Harlem at the time, Torres was an athlete who excelled at softball, baseball, and stickball, as well as fistfighting. As a member of the Puerto Rican Knights stickball team, he never realized his wish to beat the awesome Devils from 115th Street or the Furies from 109th Street and Madison Avenue.

In 1945, at age sixteen, Torres became the vocalist for Pappy Ali y Sus Rumberos. The group rehearsed their arrangements of Machito and Marcelino Guerra tunes at the Good Neighborhood Federation on 106th Street between Park and Lexington Avenues. Ali's pianist, a brilliant fourteen-year-old named Gil López (who later played with Tito Rodríguez and Tito Puente), was the spark plug that fired the group. When the Rumberos disbanded in 1947, Torres acquired a new skill that would later play an important part in his life. For the next five years, Torres drove a truck in the garment center.

One evening in early 1952, he visited El Obrero Español, an after-hours club at 102nd Street and Madison Avenue. There he renewed his friendship with Nick Jiménez, a tall, thin pianist and composer who was directing a quintet. Jiménez invited Torres to sing, and Torres's stunning English-language mambo version of "I've Got You Under My Skin" prompted Jiménez to hire him. At this same time, an instrumental group called the Joe Panama Quintet was a hot attraction at Los Muchachos, a nightclub two blocks away. The quintet was led by David "Joe Panama" Preudhomme, a pianist of Panamanian descent, with Roy Rosa on bass, Tommy Berrios on vibraphone, Jimmy Sabater on timbales, and Gilberto "Sonny" Calderón on congas.

Inexplicably, Panama fired his sidemen and replaced them with other musicians. Gil Calderón assumed control of the disbanded quintet and added Willie Torres and Nick Jiménez to what became the "Joe Panama Sextet." Machito and promoter Catalino Rolón got the group gigs at the Park Plaza, Audubon Ballroom, Hotel Diplomat, and Hunts Point Palace. One evening, while the sextet was performing at La Bamba Club in midtown Manhattan, David Preudhomme and his mother dropped by the club and warned Calderón that they held the copyright on the "Joe Panama" name. Calderón ignored them, but the musicians' union ruled in favor of Preudhomme and his mother. In 1955, Rolón renamed Calderón's group the Joe Cuba Sextet, and its reign of popularity began.

In 1956, vocalist Santitos Colón left the José Curbelo orchestra to join Tito Puente's band. Torres auditioned for Colón's spot by singing all his vocals at Curbelo's Riverdale apartment; after two hours he became Colón's replacement. Replacing Torres in the Joe Cuba Sextet was José "Cheo" Feliciano. In 1959, Curbelo became a Latin-music booking agent when he disbanded to organize the Alpha Agency. Not once during his tenure with Curbelo did Torres get to record. The vocalist kept busy by singing with several bands and recording with guitarist Randy Carlos.

In 1961 a new musical era was ushered in by the *pachanga*, which was played by charanga orchestras featuring flutes and violins. Torres joined Charlie Palmieri's charanga, La Duboney. Latin Americans now heard Torres's ballad renditions of "La Vida Es Un Sueño," "Estuve Pensando," and "Hoy Como Ayer," and the mambos "El Vendedor de Mangos" and "El Yerbero." With heartfelt sincerity, Torres said, "I owe much to Charlie Palmieri....He made me aware of majors, minors, tone changes, and many other recording tips which improved my technique." Other great recordings followed: *Qué Chévere* (1963) with Orlando Marín, *Vaya Means Go!* (1963) and *Sí Sí, La Playa* (1965) with La Playa Sextet, and a 45-rpm single titled "Olvidado" (1965) that was released by Seeco. Torres was never without work. His voice was heard on recordings or in ballrooms with the orchestras of Bobby Paunetto, Tito Puente, Joe Quijano, Pete Terrace, Ray Barretto, and Eddie Palmieri.

In 1956, Torres left Joe Cuba to sing with José Curbelo's orchestra. Was this move an error in judgment? Cheo Feliciano, his replacement, rose to become a superstar. Ten years later, in 1966, Torres replaced Feliciano in Cuba's sextet. Torres's delivery on the tunes "Triste" and "Que Son Uno" made the sextet's Tico LP *Wanted Dead or Alive* a best seller in 1966.

Four years later, after logging thousands of miles throughout the Caribbean, South America, Central America, and Mexico, Torres thought about his future and decided he needed security during his senior years. He bade the sextet farewell and became a bus driver for the New York City Transit Authority. He continued to record jingles for radio and TV commercials, as well as the hit "Undress My Mind" for Chico Mendoza's band Ocho. In 1990, after twenty years of driving a bus, Torres retired and started enjoying a monthly pension check and medical benefits.

"Musicians should think about their future," he said. "They should not only depend on their music skills. If they are not union members entitled to pension benefits, they should develop other skills so they could have a pension and enjoy retirement."

Originally published in Latin Beat *magazine, September 1999*

THIRTY-SEVEN

CHEO FELICIANO

Singer José "Cheo" Feliciano rose to the top of the Latin music world and was at one time considered king of the balladeers, but then he fell from the lofty heights of stardom into the black hole of substance abuse. In addition to losing hundreds of thousands of dollars, he almost lost his family and his life. For years he experienced the pain of daily drug cravings. He sank to a life of street dereliction, panhandling for money for a fix. His life was an indescribable hell. Dying would have been the easy way out. But he never gave up. His will to live, to regain the love of his family, and to recapture his niche in the Latin music world gave him the inspiration to beat the odds.

During 1968, 1970, and 1971, Feliciano endured the excruciating agony of quitting cold turkey until the demonic cravings finally subsided, permitting him to resume a normal life. In the December 26, 1988, issue of the *San Juan Star*, he revealed his drug problem in an interview with reporter John Ortíz, who wrote that "After thirty-one years as a salsa singing star and balladeer, Cheo Feliciano has proven a lasting exponent of Latin music. Even more, his battle to conquer drug addiction has earned him the respect and admiration of many." Feliciano is evidence that people addicted to drugs can come back to live a productive life. Perhaps his story will result in a mandatory course for high school and college students about the evils of drug abuse, and how to say no.

Cheo was born José Luis Angel Feliciano-Vega on July 3, 1935, in Ponce, Puerto Rico. During his preteen years he listened to his father singing at home. Colombian baritone Carlos Ramírez, of Hollywood fame, was another of his musical influences. Feliciano's musical education consisted of conga-thumping street-jam sessions at the Ponce Free School of Music. In 1952, at age seventeen, he relocated to New York City, where he attended Seward Park High School. He frequented the Latin-music ballrooms, which featured the popular Cuban rhythms of Machito, Tito Puente, and

Tito Rodríguez. Feliciano befriended Machito, who became his mentor. "Macho and I met at the Palladium Ballroom," said Feliciano. "He counseled me and gave me direction...he introduced me to Tito Puente and Tito Rodríguez."

Feliciano dropped out of school and played congas with beginner groups. One evening in 1956, he and some friends were at the Palladium to enjoy the music of Tito Rodríguez. One of Feliciano's friends, well known to Rodríguez, urged him to give Cheo a chart to sing. Feliciano, who knew all of Rodríguez's repertoire, was given Tito's maracas as he climbed onto the bandstand. He sailed though "Changó Tá Vení."

"I looked for Tito in the crowd," he said. "I was dying to hear what he thought. Tito walked toward me smiling, raised his arms in the air, and urged the dancers to applaud more. He turned to me and said, 'You want to sing, so sing!' I sang 'Barito.' It was the first time I sang before an audience. Nothing I've done has ever matched that thrill. I will always remember the moment because of a remark made by Julio Andino, Tito's bass player. He said, 'Now there are two of you—Tito Rodríguez and Cheo Feliciano.'"

Months later, Feliciano learned through Spanish Harlem's grapevine that Joe Cuba was searching for a vocalist to fill Willie Torres's spot. One night in 1957 at the Palladium, Tito Rodríguez told Joe Cuba about Cheo and insisted that he be given a chance. Right after Tito's trumpeter Mario Cora praised Feliciano, Cuba decided to have his timbales player, Jimmy Sabater, scout Feliciano. Sabater reported, "He is what we need." Cuba needed to be convinced, so he invited Feliciano to audition at El Club San Juan.

"That night, Cheo arrived late, and he couldn't sing our English-lyric tunes," recalled Cuba. "He showed great promise; I could hear it. He won me over with his warm personality. He knew all the Tito Rodríguez tunes....He started out banging the cowbell, [and] as we added Rodríguez tunes to our repertoire, Cheo began to sing them."

For the next few years, the Joe Cuba Sextet's performances and recordings enabled the group to soar in popularity and earn a spot among Latin music's top ten bands. In 1962, when Seeco recorded Cuba's album *Steppin' Out*, Feliciano's delivery of the ballad "Cómo Ríen" served notice that his star was on the rise. "Cómo Ríen" won him a place among Latin music's most romantic singers—Lucho Gatica, Tito Rodríguez, Vicentico Valdés, Gilberto Monroig, Graciela, and Vitín Aviles. When his rendition of "Aunque Tú," a lush ballad from the 1964 Seeco LP *Diggin' the Most*, was released, Latin music had another Frank Sinatra.

One year later, Cheo's life and star image began to decline. Those responsible were the vermin who enslave people by getting them addicted to drugs. The December 26, 1988, issue of the *San Juan Star* included reporter John Ortiz's interview with Feliciano, titled "Cheo's Tale: Beating the Drug Habit." "I started smoking marijuana only on Saturdays," Cheo told Ortíz. "After awhile I became accustomed to it and I looked for something stronger. I graduated to snorting cocaine. The drug bondage began when the drug dealers started mixing the cocaine with heroin. My next step was heroin. I became increasingly irresponsible....My life started falling apart. I spent little time at home. Before joining the sextet at the job site, I would get high. After the gig I would stay out all night and stayed high. After a few hours sleep, I would feel sick and go out again in search of more drugs.

"I would arrive to work late. I wouldn't begin singing until I was high. I was always arriving late—with only minutes before the gig started. I would invent twenty thousand excuses. I would rip my clothes and say I was mugged...but the Cuba sidemen didn't believe me." Cheo was replaced by Willie Torres in 1965 during the recording of the award-winning Tico label album *We Must Be Doing Something Right!*

"I was on my own—no job," said Feliciano. "I remember recording an album with Eddie Palmieri [1967's *Champagne*, for Tico]. At the time, I was trying to kick the habit. I took medication to ease the pain. In 1969 I was in Puerto Rico with Kako's orchestra. After a month the band returned to New York. I remained in Puerto Rico. Whatever money I earned went into my veins. At first, friends put me up...then I had no place to stay and started living like a beggar in the streets. I spent much time in La Perla—slept under houses, abandoned cars, abandoned buildings. I lived for drugs. I never stole, but I took advantage of my friends and fans and asked them for money. I roamed the streets of El Condado without taking a bath, without shaving for a month, with worn-out shoes....Everyone saw me.

"During the Christmas season of 1969, bandleader Tommy Olivencia and his trumpeter Luis Café told me of Hogar Crea, a drug rehabilitation center at Trujillo Alto just starting out. I enrolled for three years. I was tied to my bed....I felt nothing but pain....I was going cold turkey. I felt pain, fevers, nausea....When 1972 arrived I was on my way to recovery....Fania president Jerry Masucci assured me of a new future when I recorded Tite Curet Alonso's songs 'Anacaona,' 'Mi Triste Problema,' and 'Franqueza Cruel' for the Vaya LP *Cheo*. The recording was made during a two-week pass in New York. A few of Crea's officials thought I would not return. They looked surprised two weeks later when they saw me with my suitcases. I had shown them and myself that I intended to fulfill my obligations. After a few months, the album was out and I received my certificate, which confirmed that I completed my treatment. I was so proud. I learned all my weaknesses and how much I failed my profession, my family, God, and my people. I feared the outside world's rejection, that I would not be permitted to return to singing. I was accepted with open arms and was treated as if nothing had ever happened."

Jerry Masucci gave Cheo Feliciano his passport back to the Latin-music world. He signed him to a contract and selected the cream of Fania's artists, along with renowned composer Catalino "Tite" Curet Alonso to pen six tunes. The liner notes hinted of Cheo's three-year absence. The album cover was a photo of a pensive Feliciano staring out to sea at Old San Juan's El Morro Castle as he contemplated his future. When I heard his lush treatment of the ballad "Poema de Otoño," I figured that Cheo was back.

In September 1972, the Vaya label LP *La Voz Sensual de Cheo* was released. It's my favorite of all his albums. Masucci made sure it received exposure. Feliciano was the opening act for Larry Harlow's salsa "opera" *Hommy*, which was presented at Carnegie Hall on March 29, 1973. At 8:20 P.M., *Latin New York* magazine publisher Izzy Sanabria introduced Jorge Calandrelli, the Argentine musician who orchestrated the violins for Cheo's album. After Calandrelli mounted the conductor's stand and the spotlight focused on Cheo in his blue velvet tuxedo, a tremendous roar of applause and high-pitched, feminine shrieks washed over five tiers of standing people. Visibly moved by the overwhelming audience response, Cheo seemed to choke up. His Adam's apple bobbed a few times and his eyes became teary. He waved, bowed his head in several directions, looked up and around at the audience, and threw kisses to the people seated above the orchestra.

Three minutes later, when the applause diminished, the house lights dimmed and a romantic mood ensued. Then, very softly, violin music began. A high-intensity spotlight focused on Cheo's handsome face as he held the microphone close to his mouth. He closed his eyes and began to sing the first of five ballads, "Contigo a la Distancia," in his sensual, resonant voice.

Between songs, Cheo surprised everyone with his bilingual articulateness and fluency. Like a true Nuyorican, he started one sentence in Spanish and ended in English. After being knocked out by the ballads "Cómo Ríen," "Siempre de Tí," "Nuestra Vida," and "Juégate," the audience tried to prolong its euphoria by refusing to let Cheo leave the stage. Then the unexpected happened. Izzy Sanabria brought the audience to its feet with clamorous applause when he paid a ringing tribute to the king of the bolero, Tito Rodríguez. Sanabria, looking at the audience and pointing to Feliciano, said, "Tito's gone, and now I want to have Cheo take his place."

Sanabria and the audience crowned Cheo Feliciano the new king of the bolero.

Since his return from purgatory in 1971, Feliciano has garnered various awards for his recordings of "Cómo Ríen," "Juégate," "Contigo a la Distancia," "Delirio," "Poema de Otoño," "Yo Quiero Ser Tu Amante," "Amada Mía," and "Canta," one of the best recordings of 1976. He won the *Latin New York* magazine award for best vocalist of 1975. On October 13, 1984, a sold-out crowd witnessed a Cheo Feliciano tribute at Madison Square Garden. On Esta Noche Sensacional, as the show was billed, Feliciano was acknowledged as one of Puerto Rico's greatest artists.

At this point in his life, Cheo had experienced all types of thrills, but he never realized his dream of singing duets with the great Cuban vocalists Beny Moré and Elena Burke. He often thought about working with them, as well as with Cuban composer César Portillo de la Luz, who composed "Tú Mi Delirio" and "Contigo a la Distancia."

During the third week of November 1997, Feliciano and his wife accepted an invitation to visit Cuba. His dream became a reality. The November 23 issue of the newspaper *Nuevo Día* carried an article by writer Javier Santiago that described the visit under the headline "Cheo en Cuba."

"The streets of Old Havana were immaculately clean," the article read. "Old buildings with their weather-beaten façades were the background of the '50s. American-manufactured Buicks, Pontiacs, and Fords were parked in the streets. On sidewalks alive with human activity were heard voices discussing the Pope's scheduled visit, and daily hunger because of food rationing and the American blockade. All of a sudden a woman stopped in front of a couple, leaned forward for a better look, then said, 'Cheo, thanks for coming.' Like an uncontrollable brushfire, word spread throughout Havana and Varadero that Cheo Feliciano was in Cuba to sing for them."

"When the Fania All Stars visited Havana [in 1979]," said Feliciano, "I was told that Cubans were yelling my name, that they wanted to hear me sing." The outpouring of love and the Cuban people's warmth toward him were overwhelming. "Everywhere I went," said Cheo, "it was the same…they had me crying all six days I was there. My wish to meet Orquesta Aragón, Elena Burke, and Portillo de la Luz came true. First we went to Varadero. The press and TV cameras greeted us. A caravan of cars followed us to a hotel."

Hours later, Cheo was on stage; he sang for three hours. The Cubans loved every second of his performance, applauding enthusiastically and encouraging him to sing "El Ratón," "Anacaona," "Amada Mía," and hits from his well-known repertoire, which was on a cassette that had been dubbed hundreds of times by Feliciano aficionados. Next evening, Cheo was the featured act at El Club Tropicana. On stage, he scanned the few hundred people in the audience and uttered words of praise to César Portillo de la Luz, who joined him on stage. At long last, part of his dream came true, and he warmly embraced Portillo de la Luz. Cheo was singing an up-tempo tune when suddenly he was joined by vocalists Pedro Calvo, Ismael Miranda (from Puerto Rico), and Issac Delgado.

During his free time in Cuba, Cheo walked the streets of Havana. Another part of his wish came true when he met and embraced Elena Burke. He shook hands with musicians, with the grandson of the late vocalist Miguelito Cuní, with composer Nico Rojas, with vocalist Puntillita, and with the granddaughter of Chano Pozo. Cheo was showered with flowers. He and his wife visited a church and left some of the flowers on the altar of La Virgen de la Caridad. Outside the church, the Felicianos encountered a crowd of school kids who kept yelling his name. His voice quivered and cracked while tears swelled in his eyes. "It was an emotional moment," Cheo said. "Now I understand why Cubans and Puerto Ricans *somos de un pájaro las dos alas* [are birds of a feather]....Our countries have much in common....We never discussed politics, we spoke about music....The people I spoke to know about Gilberto Santa Rosa, Marc Anthony, La India, Ismael Miranda, El Gran Combo, La Sonora Ponceña, even Joe Cuba....I don't think that anyone will be offended by my visit here....I have been part of a cultural exchange....If my musical career ends with this visit, I will accept it, because it was like graduating from college."

Originally published in Latin Beat *magazine, December/January 1999*

THIRTY-EIGHT

JOE BATAAN

New York City's East Harlem during the 1940s and 1950s was notorious for gang wars that contributed to a high incidence of teenage crime and death. Every block between 100th and 125th Streets had gangs that either played stickball or fought. The teenage Harlemite had few role models besides sports figures and musicians.

During the mid-1940s, performers like Miguelito Valdés, Machito, Noro Morales, and Marcelino Guerra attracted youngsters to the Latin music world. Tito Puente, Tito Rodríguez, Cal Tjader, Johnny Pacheco, Ray Barretto, and Eddie Palmieri were inspirations for youngsters in the 1950s and '60s. That is when Joe Bataan gained the appreciation for Latin music that would determine the course of his life.

He was born Peter Nitollano Jr. in Harlem Hospital on May 15, 1942. His African-American mother was from Newport, Virginia, and his father was Filipino. The family lived in several tenements before settling at 104th Street between Lexington and Park Avenues in 1947. He started school at PS 72, continued at Patrick Henry Junior High, then went on to Commerce High School, but dropped out after a year.

"My earliest recollection of music was when I was five," said Bataan. "I sang along with whatever came on over the radio. Later I hung out at Gitch's candy store at 103rd Street and Lexington Avenue, where I bought the monthly *Hit Parade* magazine, which listed the current popular hits. I learned the lyrics and sang along to tunes like 'Tennessee Waltz,' 'Cruising Down the River,' 'Stranger in Paradise,' 'Cry,' and 'Oh! My Papa.' My Latin music appreciation began with 'Anabacoa,' 'Ran Kan Kan,' Alfredito's 'Chinese Mambo,' and the merengue 'A Lo Oscuro.' Then in 1955 I was influenced by Frankie Lyman's 'Why Do Fools Fall in Love.' I was one of a thousand kids at the Brooklyn Paramount who saw the Harptones, the Chantels, the Heartbeats, Bo Diddley, and Fats Domino. As teenagers we had a music that was ours....We identified with the young artists and the lyrics....I say this because parents tend to forget they were once teenagers, that they had yearnings, pangs of puppy love, and that they also wanted to be treated like adults. Teenage blacks and Puerto Ricans born in ghettos have no say about the poverty and oppression we are born into, but we had our beautiful sisters and a music that enabled us to be just as rich as the kids living in affluent areas."

During Bataan's adolescence, his adept fighting skills and swift hands were legendary in East Harlem, where he was known as the Afro-Filipino Sugar Ray Robinson. "Girls were always the reasons for fights," he said. "It would begin with a guy rapping to another guy's girlfriend; it offended her man, who would seek revenge with his gang....Then the opposing gang wanted its revenge...it never ended....Being bad got me attention...I wanted an identity. Guys who stood on corners and looked bad were impressive, though no one wanted to belong to a gang of thugs, so the group called itself a 'social athletic club.'...They became unsociable at the weekly grind-'em-ups [where dancers embraced and gyrated their lower torsos]."

In 1959, a housing police officer caught Bataan driving a stolen vehicle, and he was sentenced to serve five years at the state prison in Coxsackie, New York. While incarcerated, Bataan learned the rudiments of music under the tutelage of Mark Francis. "Music was my salvation," said Bataan. "It taught me discipline. I acquired a mature attitude about life. I was paroled after two years, and at this time I had already read many books and earned my high school diploma. In the evening I hung out at the William Ettinger Youth Center at 106th Street between Madison and Park Avenues, and I learned to play piano by reading a beginners' instruction book. I copied the style of my man Eddie Palmieri. I learned Latin dancing at the Chez José, got married, and was expecting a child when in 1964 I violated my parole and returned to Coxsackie."

One day in prison he thought about the huge number of African-Americans and Hispanics his age who filled the place. He began analyzing lyrics and reinterpreting the world after listening to the Teen Queens' "Eddie My Love," the Cadillacs' "Gloria," and the Skyliners' "Since I Don't Have You." He picked up on their positive messages and set out to write songs that would change people's attitudes about life. A different Bataan emerged after a prison guard advised him that "acquisition of knowledge would help one sidestep the traps in life which usually lead to prison time and death."

One year later, the new Joe Bataan was released from prison. He organized his band by recruiting whoever entered the Ettinger Center with an instrument case. He rehearsed his group five days a week. When he needed vocalists, he called upon two old friends, doo-woppers Tito Ramos and Tito Rojas, who declined because they were singing for the newly organized Johnny Colón orchestra.

"Colón's band was holding rehearsals at the Banana Club at 102nd Street and First Avenue," said Bataan. "Both Titos said that Johnny would not permit anyone to hear his band. But that didn't apply to me because Johnny and I were tight. We attended Commerce High School together. I walked into the club and sat down in a dark area. I was turned on by the trombone sound and Milton Cardona's conga drumming. I approached Johnny, who was sitting at the piano, wanting to congratulate him. In a nasty tone he demanded I leave. I became angry. It was his belligerent attitude that fired me up. I wanted revenge, so instead of kicking his ass, I thought about directing a band better than his. I set out to create a new sound, a fusion of R&B and Latin. Every day for the following six months my band improved, and I began using the name 'Bataan.' My boys were ready for gigs after our repertoire added both original tunes and vocalist Georgie Pagán.

"In the lobby of the Boricua Theatre at 107th Street and Lexington Avenue, I approached Federico Pagani and told him I had a band looking for work. I gave him a business card that was given to me that same day. On the card was printed 'Joe.'" He no longer remembers who "Joe" was, but he wrote his new stage surname on the card, and his phone number. "That evening we debuted at the Bronx Tropicana, and I looked on the poster and realized Pagani combined Joe's name and 'Bataan.'...Ever since then I have been Joe Bataan."

After Bataan's first set, Pagani offered him a steady job. "I finally was going to earn money, but my sidemen were in their teens and had a 10 P.M. curfew. I pleaded with their mothers, who gave me a hard time because of my gang-leader reputation. I convinced them I was a new Bataan, to give me a chance to prove it. Pagani provided gigs at the Tropicoro, Colgate Gardens, and Bronx Casino, and he paid us well."

Georgie Pagán's noticeable Spanish accent was the reason Bataan began singing. He changed the lyrics of "Gypsy Woman," sang it, and received a favorable response. George Goldner and Stan Lewis, who founded the Cotique label, heard Bataan audition at the Ettinger Center.

"My band played and I sang. Goldner said, 'Great, but you don't want to sing. You sound sweet; you need a masculine tone.' I became angry, and had I not become the new Bataan, I would have knocked him on his ass. I cooled off. My pride was wounded, so I said 'OK, I'll record with someone else.' Goldner said, 'Don't get upset. I want to record you. What do you care? You're the leader of the band; let someone else sing.' He told me in a nice way I couldn't sing. Mr. Goldner gave me a blank contract to sign, and I signed it with my pseudonym, Joe Bataan. George Rosas, my manager, introduced me to DJ Dick 'Ricardo' Sugar, whose contract I also signed as Joe Bataan."

Days later, Bataan signed a contract with booking agent José Curbelo's Alpha Agency. Curbelo introduced Bataan to Jack Hooke, the promoter for the Village Gate nightclub. Hooke told him that Atlantic Records would record him if he agreed to do it without getting paid. When Curbelo learned of the terms, he introduced Bataan to Morris Levy, president of Tico-Roulette Records, at Levy's office. "What do you want?" Levy asked Bataan. "I want to record," was the reply. "OK, you got it," said Levy. "The kid wants to publish his music and get paid for the recording," said Curbelo. "He's got it," responded Levy. "I'll schedule a session next week."

In walked George Goldner, who saw Bataan and asked him what he was doing there. Curbelo and Levy looked at each other, bewildered. "I have this kid on contract," said Goldner. "Wise guy, huh?" said Levy, looking at Bataan. Levy asked Curbelo and Bataan to leave so he could discuss the problem with Goldner, but Goldner retorted that there was nothing to discuss, since he had a signed contract. Levy became enraged and demanded that Goldner leave his office.

"Here I was in a big mess," said Bataan. "I had signed 'Joe Bataan' to contracts with George Rosas, Dick Sugar, Jack Hooke, José Curbelo, and Symphony Sid. I did it to get the best possible deal, and whoever tried to shaft me, I would renege on the contract, because Joe Bataan was not my true name. They all nutted up on me. I was locked out of dance halls and didn't work for a while. Eventually I decided to record for Fania, because Jerry Masucci was not part of that clique. Jerry paid me for the arrangements and the recordings."

The night Dick Sugar aired "Gypsy Woman" for the first time, the entire Joe Bataan orchestra and a few hundred neighborhood friends congregated at a housing project playground at 103rd Street and listened to their portable radios. "It had all the excitement of a championship bout," said Bataan. "About twenty minutes into Sugar's show he played it, and it was the greatest feeling in the world. For the following weeks our fans called Dick Sugar and requested 'Gypsy Woman.' One evening, Sugar's words had me choking with emotion. I began to cry when he said that the number of requests for 'Gypsy Woman' was incredible and that it couldn't happen to a nicer guy. It was a dream come true. You have no idea what it means to guys like me to rise from poverty to recognition, to experience the acceptance of my music after working so hard. I was now Joe Bataan, musician and bandleader. My band performed at Latin and black dances."

"Gypsy Woman" landed the number sixteen spot on WWRL's charts. Three months after the *Gypsy Woman* LP was released, Bataan recorded two other albums, *Subway Joe* and *Riot!* It did not matter that his sound was not *típico*. He was singing about the daily events in El Barrio, and he was singing about the people. As he sang, the outside world heard about ordinary guys, unwed mothers, subway rides, and love for a woman. Bataan's orchestra was among Latin music's top five in record sales. "Polito Vega is responsible for the tremendous sales of *Subway Joe*," said Bataan. "He aired more of my recordings than any other DJ."

The sounds of Johnny Colón, Joe Cuba, King Nando, the Lebrón Brothers, Pete Rodríguez, Joey Pastrana, and Joe Bataan were all the rage, but except for Joe Cuba, they all were paid much less than established bands, and they got second billing. There was talk about Latin-soul bandleaders uniting to protest this injustice, but nothing ever came of it. "I was taking home four hundred dollars a night," said Bataan, "but after paying off commissions to everyone who owned a piece of me, I ended up with one hundred dollars."

"In 1968, Tommy James and the Shondells sold two and a half million copies of 'Crystal Blue Persuasion' for Morris Levy's Roulette label, and it rose to the number six spot on the New York City charts. This was the beginning of my involvement in the American pop field. Jerry had me record it for his new label, Uptite Records, and it sold well."

Bataan left Fania before his contract expired and founded Ghetto Records with George Febo. Since he could not record until his Fania contract ended, he went the live concert route and made personal appearances. Within months, Ghetto Records folded. In 1973, Bataan got his release from Fania and signed with Mericana Records. One week after his LP *Salsoul* (1973) was released, it was so well promoted by WBLS DJ Frankie Crocker that it sold more than twenty thousand copies. The Salsoul label LP *Afrofilipino* also sold well and placed Bataan on the road to American pop stardom. In 1975, the French sextet Blonde Latin recorded Marty Sheller's arrangement of Bataan's "Johnny's No Good." It was played throughout France and subsequently earned Bataan more money than any of his other compositions. Then, disagreements with Joe Cayre led to the termination of Bataan's contract with Salsoul. The album *Mestizo* (1980), which included "Rap-O Clap-O," reflected the beginning of the rap era.

Since the mid-1980s, Bataan has spent more of his time as a youth counselor and has helped troubled teenagers become productive citizens. Still, music has called him, and on April 27, 1995, he made a successful comeback at a concert held at the Hostos College Center for the Arts.

"Everything good that has happened to me, I owe to God," said Bataan. "People are now wondering which Bataan I am, the old or the new. Well, tell them the real Bataan is back."

Originally published in Latin Beat *magazine, August 1995*

THIRTY-NINE

SALSA ORIGINS

Popular use of the word "salsa" for danceable Latin music began in 1933, when Cuban song composer Ignacio Piñeiro wrote the tune "Échale Salsita." According to the late Alfredito Valdés Sr., whom I interviewed in 1974, "On July 6, 1933, I married Anita Purmuy, guitarist for the all-female band La Anacaona. I didn't have a honeymoon because hours later I was on a boat with [Septeto] Nacional headed toward Miami...then to the world's fair in Chicago. On the train I rehearsed Ignacio's new tune, 'Echale Salsita.' He got the idea after tasting food that lacked the Cuban spices. It was a protest against tasteless foods."

During the late 1930s, as the Hispanic community was sprouting in Spanish Harlem, Gabriel Oller, proprietor of Tatay's Spanish Music Center on the corner of 110th Street and 5th Avenue, remembers shouts of *"échale pique, caliéntalo, menéalo que se empelota"* (put some spice in it, heat it up, shake it till it blows) used to describe the thrilling Afro-Cuban dance rhythms of rumbas and *guarachas*. The term "salsa" remained dormant until 1962, when Seeco Records released Joe Cuba's *Steppin' Out* LP. In Jimmy Sabater's tune "Salsa y Bembé," vocalist Cheo Feliciano wants his main squeeze to add salsa to the *bembé*—the dance—when she does her steps. The lyrics suggest a request for the dancer to liven or spice up her performance. "When I wrote this tune," said Sabater, "I was labeling the music as 'salsa'...you know, exciting. When musicians were asked to spice up the music, there were shouts of *'guataca.'* While the band was executing the mambo part, I heard shouts of *'guapachosa.'* These were labels which never caught on. My use of 'salsa' was to describe the music, not the food."

A year later, Alegre Records released Charlie Palmieri's charanga LP *Salsa Na' Ma'*. In the Henry Alvarez tune with the same name, the chorus of Víctor Velásquez and Willie Torres suggests that when they dance with their partners it is *salsa na' ma', qué cosa rica*—only salsa, what a joy." However, Al Santiago called the music "salsa" in his liner notes that describe La Duboney (Palmieri's band) as "a musical aggregation that functions as an individual unit and possesses that all important 'sauce' necessary for satisfying the most demanding of musical tastes. It is for this reason that the LP album offering is titled *Salsa Na' Ma'*."

On November 20, 1964, the Cal Tjader Quintet Plus Five had just finished recording a long version of "Guachi Guaro," another version of Tjader's first hit recording in 1954, "Wachi Wara" (adapted from Chano Pozo's composition "Guarachi Guaro"). After hearing it played back, Tjader was dissatisfied: it lacked something, but he did not know what. Creed Taylor, producer of the album (which had no title at that moment), suggested a shorter version and a new title, since "Guachi Guaro" would be difficult to pronounce and did not mean anything. Tjader invited Willie Bobo to dub the *quijada*—the jawbone. Bobo did so, and his interpretations of "Sabor, Sabor" and "Salsa Ahí Na' Ma'" satisfied Tjader and gave him the idea for the album's name, *Soul Sauce (Salsa del Alma)*. Bobo explained to Tjader that this track and the others—"Pantano," "Maramoor Mambo," "Tanya," and "Leyte"—were fiery and exciting, like well-seasoned sauce. The *Soul Sauce* album cover thus sports a fork on a plate of red beans and chili, along with an open bottle of Tabasco sauce labeled *Cal Tjader Soul Sauce*. This was the third time such music had been called "salsa," and in San Francisco, Tjader's Mexican-American fans began using the word to describe his brand of music. The term spread to Los Angeles, to other California cities, and eastward via Spanish-language stations across the United States, and also via rhythm-and-blues and jazz programs throughout the country. Such stations had never before aired Latin music. Now they helped Tjader sell 150,000 albums.

In 1965, while West Coast Mexican-Americans were using the word "salsa" for up-tempo Latin music, African-Americans in New York were starting another trend. What was "salsa" on the West Coast was "asooka" (from the Spanish *azúcar*, meaning sugar) in New York City. "Please, Eddie [Palmieri], sweeten it…give us a little sugar," was a request to spice up the music with a unique Palmieri *montuno*. Palmieri composed and recorded the blockbuster "Azúcar," but the word never caught on outside New York. Four years later, Carlos Santana's "Oye Como Va" (a rock version of a Tito Puente tune) attracted youths of all ethnic backgrounds to his music, and conga drums sold like never before across the United States.

On August 26, 1971, the Fania Records artists congregated at El Cheetah nightclub in midtown Manhattan for a filmed dance concert that resulted in the movie *Our Latin Thing*. It premiered July 19, 1972, at the Line 2 theater at Forty-eighth Street and Seventh Avenue in New York City and received favorable reviews from the *Daily News* and *New York Times*.

Nowhere in the film is "salsa" mentioned; the word does not appear in the reviews, either.

Still, the word kept cropping up in songs. In the 1972 Mericana LP *Rey Roig Aquí Llegó*, vocalist Julian Llano's lyrics in the *bomba-son* "Traigo Salsa" were about bringing the sauce for his attractive female neighbor. In January 1973, Peter Rios gave illustrator/publisher Izzy Sanabria the right to use the *Latin New York* magazine title, which Rios owned from 1967 to 1968. *Latin New York* issue number four, dated April 16, 1973, has an ad displaying the cover of Roberto Anglero's LP *Guaya Salsa*. In the next issue, dated May 28, 1973, are ads with photos of Mericana LPs *Salsa Hits from Orquesta Power* and *Tempo 70*, as well as Louie Colón's United Artists LP *Más Salsa Que Pescao*. Issue number eight, from September/October 1973, has ads for El Cheetah Club that refer to it as "Cheetah, Home of the Salsa." The same issue advertises Vicentico Valdés's new Tico release, *Amor con Salsa*. Issue number nine, from November 1973, has an ad for vocalist Roberto Torres's Mericana LP *El Castigador Is the New Salsa Sensation*. Also in this issue is a cartoon of Izzy Sanabria announcing "a new Salsa music TV show on WXTU channel 41, premiering Saturday, November 17, 1973, at 6:30 P.M." As well, an ad for DJ Polito Vega's show reads "100% Salsa WBNX Mon–Fri 7:30 to 9:30 P.M." On the other hand, issue number twelve, dated February 1974, contains a full-page ad of the fifth Latin Music Festival, featuring Celia Cruz, Ray Barretto, Johnny Pacheco, Típica 73, the Machito Orquesta, and the Apollo Sound. Not once is "salsa" mentioned.

In March 1974, Mericana Records released Rey Roig's LP *Otra Vez*, in which Julian Llano sings *Pescao en Salsa*. During the same month, Fania Records released Larry Harlow's *Salsa*, recorded November 26 and 27, 1973. This album placed Harlow among the top five most popular bandleaders, and the LP enjoyed tremendous sales. After this, almost every recording of Afro-Cuban rhythms and anything that was exciting in Latin music was labeled "salsa." Now the Anglo market—which had abandoned the music when the *cha-cha-chá* followed the mambo's 1956 decline in popularity—came back into the fold. *Billboard* magazine's June 12, 1976, issue was dedicated to Latin music and included a twenty-four-page supplement titled "Salsa Explosion." It contained stories are about salsa, photos of salsa artists, and names of individuals who supposedly were the core of salsa. I read each article and extracted what was germane to this story.

In "Salsa Is Exploding," by Rudy Garcia of the New York *Daily News*, Garcia wrote about the "salsa explosion" and noted that "some call it political and social expression of young Puerto Rican New Yorkers, others the product of promotional genius by clever recording execs....The term began appearing on album jackets around fifteen years ago to describe the 'hot and saucy' nature of the music." Garcia continued by discussing Jerry Masucci, the president of Fania: "Masucci produced two films, *Our Latin Thing* and *Salsa*, both of which have gone a long way towards promoting the musical genre....At one point Masucci produced seventy-five hours a week of salsa programming for five Spanish-language radio stations in major Latin markets....Masucci has gotten salsa recordings played on major R&B and rock outlets in the U.S. and has helped promote salsa concerts in Europe, Africa, and South America....There is no doubting the Afro-Cuban rhythms which formed the basis for much of the music and most of the leading exponents of what has since become known as salsa music had its root in the Cuban experience....Despite the dominance of such labels as Fania, which has about seventy percent of the $8 million a year salsa market...there are other smaller labels who have managed to carve or maintain a niche for themselves....Seeco, a traditionally Latin music company, has been re-releasing salsa product from its old catalog....Seeco was in business long before Masucci's Fania....Seeco provides great material for tracing the development of the genre."

David Medina's article "Salsa Is Also a Political Force" was reprinted from the *Daily News*. "They used to call it El Ritmo Caliente," Medina wrote, "and after that El Mambo...now it has caught on all over again under the name Salsa....Salsa has helped give Latinos a sense of national identity and political unity....Salsa is also beginning to creep into the playlists of many an English language radio station here....Although any number of people are taking credit for having coined the word, the very first documented use of the word occurred in 1963 on a Charlie Palmieri record album titled *Salsa Na Mas* [sic]....Three years later the word cropped up again in Cal Tjader's *Soul Sauce* album, a runaway success....With repeated use, salsa went from a word to a full blown concept in 1971."

Geraldo Feeny wrote in "Los Angeles Swings to Salsa Beat" that "in Los Angeles and Orange counties there are 1,449,000 Spanish residents according to the 1970 U.S. census....The obstacle to salsa in L.A. is that the Spanish-speaking population doesn't identify with salsa....This changed with Latino youth at the time Carlos Santana triumphed with 'Oye Como Va'...suddenly Chicanos could identify with the salsa sound. There have also been many pioneers of salsa on the radio, the most notable of whom are Chico Sésma, Al 'Pablito' Fox, Richard Leon, Rolando Ullóa, and an organization known as Los Locutores (the DJs)...each one greatly contributed to the exposure of salsa through English-language media."

And Anam Munar's "Miami's Cubans Love Old Salsa" let readers know that "WFAB has a three-hour, daily salsa show programmed by Fania

Records; and most other Spanish-language stations program at least some salsa as part of their playlists."

In sum, it appears that Jimmy Sabater coined the word "salsa" to mean up-tempo Latin music. Cal Tjader's *Soul Sauce* and Santana's "Oye Como Va" gave the salsa movement thrust, beginning with Mexican-Americans in San Francisco. But "salsa" did not enter popular usage until *Latin New York* magazine used it repeatedly and the Fania All Stars started employing the term to describe their music when the group played outside New York City. Salsa finally exploded in the 1972 film *Our Latin Thing*, after a kid in the opening scene kicked a can and Luis Cruz Jr.'s wah-wah synthesizer sounded in Ray Barretto's rendition of "Cocinando Suave." Goose bumps broke out on the flesh of moviegoers, marking salsa's detonation. Since then, the fallout from its mushroom cloud has been felt worldwide.

Originally published in Latin Beat *magazine, November 1991*

FORTY

JERRY MASUCCI

On Sunday, December 21, 1997, Jerry Masucci, president of Fania Records, died in Buenos Aires, Argentina. The previous Friday, he had experienced stomach pains while playing tennis. During exploratory surgery on Sunday, he expired on the operating table. The cause of death was a brain aneurysm. The following week, his body was flown to New York, and his remains rested at the Frank E. Campbell Funeral Home at Eighty-first Street and Madison Avenue. On Friday, January 2, 1998, the public paid its respects. The next day, during a private ceremony attended by well-known musicians, family, friends, and VIPs, Celia Cruz could be heard singing "Ave Maria," and eulogies were given by vocalist-turned-minister Bobby Cruz, and by Ralph Mercado. After the ceremony, Masucci was reportedly cremated.

Gennaro Masucci was born on October 7, 1934, to Elvira and Urbano Masucci, who lived in Brooklyn at the time. Gennaro—or Jerry, the name he preferred—became a high school dropout who earned his diploma while serving in the U.S. Navy at Guantanamo Bay, Cuba. There he was moved by the sound of typical Cuban music, and he learned to speak Spanish. After his honorable discharge, he studied business administration in Mexico, became a New York City police officer, and earned a law degree at New York Law School.

In late 1962, while he was at the law offices of Pariser and Masucci, bandleader Johnny Pacheco, Latin music's hottest attraction at the time, met Masucci. The two of them decided to establish the Fania recording company with five thousand dollars. Pacheco's first album, *Cañonazo*, along with his second release, *At the New York World's Fair*, enjoyed tremendous sales and bankrolled the recordings of Larry Harlow, Ralph Robles, Bobby Valentín, Willie Colón, and Ray Barretto. In 1967, Barretto's album *Acid* was one of the hottest sellers; his band's performance of the outstanding track "Soul Drummer" at Harlem's Mount Morris Park was broadcast on television.

The following year, Peter Rios, a commercial artist, founded the original *Latin New York* magazine. Masucci helped pay the printing costs by buying advertising. Rios decided to present awards for the best recordings of 1967 on November 8 at New York City's Hotel Americana. Slated to win were Ray Barretto for "Soul Drummer" and Eddie Palmieri for the album *Champagne*. On the night of the awards, neither artist was mentioned. The following week, Masucci learned that the person who had supplied the live music for the event threatened to withhold it unless someone else won the awards intended for Barretto and Palmieri. Masucci exploded with anger and vowed that he would never again be vulnerable to the underhanded business-as-usual that prevails in the Latin music industry. Masucci withheld his financial support, and *Latin New York* magazine folded.

In 1970, the boogaloo's reign ended, and a modern variation of the Cuban *son* was created by Fania recording artists Pacheco, Harlow, and Barretto. It was called Cuban music, but it was really Latin music created in New York by New York musicians.

In 1973, commercial artist Izzy Sanabria revived *Latin New York* magazine and began using the word "salsa." Masucci paid for the front and back covers and for articles about Fania recording artists. Setting out to dominate the Latin-music world with movies and salsa music, he signed sixty exceptional musicians to five-year contracts. He also bought airtime on popular radio programs—Polito Vega's three-hour weekday afternoon show on WBNX in New York, Chico Sesma's show in Los Angeles, and shows in Philadelphia and San Juan, Puerto Rico. Masucci also paid for tours outside New York City. "Fame costs," said Masucci. "I paid for the recording sessions, I paid for music arrangements...I bought La Tierra Recording Studios."

Throughout his tenure as salsa's most powerful impresario, Masucci was a no-nonsense businessman. He was generous, sponsoring lavish parties and buying everyone lunch at the Fania All Stars rehearsals. In 1976, the Tito Puente orchestra had sunk in popularity, and Puente had not recorded in two years. Masucci revived Puente's career by buying television time on the popular *Dinah Shore Show*. On Friday, July 30, 1976, the Puente orchestra was seen coast-to-coast at 4 P.M. performing "Fiesta a la King"; Puente's tenor saxophonist, Al Shikaly, blew everyone away. Puente began his comeback to the top of the world; meanwhile, his performance on *Dinah Shore* cost Masucci fifteen thousand dollars. Months later, Puente's orchestra was seen on the *Donny & Marie* show.

In 1977, Masucci owned eleven recording companies—Fania, Vaya, Cotique, Tico, Alegre, Mardi Gras, Sonido, Exitos, International, Bronco, and Karen (the last recorded Dominican bands). He almost acquired Puerto Rico's Montilla label, but the deal fell through. He also earned money from real estate investments and as part owner of the Fame model agency. Throughout the 1970s, Masucci was vilified. His sin was that he was a successful businessman and had a knack for making money.

Originally published in Latin Beat *magazine, February 1998*

FORTY-ONE

THE CORSO

On May 1, 1966, the Palladium Ballroom—the mecca of New York City's mambo dancers—closed its doors for the last time. The new in place became the Chez José, located at the Park Plaza Hotel at 50 West Seventy-seventh Street, between Central Park West and Columbus Avenue. It was a posh club with black double doors that led downstairs from the street-level entrance. The Chez José opened for business on a Friday evening in mid-1965, with the Larry Harlow orchestra as its first attraction. There was no advertising or marquee trumpeting the names of the featured bands, so dancers never knew who was going to perform until they entered the ballroom. Nevertheless, the club attracted a huge following. Between 1965 and 1970, New York's elite salsa, charanga, and boogaloo orchestras performed their swinging music, attracting beautiful, elegantly dressed people who danced till the wee hours of the morning.

After the Chez José closed in 1970, the new place to be was the Corso at 205 East Eighty-sixth Street, off the corner of Third Avenue. The site had first opened for business in 1927, but until the end of World War II it was a restaurant catering predominately to the German-Americans who lived in the neighborhood. As late as 1968, when Tony Raimone became the proprietor, the Corso was still featuring "Continental music" from Europe. Raimone had been a regular customer at the Corso for fourteen years before he decided to buy it. He opened for business in May and featured the Glenn Miller Orchestra led by Buddy DeFranco. The Miller group was followed by Lionel Hampton's band. But neither orchestra attracted crowds.

One evening, Pete Bonet, a vocalist born in Santurce, Puerto Rico, persuaded the owner to let him promote a Latin-music night. Bonet had recently cut a hot-selling album called *Soul Drummer* with Ray Barretto's orchestra. Now he hired the Barretto band and filled every square inch of the club. Subsequently, Bonet and his brother Julio filled the club every evening from Wednesday through Sunday by booking popular bands such as those of Tito Puente, Machito, Eddie Palmieri, Johnny Pacheco, and José Fajardo, as well as Orquesta Broadway, Típica Novel, and La Sonora Matancera. The Wednesday-night crowd was treated to special shows, where Cuban Pete, Mike Vásquez, Freddie Rios, Carlos Arroyo, and Mike Ramos, among other well-known dancers, thrilled spectators with their exhibitions of the latest dance crazes and steps.

On August 2, 1968, the twelve-man Pete Bonet orchestra, under the music directorship of Louie Ramírez, made its club debut. The group overwhelmed dancers with original Ramírez compositions and arrangements that reminded me of the Tito Puente sound (listen to Bonet's 1968 Swinger album *The Odds Are On* and to Bonet and Ramírez's 1969 Fania album *Pete & Louie: The Beautiful People*). The Bonet brothers were on a roll, so they went Latin on Monday nights, which drew aficionados away from the Monday Latin-jazz shows at the Village Gate. Contributing to the popularity of the Corso were ads like this one I wrote, titled "The Corso, the Home of the Typical Sound," for the newly founded *Latin New York* magazine:

> Ever feel blue, lonely, and don't know what to do? Want to meet a beautiful doll and dance to music that will arouse the both of you? If your answer is yes, visit the Corso any Monday, Wednesday, Friday, Saturday, or Sunday evening. No matter what your problem is, once you pass through the portals to the entrance of the Corso, the typical music will infect you and enable you to escape from your problems for a few hours. Something different is always happening. Someone is always getting infected.
>
> The capacity crowd on Mother's Day, May 13, 1973, was infected by the typical music of Orquesta Broadway, Ray Barretto, and Johnny Pacheco. Eddie Zervigón, flutist and director of Orquesta Broadway, thrilled the dancers with an arousing-sounding "Pa' Africa" from their most recent recording. Try to imagine his rapidly moving fingers on a black wooden flute blowing a minor chord in a low register and then rising three octaves above every other note. Try to picture sweat beads dripping from the nose of Ray Barretto while he sings *coro* and his hands thump the skins of his drums. Can you see Johnny Pacheco suffering with a head cold, unable to sing and asking a sensuous, five-foot-five-inch, shapely, doe-eyed Latin doll to sing *coro* in his place because his sore throat did not permit him to reach the high notes? No, don't try to imagine it. See and hear it at the Home of the Typical Sound. Drop by the Corso—and get infected!

And in an article I wrote for *Latin New York*'s August 1973 issue, I talked about the capacity crowd that had turned out two months earlier to hear the new, electrified sound of Eddie Palmieri at the Corso.

> [The huge turnout was like] the people who lined up along Fifth Avenue to greet the grand marshal of the Puerto Rican Day Parade. They stood five deep in a semicircle around the front of the bandstand and looked up at the pianist; others filled every square inch of the dimly lit club. With arms extended outward and his nimble fingers tickling out the *montuno* to "Pa' Huele," the goateed Palmieri—head tilted upwards, eyes closed, and wearing a look of sensual satisfaction—appeared to have been anesthetized by his own music. The new "Pa' Huele" was highlighted by the stirring amplified violin artistry of Alfredo de la Fé, whose head, shoulders, and right arm jerked and quivered spasmodically while his bow passed over the strings....Following de la Fé's mesmerizing three-minute solo was the arousing flute of Mario Rivera and an inspired, unheard-of solo from the adroit fingers of bassist Andy González, which made this tune better than the recording. "Pa' Huele" was so incredibly good that every tune played after it could not raise the same fever pitch.

There were many unforgettable nights at the Corso, but the one I enjoyed most was when Vicentico Valdés and Tito Puente reunited after their split twenty-one years earlier. In 1954, a misunderstanding between the two musicians resulted in Valdés leaving the Puente orchestra and forming his own group, which was an immediate success. For years, Latin New Yorkers hoped the two musicians would talk and bury the past.

On April 18, 1975, the historic reunion of Puente and Valdés took place at the Corso. At 1 A.M., shortly after Johnny Pacheco's *conjunto* had finished swinging a fiery *guaracha*, the dimly lit dance floor was lit up with white ceiling lights as dancers hurried to find a spot to view the floor show. According to Machito and Miguelito Valdés, the Tito Puente of the mid-1970s was a mature person who had expressed a desire to be on the same bill with Tito Rodríguez and Vicentico Valdés. Anticipation of what would happen next was the piston pumping my fast-flowing adrenaline.

Marty Arrett, the Corso's master of ceremonies, began the historic occasion by welcoming Puente back to the Corso after a two-and-a-half year absence. The white-haired Puente, dressed nattily in a blue suit, white shirt, and red tie, bowed to the applauding crowd and signaled drummer Mike Collazo, whose drum roll accompanied Arrett's words: "Ladies and gentlemen, the King, Tito Puente, and Vicentico Valdés."

Thunderous applause and a standing ovation followed. Valdés, attired in a cream-colored safari jacket, sport shirt, and slacks, broke away from a cluster of women, smiled, walked calmly toward Arrett, shook hands, accepted a microphone, nodded to Puente, and began singing the ballad

"Corazón No Llores." Three more ballads followed; each elicited enthusiastic applause. When the familiar introduction to "La Gloria Eres Tú" began, the din of applause and whistles drowned Valdés out. Within seconds I was mentally transported to the year 1952. I imagined Puente's mellow vibraphone and had visions of cheek-to-cheek dancers crowding the Palladium Ballroom's dance floor. When the band began swinging on "Babarabatiri" and followed with "Abaniquito," the patrons responded like madmen. It was just one of many historic moments in the up-tempo Latin-music history that unfolded between 1969 and 1985 at the Corso, the "Home of the Typical Latin Sound."

Originally published in Latin Beat *magazine, September 2000*

FORTY-TWO

WILLIE ROSARIO

Yes, there is a *timbalero*-bandleader who has hardly ever soloed and whose band is in great demand. He is Willie Rosario, and he is a "rhythmic drummer"—one who never deviates from the beats.

This writer was the host of *The Latin Musicians Show*, which used to be heard on Saturdays between 2 and 4 P.M on WKCR-FM in New York. From May 1984 to early 1985, my music diary records letters and phone calls from listeners about Rosario's Bronco LP *New Horizons*. Week after week I got requests to play "Babarabatiri," "Lluvia," "Changó Tá Bení," "El Plantao," and "Laura." This may have been Rosario's best album, because shortly after it was released, his vocalists Tony Vega and Gilberto Santa Rosa were being talked about in Latin communities, and they subsequently both became stars in their own right.

The Rosario orchestra was a veritable college for musicianship. Many salsa and Latin jazz stars graduated from this school, and they will tell you that there is not a group on any bandstand in the world that outswings the Willie Rosario orchestra.

Born Fernando Luis Rosario-Marín on May 6, 1930, in Coamo, Puerto Rico, he was weaned on Puerto Rican trio music, Rafael Muñoz, and the then-Sinatra of Borinquen, Jose Luis Monero. At eight he was tapping out *típico* rhythms on a big empty lard can. His mother encouraged him to play guitar, but he dropped that instrument for the saxophone, then settled on the acoustic bass.

In 1951, he moved to the Bronx. One evening at the Palladium Ballroom, a Tito Puente performance mesmerized him. Puente stood center stage playing "Mambo la Roca." He held his feet slightly apart, striking the metal sides and tops of the drums with precise piston-like movements. Rosario decided then and there to learn the drums, and was tutored by Henry Adler until he was proficient enough to land a job with El Trio Río Piedras. Other one-night gigs followed until 1953, when he remained for a few months with Noro Morales's orchestra. Late in 1953 he began the first of his five years with Johnny Seguí, whose *conjunto* was among the first to utilize three trumpets. Seguí's vocalist was Yayo El Indio, and his pianist was a young man named Eddie Palmieri.

In 1958, Seguí moved to Puerto Rico, and Rosario held on to the sidemen. He visited the Little Neck, Long Island, home of vocalist-bandleader Tito Rodríguez, who taught him to administer and direct a disciplined organization of musicians. Rosario also learned from Rodríguez to develop his own style of relaxed but fiery swing. In the spirit of "helping one of our own," fellow Puerto Ricans Tito Rodríguez and Tito Puente helped the Rosario band to get started with charts from their books. The band's first club date was at the Broadway Casino, then located at 137th Street and Broadway.

In 1962, Al Santiago signed Rosario to record for his newly created Alegre label. The search for a vocalist ended one evening at El Club Caborojeño, when Rosario heard Carlos Pizarro's conga drummer sing a merengue. The *conguero* laughed at the invitation to become a lead vocalist. Rosario was adamant; his ears heard great potential. Two weeks later, the conga drummer, Frankie Figueroa, recorded for Rosario's Alegre LP *El Bravo Soy Yo*; his rendition of Tito Rodríguez's composition "Guaguancó Bonito" hit after much airplay. Figueroa went on to become a good vocalist and years later became Tito Puente's lead singer, after Santos Colón began his solo career in 1970.

During the charanga craze of the early 1960s, Al Santiago kept Rosario's band busy working club dates. After Alegre folded and godfather Santiago lost his power, Rosario learned about the reality of New York's Latin music world. He soon found out that booking dance bands for club dates was like the Barnum & Bailey Circus: the same shows traveled from club to club, and acts that had no agents were not permitted to earn a living. Popular Latin music DJ Dick "Ricardo" Sugar got Rosario a recording date, and on the liner notes of the Atco label LP *Boogaloo y Guaguancó*, Sugar wrote: "Success unfortunately is usually measured in monetary terms…if it were in terms of ability, then one of Latin's music's most successful artists would be Willie Rosario."

To support his family, Rosario took on odd jobs; one was as a percussion teacher. Bill Lester, a student of Rosario's who lived on the same block (160th Street between Broadway and Amsterdam Avenue), years later became director of one Los Angeles's hottest Latin-jazz groups, Shades of Jade. Rosario also sold grocery products for a food distributor during the daytime and at night was a mailroom supervisor.

In 1967 he hosted a Latin-jazz radio program for WADO that was heard

Monday through Friday from 10 P.M. to 5 A.M. The program, in Spanish, included material about the history of Latin music and the origins of its rhythms, as well as anecdotes. The Thursday evening show featured guests like Tito Rodríguez, Larry Harlow, Joe Quijano, La Lupe, and Raul Marrero, who would drop by for informal chats. Rosario had much of Latin New York listening to him.

His most memorable show was with guest Tito Rodríguez, who was involved at that time in a top-billing war with his childhood friend Tito Puente. Puente's agent, José Curbelo, made it difficult for Rodríguez to work at the top New York clubs, yet Rodríguez, in answering Rosario's question of whether he had enemies, said, "I have no enemies....Everyone in this industry is a friend of mine." I took Rodriguez's statement to mean that Puente and Curbelo did not hate him, that their actions were not personal, and that their war was merely business as usual—an attitude that has been part of the New York Latin music scene since its inception.

Rosario just couldn't stay away from music. He organized a band and looked for work but was told that without a current recording, it would be almost impossible to get gigs. Pete Bonet was Louie Ramirez's vocalist at the time, and he also booked bands at the Corso ballroom. He gave Rosario twelve dates, but in 1970 a new Corso administration ended the contract.

The following year Rosario's situation improved, after his Inca label recording of "El Barrio Obrero a la Quince" rose to the number-one slot in Puerto Rico. "'El Barrio Oberero' is my biggest hit," said Rosario. "I've had others like 'Cuesta de la Fama,' but they haven't topped 'Barrio Obrero.'"

He moved to Puerto Rico, and a new world opened up for him. After six months his band was working steadily. They signed to record for Bobby Valentín's Bronco label. In 1973 his version of "Last Tango in Paris," from the Inca LP *Infinito*, was receiving airplay on jazz stations. But in the early 1980s an invasion of Domincan merengue bands, who underpriced the Puerto Rican groups, compelled Puerto Rican musicians to resign from the Federation of Musicians.

Rosario and Valentín became co-owners of a nightclub, and it kept both bands working, along with other Puerto Rican groups. By the early 1990s, Rosario had recorded thirty albums, a few of which were Grammy nominees. My favorites among his songs are "Cuca la Loca," "My Favorite Things," "Devuelve Mi Alegría," "Nico Cadeon," "Nicolás," "Soy Rumbero," and "Antonia."

Originally published in Latin Beat *magazine, March 1993*

FORTY-THREE

HECTOR LAVOE

In February 1976, *Latin New York* magazine's second Latin Music Awards contest was in progress. Ballots listing forty-one music categories had been mailed and were being sent back. All the categories were close except for Best Male Vocalist: eight out of every ten ballots had a vote for Hector Lavoe. Izzy Sanabria, the magazine's publisher, assigned me to write about Lavoe.

At noon on Thursday, February 5, 1976, Lavoe and I sat in a small room on the magazine's premises. His frankness in answering questions startled me. He hid nothing and spoke with complete lack of inhibition about his drug problem—how at first the drugs were free, but then the habit started costing him thousands of dollars. At the moment he was making these revelations to me, he was salsa music's rising star. I decided not to mention his drug problem for fear it could ruin his career. The following was published in the March 1976 issue of *Latin New York*, headlined "Hector Lavoe: 'I Have Something to Prove.'"

> After I met Hector Lavoe for the first time, I realized that rumors and images drawn from an album cover could be misleading. Ever since 1967, when Willie Colón's first LP, *El Malo*, introduced Lavoe's voice, I believed Colón and Lavoe to be two thugs who loved to hear their knuckles crunch against jaws for the hell of it. This belief was furthered by the reported fistfights at their dances, by Colón's being hospitalized on one occasion, and by Lavoe's surly look while wearing a black, wide-brimmed gangster hat, a cigar protruding from his mouth, on the cover of the album *Crime Pays*. I was waiting to hear Lavoe speak from the side of his mouth like Bogart. But after hearing him speak, my preconceived image of Lavoe disappeared fast. Here I was, locked in with him in a closet where the back issues of *Latin New York* magazine are stored. A microphone extended from my cassette recorder and sat on top of a large speaker that separated us in the cramped quarters. Then, speaking English with a slight Spanish accent in his

warm, soft voice, he startled me with candid accounts of his personal life. If you had heard it, you would probably say, "So what? His story has been told a million times." True. But no one knows how it has affected him and what he's done to overcome his handicaps. The Hector Lavoe story contains all the dismal features of life—poverty, a broken home, the death of his mother at a time she was most needed, a limited education, and a brother's death on the streets of New York from a drug overdose. But he is determined that his life will not have a tragic ending.

He has a burning ambition, and nothing will deter him. His quest for recognition is so intense that nothing will stop him. "I want to be known throughout the world," he said in a serious tone. "Identity, to me, is more important than anything else. I have something to prove."

For the last sixteen years he's been unable to prove anything to his father. To understand this story intelligently we must start thirty years ago, on September 30, 1946, when Hector Pérez was born to parents Panchita and Luis in Ponce, Puerto Rico. His father, a musician, supported his wife and eight children with money he earned singing and playing guitar with trios and big bands. The senior Pérez's musical influence was the inspiration that spurred six-year-old Hector to stand by the radio and shout out the *jíbaro* [Puerto Rican hillbilly] songs with [legendary *jíbaro* singer] Chuito. Daily tutoring by his dad lasted a few years, until he enrolled in the Juan Morell Campos Music School. He took up the saxophone but lost interest in it fast. If only he could play the piano like the tot called Papo Lucca, the instrument would interest him.

In 1960, at age fourteen, Lavoe was earning eighteen dollars a night singing for a ten-piece band in Ponce's Club Suevia. "I didn't feel I was accomplishing anything," he told me. "I dropped out of school....I was always in trouble...so when I was seventeen I decided to live in New York and earn lots of money." Instead of giving his blessing, his father discouraged his trip, saying, "New York is not for you. Remember what happened to your brother. I forbid you to go." His father made it sound as if Hector didn't love him, his family, or Puerto Rico.

Despite his father's objections, he boarded a jet in San Juan on May 3, 1963, and saw the island disappear from view through the round window. While the jet was zooming toward New York, a lump stuck in his throat when he considered his father's last words: "If you go to New York, forget you have a father." He thought, "I'll change his mind about me and New York. I'll earn a lot of money working in a factory and someday return to Ponce a rich man."

Three hours later the plane began to descend. He felt the wheels touch the gourd, screech a few times, and slowly move toward the unloading gate. Waiting to greet him was his sister Priscilla. When she saw his five-foot-eight-inch, 102-pound frame, the first thing she wanted to do was get him a meal. He didn't want to eat. All he wanted to do was see that much-talked-about barrio on the Upper

East Side. Not long after their car weaved in and out of the streets of Spanish Harlem, a look of disappointment covered his face. There were no Cadillacs, no tall marble skyscrapers, and no tree-lined streets. Instead he saw much litter and many six-story brick buildings with weather-beaten façades.

Priscilla's Bronx apartment on Bryant Avenue was better. One week later, Roberto García, a childhood friend, came to visit him. García, a musician, invited him to a rehearsal of a sextet that was being formed. When they played the bolero "Tus Ojos," Lavoe noticed that the singer was murdering it. As a gesture of goodwill, he volunteered to sing it and show the other vocalist how it was supposed to sound. He mounted the bandstand, nodded to the leader, and began to create a romantic aura. He sang in key, giving each note its full value while he sang, *"Hoy miré tus ojos, tus ojos tan lindos, más verdes que el mar."* The musicians began looking at each other as if to say, "This is what is missing." Lavoe ended up with the vocalist's job. With the sextet, he worked three nights and was paid twenty dollars. Other jobs followed with Orquesta New Yorker, Kako's All-Stars, and Johnny Pacheco before his meeting with Willie Colón in February 1967.

He recorded the vocals slated for Colón's first Fania LP, *El Malo*. After he heard the playback of the tunes "Jazzy," "Chonquí," and "Quimbombó," he no longer believed, as he originally had, that Colón's group was "a terrible-sounding band." "Willie never asked me to join the band," said Lavoe. "After the recording, he said, 'On Saturday we start at El Tropicoro at 10 P.M.'"

The success of that first album changed Lavoe's life radically. He received instant recognition, steady work, and a wad of money that provided a comfortable life. It happened so fast that he didn't know how to cope with it. "I began showing up to gigs late and then not at all," he said. "I had encountered a serious problem. Willie got fed up and fired me. When Willie learned what my problem was, he helped me to overcome it. I love Willie like a brother...he took a lot of crap from me and he never gave up on me. No one has taken an interest in me the way Willie has."

When Colón disbanded his group in 1973 to broaden his studies, Lavoe took the band over. Since then, the vocalist has globetrotted, and his ambition to be known the world over will be realized within a few years. Lavoe's success can be attributed to his unique "*jíbaro* salsa" flavor. He doesn't resent being called a hick. *"Soy un jíbaro,"* he said rather proudly. He didn't have to convince me of his pride. I've known it for years. I've heard it in the lyrics of many of his recordings with Colón. A good example is "Paraíso de Dulzura," a tune Lavoe wrote for his first solo LP, *La Voz*: *"Que de adonde vengo...que pa' donde voy, vengo de la tierra de gran dulzura, la sabrosura y sandunguera, que Puerto Rico puede dar, lo lei lo lei lo lei lo lei, esa tierra es mi locura, Puerto Rico yo te adoro, tierra santa, tierra pura."*

Listen to it well, Mr. Luis Pérez. It's your son singing from his heart. He's never been sprawled out on a street, and he's been paying his own way since 1963. He's already sung at Carnegie Hall, Madison Square Garden, and the concert halls of London, Paris, and Berlin with the Newport Jazz Festival in November 1975. What more does he have to do or prove? Forget your pride and dismiss your cruel words, which were uttered in a moment of anger. His beautiful lyrics are an indication that he loves the land of his birth and everything connected with it. Your son Hector Lavoe is another *jíbaro* from Ponce who is going to make it big in the Latin music world. With a brother like Willie Colón in his corner, how can he miss?

On Sunday, May 16, 1976, Lavoe, attired in white from hat to shoes, held two fingers of his right hand in a *V* above his head when he accepted the *Latin New York* magazine award for Best Vocalist and Best Conjunto. "These trophies," he said, "are for Puerto Rico." In 1973, after years of enduring the tag "kiddie band" from envious musicians, Willie Colón left the group to Lavoe. With Colón gone, jealous musicians could no longer call the band "kiddie": three Lavoe LPs, *De Mi Depende, La Voz,* and *Comedia,* became hot sellers. From then on, Lavoe joined the elite club of international stars that included Lucho Gatica, Vicentico Valdés, Cheo Feliciano, and Vitín Aviles.

But during the summer of 1987, his life seemed to be falling apart. It happened after the death of his sixteen-year-old son, Hector Jr., in what was reportedly an accident at a friend's home. During the same period, Lavoe's apartment in Rego Park, Queens, was destroyed by fire. One year later, on June 25, he was in San Juan, along with Johnny Pacheco, Willie Colón, Luis "Perico" Ortíz, and Pete "El Conde" Rodríguez, for the Fania concert titled Pulseo Salsero con los Titanes de la Salsa, scheduled for Bayamón's Rubén Rodríguez Coliseum. Two hours before concert time, the event was cancelled. According to Lavoe's wife, Nilda, the vocalist had been depressed, and things had worsened with the bad news of his son's death and the fire. They were in room 907 of the Regency Hotel at Condado Beach. "We had just finished dinner," said Nilda, "and were getting ready to go to the beach. He gave me his glasses. I put them on the table and walked toward the door. I turned around and saw him jump over the balcony."

An emergency crew found Lavoe lying face down on top of the thick foam cushioning over an air-conditioning duct, which apparently saved his life. He was conscious and bleeding profusely. Dr. Blas Arroyo, of the University of Puerto Rico Medical Center at Rio Piedras, said the singer suffered multiple fractures of his arms, legs, and other parts of his body. This and subsequent tragedies continued to plague Lavoe until the afternoon of June 29, 1993, when he died at St. Clare's Hospital in

Manhattan from an AIDS-related condition caused by infected hypodermic needles.

Thousands of mourners paid their respects on June 30 and 31 at the Frank E. Campbell Funeral Home on East 81st Street and Madison Avenue. On July 2, after a mass at Spanish Harlem's St. Cecilia's Church, Lavoe was buried at St. Raymond's Cemetery in the Bronx. His tragic death contains a quintessential lesson for all youngsters, and especially for aspiring musicians: heroin, cocaine, and crack will kill you. All music schools should include at least one drug-abuse prevention course.

Originally published in Latin Beat *magazine, September 1993*

FORTY-FOUR

WILLIE RODRÍGUEZ

It was 9 P.M. on May 11, 1994. I was enjoying a meal at Willie's Steak House on Westchester Avenue—the place to listen to Latin New York's best musicians jam on Wednesday evenings. On stage was Sonny Rivera's Latin Jazz Quintet. Rivera, on vibraharp, opened with "Mambo Diablo," and the Bronx eatery was in *montuno* heaven. Contributing to the manic spell were the novel ad-libs of pianist Willie Rodríguez. All evening, he captivated listeners with his keyboard mastery on the tunes "Sonny," "Pare Cochero," "When Sonny Gets Blue," and "Wachi Wara." The quintet, consisting of Rivera, Jimmy Sabater on timbales, Eddie Montalvo on congas, and Johnny Torres on bass, was great. But Willie Rodríguez's performance was outstanding. It was historical.

The Willie Rodríguez story is about a person from the South Bronx who overcomes the pitfalls of life by educating himself. Willie, the youngest of three children, was born to Carmen Nieves and José Rodríguez on July 20, 1951, while the family resided at Eleventh Street and Lexington Avenue. Five years after his father abandoned the family, the Rodríguezes moved to a tenement at Alexander Avenue and 134th Street. Willie's mother's religious faith was the inspiration that maintained the family base. They attended Sunday services at the Bethany Presbyterian Church, where Willie made sure he sat behind the pianist. At Burger Junior High School on 141st Street and Brook Avenue, he joined the church choir and acted in plays sponsored by Burger's South Bronx Community Action Theater. He was a clarinetist at Burger, while Wayne Gorbea and Willie Colón were trumpeters. At thirteen he was the only Burger student awarded a drama scholarship to the School of Performing Arts. He declined the award and accepted one offered by a prep school in Kingsville, Texas.

Willie was one of one hundred students from across the United States who were given this special chance. For months his day consisted of dormitory, classroom, dining hall, library, and dormitory once again. It was at this point that he decided to get serious about music. He studied piano and played the instrument at Sunday services. For the remainder of his school tenure, he learned to play classical and church music on piano, and to sing.

In May 1969, he graduated and returned to New York. "I needed a car and a piano, so I went to work for a year before I entered college," said Rodríguez. "I dropped by the dance clubs and was moved by Ray Barretto's pianist Louis Cruz and by Larry Harlow. I began freelancing with several bands...my mind was focused on music so I dropped out of Brooklyn College during my second year...I joined Wayne Gorbea's Orquesta Cuda. One day while Cuda rehearsed at Burger, Wayne gave me a chart which read 'Guaguancó in Key of G'...There were no notes in four bars...I didn't know what to do. Wayne then sang the *guaguancó* part, and this is how I began my Latin dance-music education."

From this point on, Willie developed into a seasoned keyboardist, thanks to the tutelage of two proficient pianists, the Dominican Francisco "Popi" Peña and the Panamanian Nicholas Rodríguez. After six months with Cuda, Willie joined Ernie Agosto's La Conspiración in 1972 and continued piano studies with Paquito Pastor, who prepared him to read Orlando Marín's charts for the gigs at the Westchester Avenue clubs Chaparral, Maxie's, Mediterranean Lounge, B'Que, and Alex and Henry's. On Valentine's Day 1976, Willie began working with Pete "El Conde" Rodríguez at Manhattan's Havana–San Juan Club. This was followed by gigs with Kako until Willie joined the Machito orchestra in 1977.

"While I attended the Machito university in 1977 and 1978, I worked the top clubs—the Corso, the Casablanca," said Rodríguez. A trip to Puerto Rico included Charlie Palmieri, Johnny Pacheco, and Miguelito Valdés....In 1978 there was a Latin-jazz tribute at Alice Tully Hall....Tito Puente wrote an arrangement of [the theme from] *2001: A Space Odyssey*, in which his band and Machito's performed simultaneously....I was with the original Charanga America before I moved to Tampa, Florida."

Willie performed on keyboards at a Latin nightclub in Tampa until mid-1979, when the club closed for renovation. As pianist for Jerry Jerome's trio, he earned top dollar for gigs at many posh venues, including Chicago's Playboy Club. Upon hearing that his mother was ill, he returned to New York and immediately found work as a pianist, organist, and choir director at the Fort Washington Heights Presbyterian Church. In sixteen years, Willie missed fewer than two months of Sunday services because of tours. "One evening while working with Machito at the Corso, I mentioned that my mother was a patient at the Columbia Presbyterian Medical Center. The following day Machito and Graciela visited my mother. Machito told her, 'Your son is one of the best pianists to play with my orchestra.' Machito and Graciela's visit was the best medicine my mother received that day…she died shortly thereafter."

Before his mother's death, Willie promised he would earn a college degree. He enrolled at Lehman College and one and a half years later earned a BSA in psychology with a minor in music, which enabled him to teach. In the interim were gigs and recordings with Charanga America and Luis "Perico" Ortíz, and a three-week tour of Europe with the Machito Orchestra, with whom he recorded the 1982 Grammy-winning album *Machito and His Salsa Big Band*. During the same year, Willie married a young lady he met at a Sunday service. It was the same year salsa recordings lost most of their airplay because commercial Latin radio stations were favoring merengues and ballads. The salsa drought lasted until 1988, and most New York salsa musicians suffered economically. Willie was fortunate, as his teaching credentials landing him a teaching job at the Bronx's PS 138.

In February 1992, the pianist was in a car accident that ended up incapacitating him for most of the year. He got by because of the vacation time and sick leave that he had accrued as a teacher. It was Dr. Ken Leo Rosa, a music-loving Bronx chiropractor, who healed him after eight months.

In 1993 Willie began his first year with Conjunto Libre, just after Libre's recording of "Little Sunflower" won the group the annual title of "King of Latin Jazz." Before the year was out, Willie had earned a master's degree in education at Lehman College. "It permitted me to earn more money.…I taught students English through singing. At Queens College, I earned a degree in supervision administration, which will permit me to be a principal of a junior high school."

Willie Rodríguez returned to the Latin music spotlight when New York City's FM stations and Vicki Sola's popular Saturday noon show started airing his English vocal of "Sabor A Mi," from the Libre CD *Ahora*. At the moment, his English-language version of "Speak Low," from Libre's Milestone CD *Mejor Que Nunca*, is responsible for his Friday night gigs as a soloist at Willie's Steak House. Willie sings in English, and his piano solos are breathtaking.

"Education," he said, "has made me an independent person. Most sidemen have no health or unemployment protection. I do, because education has enabled that. Musicians must have something to fall back on when the performing days are over. Thank God I earned teaching credentials."

Originally published in Latin Beat *magazine, April 1995*

INDEX

"A Beny Moré," 172
"A Las Seis," 233
"A Mi Manera," 63
"A Mí Qué," 180, 190
Abalon Ballroom, Le (Bronx), 224
"Abaniquito," 90, 98, 108, 114, 129, 135, 141, 144, 164, 207, 228, 268
Abraham, Norman, 212
"Acércate Más," 112
Acevedo, Placido, 29
Acid, 261
Acosta, Leonardo, 179
Acuña, Alex, 104
"Adelante," 200–201
"Adios," 9
Adler, Henry, 269
"Africa Canta y Llora," 41
African-American influences, 7, 54
Africando, Vol. 1: Trovador, 186
"Africanerías," 49, 139
Afro-Cuban jazz, 11, 34, 46, 65–66, 71
"Afro Cuban Serenade," 108, 128
Afrofilipino, 253
"After Hours," 7
Agosto, Ernie, 280
"Agua de Tinajón," 88
"Agua del Clavelito, El," 179
"Agua Limpia Todo," 156
"Agua No, El," 233
Aguabella, Francisco, 101
"Aguardiente, El," 180, 190, 191
Aguilar, Pedro "Cuban Pete," 92, 159, 266
Ahora, 281
"Ahora Seremos Felices," 13
"Ahora Sí Somos Felices," 70

Alarcón, Raúl, 10
Albino, Johnny, 123
Alegre All Stars, 219, 221–22
"Alegre Mambo," 233
Alegre Records, 50, 78, 110, 116, 149, 165–66, 198, 199, 224, 255, 262, 270
Alfredito, 159, 161, 162
Alhambra Lounge (Bronx), 165
Alice Tully Hall (Manhattan), 280
Alicea, Maria, 109
Allende, Pedro "Pullidor," 10
Alma Boricua septet, 160
Alma Dance Studios, 84, 128
"Alma Llanera," 9
Almacenes Hernández. *See* Casa Hernández (music store)
Alonso, Catalino "Tite" Curet, 245–46
Alpha Artists booking agency, 95–99, 116, 162, 252
"Alturas de Simpson, Las," 176
Alvarez, Chico, 120, 192
Alvarez, Fernando, 48, 75, 76, 127, 196
Alvarez, Henry, 255
Alvarez, Paulina, 97, 177, 188
Alvarez, René, 188
"Am I Blue," 125
"Amada Mía," 247
"Amapola," 2, 9, 22, 54
Ambassadeurs Club, Les (Paris), 56–57
"América Club," 182
American Federation of Musicians (union), 9–10, 11, 44, 107, 239–40
American Legion Hall (Manhattan), 107

Amitin, Mike, 212
Amor con Salsa, 257
"Amor Gigante," 64
"Ampárame," 160
"Anacaona," 245, 247
Anacaona Septet, La, 56–57, 255
Andino, Julio, 75, 77, 78, 90, 244
Andreu, José, 210, 221
"Angelitos Negros," 41
Angeloro, Al, 185, 202, 215, 217
Anglero, Roberto, 257
"Angoa," 180, 190
"Anna Boroco Tinde," 44
"Año 1963," 191
"Año 1965," 209
"Añoro," 145
Ansonia Records, 11, 73, 78, 116, 149
Anthony, Marc, 248
"Antonia," 271
Apollo Sound, 257
Apollo Theatre (Manhattan), 77
"Apóyate En Mi Alma," 155, 156
"Aprende a Querer," 166
"Aprieta el Pollo," 145
Aragón, Orestes, 179
Arcadio Ballroom (Manhattan), 89
Arcaño, Antonio, 7, 84, 178–80, 188–89, 207, 209
Arcaño y Sus Maravillas, 60, 84, 88, 179
"Aretes de la Luna, Los," 145
Argueso, Ramon, 75, 76, 139, 159, 162
Armandito (trumpeter), 3
Armenteros, Alfredo "Chocolate," 93
Armstrong, Louis, 54
Arnaz, Desi, 6, 7, 42, 105, 108–9
Aroche, Elizardo, 183
Arraya, Anna, 216–17
"Arrebato, El," 90, 115
Arrett, Marty, 213–14, 267
Arrímate Pa' Ca, 211
"Arrollando," 145
Arroyo, Carlos, 266
Arsenio Rodríguez y Su Conjunto de Estrellas, 88
Artau, Mariano, 111, 148
Arthur Godfrey Show (radio show), 72
"Arthur Murray Rhumba," 108, 128
Arvelo, Pepito, 17
ASCAP radio ban, 8, 29
"Así No Se Quiere A Nadie," 67

"Asia Minor," 73, 221
Asia No. 1 (Manhattan Cuban restaurant), 49
Astaire, Fred, 44
At Last|—La Magnífica, 224
At the New York World's Fair, 261
"At the Party," 221
Atco label, 270
Atlantic Records, 252
Audinot, Rafael, 29, 196
Audubon Ballroom (Manhattan), 43, 66, 84, 109, 241
Augie and Margo (dancers), 92
"Aunque Tú," 234
"Ausencia," 13, 16
Avellanet, Roberto, 173
"Aventura Más, Una," 145
"Averigua," 224
Avery Fisher Hall (Manhattan), 200
Aviles, Vitín, 48, 99, 108, 118, 123, **147–49,** 151, 160, 197, 225, 234, 244, 276
"Ay, Qué Frio," 190
"Ay Cariño," 156, 157
"Ay Qué Frío," 180
Ayala, Frank Gilberto, 34, 66, 76, 195, 196
"Ayúdame San Antonio," 185
Azcárraga, Lucho, 38
Azpiazu, Don, 2–3
"Azúcar," 223, 256

"Babalú," 6, 9, 42, 43, 61
Babalú, El (Manhattan restaurant), 66
"Babarabatiri," 90, 130, 135, 144, 156, 268, 269
Baez, Onix, 118
"Baila Vicente," 179
Bailadores, 234
Baile de los Cocos Pelaos, El, 83
"Baile Mi Mambo," 145
"Baja del Caballo," 67
"Bajo de Chapotín, El," 127
Baker, Josephine, 54
"Bamba, La," 9
Bamba Club, La (Manhattan), 241
"Bambaram Bam Bam," 152
"Bambarito," 43
"Ban Ban Queré," 160
Banana Club (Manhattan), 251

index

Bandaide, 79
"Bandolera," 161
"Bang Bang," 235–36
"Bangin' the Bongo," 23, 66, 71, 72, 160
Banguela, Miguel Angel, 65
"Barco Sin Puerto," 191
Baretto, Justo, 51
"Barito," 244
Barnet, Charlie, 52, 102
Baró, Evaristo "Guajarón," 161
Barraca, La (Manhattan club), 170, 191
Barrère, Georges, 53
Barreto, Luis, 103, 113, 139, 236
Barretto, Ray, 50, 101, 104, 130, 137, 157, 220, 221, 224, 249, 257, 259, 261–62
   orchestra of, 95, 185, 213, 219, 242, 265–66, 280
"Barrio del Pilar," 214
"Barrio Obrero a la Quince, El," 207, 271
Barroso, Abelardo, 23, 143, 177
Basie, Count, 7, 190
Basin Street East (Manhattan club), 191
Bass Clef (London club), 202
Bassey, Shirley, 118
"Basura, La," 149
Bataan, Joe, **249–54**
"Batamú," 64
Batamú dance troupe, 64
"Batanga," 145
Batista, Fulgencio, 64
Battle of the Baritones (radio show), 159–60
Bauzá, Estella, 6
Bauzá, Mario, 6, 7, 11, 21, 43, 47, 49, 50, 57, 59, 65, 67, 75, 77, 102, 105, 141, 144
   as Alma Dance Studios promoter, 84
   in Sigler's band, 2
   as Machito's music director, 9–10, 33, 34, 45–46, 76, 88–89, 160
   orchestra of, 67–68
Baxter, Les, 87
"Bayamón," 207
Beck, Al, 161
Becké, Pepé, 45, 47
"Beeree Bee Cum Bee," 220
"Begin the Beguine," 71, 72
"Bei Mir Bist Du Schoen," 77
Beicuz, Remberto, 60
Beltone Studios, 24, 114

Benjamín, Luisito, 48, 220
Bennett, Tony, 104, 118
Bennett, Walter, 54
Berrios, Ruben, 108
Berrios, Steve, 66, 102
Berrios, Tommy, 227, 229, 230, 234, 236, 237, 241
Bert, Eddie, 135
"Bésame la Bembita," 90, 115
"Bésame Mucho," 8
"Besitos Pa' Tí," 170
Billar de los Músicos, El (Manhattan billiard parlor), 2–3, 33
Billboard magazine, 44
"Bim Bam Bum," 9, 44, 70, 112
Birdland (Manhattan club), 77, 92, 130, 134, 190, 197
"Black is Black," 211
Blanco, 56
Blanco, Julio, 64–65
"Blen Blen Blen," 43
Blen Blen Blen Club (Manhattan), 89
Blonde Latin Sextet, 253
"Blue Moon," 75
Blue Note Club (Chicago), 77
"Blues in the Night," 75, 77
BMI (Braodcast Music, Inc.), 8, 9
"Bobby," 224
"Bobby: Bajo y Clarinete," 221–22
Bobby Rodríguez y La Compañia, 172
Bobo, Willie, 30, 101, 105–6, 109, 110, 135, 149, 152, 161, 182, 184, 220, 227, 229, 231, 234, 256
   Puente and, 93, 104, 130
Boborosa, Willie, 130
Boggs, Vernon, 87
bolero, 16
"Bom Bon, El," 185
"Bombín de Barretto, El," 177
Bonds, Margaret, 197
Bonet, Pete, 265–66, 271
Bongo Logic, 186
Bonilla, Benny, 147, 224
"Bonito y Sabroso," 191
Bonnemere, Eddie, 57, 58
boogaloo, 95–96, 135, 136, 223, 235
Boogaloo y Guaguancó, 270
Booth, Shirley, 87
Boricua Theatre (Manhattan), 251
"Borinqueña, La," 3

285

"Botecito, El," 233
"Botellero, El," 10, 126
"Bottomland," 52
Boufartique, Oscar, 57, 64
Boy, El. *See* Torres, Juan "El Boy"
Brachfeld, Andrea, 186
Brando, Marlon, 87
Bravet, Leonel, 183
Bravo, Sonny, 30, 181
Bravo Soy Yo, El, 270
Bravos de Cuba, Los, 23
Briggs, Karen, 186
Brito, Alfredo, 97
Brito, Felo, 199
Broadway Casino (Manhattan dance hall), 239, 270
Bronco label, 271
Bronco Records, 146, 262, 269
Bronx Casino, 84
Brown, Les, 87
"Bruca Maniguá," 40, 41, 66, 198
Brunswick Records, 55
"Buchi Pluma Na' Ma'", 13, 16
Budet, José, 34, 107
"Buena Noche Cha Cha," 172
Bulog, Puchi, 137
Burke, Elena, 247, 248
"Busca Lo Tuyo," 67
"Buscando la Melodía," 64
"Busco Una Chinita," 191
Buttery Room (Chicago), 197
Byron and Tybee (dancers), 92

Cabaret La Red (Havana), 170
"Cabildo," 41, 45
Caborojeño, El (Manhattan dance hall), 239, 270
Cabrera, Julian, 183
"Cachao." *See* López, Israel "Cachao"
Cachao 77, 201
Cachao y Su Descarga 77, Volumes I and II, 182
"Cachita," 13, 126
Café, Luis, 245
Cain, Joe, 145, 149, 233
"Cal Miller Mambo," 130
Cal Tjader Quintet Plus Five, 256
Cal Tjader Soul Sauce, 256
Cala, Portuondo, 56
Calandrelli, Jorge, 246

Calderón, Alberto, 2
Calderón, Gil "Sonny." *See* Cuba, Joe
"Call of the Jungle Birds," 57
Calloway, Cab, 7, 36, 52, 54
Calvo, Pedro, 248
Calzado, Rudy, 183, 186, 192, 219, 221
Camacho, Nevia, 112
"Camaguey," 144
Camero, Candido, 101
"Camina Camarón," 145
"Campanitas de Cristal," 13, 73
Campo, Pupi, 77, 160, 197, 231
  orchestra of, 63, 75, 76, 89–90, 105, 107, 108, 114, 127–28, 134, 140, 148
Campo Amor, El (Manhattan), 4, 17, 54, 55–56
Canario, El, 21
"Canelina," 98
Caney. *See* Conjunto Caney
Caney, Rey, 219
Cañonazo, 261
Canoura, José, 184
"Canta," 247
"Canta Bajo," 170
"Canta Pajarito," 16
"Capitán, El," 225
Capitol Theatre (Manhattan), 106
Capó, Bobby, 17, 21, 36, 44, 67, 83, 111, 151, 159
"Capullito de Alelí," 13, 16, 17, 73, 76, 148
"Cara de Payaso," 116
"Cara Suica," 233
"Caramelos," 156, 184
Caravana Club (Bronx), 84, 198
Carbo Menéndez, José, 148
"Carbonero, El," 196
Cardona, Eliseo, 192
Cardona, Milton, 251
"Caress Me," 221, 236
Caribe Latino (radio show), 147
Carl Webster's Yale Collegians, 54
Carlos, Randy, 224, 241
"Carmela," 220
Carnaval En Harlem, 156
Carnegie Hall (Manhattan), 57, 77
Carnival Room (Manhattan), 140
Carp, David, 87
Carpentier, Alejo, 175

index

The Music of Cuba, 176
"Carreteros, Los," 13–14, 18, 70, 169–70
Carrillo, Isolina, 65
Carrillo, Luis, 60
Carroll, Diahann, 161
"Carta, La," 224, 226
Cartagena, Ralfi, 225
Carter, Benny, 52, 56
Casa Hernández (music store), 14, 21–22, 33
Casablanca (Hotel Riverside), 185, 214, 280
Casino de la Playa (orchestra), 5, 6, 33–34, 40–41, 42, 59, 61, 126, 147, 240
Castellanos, Al, 90
Castigador Is the New Salsa Sensation, El, 257
Castillo, Carlos del, 188
Castro, Armando, 75, 102, 148
Castro, Concepción "Cuchito," 56
Castro, Fidel, 210
Castro, George, 184
Castro, Hector, 224, 228
Castro, Juanito, 60
Castro, Manolo, 39, 60
Castro, Ramon, 41
Castro sisters, 56
Castroviejo, Ramón, 67
Catalano, Michael, 90
"Cataño," 207
Catskills resorts, 5, 35, 61, 89, 98, 106, 107, 161, 208, 231
Cavallero, Carmen, 160
Cayre, Joe, 253
"Cayuco, El," 135, 156
"Cayuga, La," 182
"Cenizas," 152
Centeno, Joe, 92
"Cero Codazos, Cero Cabezazos," 179
"Cero Tú," 113
Cesta Records, 206
Cha-Cha Boys, 230
cha-cha-chá, 48, 75, 78, 85, 103, 130, 135, 181, 182–83, 220–21, 257
Cha Cha Cha Goes Modern, 161, 162
"Cha Cha Chá in Blue," 99, 231
Cha Cha Cha in Havana, 190
Cha-Cha-Charanga, 186
"Chacumbele," 10, 98
Champagne, 245, 262
"Champú de Cariño," 148

"Chang," 48, 128
"Changó Tá Bení," 269
"Changó Tá Vení," 232, 244
"Chanhullo," 178
"Chano Pozo," 47
charanga, 35, 135, **175–87,** 205–6, 241
Charanga, 116
"Charanga, La," 191
Charanga 76, 186
Charanga America, 185–86, 280, 281
Charanga Casino, 186
Charanga Colonial, 186, 215
Charanga De La 4, 186
Charanga Soul, 186
Charanson, 186
Charles, Ezzard, 87
Chateau Madrid (Manhattan), 190
Chateau Madrid label, 184
Chateau Renaissance (North Bergen), 117
Cheatham, Doc, 66
Cheetah Club (Manhattan), 85, 199–200, 256, 257
"Chen Chen Ko," 73
Cheo, 245
"Cherry Pink and Apple Blossom White," 78, 115, 183
Chesna, Otto, 197
Chez José (Manhattan), 265
Chicago Serenaders, the, 54
China Doll (Manhattan club), 72–73, 106, 107, 108, 113, 134, 220
Chino Gueits y sus Almas Tropicales, 164
"Chiquita Banana," 103
Chirino, Willy, 171
"Chop Suey Mambo," 93
"Chua Chua," 165
Chuito, 274
"Chun-Ko," 198
"Chupa Chupa," 35
Clark, Buddy, 231
"Clave Misteriosa, La," 64
"Close Your Eyes," 198
Club Broadway (Manhattan), 202
Club Cuba (Manhattan), 34
Club Cubanacán (Manhattan), 4, 54–55, 66
Club Embassy. *See* Embassy Club
Club London (Manhattan), 106
Club Los Muchachos (Manhattan), 229
Club Ronde, El (Miami), 62

287

Club San Juan. *See* San Juan Club
Club Tapestry (Bronx), 216
Club Tico Tico (Manhattan), 23, 46, 66
Club Triton (Bronx), 219
Club Tropicana, El (Havana), 248
Club Tropicoro (Manhattan), 84
Coche Records, 237
"Cocinando Suave," 259
"Coco," 149
Coco Records, 191, 214, 215
"Coco Seco," 149, 224
Cocolia, 15
Coda Records, 19–20, 23–25, 27, 35, 46–47, 66, 71, 72–73, 98, 113
Coen, Augusto, 2, 5, 6, 13, 21, 34, 36, 52, 54, 55–56, 70, 82–83
Coen-Concepción, Ray, 109, 145, 149, 161, 162
Cofresi, Tony, 223
Cohen, Martin, 131
Cohn, Al, 99
Cole, Jack, 10
Cole, Sylvia, 88
Colgate Gardens (Bronx), 35, 84, 210
Colindres, Roy, 194
Collazo, Fernando, 177, 178
Collazo, Mike, 117, 137, 163, 207, 267
Colón, Eddie, 123, 224
Colón, Frankie, 49, 69, 102, 128, 129, 135, 137, **139–41**, 144, 145, 147
Colón, Johnny, 130, 199, 234, 251, 253
Colón, Louie, 257
Colón, Santitos, 99, 152, **155–57**, 161
Colón, Santos, 48, 99, 130, 135, 219, 270
Colón, Willie, 261, 273, 275, 276, 279
Colony Club (Chicago), 29, 61, 126
Colorao, El, 179
Columbia Records, 35, 43, 44, 52, 54, 70, 78, 112, 191, 220, 239
Combo Gigante, El, 202, 237
Comedia, 276
"Cómetelo Tú," 46, 113
"Comimos La Paella, Los," 77
Comin' at You, 234
Como, Perry, 104, 160
"Como Camina María," 209, 211
"Cómo Está Miguel," 156
"Como Fue," 145
Como Me Gusta, 212
"Cómo Ríen," 233, 234, 244, 246, 247

Como Su Ritmo No Hay Dos (film), 182
"Como Yo No Hay Quien Baile El Muñeco," 70
"Comparsa Baracón," 66
"Complicación," 156
Con el Ritmo de Cachao, 181–82
"Con Mi Mambo," 233
"Con Tu Negro," 70
Concepción, César, 85, 101, 102
Concha Club, La (San Juan), 104
Concord Jazz Picante label, 131
"Confesiones," 152
conga, 6
"Conga, La," 126
Conga, La (Manhattan club), 6, 44, 61, 65, 71, 98, 106, 113, 148
Conjunto Alfarona X, El, 228
Conjunto Batamu, 25, 46
Conjunto Cachana, 206
Conjunto Candela, 224
Conjunto Caney, 21, 22, 24, **27–30**
Conjunto Hatuey, 65
Conjunto Libre, 281
Conjunto Pin Pin, El, 197
Conjunto Rapindey, 66
Conjunto Saoco, 84
Conjunto Siboney, 112
Connie's Inn (Manhattan), 55
Conquet, Johnny, 101, 103–4, 160, 208, 231
Conspiración, La, 280
"Contéstame," 67
"Contigo a la Distancia," 246, 247
Continental label, 220
contradanza, 176
contredanse, 175
"Convergencia," 67
Cookie (dancer), 92
Copacabana (Manhattan club), 71, 127
Copacabana Club (Santurce), 148
Copacabana Samba Band, 76, 196
Cora, Luis, 24
Cora, Mario, 162, 183, 197, 244
"Corazón, Un," 129
"Corazón No Llores," 13, 268
Cordero, Jules "Slim," 229–30, 236, 237
Corea, Chick, 109
Corso Ballroom (Manhattan), 146, **265–68**, 280
Cortijo, Rafael, 30, 101

Cosby, Bill, 137
"Cose, Cose, Cose," 47
Costello, Diosa, 5, 7, 44–45
Cotique Records, 162, 251, 262
Cotto, Gilberto "Tico Tico," 106
Cotton Club (Manhattan), 55
Courtney, Chris, 48
Creole Stars, the, 53–54
Crime Pays, 273
Criss Cross (film), 72
Crocker, Frankie, 253
Crosby, Bing, 160
Crusellas, Ramon, 40
Cruz, Bobby, 261
Cruz, Carmen, 92
Cruz, Celia, 96, 157, 169, 170, 257, 261
Cruz, Gustavo, 186
Cruz, José Antonio, 180, 187, 189
Cruz, Luis, Jr., 259, 280
Cruz, Tony, 216
"Crystal Blue Persuasion," 253
"Cua Cua," 135, 156
"Cuándo, Cuándo," 116
"Cuando Caliente el Sol," 156
"Cuando Te Vas," 108
"Cuando Te Vea," 76, 127, 156
"Cuánto Le Gusta," 9
"Cuarenta Que Son Uno," 182
Cuarteto Borinquén, El, 28
Cuarteto Caney, 63
Cuarteto Mayari, 29
Cuarteto Victoria, El, 16–17, 21
"Cuatro Personas," 13
Cuba, Joe, 116, 118, 130, 164, 199, 219, 221, 223, **227–37,** 241, 244, 248, 253, 255
Cuba, racial discrimination in, 1, 31–33, 41–42, 51, 54, 58, 88, 189–90
Cuban Carnival, 108, 109, 156, 161
"Cuban Cutie," 115
"Cuban Fantasy," 109
Cuban Jam Session, Volume 5, 191
Cuban Love Song (film), 2
"Cuban Mambo," 103
Cuban Pete. *See* Aguilar, Pedro "Cuban Pete"
Cuban Pete (film), 71, 126
Cubop, 129–30
"Cuca la Loca," 271
Cuesta Abajo (film), 4

"Cuesta de la Fama," 271
Cueva, Luis, 66
Cuevas, Julio, 3, 88
Cugat, Xavier, 42–44, 45, 67, 84, 109, 118, 160, 231
   orchestra of, 8, 9, 13, 22, 29, 35, 43–44, 61, 69, 71, 72, 76, 85, 97–98, 101, 105, 106, 112, 197, 229
"Cumbanchero, El," 13, 207
Cuní, Miguelito, 248
Curbelo, Fausto, 52, 159, 161
Curbelo, José, 19, 72, **95–99,** 106, 112, 116–17, 126, 130, 151, 152, 160, 161, 231, 232, 252, 271
   orchestra of, 63, 65–66, 89, 97–98, 101, 105, 107, 113, 127, 156, 159, 241, 242
Curbelo, Nilo, 107, 108
Curtis, Tony, 72

Dance Mania, Vol. 1, 104, 130, 156
Dance Mania, Vol. 2, 156
"Dandys, Los," 196
danzón, 175–79
"Danzón Antiqua, El," 177
danzón-mambo, 6–7, 182
Davidson, Eduardo, 205
Dávila, Chivirico, 165
Dávila, Frank "Paquito," 162
Dávila, Ray, 106
Davilita, 5, 11, 16, 21, 52, 55, 70, 159
Davis, Sammy, Jr., 87, 118
Davis label, 35
Dawson, Roger, 200
De Carlo, Yvonne, 72
De La Fé, Alfredo, 186, 200, 267
De Mi Depende, 276
De Mí Para Tí, 156
"De Todo un Poco," 185
DeCastro Sisters, 231
Decca Records, 22, 27, 28, 35, 52, 63, 70, 73, 103, 106, 126, 139
DeFranco, Buddy, 265
Del Campo, Luis, 106–7
Delgado, Isaac, 248
"Delirio," 247
Demetrios Katsaris Orchestra, 149
Dengue, 211
Depiní, Carmen Delia, 155
Derecho Y Virao, 234

289

DeRisi, Al, 108, 128, 152
DeRisi, Tony, 108, 128, 140, 141, 144
"Derroche de Felicidad," 145
"Descarga Charanga," 208
Descargas: Cuban Jam Sessions, 181
"Desconfianza," 196
"Desert Dance, The," 90, 115, 144
"Despacito," 148
"Desvelo de Amor," 16
"Devuelve Mi Alegría," 271
"Diablo de Esa Mujer, El," 152
Diago, Virgilio, 32, 60
Diana, La (Havana café), 177
Díaz, Aniceto, 177
Díaz, Carmelo, 69
Díaz, Herman, Jr., 73
Díaz, Phil, 236
Díaz, Rafael, 3, 10
Díaz, Ulpiano, 60
Díaz Ayala, Cristóbal, 63
"Dice Mi Gallo," 66
Díez, Barbarito, 177
Diggin' the Most, 231, 234, 244
Dinah Shore Show (television show), 136, 262
Dirty Dancing (film), 185
Dixon, Mary, 52
Do Their Thing, 211–12
"Dolor Cobarde," 5, 34, 40–41, 126
Don Julio Club (Greenwich Village), 160
Donay, Millie, 92
"Donkey Serenade, The," 115
Donny & Marie Show (television show), 136, 262
Doroteo, 107, 159
Dorsey, Tommy, 52, 102
"Dos, Los," 221, 236
"Dos Letras," 13
Dos Tiempos de Monroig concert, 152
Dove, Don, 172–73
Down Argentine Way (film), 8
Dreamland Dancing Academy, Inc., 88
Drennon, Eddie, 184, 186, 200
"Drum Boogie," 102
"Drume Negrita," 10, 41
"Drume Negro," 108
Duboney, La, 182, 183–84, 199, 211, 233, 241, 256
Duchesne, Chuck, 102
Dumont, Mario, 102
Durante, Jimmy, 2

Dynasonic label, 4, 19, 22

"Earl Wilson Mambo, The," 76, 127
Eberly, Bob and Ray, 160
"Echa Martín," 67
"Échale Salsita," 255
"Echale Taquito," 149
Echevarría, Domingo, 131, 156
"Eco," 10, 126
Ecos de Cuba, Los, 28–29
Ed Sullivan Theater (Manhattan), 108
Edreira, René, 1, 2, 52
Edward B. Marks Music Company, 63
"Egoísmo," 152
Egües, Eduardo, 210
Egües, Richard, 179, 187, 209, 210
Either You Have It or You Don't, 199
El. *See next word of title*
El Sonido label, 185
"Elena," 16
Ella (film), 71, 126
Ellington, Duke, 54, 58
Elter, Gary, 37
Embassy Ballroom (Manhattan), 84
Embassy Club (Manhattan), 90, 127, 134
"En Mi Viejo San Juan," 207
"Encanto Cubano," 24, 108
"Enchanted Cubano," 128
"Engañadora, La," 180, 181, 190
"Enlloro," 41
Ensley, Ernie, 92, 213
"Entre Juanita y José," 67
Epic Records, 219, 221
"Eque Tumbao," 161
Escambrón Beach Club, El (Puerto Rico), 102
Escobar, Al, 76, 108, 128, 220
Escollies, Tony, 34, 102, 126
Escoto, Bobby, 99
"Escucha Mi Son," 72
Eskilssen-Tejada, Vera, 38–39
Espinosa, Pedro, 212
Está en Algo, 166
"Está Frizao," 47, 127
Este es Mi Mundo, 124
Estévez, José. *See* Loco, Joe
Esto Es Lo Nuestro (television show), 225
Estoy Como Nunca, 119
"Estoy Siempre Junto a Tí," 156
Estrellas Cubanas, Las, 24, 210

index

Estrellas del Ritmo, 186, 215
"Estuve Pensando," 241
"Esy," 130
Esy Morales Orchestra, 72
Exitante Ritmo, 156
Exitos Records, 262

Failde-Pérez, Miguel, 176
Fajardo, José, 30, 50, 93, 179–81, 185, **187–92,** 209, 266
"Fajardo Está de Bala," 180, 190
Fajardo Llegó a Miami, 191
"Fajardo y Su Flauta," 191
"Familia, La," 99
Familia Socarrás Orchestra, La, 53
"Fango," 224
Fania All Stars, 206, 247, 259
Fania All Stars concerts, 135
Fania Records, 49, 131, 135, 156–57, 173, 192, 200, 235, 245, 253, 256, 257, 258–59, 261–63, 266, 276
Fantasy Records, 78, 92, 184
Febo, George, 253
Feeny, Geraldo, 258
"Fefita," 209, 213
Feliciano, José "Cheo," 151, 173, 227, 232–35, 240, 241, 242, **243–48,** 255, 276
Feliu, Izzy, 165, 171
Felix, Alvaro, 34
Fellove, Francisco, 165
"Ferias de las Flores, Las," 240
Fernández, Gonzalo, 200
Fernández, Joseito, 177
Fernández, Ruth, 155
Fernando, Hector, 171
Ferrer, 56
Ferrer, José, 87, 118
Ferrer, Mel, 87
"Fever," 223
"Fiel," 157
"Fiesta en el Cielo," 123
Fiesta en Harlem, 25
Fiesta Records, 99, 103, 156, 162, 164, 166, 231
Figueroa, Frankie, 147, 270
Fisher, Clifford, 56
Fishkill Correctional Facility (New York State), 191–92
Fisk, Charles, 104

"Flauta de José, La," 191
Flemming, Leo, 147
"Flor de Amor," 191
"Flor de Ausencia," 143
"Florecita, La," 67
Flores, Marcial, 4, 54
Flores, Payo, 36
Flores, Pedro, 5, 13, 21, 155
Foley, Roberto, 184
Folis, Daniel de, 40
Fonda, Henry, 87
Font, Rafael, 109
Fontainebleau Hotel (Miami), 62
Forestier, Eddie, 220
Foster, Stephen, 8
Four Points label, 221
Fox, Al "Pablito," 258
Fox, Charlie, 186, 208
Francis, Mark, 250
Franklin, Al, 77
Franklin, Marty, 231
"Franqueza Cruel," 245–46
Frazier, Charlie, 58
"Frisao," 114
"Frisao con Gusto," 128
Frisaura, Jimmy, 108, 128, **133–37,** 139, 140, 141, 144, 149, 152, 155, 161, 232
"Fristi Popo," 77
Frohman, Mitch, 137
From the Drum to the Synthesizer (Acosta), 179
Fuentes, Levio, 109
Fuentes, Lydio, 161
"Fufulando," 40
Fuller, Gil, 221
"Funny," 236

Gains, Joe, 124
Galíndez, Polito, 21, 75, 106, 159, 196, 229
"Gandinga," 47
Garcia, Andy, 182
García, Elmo, 219, 220, 221
García, Frank "Hot Lips," 66
García, Gilberto, 216
García, José "Belingi," 66
García, Mike, 184
García, Oscar, 117–19, 165, 236–37
García, Ramón, 195
García, Roberto, 275

Garcia, Rudy, 257–58
García, Tommy, 163, 220
García, Willie, 236
García, Willy, 170
Gardel, Carlos, 4
"Garrotín, El," 177
Gatica, Lucho, 49, 234, 244, 276
"Gaucho Serenade, The," 198
Gay Ranchero, The (film), 71, 126
Gema label, 178
Ghetto Records, 253
Gibbs, Terry, 105
Gigante del Teclado, El, 149
Gilbert, Dick, 8–9, 44
Gillespie, Dizzy, 45–46, 57, 134, 156, 235
Glen Island Casino, 52
Glenn Miller Orchestra, 265
"Gloria Eres Tú, La," 134, 145, 164, 207, 268
"Gloria Maceo," 178
Gloria Theater (Manhattan), 60
Glow, Bernie, 135, 149
GNP (Gene Norman Presents) label, 78, 183
Godfrey, Arthur, 72
Goicochea, Lou, 163, 206
"Goin' Conga," 35, 36
Going Loco, 78
Golden Casino Ballroom (Manhattan), 55, 66, 81, 83
Goldner, George, 77–78, 90, 114, 251–52
"Golpecito," 90, 115, 144–45
Gómez, Eddie, 149
Gómez, Juan (Venezuelan president), 69
González, Andy, 267
González, Daniel, 221
González, Gabriel "Chino," 108, 113, 127, 128, 134, 140, 141, 144
González, Herman, 206
Gonzalez, Neno, Jr., 210
González, René, 179
Goodman, Benny, 52, 102, 230
Gorbea, Wayne, 279, 280
Goris, Jesús, 180
"Goza el Montuno," 191
Graciela, 56, 57, 67, 129, 141, 234, 244, 280–81
Gran Cachao, El, 182
Gran Combo, El, 248

Gran Combo de Puerto Rico, El, 215
Gran Federico, El. *See* Pagani, Federico
"Gran Machito, El," 172
Grand Plaza (Bronx), 43
Green, Lenny, 113
Grevi, Santiago, 10
Grillo, Frank "Machito." *See* Machito
Grillo, Mario, 172
Gringo and His Brazilians, El, 57
Gross, Ben, 57
Grossinger's (Catskills resort), 35, 107, 161, 232, 233
Grossman, Connie, 167, 186, 192
"Guachi Guaro," 256
Guagenti, Mike "Pasquale Caputo," 123, 236
"Guaguancó a Todos Los Barrios," 209
"Guaguancó Bonito," 270
"Guaguancó en Nueva York," 161
"Guaguancó en Tropicana," 145
"Guaguancó Margarito," 162
Guajira con Boogaloo, 162
"Guajirando," 191
"Guanguancó Margarito," 156
"Guantanamera," 24, 184
"Guarachi Guaro," 256
"Guararé," 114, 128
"Guardia Con el Tolete, El," 67
Guaya Salsa, 257
"Guayaba," 90, 161
Guerilla, La, 83, 107
Guerra, Marcelino "Rapindey," 19, 24–25, 46, **63–68**, 76, 83, 106, 144, 160, 207, 240, 249
  orchestra of, 75, 85, 89, 107
Guerra, Orlando "Cascarita," 147
"Guieta Caiman," 149
"Guili Guili," 73
Guilli Guilli, 73
Guillot, Olga, 20, 23, 45–47, 67, 170
"Güira, La," 134, 145
"Güiro de Macorina," 205
Guizar, Tito, 83
Gutiérrez, Julio, 171, 182
Gutiérrez, Peter. *See* Terrace, Pete
"Guyabero, El," 164
Guzmán, Paquito, 206
"Gypsy in My Soul," 75
"Gypsy Woman," 251, 252–53

Gypsy Woman, 253

Haiti, 175
Hamill, Pete, 173
Hampton, Lionel, 265
Hangin' Out, 234
Hansen, Susie, 186
Happy Boys, Los, 5, 34, 83, 107
"Harlem Special," 23, 47–48
Harlow, Larry, 130, 225, 246, 257, 261, 262, 265, 271, 280
Harris, Bob "Pedro," 10, 182
Harris, Jack, 61
Harry Smith Recording Studio, 47
Harvest Moon Ball *(New York Daily News),* 71
Havana, Cuba, 37–38, 175–76
Havana-Madrid Club (Manhattan), 42, 56, 61, 98, 107
Havana Philharmonic, 33
Havana Sport (ballroom), 65
"Have You Ever Felt That Way?", 52
Hawkins, Erskine, 7, 56
Haymes, Dick, 160
Hayworth, Rita, 44, 79
Heart of Cuba, 183
Hechos No Palabras, 152
Hecto-Mania, 221
Hector Rivera Quintet, 221
Heller, Eddie, 231
Herman, Woody, 87, 134
Hermanos Castro, Los, 39, 60–61
Hermanos Lebartard, Los, 97
Hermanos Marcano, Los, 21
Hermanos Mercado, Los, 160
Hermanos Palau, Los, 28
"Hermosa Ofelia," 180, 190
Hernández, Bartolo, 75, 101, 103, 107, 196
Hernández, George, 182
Hernández, Rafael, 1–2, 5, **13–18,** 21–22, 36, 69, 70, 72–73, 120, 169–70
Hernández, René, 20, 24, 47–48, 49, 57, 76, 88, 105, 113, 114, 117, 145, 149, 208
Hernández, René "El Látigo," 183, 189, 219–20
Hernández, Victoria, 1–2, 13–18, 21–22, 70

Herscher, David, 211
Herscher, Ira, 211–12
Hersh, Anna, 82
"Hi, Hi, Hi," 148
Hidalgo, Giovanni, 101
"Hija de Lola, La," 149
"Hijos de Buda, Los," 126
History of La Conga, The (Decca Records), 6
Hit Parade (radio show), 98
Hitchcock, Jack, 99
Hollywood, Latin music in, 8–9, 22, 44–45, 46, 71, 126
Holmes, Marty, 137
Homenaje a Rafael Hernández, 169
Hommy (Harlow salsa opera), 246
"Hong Kong Mambo," 156
Hooke, Jack, 234, 252
Hora Continental, La (radio show), 8
"Hora Staccato," 57
"Horas y Minutos," 155
Horne, Lena, 87
Hornedo, Alfonso, 39
Hotel Americana (Manhattan), 84
Hotel Diplomat (Manhattan), 163, 241
Hotel Lucerne (Manhattan), 228
Hotel McAlpin (Manhattan), 54
Hotel Normandy (San Juan), 102
Hotel Riviera (Las Vegas), 116
Hotel San Juan (Puerto Rico), 62
Hotel Seville (Havana), 53–54
house parties, 4, 16
"How High the Moon," 75, 76, 127, 134
"Hoy Como Ayer," 241
Hoya, Oscar de la, 97
"Hueso, El," 224
Hunts Point Palace (Bronx), 83, 165, 205, 207, 220, 241
Hyman, Max, 90–92, 93, 114–15, 116, 210–11

"I Like It Like That," 224
"I Talk to the Trees," 233
Ideal, La, 210
"Imágenes," 156
Imperial Records, 78
"Impression," 66
Imprudencia (film), 45
"In the Still of the Night," 75
Inca label, 271

"Incertidumbre," 5, 9
India, La, 173, 248
"Indio," 41
Infierno Cabaret (Havana), 64
Infinito, 271
Ink Spots, the, 7, 125
"Inolvidable," 117, 123
Inolvidable, 119
International Casino (Manhattan), 95
International Records, 262
International Workers Order Symphony Orchestra, 33
"Isla del Encanto," 209, 214
"Isla Verde," 73
Ithier, Salvador, 16
"I've Got You under My Skin," 229, 241
Iznaga, Alberto, 1, 2, 6, 7, 19, 21, **31–36**, 43, 59, 83, 84, 102, 107, 160, 182

Jack Cole Dancers, 101, 126
"Jacobo Basura," 113
"Jamaiquino, El," 182, 220
James, Harry, 102, 133–34, 224
Jazz Espagnole, 78
Jazz Singer, The (film), 1
Jefferson, Walter, 165
Jerome, Jerry, 280
Jewish people in Harlem, 22, 82
"Jibarito, El," 98
"Jíbaro en Nueva York, Un," 207
Jiménez, Cheo, 143
Jiménez, Nick, 227, 229, 230, 231–37, 241
Jiménez, Tito, 165
Joe Cuba Presents the Velvet Voice of Jimmy Sabater, 221
Joe Cuba Sextet, 230–37, 244
"Joe Cuba's Madness," 118
"Joe Cuba's Mambo," 233
Joe Loco Trio, 77
"Joe Lustig Mambo," 90, 115
Joe Panama Quintet, 241
Joe Panama Sextet, 241
"Johnny's No Good," 253
Jones, Robin, 202
Jordan, Louis, 228
Jorrín, Enrique, 180, 181, 190
José Budet y Sus Tropicales, 160, 196
José Curbelo Orchestra, 89
José Panama Quintet, 228, 229
Joseph, Karen, 186, 192

"Jóvenes de la Defensa Pueblo Nuevo," 182
Jóvenes del Cayo, Los, 20
"Jóvenes del Ritmo," 200
Juan Alberto de Regla Hall (Cuba), 189
"Juaniquita," 191
"Juégate," 246, 247
"Jugué y Perdí," 171
Juilliard School of Music (Manhattan), 34
Julia, Raul, 169
Julio Andino Orchestra, 77
Julio "El Vaquero," 161
Julio Gutiérrez Quintet, 170–71
"Julito y Sus Flautas," 182
"Jungalarero," 72
"Jungle Fantasy," 72
"Jungle Holiday," 57
Just for Fun, 186

Kahn, Lewis, 186
Kako, 245, 280
Kako's All-Stars, 275
Karen Records, 263
Katherine Dunham Dance Company, 35
Kenny, Nick, 57
Kenton, Stan, 101, 102, 105, 134
Kid Chocolate, 3, 38
"Kikirikí," 190
King, The, 156
King Salsa (band), 202
"Koki Koka," 59, 61
Koppe, Edmundo, 211
Krane, Bernie, 112, 114, 123
Krazy Kats, Los, 28
Krupa, Gene, 102–3, 126, 163, 230
Kubaney label, 181–82
Kurtzer, Dave, 137

La. *See next word of title*
"La-La-La," 161
La Negra, Tonia, 83
La Playa Sextet, 63, 67, 95, 105, 149, 162, 182, 196, 220, 224, 229, 242
Labah Sosseh with Orquesta Aragón, 186
LaBarron, Eddie, 112
LaCalle, José, 54
"Lamento Borincano," 13–14, 16, 22
Lancaster, Burt, 72
Lane, Abbe, 87, 197
Laredo, Junior, 155

LaSalle Cafeteria (Manhattan), 107, 128, 140, 144
Laserie, Rolando, 18, 93, 190
"Last Tango in Paris," 271
Latin Dimensions, 186
Latin Dimensions, 187
Latin hustle, 135
Latin Jazz Quintet, 279
Latin music, development in New York City, **1–12**
Latin Musicians Show, The (radio show), 131, 215, 269
Latin New York (magazine), 37, 84, 96–97, 112, 114, 200, 262, 266–67, 273, 276
Latin Nostalgia (radio show), 59
Latin Quarter (Manhattan club), 98
Latin Rendezvous, 186
"Laura," 269
Lavoe, Hector, 151, 162, **273–77**
Lay, Rafael, 179
Lazy Levee Loungers, 54
Lebrón Brothers, 253
LeCompte, Maria Luisa, 7
Lecuona, Margarita, 42
Lecuona Cuban Boys, 229
Lee, Peggy, 223
Lefkowitz, Louis J., 88
Legarreta, Pupi, 183, 184, 200, 210
Legreti, Pepe, 15
Leight, Don, 161
Leña, Moncho, 93, 164, 219, 220
León, Alfredo, 65
Leon, Richard, 258
Leslie, Lew, 52, 54
Lester, Bill, 270
"Letargo," 50
Let's Cha Cha Cha with Hector Rivera, 221
Let's Dance the Charanga, 205
"Levántate Manuel," 103
Levine, Louis, 88
Levy, Al "Alfredito," 93, 109, 151, 164, 208, 220
  orchestra of, 101, 105
Levy, Morris, 49, 78, 115, 136, 171, 234, 235, 252, 253
Lew, Ralph, 92, 187
Lew Leslie's Blackbirds, 52, 54
Lewis, Jack, 198
Lewis, Stan, 251

Leyda, Linda, 99
"Leyte," 256
Libre label, 281
Liceo Artístico y Literario, El, 176
"Light My Fire," 185–86
Limbo Lounge (Queens), 165
Lincoln Square Center (Manhattan), 107
"Linda Mujer," 160
"Little Brown Jug," 75
"Little Sunflower," 281
Live at the Palladium, 116
Llano, Julian, 257
"Llego Mijan," 156
"Llegué," 166
"Llora," 98
"Llora Timbero," 156
"Lluvia," 269
"Lo Dicen Todos," 90
"Lo Siento Por Tí," 13
Lobo y Melón, 165
Loco, Joe, 5, 7, 16, **75–79,** 83, 105, 106, 107, 108, 112, 115, 118, 127, 134, 149, 196, 220
Loco Recording and Publishing Company, 79
"Locorama," 77
Locutores, Los, 258
Loews Boulevard Theater (Bronx), 170
Loop Lounge, 156
Lopati label, 35
López, Alfredo, 184
López, Angel, 42
López, Belisario, 97, 177, 187, 189
López, Elias, 223
López, Freddie, 77
López, Gil, 107, 113, 114, 129, 137, 141, 145, 197, 213, 240–41
López, Israel "Cachao," 6–7, 84, 178, 181–82, 186, 189, 194, 200
López, Jack, 76
López, Jesús, 179, 189
López, Johnny, 5, 159
López, Jorge, 156
López, Many, 105
López, Nico, 43
López, Orestes "Macho," 6–7, 84, 178–79
López, Paco, 16
López, Paul, 73, 105, 108, 137
López, Pedro, 60
López, René, 147

López, Tommy, 234
López, Vincent, 2, 52, 56, 76, 126
Lopinto, Frank, 135
Los. *See next word of title*
"Louie's Saxofobia," 166
"Love for Sale," 75, 79
Loyola, Efrán, 179
Lozano, Robertico, 171
Lozano, Rolando, 179, 183, 184, 186, 187, 209
Luhtala, Pere, 215
Luis, Fernando, 55–56
"Luis A. Ferré Performing Arts Center (Puerto Rico), 152
Luis Muñoz Marin Amphitheater (Hato Rey), 157
"Luna de Miel," 103
Lunn, Bobbie, 231
Lupe, La, 99, 157, **169–73,** 271
Lustig, Joe, 92
"Luz a Babalú," 50
Lyman, Frankie, 249

Machado, Gerardo, 64
Machín, Antonio, 2
Machito, 6, 13, 21, 35, 59, 63, 65, 83, 112, 123, 159, 160, 195, 207, 214, 219, 240, 241, 243–44, 249, 280–81
  with Cugat, 7
  in La Siboney, 34
  marriage of, 5
  orchestra of, 5, 9–10, 11, 20, 23, 24, 33, 34, 44, 45–47, 50, 57, 63, 69, 71, 75, 76–77, 84–85, 88–89, 90, 95, 97–98, 101, 105, 106, 108, 113, 114, 120, 126–27, 135, 139, 143, 171–72, 182–83, 220, 221, 232, 239, 257, 266, 281
  Valdés and, 43, 50
  views on Curbelo, 96
  views on Oller, 19
  views on Puente, 267
Machito and His Salsa Big Band, 281
Machito at the Concord, 110
"Mack the Knife," 198
Macucho, 36, 110, 182
"Macurijes," 43
Madera, Frank, 155
Madera, José "Pin," 11, 155

Madison Square Garden (Manhattan), 120–21, 135, 136
Madriguera, Enric, 42, 52, 54, 75, 101, 112
Maganette, La (Manhattan club), 166, 191, 192
"Mago del tres, El," 67
Majestic Records, 72
Make Believe Ballroom, The (radio show), 11
"Mala Lengua," 59
"Malcriada," 152, 153
"Malditos Celos," 17, 73
Maldonado, Carlos, 160
Maldonado, David, 131
Maldonado, Jorge, 186
Malo, El, 273, 275
"Mamá Güela," 121
"Mamá Yo Quiero," 8
mambo, 178
"Mambo," 178
mambo, birth of, 11–12, 48, 67, 85, 92, 113–14
"Mambo Birdland," 134
Mambo Boys, 108
"Mambo City," 130
"Mambo Con Puente," 145
"Mambo de Broadway, El," 24, 128
Mambo Devils, 114
"Mambo Diablo," 134, 197, 230, 279
"Mambo en Broadway, El," 108
"Mambo Gozón," 156
"Mambo Inn," 130, 220
"Mambo Inspiración," 179
Mambo Kings, The (film), 137
"Mambo la Roca," 90, 269
"Mambo Macoco," 129, 144
Mambo Madness (film), 103
"Mambo Mona," 90, 115, 144
"Mambo No. 5," 24, 87, 113–14
"Mambo of the Pines," 231
"Mambo of the Times," 231, 233
"Mambo Rhapsody," 76
"Mambo se Ha Puesto Duro, El," 108
"Mambo Show," 202
"Mambo USA," 77
Mambo USA tour, 77–78
Mambo with Noro, 73
Mambo with Tjader, 92
"Mambo Wolves," 114
"Mambolino," 230

"Managua, Nicaragua," 98
"Mango del Monte," 114, 128
Mangrella, Frank, 90
Mangual, José, 10, 75, 76, 101, 110
Mangual, José, Sr., 231
Mangual, Luis, 147
Manhattan Center (Manhattan), 23, 46, 47, 66, 85, 161
Manhattan Groove, 186
Manicero, El, 199
Mann, Herbie, 101
Manor Ballroom (Queens), 165
Manquina, Louie, 92
"Manteca," 235
Mantilla, Ray, 147
Manzano, Guillermo, 151
"Maramoor Mambo," 256
Maravilla del Siglo, La, 178
Marcano, Pedro, 5, 7, 10, 13
Marcano, Piquito, 106, 159
"Marcianos, Los," 149
Marden, Ben, 43
Mardi Gras label, 233, 262
Marguerite LeCompte Music Studio, 140
"María Cervantes," 202
"María Teresa," 177
"Marijuana," 145, 149
marímbula, 29
Marín, Frankie, 224
Marín, Orlando, 93, 101, 137, **163–67,** 202, 207, 219, 220, 224, 242, 280
  orchestra of, 95, 105
Marini, Leo, 70
Marquetti, Cheo, 23, 143
Marrero, Nicky, 101, 192
Marrero, Raul, 271
Martha, 116, 123
Martí, Frank, 127
Martínez, Cacha, 45, 47
Martinez, Cito, 236
Martínez, Cuco, 183
Martínez, Johnny, 105
Martínez, Mike, 211
Martínez, Osvaldo "Chihuahua," 181, 186, 189, 191
Martínez, René, 106
Martínez, Rogelio, 52
Martínez, Sabú, 78, 98, 101, 163, 228

Martinique, La (Manhattan club), 44–45, 61
"Mary Ann," 231
Más Salsa Que Pescao, 257
Masucci, Jerry, 131, 135, 156, 173, 235, 245–46, 252, 258, **261–63**
"Mátala," 66
Matamoros, Miguel, 3, 10
Mateo, Joseito, 89
"Material, El," 214
Máximo, Lo, 162
"Mayaguez," 207
Maysonet, George and Margie, 185
McKibbon, Al, 92
McRae, Carmen, 104
"Me Dejan Solito," 220
"Me Lo Dijo Adela," 115, 183
"Me Voy Pa' Morón," 214
Mechita, 99
Medina, David, 258
Medina, Henry, 147
Mejor Que Nunca, 281
"Meletón," 178
Melody Lounge (Denver), 77
Méndez, José Antonio, 145
Mendoza, Chico, 242
"Menéalo Que Se Empelote," 16
Menéndez, Nilo, 1, 2, 5, 54
Menéndez, Pedro, 97
Meñique, 157, 162
"Mentiras Criollas," 179
Mercado, Ralph, 200, 224, 261
Mercerón, Mariano, 63
Mercury Artists, 113
Mercury Records, 73, 221
"Merengue Pa' Tí," 113
Mericana Records, 187, 253, 257
"Mesa, La," 164, 165, 166, 220
Mesa, Oro, 188
Mesa, Señor, 16
Mestizo, 253
Mexican Jumping Bean (film), 71, 126
Mexico, film industry in, 45, 70, 181
MGM Records, 73
"Mi Bomba Sono," 156
"Mi Chiquita Quiere Bembe," 156
"Mi Guajira," 73
"Mi Jaragual," 152
"Mi Jevita," 166

"Mi Loca Tentación," 152
"Mi Mambo," 164, 208, 220
"Mi Tonada," 191
"Mi Triste Problema," 245–46
"Mi Vecina," 149
"Micaela," 224
Midnight Serenaders, the, 69
"Miedo de Tí," 66
Millan, Willie, 99
Miller, Glenn, 52, 102
Millian, Professor, 126
Minguella, Panchito, 102
"Mio," 119
"Mírame Más," 156, 157
Miranda, Carmen, 8, 22
Miranda, Ismael, 155, 248
Miranda, Juan Pablo, 187
Miranda, Luis, 107
Miranda, Miguelito, 102, 148, 155
Miranda, Santos, 228, 229
Mirros, Hilda, 225
"Mis Amores," 127
"Moanga," 209
Mocambo (Hollywood), 44–45
Modern Drummer (magazine), 104
Mojica, José, 38
Molina, Tony, 48, 99, 109, 110, **159–62,** 161
Mollick, Stan, 161
"Mondongo," 23, 47
Monero, Jose Luis, 269
Monge Funeral Parlor (Manhattan), 3
Mongo Introduces La Lupe, 170
Monogram label, 48
Monroig, Gilberto, 48, 99, 130, 135, **151–53,** 156, 161, 232, 244
Monroig, Glenn, 152
Monsanto, Quique, 224
Montagne, Davy, 165
Montalvo, Eddie, 279
"Montaña, La," 145
Montañez, Andy, 173
Monte Carlo (Manhattan), 35, 183, 197
"Monterrey," 134
Montesino, 21, 34, 75, 83, 107
Montilla label, 263
Montmartre (Havana nightclub), 40, 54, 71, 109
montuno, 177
Montuno (radio show), 202, 215

"Montuno in A-Flat," 23, 71, 72
"Montuno in G," 72
Mood Latino, 186
Morales, Esy, 70, 72, 105, 108
Morales, Humberto, 70, 103
Morales, Luis, 69
Morales, Noro, 7, 52, 59, 66, 67, **69–73,** 82–83, 84, 93, 112, 160, 195, 196, 206, 207, 219–20, 239, 249
 film shorts of, 71, 126
 Oller and, 19, 21, 22, 23, 24
 orchestra of, 5, 10, 45, 63, 76, 89, 95, 98, 101, 103, 105, 106, 107, 108, 109, 114, 139, 143, 270
 quartet of, 228
 Socarrás and, 55
Morales, Pepito (also Mandinga), 70
Morales Brothers Puerto Rican Orchestra, the, 70–71, 72
Morand, José, 5, 162, 164
Moré, Beny, 48, 207, 247
"More I See You, The," 236
Morena, Rosita, 15
Moreno, José Luis, 35
Morro, El, 97, 177, 187
Mortimer, Lee, 112–13
Morton, Tommy, 88–90, 160
Mount Morris Theater (Manhattan), 54
Mountain, Blue, 125
Mucho Mucho Machito, 67
"Muerto Se Fue de Rumba, El," 139
"Mujer Divina," 221
Munar, Anam, 258
Mundo de Tito Puente, El (television show), 130–31, 199
"Muñequita Linda," 233
Muñoz, Monchito, **101–4,** 161, 227
Muñoz, Rafael, 69, 101, 102–3, 196, 269
Muñoz Marin, Luis, 14
Museo del Barrio (Manhattan), 157
Music of Cuba, The (Carpentier), 176
Music of Gonzalo Curiel, The, 78
Music of Rafael Hernández, The, 78
Música (documentary), 57
Musicor label, 119, 211
Musicraft Records, 45
"My Favorite Things," 271

Nader, Richard, 120–21, 124, 136
"Nague," 10, 35, 98, 106, 139

index

"Nana Seré," 225
Nando, King, 253
Navarro, Paquito, 123
"Negra Consentida," 148
"Negra Leona," 43
Negrete, Jorge, 70, 83
"Negro," 41
Nelson, Bobby, 165, 184, 215
New Horizons, 269
New York City Salsa, 215
New York World's Fair (1938|-39), 6
"Niche, El," 183
"Nico Cadeon," 271
"Nicolás," 271
Nieto, Uba, 227
Night in Mambo Jazzland, A, 78
Night in the Tropics (film), 46
"Nina," 149
"No Blues Noro," 73
"No Me Quieras Tanto," 13
"No Te Olvides De Mi," 221
"No Te Quedes Con Las Ganas," 191
"Nobody Here but Us Chickens," 228
"Noche de Ronda," 155
Noche en Montmartre, Una, 190
Nola Penthouse Studios, 46
Norales, Noro, 11, 13
Norman, Abraham, 211
"Noro in Rumbaland," 71, 89
Novak, Kim, 87
Novos, Tony, 156
Nuestra Herencia, 184
"Nuestra Vida," 246
"Nueva Conga," 43
Nuevo Ritmo, 184
"Núnca," 232
Núñez, Arturo, 143
Núñez, Joseito, 65

Obrero Español, El (Manhattan club), 241
"Obsesión," 143
Ocho, 242
Odd Fellows Temple (Manhattan), 66, 83, 106
Odds Are On, The, 266
Of Latin Extraction, 184
O'Farrill, Chico, 108, 141, 157
　orchestra of, 105, 139
"Oh Yeah," 235

"Ojos Verdes," 22
Oliva, Carlos, 171
Olivencia, Roberto "Chinky," 102, 139–40
Olivencia, Tommy, 245
Oller, Gabriel, 3–4, 11, **19–25,** 27, 29, 46, 47, 71, 72–73, 77, 82, 84, 113–14, 128, 255
Oller, Gabriel, Sr., 20
Oller, Vicente, 21
"Olvidado," 242
"One O'Clock Jump," 7
One of a Kind, 173
"110 Street and Fifth Avenue," 73, 108, 220
"Opus Esy," 72
Oquendo, Manny, 130, 141, 144, 145, 219, 220
Orchard Beach (Bronx), 110
Orfeon label, 78
"Oriente," 169, 171, 172
Original de Manzanillo, 182
Orlando Marín Conjunto, 207
"Orlando's Saxofobia," 166
Orquesta Alimen, 182
Orquesta América, 180, 181
Orquesta Antillana, 186
Orquesta Aragón, 197, 207, 208, 210, 247
Orquesta Broadway, 84, 93, 95, 163, 181, 182, 185, 186, 191, 192, 209, 211–17, 266
Orquesta Broadway Loves New York, 215
Orquesta Cosmopólita, 143
Orquesta Cuda, 280
Orquesta Francesca de Tata Pereira, 60
Orquesta Gilberto Valdés, 182
Orquesta Gris, 178
Orquesta Havana-Riverside, 97
Orquesta Ideal, 188
Orquesta Ilda, La, 187
Orquesta Melodías del 40, 210
Orquesta Metropolitana, 186
Orquesta Neno González, 189
Orquesta New Yorker, 275
Orquesta Novel, 184
Orquesta Nuevo Ritmo, 183
Orquesta Pablo Valenzuela, 177
Orquesta Quisqueya, 160
Orquesta Revé, 182
Orquesta Ritmo Tropical, 196

299

Orquesta Sensación, 210
Orquesta Serenata Tropical, 148
Orquesta Tropicana, La, 155
Ortiz, Carlos, 84, 237
Ortíz, John, 243, 245
Ortíz, Luis, 162
Ortíz, Luis "Perico," 50, 208, 276, 281
Ortíz-Dávila, Pedro. *See* Davilita
Osácar, Elio, 29–30
Osácar, Elio, Jr. *See* Bravo, Sonny
Osmond, Marie, 136
Otra Vez, 257
Our Latin Thing (film), 256–57, 258, 259
"Oye Como Va," 178, 256, 258, 259
"Oye Heck," 221
"Oye Mi Bajo," 112, 214
"Oye Mi Son Cha-Cha-Cha," 164
"Oye Negra," 10, 126
"Oyeme Mulata," 184, 205

"Pa' Africa," 209, 212, 266
"Pa' Coco Solo," 191
"Pa' Huele," 267
Paar, Jack, 197
Pabón, Tony, **223–26**
pachanga, 78, 84, 85, 136, 198–99, 205–6, 241
"Pachanga, La," 205
Pachanga at the Caravana Club, 198
Pachanga Con Puente, 156
"Pachanga 'n Charanga," 208
"Pachanga Oriental," 221
"Pachanga Se Baila Así, La," 198–99, 206, 208
"Pachanga Suavecito," 221
Pachanga with Barretto, 221
Pachanga with Joe Loco, 78, 184
Pachanga y Charanga!, 219
Pacheco, Johnny, 50, 91, 95, 130, 183, 197–98, 202, 205, 219, 224, 249, 257, 261, 262, 276, 280
  creation of *pachanga*, 85, 206
  orchestra of, 182, 184, 210, 221, 266, 267, 275
Pacheco, Mary, 155
"Paella, La," 10, 98
Pagán, Georgie, 251
Pagan, Howie, 196
Pagani, Arsenio. *See* Pagani, Federico
Pagani, Federico, 2, 46, 49, 66, 67, **81–85,** 89, 106, 107, 112, 127–28, 134, 164, 251
Pagani, Papi, 102, 104, 139–40, 182, 227
Palacios, Hortensia, 56
Pa'Lante, 157
Palau, Rafael "Tat," 152
Palladium (Hollywood), 117
Palladium Ballroom (Manhattan), 11, 84, **87–93,** 111, 114–15, 119, 128–29, 134, 135, 140, 144, 148, 151, 160, 161, 164, 180, 182–83, 190, 197, 207–8, 210–11, 220, 232, 234, 244, 265, 268, 269
Palladium Memories, 120
"Palladium Stomp," 48
Palm Gardens Ballroom (Manhattan), 115, 223
Palmer, Robert, 84
Palmieri, Charlie, 5, 50, 59, 69, 77, 79, 91, 104, 108, 109, 116, 130, 149, 152, 163–64, 185, 190, **193–203,** 220, 236, 237, 258, 280
  creation of *pachanga*, 85, 205–6, 208
  in Terrace's quintet, 78
  with Muñoz band, 103
  orchestra (charanga) of, 84, 101, 165, 182, 183–84, 211, 233, 241–42, 255–56
  with Picadilly Boys, 107, 128
  with Puente band, 129, 141, 145
  quintet of, 95
Palmieri, Eddie, 104, 130, 163, 165, 173, 195, 207, 220, 223, 227, 249, 250, 256, 262, 267, 270
  in Rodríguez's band, 115–16
  orchestra of, 84, 93, 101, 182, 234, 242, 245, 266
Palmieri, Esther, 203
"Palo Tiene Jutía," 113
Palomo, Johnny, 211
Pan American Lounge (Queens), 156
"Pan Sobao, El," 149
Panama, 38–39
Panama, José. *See* Preudhomme, David "Joe Panama"
Panart Records, 49, 180, 181, 190–91
Panchito "Flauta Mágica," 97, 177, 187
Pancho's Club Tico Tico (radio show), 23, 46
"Pantano," 256
Pantoja, Victor "El Negrito," 106, 228,

229
Pappy Ali y Sus Rumberos, 240
Pappy y Sus Rumberos, 229
"Paraíso de Dulzura," 275
Paramount Theatre (Manhattan), 43
"Pare Cochero," 63, 65, 93, 179, 214, 279
Paredes, Gustavo, 57
Pareles, Jon, 193–94
Parish, Avery, 7
Park Palace (Manhattan), 9, 21, 66, 77, 81, 83, 106, 107, 115, 144–45
Park Plaza (Manhattan), 17, 43, 55, 84, 241
Pasaporte, 214
"Pasó en Tampa," 46, 113
Pastor, Paquito, 165, 208, 212, 280
Pastrana, Joey, 224, 253
Pastrana, Willie, 123, 224
Patio Club, El (Atlantic Beach), 90, 103, 128, 134, 140, 161
Patot, Manuel, 108, 127, 128, 135, 140, 141, 144, 152
"Patricia," 183
"Paula," 98
Paunetto, Bobby, 242
Paz, Rafael de la, 143
"Peanut Vendor, The," 2, 73, 104, 167
Peer, Ralph, 9
Peer International, 60
"Peluca, La," 162
Peña, Enrique, 177
Peña, Francisco "Popi," 280
Peña, José, 39
"Penjamo," 145
"Pensar," 221, 236
Peraza, Armando, 101
Perdido, 221–22
"Perdiendo la Cabeza," 149
Pereira, Tata, 60
Pérez, Chicky, 163, 220
Pérez, David, 224
Pérez, Graciela. *See* Graciela
Pérez, Juan Irene, 147
Pérez, Lou, 5, 37, 69, 171, 184–85, 186, 210
  orchestra of, 105, 182
Pérez, Luis "Chicky," 206
Perez, Miguel, 216
"Perfume de Gardenias," 73

Perieda, Liduvino, 39
Permuy, Ana, 56
Pesante, Rafael, 34
Pescao en Salsa, 257
Pete & Louie: The Beautiful People, 266
Pete Terrace Quintet, 78
"Pete's Boogaloo," 223
Petit Lounge (Chicago), 183
"Petite," 221
Petrillo, James, 9–10, 11, 44
"Philadelphia Mambo," 93, 230
Photoplay Theater, 82
piano solos, 41
"Picadillo," 48, 90, 108, 128, 202. *See also* "Chang"
Picadilly Boys, the, 24, 90, 107–8, 128, 134, 140, 148
"Picao y Tostao," 152, 153
Pickells, Charles, 76
"Piérdete," 127
"Pilarena," 76, 108, 127
Piñeiro, Ignacio, 63, 88, 255
Pines (Catskills resort), 231
Piro, Killer Joe, 92
"Pito, El," 235, 236
Pizarro, Carlos, 35, 36, 270
"Plantao, El," 269
"Plaza Stomp Mambo," 77
"Plazos Tracioneros," 145
Plus label, 164, 208
"Poco Pelo," 161
"Poema de Otoño," 246, 247
"Ponce," 73, 108, 220
Pop Art label, 171
"Poquito Más, Un," 66
"Por Qué Ahora," 149
"Por Tu Amor," 115, 136, 230
"Porque Tú Sufres," 46, 113
Portela, Guillermo, 39, 61
Portillo de la Luz, César, 247–48
Portrait of Santos Colón, 157
Pouchie, Steve, 147
Pous, Arquimedes, 53
Pozo, Chano, 20, 23, 24, 41, 63, 67, 75, 105, 113, 140, 248, 256
  murder of, 47
  Valdés and, 45–47
Pozo, Chino, 10, 101, 106, 108, 126, 128, 140, 141, 144

301

Prado, Pérez, 24, 78, 85, 87, 101, 107, 113–14, 115, 148, 183
"Preciosa," 13–14
"Preludio en Ritmo," 149
Preudhomme, David "Joe Panama," 228, 229, 241
Prima, Louie, 161
Primera Maravilla del Siglo, La, 178
"Príncipe Niño, El," 182
Protesta, La, 224–25
"Pruébalo," 235
Puchito Records, 180, 190
"Pueblo Nuevo," 189
Puente, Anna, 125, 127
Puente, Tito, 7, 10, 48, 57, 59, 69, 76, 78, 79, 107–10, 112, 123, **125–31,** 155, 169, 170–71, 178, 190, 199, 220, 227, 230, 231, 232, 235, 243–44, 249, 270, 280
  drafted into Navy, 10, 11, 126–27
  early years, 4–5, 61, 71
  fitieth anniversary celebration, 157
  Hernández and, 16
  on "Dolor Cobarde," 41
  orchestras and bands of, 24, 30, 72, 75, 84, 85, 90–92, 95, 96–97, 101, 103, 104, 105, 133, 135–36, 139, 140–41, 144, 148, 151–52, 159, 161–62, 163, 165–66, 182–83, 196–97, 206, 207, 232, 233, 239, 241, 242, 262, 266, 267–68, 269
  rivalry with Bobo, 93, 104, 130
  rivalry with Rodríguez, 49, 90–91, 109, 114–15, 116–17, 120, 129–30, 141, 144, 198, 271
  Valdés and, 143–46
"Puerta de Tierra," 73, 207
Puerto Rican politics, 13–14
Puerto Rican Symphonette, 17
Puerto Ricans, early New York immigrants, 1–2, 20–21
Puerto Rico 67, 79
Puerto Rico Theater (Bronx), 171
Puig, Cheo Belén, 20, 143
Pullman, Shep, 152
Puntillita, 248
Purmuy, Anita, 255
"Push Push Push," 235

QRS label, 52

"Qué Bonito Es," 180, 190
Qué Chévere, 165, 242
"Qué Me Pasa," 47
"Que No, Que No," 98
"Qué Pena Me Da," 49, 139
Qué Problema, 234
"Qué Sabes Tú," 152
"Que Se Fuñan," 99, 103, 156
"Qué Será Mi China," 110, 161
"Que Son Uno," 236, 242
"Qué Te Importa," 13
"Qué Te Pedí," 169, 171, 172
"Que Usted Conoce, El," 156
Que Viva la Música (radio show), 147
Quevedo, Pablo, 177
Quian, Monguito "El | 'Unico," 210
"Quiéreme y Verás," 145
Quijano, Joe, 93, 163, 164, 184, 198, 202–3, **205–8,** 220, 242, 271
  orchestra of, 105, 182
"Quinta Guajira," 212
Quintana, Miguel, 147
Quinteto Siboney, 65
"Quivican," 162

racial discrimination, 1, 10, 31–33, 41–42, 51, 54, 58, 67, 88, 189–90
radio, 4, 98
  Cuban, 40, 180, 189
  Latin music on, 8–9, 10–11, 22–23, 43–44, 46, 47, 54–55, 59, 61–62, 72, 90, 91, 114, 123, 129, 131, 135, 137, 144, 147, 149, 159–60, 185–86, 192, 206, 215, 221, 258, 270–71
  Puerto Rican, 18
Rafael Sánchez y Su Sinfónica, 69
Raimone, Tony, 265
Rainbow label, 231
"Rainfall," 197
Ramírez, Carlos, 22, 232, 243
Ramírez, Louie, 30, 78, 105, 110, 118, 131, 157, 202, 266, 271
Ramírez, Louise, 236
Ramos, Danny Hinton, 184
Ramos, Mike, 159, 266
Ramos, Nick, 165
Ramos, Tito, 251
"Ran Kan Kan," 90, 108, 130, 135, 148
"Rap-O Clap-O," 253

Rapetti, Gene, 133–34, 135, 137, 152
"Ratón, El," 247
Ray, Ricardo, 93, 199, 223, 234
Raymond, Art "Pancho," 10, 19, 23, 46, 47, 84, 90, 114
RCA Victor, 2, 16, 24, 35, 57, 78, 98, 104, 108, 109, 112, 115, 135, 156, 161, 239
records, 78-rpm, 6, 145, 151–52
Reencarnación, La, 224
Reilly, Betty, 46
"Reina, La," 106, 112
Reinhardt, Django, 57
"Reloj, El," 16
"Relojito Travieso, El," 191
Remo Records, 224
"Rendezvous," 156
René, Angel, 111, 112, 120–21, 124, 146
rent parties, 4, 16
"Renta, La," 114
Reunión, 49
Reunion: Miguelito Valdés with Machito and his Orchestra, 139
Rey Roig Aquí Llegó, 257
Rey y Yo, El, 169
Reyes, Emilio, 101, 103
Reyes, Eulogio, 170
Reyes, Freddie, 113
Reyes, Walfredo de los, 39, 40, 219
Reyna, Felix, 189, 210
"Reza del Meletón," 178
"Rhapsody in Blue," 57
"Rhumba Rhapsody" (earlier "Rhumba Flamenco"), 29, 45, 66, 71, 72, 160
Rica Charanga, 186
"Rica Pulpa," 10
Rich, Buddy, 163
Ricky Gardel Orchestra, 229
"Rico Vacilón," 182–83
"Rinconcito, El," 103
Rios, Freddie, 159, 266
Rios, Peter, 84, 216, 257, 262
Riot!, 253
Riset, Panchito, 64, 159, 207
Rítmica Aragón, La, 179
"Ritmo Bembé," 165
Ritmo Con Ache (radio show), 147
"Ritmo de Pollos," 180, 190
Ritmo de Pollos, 180, 190
"Ritmo Melón," 185

Ritmo Records, 226
Rivera, Bobby, 35–36
Rivera, Eddie "Gua Gua," 194
Rivera, Facundo, 65
Rivera, Geraldo, 124
Rivera, Hector, 69, 162, 163, 206, 208, **219–22,** 221, 234, 235
Rivera, Ismael, 18, 39, 151, 225
Rivera, Joe, 206
Rivera, Mario, 267
Rivera, Mon, 93, 99, 151, 164
Rivera, Ray, 77
Rivera, Sonny, 279
Rivero, Don, 113
Riverside Records, 170, 221
Riviera Nightclub (Englewood Cliffs), 43
Rizo, Marco, 57, 58
RKO Theater (Manhattan), 2
Robbins, Fred, 46
Robbins Music Corporation, 60, 65
Roberts, John Storm, 131
Robinson, Bill "Bojangles," 54
Robles, Ralph, 261
Rodríguez, Alfredo, 236
Rodríguez, Arsenio, 6, 20, 24–25, 35, 41, 46, 65, 67, 88, 113, 179, 207, 210, 220, 221, 233
Rodríguez, Bobby, 50, 106, 123, 219
Rodríguez, Chucho, 143
Rodríguez, John "Big Daddy; La Vaca," 5, 71, 76–77, **105–10,** 134, 140, 149, 161
Rodríguez, Johnny, 10, 70, 111, 112, 126, 159
Rodríguez, Johnny "Dandy," 50, 105, 117, 137, 231
Rodríguez, Lalo, 50
Rodríguez, Nancy, 137, 147
Rodríguez, Nano, 42
Rodríguez, Nicholas, 280
Rodríguez, Nora, 165–66
Rodríguez, Pablo. *See* Rodríguez, Tito
Rodríguez, Pellín, 71, 109, 161, 183, 225
Rodríguez, Pete, 199, 223, 224, 234, 253
Rodríguez, Pete "El Conde," 224, 276, 280
Rodríguez, Quique, 179
Rodríguez, Roberto, 215
Rodríguez, Tito, 20, 29, 44, 46, 48, 69, 71, 98, 106, **111–24,** 126, 144–45,

303

151, 205, 220, 221, 231–32, 234, 244, 246, 249, 267, 270
orchestra of, 95, 101, 103, 104, 135, 163, 182–83, 197, 206, 207, 232, 239, 240–41
quintet of, 104, 107, 113
rivalry with Puente, 49, 90–91, 109, 114–15, 116–17, 120, 129–30, 141, 144, 198, 271
Rodríguez, Tobi, 111–12, 113, 115, 116, 118, 120–23, 124
Rodríguez, Tony, 166–67
Rodríguez, Tony "Hardware," 192, 216
Rodríguez, Willie, 103, 221, 227, **279–81**
Rodríguez-Fuentes, José, 112
Roena, Roberto, 225
Roig, Rey, 257
Rojas, Nico, 248
Rojas, Tito, 251
Rolón, Catalino, 84, 103, 190, 207–8, 211, 230, 233, 241
Román, Joseíto, 159, 160
Roman, Manny, 194
Roman, Papy, 223
"Romance," 13
Romero, Elliot, 211, 221
Romero, Ray, 48
Romero, Rudy, 147
Romeu, Antonio María, 41, 97, 177
"Rompiendo la Rutina," 177
Rosa, Angel, 108, 128, 135, 140, 148
Rosa, Ken, 59, 69
Rosa, Roy, 229, 236, 241
Rosario, Carlos, 147
Rosario, Pablito, 194
Rosario, Willie, **269–71**
Rosas, George, 252
Roseff, Howard, 10
Roseland Ballroom (Manhattan), 49, 84, 89, 113, 144, 239
Roseland Ballroom Orchestra, 162
Roulette label, 253
Roundtable (Manhattan club), 185, 191
Royal, Ernie, 135
Rubalcaba, Gonzalo, 192
Rubalcaba, Guillermo, 192
Rubio, Luis, 39
"Rueda," 70
rumba, 85
"Rumba Clásica," 57

"Rumba en Navidad," 208
"Rumba en Swing," 46, 113
Rumba Revue (radio show), 43
"Rumba Rumbero," 10, 43, 66
"Rumba Soy Yo, La," 10
"Rumbambola," 71, 89
Russell, Andy, 8, 160
Russell Wooding's Grand Central Redcaps, 54

Sabater, Jimmy, 202, 227–28, 229, 234, 236, 237, 241, 244, 255, 259, 279
"Sabor, Sabor," 256
"Sabor A Mi," 281
Sabor Guajiro, 191
"Sabor y Africanerías," 41
Sabrosa Pachanga, 191
"Saca Tu Mujer," 156
"Sácale Brillo al Piso," 67
Sacasas, Anselmo, 5, 9, 34, 36, 39, 40–41, 43, **59–62,** 109, 125–26, 126, 195
orchestra of, 98, 107
"Sahara," 47
Sahara Hotel (Las Vegas), 79
St. Nicholas Arena (Manhattan), 107
"Sallita, La," 191
salsa, 12, 61, 135, **255–59**
Salsa (film), 258
Salsa (Harlow record), 257
Salsa (radio show), 135
"Salsa Ahí Na' Ma'", 256
Salsa Hits from Orquesta Power, 257
Salsa Na' Ma', 255–56, 258
"Salsa y Bembé," 255
Salsoul, 253
Salsoul label, 182, 201
"Salta Perico," 149
Saludos Amigos (radio show), 22
Saludos from Fajardo, 190–91
Salvaje, 214
"Sambia," 220
Sampson, Edgar, 9
"San Juan," 124
San Juan, Olga, 4–5, 125, 127
San Juan, Pedro, 60
San Juan Club (Manhattan), 229, 230, 244
San Juan Hotel (Puerto Rico), 104
"San Pascual Bailón," 175
Sanabria, Ignacio "Nacho," 220
Sanabria, Izzy, 96–97, 112, 200, 214–15,

216, 246–47, 257, 262, 273
Sanabria, Juanito, 5, 83, 97, 229
Sánchez, Antonio, 180, 189
Sánchez, Armando, 68, 183
Sánchez, "El Yucateco," 184
Sánchez, Fernando, 187–88
Sanchez, Nestor, 224–25
Sánchez, Rod Luis, 184, 199, 219, 221
Sánchez, Tony, 102
Sancho, Bob, 147
Sands Hotel (Las Vegas), 161
Sanfino, Jerry, 110
Sans Souci (Havana nightclub), 64
Santa Rosa, Gilberto, 248, 269
Santamaría, Ramón "Mongo," 20, 78, 101, 104, 109, 110, 129, 130, 134, 141, 145, 152, 161, 165, 170, 184
Santana, Carlos, 256, 258, 259
Santana, German, 147
Santería religion, 39
Santiago, Adalberto, 210
Santiago, Al, 50, 116, 166, 199, 212, 255–56, 270
Santiago, Javier, 247
Santiago, Jimmy "La Vaca," 99, 107
Santos, Daniel, 13, 67, 83
Santos, Ray, 117
Saoco, 99
Sapphire Blues Orchestra, 133
SAR label, 186
Saratoga Springs, 107
"Satin Doll," 57, 58
Savino, Domenico, 60
Savoy Ballroom (Manhattan), 7
Savoy Club (Manhattan), 55
Saxofobia, Vol. 1, 166
Saxofónica, La, 166
Saxony Hotel (Miami Beach), 134
Sayre, Sid, 231
Scavone, Sammy, 135
Schatz, Ziggy, 109, 161
Scorzo, Harry, 186
"Se Fue la Comparsa," 112
Se Te Quemó La Casa, 165
"Se Va el Caramelero," 41
"Se Va la Rumba," 196
Seeco Records, 10–11, 45, 71, 76, 106, 108, 112, 145, 231, 233, 234, 244, 255, 258
Segarra, Candido, 102

Seguí, Johnny, 19–20, 164, 197, 270
Seijo, Ralph, 208
Selasie, Osario, 196
Selecciones Clásicas, 191
Senatore, Andy, 137
Señor Tito Rodríguez, 115
Sensamaya Kids, La, 106, 160
"Sepárala También," 156
Septeto Cienfuegos, 64
Septeto Habanero, 64
Septeto Nacional, 63, 65, 88, 255
Septeto Son de la Loma, 68
"Serenade," 46
"Serenade in Blue," 75
"Serenata Rítmica," 10, 70, 71, 72, 89, 93
"Serende," 67
Serrano, Hector, 186
Sesma, Chico, 116–17, 258, 262
"Seven Seven," 67
Severinsen, Doc, 73, 103, 135
Sexteto Batamú, 66
Sexteto Cauto, 64, 143
Sexteto Habanero, 28, 65
Sexteto Habanero Juvenil, El, 38
Sexteto Nacional, 143
Sexteto Otra Vez, El, 237
"Sha-Wan-Ga Mambo," 103
Shades of Jade, 270
Shaw, Artie, 102
Shearing, George, 87, 92, 186
Shearing Spell, The, 92
Sheller, Marty, 131, 253
Shields, Dale, 235
Shikaly, Al, 262
Shore, Dinah, 136, 231, 262
Show de Rodríguez, El (television show), 118
Sí, Sí, La Playa, 67, 242
"Sí Sí, No No," 220
"Si Te Dicen," 145
Siboney, La, 34–35, 43, 84, 107, 160
Siegel, Sidney, 10–11, 233
"Siempre de Tí," 246
Sigel, Hyman, 88
Sigler, Vicente, 1, 2, 5, 16, 33, 54, 82
"Silencio," 73
Silhouette Club (Brooklyn), 110
Silva, Henry, 240
Silva, José "Chombo," 170, 171, 184, 199, 221
Silva, Myrta, 17, 83

"Silver Star, El," 180, 181, 190
Simón, Moisés, 2
"Simplemente Una Ilusión," 152
"Sin Comprender," 66
"Sin San Sore," 66
Sinatra, Frank, 9, 160, 240
"Sing, Sing, Sing," 102, 230
Sirena Records, 191
"Situation in F Minor," 162
Small's Paradise (Manhattan), 55
SMC (Spanish Music Center) label, 19, 23, 47–48, 57, 71, 77, 113
Smith, Joe, studios of, 10
Smith, Mauricio, 184, 186, 192
"Smoke," 224
Socarrás, Alberto, 1, 2, 4, 5, 7, 20, **51–58**, 83, 135
  octet of, 52–53
  orchestra of, 69–70
Socarrás, Dolores "Lolo," 53
Socarrás, Juana "Estrella" (or "Estrellita"), 32, 53
Sola, Vicki, 147, 281
Solo Flight, 186
"Solo Tú y Yo," 129
"Son de la Loma," 3, 28, 76, 127
"Son de Pachanga," 25, 198
Son Primero, 186
Songs Mama Never Taught Me, 234
Sonido Records, 262
"Sonny," 279
Sonora Matancera, La, 45, 145, 208, 266
Sonora Ponceña, La, 248
"Sopa de Pichón," 195, 219
"Soplón, El," 73
Sosa, Paquito, 47, 129, 140, 144
"Soul Drummer," 261
Soul Drummer, 265
Soul of Spanish Harlem, The, 234
Soul Sauce (Salsa del Alma), 256, 258, 259
"South American Way," 8
"Soy Rumbero," 271
Spanish Music Center (Manhattan), 3, 19, 27, 82, 128
"Speak Low," 281
Standards label, 35
Stardust Ballroom (Bronx), 231
Stardust Ballroom (Manhattan), 134
Starlight Ballroom (Bronx), 230
Statler-Hilton (Manhattan), 123

Steppin' Out, 233, 234, 244, 255
"Stop 21," 11, 71, 89
Storch, Fernando "Caney." *See* Caney
Storch, Lydia, 30
Stork Club (Manhattan), 71, 126
Strand Theatre (Manhattan), 48, 102–3
Suárez, Gil, 185, 210, 212, 213–14
Suárez, Manolo, 29
Suarez, Senen, 207
Suave Swing Orchestra, 126
Subway Joe, 253
Sugar, Dick "Ricardo," 10, 90, 91, 114, 123–24, 129, 144, 149, 159, 182, 206, 221, 231, 252, 270
"Sun Sun Babae," 103, 161, 164, 207
Sweeny, Kevin, 184
"Sweet and Lovely," 75
"Sweet Sue, Just You," 125
Swinger label, 266
"Swinging the Mambo," 90
Symphony Sid, 252

"Taboga," 40
"Take the 'A' Train," 135
Talamante, Eddie, 105
"Tambó," 41, 72
Tambo, 57, 135
"Tamboleo," 185
"Tanga," 11, 46, 73
"Tanya," 256
"Taraeo," 108
Tatay, Andrew, 25
Tatay, Vicente, 25
Tatay's Spanish Music Center, 21, 82, 255. *See also* Spanish Music Center
"Tatilibaba," 145
"taxi dancers," 88
Taylor, Billy, 101
Taylor, Creed, 256
Taylor, Eva, 52
"Te Desafio," 156
"Te Venido a Buscar," 48
"Tea for Two," 72, 76, 89
Teatro San José, El (Manhattan), 5, 16–17, 21, 82
"Telaraña," 156
"Televisión, La," 148, 160
Tempo 70, 257
"Temptation," 72
"Ten Jabón," 72

index

"Tenderly," 77, 145
"Tengo Una Novia," 180
Terrace, Mike and Elita, 92
Terrace, Pete, 5, 69, 76, 77, 78, 197, 242
   orchestra of, 95, 105
Texeira, Anibal "Big Tex," 147, 196
Third World Gallery, 192
"This Is My Mambo," 170
Three Loves Have I, 115
"3-D Mambo," 156
Tibbett, Lawrence, 2
Tico All-Stars, 219
Tico and Fania All Stars, 157
Tico Records, 24, 48, 49, 72, 73, 77, 78, 90, 98, 103, 114, 115, 129, 131, 134, 140, 143, 144–45, 151, 161, 162, 169, 171, 184, 197, 198, 208, 221, 231, 234, 235–36, 242, 245, 257, 262
Tico-Roulette Records, 252
"Tico Tico," 9
Tico Tico Time (radio show), 47
"Tierra Va Temblá," 66
"Tierra Va Temblar," 41, 45
"Timbal, El," 227
Timothy, Tom, 76
"Tinajón," 88
"Tingo Talango," 10, 139
Típica 73, 30, 257
Típica Ideal, 185
"Típica Ideal," 214
Típica Novel, La, 185, 186, 191, 225, 266
Tiqui, Tiqui, 211
Tito Puente and Friends, 145
Tito Puente in Puerto Rico, 156
Tito Puente Roast, The (television show), 206
Tito Puente Swings—The Exciting La Lupe Sings, 169
Tito Rodríguez y Sus Lobos del Mambo, 114
"Tito Timbero," 164
Tito Unlimited, 131, 136
Tizol, Manolo, 15
Tjader, Cal, 87, 92, 104, 249, 256, 258, 259
"To Be with You," 230, 232, 233, 234, 237
"Toalla, La," 115, 207
"Tocoloro," 24
Today Show (television show), 197

Toja Cabaret, La (Staten Island), 34
Tommy James and the Shondells, 253
"Tonight I Am in Heaven," 231
"Tony and Lucille Mambo," 90, 115, 144
Too Many Girls (Broadway revue), 6
"Too Marvelous for Words," 75
Toreador, El (Manhattan restaurant), 17, 29
Torero, El (Cuban New York restaurant), 170
Tormé, Mel, 229, 240
Torres, Albert, 159, 162
Torres, Hilda, 5, 43
Torres, Johnny, 279
Torres, Juan "El Boy," 20, 35, 67, 71, 83
Torres, Nestor, 186
Torres, Pepito, 102
Torres, Pupi, 106, 228, 229
Torres, Roberto, 187, 209, 210, 211, 257
Torres, Willie, 48, 99, 147, 156, 194, 199, 206, 227, 229, 230, 231–34, 236, 237, **239–42**, 244, 245, 255
Touch of Brass, A, 186
Touzet, René, 48, 72, 101, 105
TR Record Company, 119–20
"Traigo Salsa," 257
"Tres Lindas Cubanas," 177, 179, 197
Triboro Theatre (Manhattan), 83
Tribute to Beny Moré, 136
Trio Borinquen, El, 16
Trio Los Panchos, 10
Trio Río Piedras, El, 269
Trio San Juan, 10
"Triste," 242
"Triste Navidad," 157
Triton Ballroom (Bronx), 205
Triton Club (Bronx), 165
Tropical label, 145
Tropicana Club (Bronx), 35, 84, 160, 182, 251
Tropicoro Club (Bronx), 237
"Tú Baila Con Ella," 66
"Tú Come Pellejo," 98
"Tú Mi Delirio," 247
"Tú No Comprendes," 13
"Tú No Me Quieres," 209
"Tú No Sabes Nada," 148
"Tu Plato," 77, 149
"Tu Regreso," 106, 112
"Tú Siempre Detrás de Mí," 16

307

Tú y Yo, 169
"Tubo, El," 77
"Tumba la Caña," 183
"Tumba Que Tumba," 219
"Tumbaito," 143
"Tus Ojos," 128, 140, 144, 155, 156, 275
"Tuxedo Junction," 135
25th Anniversary Performance, 120

Ullóa, Rolando, 258
"Ultima Noche Que Pasé Contigo, La," 11
Un. *See next word of title*
"Undress My Mind," 242
union, musicians'. *See* American Federation of Musicians (union)
United Artists label, 67, 116, 119, 198, 205, 208, 221, 257
"Up and Down Mambo, The," 90, 103
Uptite Records, 253
Urfe, José, 177
Usera, Moncho, 75, 83, 102, 160, 196

Valdés, Abelardo, 60
Valdés, Alfredito, 19, 23–24, 56, 88, 108, 128, 143, 210, 255
Valdés, Alfredito, Jr., 186
Valdés, Alfredo, 192
Valdés, Bebo, 178
Valdés, Carlos "Patato," 101
Valdés, Chengue, 38
Valdés, Elio, 189
Valdés, Gilberto, 35, 97, 105, 177–78, 182, 190
Valdés, Joseito, 187
Valdés, Marcelino, 171, 219
Valdés, Miguelito, 5, 6, 9–10, 20, 22, 24, 34, **37–50,** 52, 59, 67, 83, 92, 106–7, 112, 128, 148, 157, 159, 249, 280
  Oller on, 23
  orchestra of, 47–49, 85, 101, 103, 105, 140
  Palmieri on, 195–96
  views on Puente, 267
  views on Sacasas, 60–61
Valdés, Patato, 229, 234
Valdés, Rogelio, 66, 182
Valdés, Vicentico, 48, 91, 123, **143–46,** 197, 219, 229, 234, 244, 257, 276

  orchestra of, 93, 95, 139, 190, 221
  with Puente band, 98, 128–29, 140, 141
  split with Puente, 130, 135, 151–52, 232, 233
Valdés Torres, Armando, 178
Valdescu, Demetrie, 36
Valentín, Bobby, 146, 206, 208, 261, 271
Valentín, Dave, 147, 149, 186
Valentino's (Manhattan Cuban restaurant), 7, 17
Valenzuela, Raimundo, 176
Valera, Carlos, 107
Valera, Eligio, 170
Valiente, José, 210
Valiente, Pedro "Pulidor," 106
Valladares, Dioris, 35, 183, 197
Valle, Joe, 210
"Vámanos Ya," 112
"Vamos a Gozar," 191
Varela, Carlos, 148, 160, 229
Varona, Luis, 5, 7, 65–66, 76, 108, 128, 134–35, 139, 140, 141, 144, 196, 219, 229
Varona, Orestes, 179
"Varsity Drag Mambo," 156
Vásquez, Anibal, 92
Vásquez, Leo, 123, 224
Vásquez, Mike, 266
Vásquez, Pepe, 39–40
Vaughan, Sarah, 118
Vaya label, 235, 245, 246, 262
Vaya Means Go!, 242
Vega, Armando "Mandín," 164, 208
Vega, Celso, 11
Vega, Ernesto, 39
Vega, Polito, 123, 135, 253, 262
Vega, Tony, 269
Velásquez, Victor, 165, 199, 255
Velázquez, Chelo, 8
Vélez, Kike, 210
Vélez, Lupe, 2
"Velorio," 57
"Vendedor de Mangos, El," 241
Venegas, Victor, 183
Vera, María Teresa, 38, 43
"Vereda Tropical," 5, 9
Verges, Dominica, 177
Verne Records, 45, 63, 66–67, 71, 75, 148
"Vibe Mambo," 90, 115, 129, 230
"Vibe Quintet, The," 197

Vibes Galore, 110
Vicente, Wilfredo "Chonguito," 228, 229
Victor's Café (Manhattan Cuban restaurant), 49
"Vida Es Un Sueño, La," 67, 155, 233, 241
Vidal, Bolivar, 224
Vidal, Carlos, 46, 77, 101
"Vieja Luna," 196
Viera, Mr. (trumpeter), 60
Vilató, Orestes, 101, 181
"Virgen del Cobre," 172
Virginia's (Los Angeles), 165–66
"Vitamina," 73
Viva Rivera, 219
"Vivo Orgulloso de Tí," 152
Vizcaino, Ciso, 224
Vladescu, Demetrie, 32–33
"Volví a Querer," 64
"Voodoo Moon," 35, 160
Voz, La, 276
Voz Sensual de Cheo, La, 235, 246
Voz Sensual de Jimmy Sabater, La, 236
"Vuela la Paloma," 116

Wa-Pa-Cha, The (El Guapacha), 115
"Wachi Wara," 256, 279
Waldorf-Astoria Hotel (Manhattan), 8, 43, 190
Walker, Danton, 30
Walter Bennett's Swamplanders, 54
"Walter Winchell Rhumba," 71, 106
"Wampó," 145
Wanted Dead or Alive, 235–36, 242
"Watusi, El," 185
We Must Be Doing Something Right!, 235, 245
Webb, Artie, 186
Webb, Chick, 7
Webster, Carl, 54
Webster, Margaret, 52
Wegbreit, Harold, 114, 152
Weinstein, Mark, 199
"Wha' Happen," 113
"When Sonny Gets Blue," 279
Whittington, Ricardo, Jr., 186
"Wildfire," 164, 220
Wilkins, Felix, 184
William Morris Agency, 44–45, 48
Williams, Clarence, 52
Willie Bobo Committee, 146

Willie's Steakhouse (Bronx), 167
Winchell, Walter, 45, 57, 71
Winding, Kai, 135
Wine, Women, and Cha Cha Cha, 156
Winters, Marilyn, 92
Winters, Shelley, 87
Wooding, Russell, 54
Wooding, Sam, 52, 56
Woodlen, Bobby, 108

"Ya Empezó," 112
"Ya Lo Puedes Decir," 152
"Ya No Te Puedo Querer," 162
"Ya No Te Quiero," 16
"Ya Se Formó," 219
"Yambu," 90
Yayo El Indio, 36, 110, 161, 162, 219, 270
"Yenye," 66
"Yerbero, El," 241
"Yeremico, Un," 114, 128
"Yo No Engaño a Las Nenas," 24
"Yo Quiero Ser Tu Amante," 247
"Yo Saludo," 41
"Yo Sí Como Candela," 209
"Yo Soy La Rumba," 67
"Yo Tá Namorá," 43–44
"Yo Te Saludo," 40
"Yo Tengo un Mate," 198
You Were Never Lovelier (film), 44
Your Hit Parade (radio show), 159
"Yoyo, El," 145
"Yumba," 126
"Yumbambé," 77, 149

"Zambele," 103
Zanzibar (Manhattan club), 98
"Zarabanda," 10
Zeno, Hector, 211
Zervigón, Eddy, 184, 185, 186, 192, **209–17,** 266
Zervigón, Rudy, 210, 211
zoot suits, 83

781.657 SALAZAR
Salazar Primero, Max.
Mambo kingdom : Latin
music in New York